Battle on the Seven Seas

Battle on the Seven Seas

German Cruiser Battles 1914–1918

Gary Staff

Pen & Sword
MARITIME

First published in Great Britain in 2011 by
Pen & Sword Maritime
an imprint of
Pen & Sword Books Ltd
47 Church Street
Barnsley
South Yorkshire
S70 2AS

Copyright © Gary Staff 2011

ISBN 978-1-84884-182-6

The right of Gary Staff to be identified as Author of this Work has been asserted by him in accordance with the Copyright, Designs and Patents Act 1988.

A CIP catalogue record for this book is available from the British Library.

All rights reserved. No part of this book may be reproduced or transmitted in any form or by any means, electronic or mechanical including photocopying, recording or by any information storage and retrieval system, without permission from the Publisher in writing.

Typeset in 11pt Ehrhardt by
Mac Style, Beverley, E. Yorkshire

Printed and bound in the UK by CPI

Pen & Sword Books Ltd incorporates the imprints of Pen & Sword Aviation, Pen & Sword Maritime, Pen & Sword Military, Wharncliffe Local History, Pen and Sword Select, Pen and Sword Military Classics and Leo Cooper.

For a complete list of Pen & Sword titles please contact
PEN & SWORD BOOKS LIMITED
47 Church Street, Barnsley, South Yorkshire, S70 2AS, England
E-mail: enquiries@pen-and-sword.co.uk
Website: www.pen-and-sword.co.uk

Contents

List of Maps vi
Introduction vii

1. The Battle in the Helgoland Bight, 28 August 1914 1
2. The Sea Battle at Coronel, 1 November 1914 28
3. The Sea Battle Off Cape Sarych, Balaclava, 18 November 1914 41
4. The Battle of the Falklands, 8 December 1914 58
5. The Battle on the Dogger Bank, 24 January 1915 82
6. The Sea Battle Off Östergarn, 2 July 1915 104
7. The Battles of *Emden* and *Königsberg* 127
8. The Skagerrak Battle, 31 May to 1 June 1916 147
9. The Second Battle in the Helgoland Bight, 17 November 1917 190
10. The Sea Battle Off Imbros, 20 January 1918 208

Notes 221
Bibliography 226
Index 238

List of Maps

The Battle in the Helgoland Bight, 28 August 1914 12
The Sea Battle at Coronel, 1 November 1914 37
Movements of SMS *Goeben*, 17 to 19 November 1914 45
The Battle Off Cape Sarych, 18 November 1914 50
The Battle Off the Bosporus, 10 May 1915 56
The Battle of the Falkland Islands, 8 December 1914 70
The Battle of the Falkland Islands, 8 December 1914, *Leipzig* 77
The Battle of the Falkland Islands, 8 December 1914, *Nürnberg* 79
The Battle on the Dogger Bank, 24 January 1915, 08.00 to 09.20hrs 91
The Battle on the Dogger Bank, 24 January 1915, 09.50 to 11.00hrs 93
The Battle on the Dogger Bank, 24 January 1915, 11.00 to 13.00hrs 103
The Sea Battle Off Östergarn, 2 July 1915 112
The Sea Battle Off Östergarn, 2 July 1915, 07.50 to 09.30hrs 119
The Sea Battle Off Östergarn, 2 July 1915, 09.22 to 10.20hrs 121
Prinz Adalbert Torpedoed, 13.57hrs, 2 July 1915 126
The Battle at Penang, 28 October 1914 129
The Battle at Cocos Islands, 9 November 1914 135
The Battle Off Zanzibar, 20 September 1914 142
The Battle on the Rufiji Delta, 11 July 1915 145
The Skagerrak Battle, 15.45 to 16.48hrs 156
The Skagerrak Battle, the Turn to the North, 18.10hrs 162
The Skagerrak Battle, First Battle Turn Away, 19.35hr 168
The Skagerrak Battle, Third Battle Turn Away, 20.20hrs 171
The Skagerrak Battle, the German Head Under Fire, 21.35hrs 175
The Skagerrak Battle, Night Encounters, 23.10 to 23.50hrs 186
The Battle in the Helgoland Bight, 17 November 1917, 07.00 to 10.00hrs ... 200
The Battle in the Helgoland Bight, 17 November 1917, 10.00 to 11.00hrs ... 206
The Sea Battle Off Imbros, 20 January 1918 218

Introduction

During the First World War the Kaiserliche Marine, the Imperial Navy, fought across the seven seas of the world. The Atlantic Ocean, Pacific Ocean, Black Sea, Adriatic Sea, North Sea, Baltic Sea and Indian Ocean all served as theatres of operations for the cruisers of the Imperial Navy. The battles of the German cruisers truly made World War One a global conflict, as far as the Germans were concerned more so than in World War Two. For the most part the German cruisers around the world's oceans were defeated, but this does not detract from their excellent service or importance to the German war effort. On the other hand the exploits of the cruisers based at home in the Baltic and North Sea were sometimes shining lights in a war which had settled down into a static conflict.

This book is not an academic book, it is a narrative of German cruisers in action during the First World War. It depicts historical events in an accurate and informative manner, where the story of German cruisers has often never been told before. Some of the story is told by actual participants in quotes taken directly from their written work. By using contemporary accounts it is hoped that some of the atmosphere of the time, and of a naval battle at sea, can be captured and conveyed to the reader. Contemporary accounts are extremely valuable, especially now as the last survivors of this war have passed away. Using firsthand accounts by people involved at the time often gives a better view of that time, before later political meddling and influence could take effect. Many of the participant accounts used in this book were taken as evidence from survivors after the loss of their ship. The only criticism that can be levelled is that sometimes their times are not accurate, which is understandable under the circumstances.

Likewise, contemporary books and war diaries have been used widely. German combat reports and war diaries of individual ships are excellent source material, and contain many details and thoughts. Some ships' commanders were better writers than others, however, with some reports being more replete with detail than others, which shows when command of a ship changed. The German official history of the war at sea, *Der Krieg zur See 1914–1918*, is an excellent document that was written between 1920 and 1964, with one volume being revised and updated in 2006. *Der Krieg zur See* is mostly a very exacting document, with some analysis, and almost all the action. In the various war diaries various sections of the written work are underlined in red pencil, and this was the marking left by the authors of *Der Krieg zur See* of what to include in their work. So therefore the official German history was essentially written by the participants.

One thing which is very important is not to stigmatize the events, writing and history of the First World War with the events and inhumanity of the Second World War. Many authors find themselves unable to do this. The First World War must be viewed as a standalone event, after all when it concluded nobody had any inkling that there would be a second World War, and it had been the war to end all wars. Therefore the German official history was written honestly and without an alternative agenda. Conversely many British books written since the war seek to put a post-war spin on proceedings, trying belatedly to influence events.

On the other hand the official British history, *Naval Operations*, does not contain as much detail and seems more concerned with analysing command decisions. At times it lapses into parochialism and jingoism. The British ships' logs are also not as detailed, and contain no details of damage. Even the reports contained in the excellent *Jutland Dispatches* are not so detailed, although they are concise.

Russian details of necessity are taken from books now available. Many are still in print and date back to the immediate post-war period and are written by authors who were involved in the action. Some have been influenced by the Communist Government but these books are easily recognisable by their exaggerations. Russian literature is very interesting and mostly very detailed.

In writing this book I have been assisted by various institutions and individuals. The Bundesarchiv-Militär Achiv have been very helpful. All Imperial Navy War Diaries, as well as much other important research material, are freely available there, and I have been given much assistance by Frau Webel and Frau Meier there. I must also sincerely thank Sebastian Remus for his very valuable research at the BA-MA. He is an expert at finding material on any subject in the Archiv and I am indebted to him for his work. Much help has also been given by the Marine-Offizier-Vereinigung, the Naval Officers Association, and I am sincerely thankful to Fregattenkapitän a.D. Vangerow for allowing me to look at material possessed by the Association. Two friends have also been very helpful in my search for information and photographs of the Imperial Navy. Herr Carsten Steinhorst is an expert on many aspects of the history of the Imperial Navy, in particular the cruisers, and Mr. Stuart Haller has been very helpful over a very extended period with information and photographs of the cruisers of the High Sea Fleet. I am very thankful and grateful for their help and assistance.

This book is meant to be an accurate narrative history of the battles fought by the German cruisers during the First World War, told in part by the men who fought the ships. I hope it is as enjoyable to read as it was to write and I hope that it brings new insight into a period which is too frequently forgotten.

Gary Staff
February 2010

Chapter 1

The Battle in the Helgoland Bight, 28 August 1914

Although both the Royal Navy and the Imperial Navy had been preparing materially for armed conflict for a decade or more, it is amazing to learn that they were both quite unprepared strategically. The Royal Navy, and more specifically the British Admiralty, was still undecided about what form of blockade to mount on Germany. The earliest form of the blockade plan was the close blockade, which proposed a blockade by destroyer flotillas close off the German coast, with close support by three cruiser squadrons. The principal objectives of this form of blockade were to prevent German small-scale operations being mounted from their North Sea harbours and to prevent the High Sea Fleet putting to sea without the British Admiralty knowing about it. This doctrine was little different from that of the Napoleonic Wars and was in vogue until as late as 1911. In 1912 this plan was amended, in view of expected high losses to German torpedoboats and U-boats, to a more distant 'Observational Blockade'. In this form the line of destroyers and cruisers would extend from the southern tip of Norway out into the centre of the North Sea, and then southward to Holland. The general idea was to stop German shipping from trading with the world by closing off the North Sea, and to allow the battle fleet time to bring the High Sea Fleet to battle should it proceed to sea to attack the blockading cruisers, or perform any other offensive action. This 'observational blockade' remained the official strategy for Britain until 1914, just before the beginning of the First World War. Then it was finally decided to undertake a strategy of a distant blockade. This strategy called for the Grand Fleet to be stationed in Scapa Flow in Scotland and cut off the North Sea along a line from the Orkney Islands to Norway, and for a second force, the Channel Fleet, to block off the Dover Straits. This was the strategy with which the Royal Navy went to war.

In Germany the Admiralstab was uncertain of which form of blockade the British would use. As late as 1913 they still did not know whether the Royal Navy would use a close or more distant blockade, however consideration was being given to the alternatives. In manoeuvres in March 1914 the High Sea Fleet was divided into two, with one team establishing a distant blockade and approaching the coast with only light forces. The results of this exercise were that it was considered improbable that the British would mount a close blockade. Regardless of this the main German strategy was still directed towards countering a close blockade. To do this they would employ the so-called *Kleinkrieg*, or guerrilla warfare, with U-boats, torpedoboats and mine warfare being used to wear down the blockading forces until a ratio was reached where the High Sea Fleet could engage in open battle with a reasonable chance of success. It was even suggested that the mine and U-boat warfare could be extended to the English coast. Nevertheless, some minds at the Admiralstab were thinking ahead, and in May 1914 Grossadmiral von Tirpitz raised the question with Admiral Ingenohl, commander of the High Sea Fleet: 'What will you do if they do not come?' Neither man had a satisfactory answer.

In some ways the form and extent of the British blockade against Germany at the outbreak of war in August 1914 was superfluous. Even with the most successful outcome to a fleet battle against the Royal Navy, the blockade against Germany could be maintained simply because of the geographical position of Britain across the North Sea. A blockade could be preserved with only the most modest of forces, comprising destroyers, submarines and auxiliary cruisers. Even with sea mastery, Germany's only chance of breaking the blockade would be to employ convoys with powerful escorts, and these would still be vulnerable to submarines. None of these questions had been resolved to anyone's satisfaction when hostilities commenced in early August 1914.

As the first days of the war passed the Germans still harboured the hope of causing the British losses by means of guerrilla warfare, however as the days passed and their patrols reported that the Helgoland Bight was in no way blockaded the Admiralstab decided on more far-reaching operations. On 14 August the Fleet Chief ordered that on 18 August two small cruisers should surprise the English destroyer line in the Hoofden, between Yarmouth and Holland, that had been reported by U-boat reconnaissance. Accordingly on 17 August the small cruisers *Stralsund*, commander Kapitän zur See Harder, and *Straßburg*, commander Fregattenkapitän Retzmann, put to sea along with *U19* and *U24*, which were to occupy ambush positions in support of the cruisers. Further support was provided by the cruiser *Kolberg*, Fregattenkapitän Widenmann, waiting 30 nautical miles northwest of Terschelling, whilst at the same time three German battlecruisers would wait on Schillig Roads with steam up in all boilers. The German official history, *Der Krieg zur See*, stated that this last measure 'had only a morale value for the cruisers pushed far out to sea'.[1]

The weather on the morning of 18 August was very clear and the two German cruisers continued their advance until about 30 nautical miles south of the latitude of Yarmouth. Then about 04.45hrs, when they had passed through the supposed picket line under the cover of darkness, they turned and began the counter-march, hopefully catching the English destroyers unawares from behind. Towards 06.18hrs, when approximately 20 nautical miles east of Smiths Knoll light vessel, *Straßburg* sighted two enemy submarines on the surface at a range of 105 to 85 hectometres (hm)[2]. They were the English submarines *E5* and *E7*, which were immediately taken under fire at 06.18hrs. The commander of *E7*, Lieutenant-Commander Feilman, wrote in his report:

> This morning at 6.30 a four funnelled cruiser, apparently of the improved *County* class, flying no colours, hove in sight on the port bow, steering an opposite course to ours, steaming fast. *E5* hoisted the demand which was unanswered, and when on our port beam the cruiser opened fire, at a range of two to three miles. Her ranging shot fell 25 yards from us, on our port quarter, and we dived at once, several salvos being fired at us as we went under and falling close around us, but not hitting.[3]

Aboard *Straßburg* they believed they had observed a hit, but were uncertain because of the great range. The German cruiser immediately reported the encounter by wireless. What is interesting is that aboard the submarine they believed they were dealing with a cruiser of the *Cressy* class.

Meanwhile, some 50 nautical miles to the east of this position, *Stralsund* also had an encounter with enemy forces. At 06.39hrs she sighted eight to ten British destroyers of the *Mohawk* and *Archer* classes to the northeast. To the southeast a further eight destroyers and then a light cruiser of the *Amphion* class were sighted. It was *Fearless* and the 1st Destroyer Flotilla which were running towards one-another to concentrate. *Stralsund* immediately opened fire on the northern group as they were closer, and only on the southern group as the range to them reduced to 85hm. The battle continued for half an hour or more with both sides manoeuvring vigorously to throw off the opponent's aim. Soon four approaching torpedo tracks were observed from *Stralsund*, and three passed behind the German ship, whilst one passed ahead. The gunfire from the British ships was not accurate and almost all shots fell short of *Stralsund*, whilst on the British side two destroyers appeared damaged, one veiled in black smoke and another blowing off steam. At 07.40hrs a second British cruiser was observed approaching from the south and Kapitän zur See Harder broke off the action, whilst the British destroyers and cruiser had already turned away to the southwest. From a German point of view it was determined that a stronger force was required if the British destroyer line was to be rolled up. From the British point of view they were stung into embarking on a retaliatory riposte.

On 23 August Commodore Keyes, commander of submarines based in Harwich, submitted a plan for an attack on the German picket forces off Helgoland. He was supported in his submission by the commander of Harwich forces, Commodore Tyrwhitt. The plan called for the 1st and 3rd Destroyer Flotillas, each of sixteen destroyers, together with the cruiser *Fearless* and

Commodore Tyrwhitt's flagship, from 26 August the cruiser *Arethusa*, to approach the German picket line of torpedoboats just after dawn as the day and night positions were being exchanged. The English forces would approach from the north and pass behind the German forces to the east, before turning west and rolling up the German lines. Commodore Keyes's submarines, a total of eight boats, would be deployed in two lines, the first deployed to attack German cruisers as they hurried into the Helgoland Bight, and the second on the surface to the west to draw the German guard forces to seawards. Two other submarines would operate off the Ems River. Supporting to the north would be Rear Admiral Moore with his Force K from the Humber, the battlecruisers *New Zealand* and *Invincible*. Rear Admiral Christian would support the operation to the west, off Terschelling, with his six old cruisers of the 7th Cruiser Squadron. Commodore Keyes also suggested that the 1st Battlecruiser Squadron and 1st Light Cruiser Squadron should lend support, but this proposal was rejected by the Admiralty. The Admiralty approved the remainder of the plan to conduct the sweep, with operations to commence on 26 August. Subsequently when Admiral Jellicoe learned of the advance on 26 August he suggested support. The Admiralty advised him that the Fleet was not required to cooperate, but that the battlecruisers could support if required. Admiral Jellicoe therefore dispatched the 1st Battlecruiser Squadron and the 1st Light Cruiser Squadron, but did not ensure that Commodore Keyes and Commodore Tyrwhitt were informed of this important reinforcement.

At the beginning of the war, as previously related, the German Admiralstab still expected to fight a final decisive battle almost immediately. However, the operational orders recognised the danger from English submarines and mines in the Helgoland Bight and off the river-mouths. In the beginning there was a shortage of picket boats so the torpedoboats and small cruisers had to perform picket duty, and subsequently there was a shortage of these forces to counter enemy advances and conduct long-range reconnaissance. Initially the picket lines consisted of three concentric lines of torpedoboats and U-boats at 25, 29 and 35 nautical mile intervals. However, because of the strain placed on men and equipment by these arrangements the scope and extent of the picket lines had to be reduced. The High Command considered that the use of mine barriers would restrict the sea room available to the fleet in the expected decisive battle. On the morning of 28 August the picket line consisted of nine torpedoboats arranged in the German Bight in a semi-circle between Norderney and Amrum. At night this line was pulled back, but during the day it was supported by three small cruisers behind it. On 28 August the small cruiser *Stettin* lay anchored northeast of Helgoland whilst the small cruiser *Frauenlob* lay to the south. The old obsolete cruiser prototype *Hela* lay further to the east. The small cruiser *Ariadne* lay in the entrance to the Weser River, and *Mainz* lay in the entrance to the Ems. The small cruiser *Cöln*, sistership to

Mainz, lay coaling in Wilhelmshaven. *Cöln* was the flagship of Kontreadmiral Maass, the Leader of the II Reconnaissance Group and at the same time I Leader of Torpedoboats. These were the initial German dispositions on the morning of 28 August 1914.

On the evening of 26 August, at 22.30hrs, Commodore Keyes's submarines began departing Harwich for the operation. *E4*, *E5* and *E9* departed first and were to attack any reinforcing or retreating German vessels. Then came *Lurcher* with *E6*, *E7*, and *E8*. They departed at 00.30hrs and were to be positioned 40 miles further out to sea to draw the German destroyers seawards. *D2* and *D8* left at the same time and were stationed off the Ems to attack German ships putting out from there. The destroyer *Firedrake* also followed. Early on the morning of 27 August Commodore Tyrwhitt and his forces got under weigh[4], whilst on the Humber Rear Admiral Moore and his two battlecruisers, *New Zealand* and *Invincible*, put to sea. At 05.00hrs Vice Admiral Beatty took the 1st Battlecruiser Squadron to sea. It consisted of *Lion*, *Queen Mary* and *Princess Royal*. He was accompanied by the 1st Light Cruiser Squadron, consisting of the light cruisers *Southampton*, *Birmingham*, *Nottingham*, *Lowestoft*, *Falmouth* and *Liverpool*, and commanded by Commodore Goodenough. The last British forces to depart were those of Rear Admiral Christian, which departed on the evening of 27 August. His 7th Cruiser Squadron, known as Force C, consisted of the armoured cruisers *Euryalus*, *Cressy*, *Aboukir*, *Hogue* and *Sutlej*, and was accompanied by Commodore Tyrwhitt's former flagship *Amethyst*. Vice Admiral Beatty arranged for his force to rendezvous with Rear Admiral Moore's at 05.00 on 28 August. At 03.30hrs Commodore Tyrwhitt encountered Commodore Goodenough and luckily the two forces recognised each other as friendly, however Commodore Keyes's force still remained ignorant of the presence of Vice Admiral Beatty and Commodore Goodenough.

The weather in the Helgoland Bight on the morning of Friday 28 August was a light NE breeze, the sky was overcast, there was a haze of fog, and visibility was two to three nautical miles. From the beginning the battle took the form of sporadic, individual actions between the independent German small cruisers as they arrived in the battle area, and the combined British forces, either the cruisers and destroyers of the Harwich Force, the 1st Light Cruiser Squadron, or the battlecruisers of Vice Admiral Beatty. The German Command, or more specifically the Commander of Reconnaissance Ships, or BdA[5], Kontreadmiral Hipper, who had responsibility for the security of the German Bight, was poorly informed about the conditions in the Bight. He remained unaware that in the Bight it was hazy with many fog banks until the leadership was informed at 11.35hrs after a telegram from Helgoland gave visibility of three to four nautical miles. Upon the first enemy contact Kontreadmiral Hipper dispatched small cruisers to support the Torpedoboote Flottille and these took up the pursuit individually. Only *Stettin* and *Frauenlob* were immediately available to pursue the enemy destroyers and they received orders to do so. It was not until *Mainz*'s last message at 13.02hrs that she was being pursued by battlecruisers that it became apparent that this was a raid of the heaviest magnitude, but it was too late and the German small cruisers were scattered about the Bight in patchy weather.

After several contacts with enemy submarines early in the morning, the first German contact with British surface forces occurred at 07.57hrs when the torpedoboat *G194* found herself confronted by several destroyers at a range of just two nautical miles. The recognition signal was given by searchlight but went unanswered so that *G194* made a turn and ran off to the southeast at high speed. Only 15 minutes later were approximately nine destroyers and two light cruisers made out. With the range just 2,000 metres the British fire was answered. Several attempts to wireless the I FdT[6] Kontreadmiral Maass, aboard the small cruiser *Cöln*, failed and it was not until 08.25hrs that a call got through. The neighbouring boats, *G196* and *G9* joined the battle as they turned away and headed towards Helgoland. Then *V6*, *S13* and *V1* also joined battle with the English boats. The German boats were making maximum speed and dense black smoke issued from the funnels of the coal-burning boats, whilst the sterns of the boats were sucked deeply down with the high speed. Because the German boats were relatively weakly armed, with 8.8cm guns against 4-inch pieces, and because only their stern cannon could shoot, their ammunition expenditure was low and their fire was relatively ineffective. The sterns being pulled under and smoke interference did not help either. Whilst *G194* was only hit once the other boats began to suffer. *S13* had boiler firing problems and could make only 20 knots, reducing the range to the enemy. Then at 08.50hrs *V1* suffered a hit in the forward boiler room and her speed was also reduced to 20 knots. The German boats were having a hard time of it and it was fortunate that the small cruiser *Stettin* now intervened.

The guard position of *Stettin* on the morning of 28 August was anchored to the NNE of Helgoland Island. At this early stage of the war it was not unusual to remain anchored whilst on picket and the cruiser was protected against submarine attack by the shallow water depth. The visibility conditions were poor, fluctuating between 50 and 85hm. At 08.20hrs shooting was heard in a northern direction, but this was mistaken for the Torpedoboote Flottille conducting a planned calibre shoot. Then at 08.32hrs a wireless message arrived from the V Flottille about being in combat with enemy destroyers. *Stettin* immediately weighed anchor and steamed NNW at 15 and then 18 knots. However, the cruiser only had steam up in eight out of eleven boilers and therefore maximum speed could not be reached. At 08.55hrs the enemy could be made out and at 08.58hrs *Stettin* opened fire on the middle group of destroyers at 85hm, and reported to the BdA: 'Am in battle with destroyers'. The destroyers mostly turned off to the west and, as they numbered approximately twenty boats armed with 4-inch cannon, support was urgently requested from the BdA. The commander of *Stettin*, Korvettenkapitän Nerger[7] wrote in his combat report:[8]

> Towards 9.05am behind the enemy formation a cruiser with 4 funnels[9] was seen for a brief time and this observation was reported to the I BdA: 'enemy cruiser found with the enemy flotilla'. Whether he intervened in the battle is not known. The impact of the enemy shells in the immediate vicinity of the ship was so numerous, that it did not allow observation. According to a communication of the Commander of the V Flottille the impacts gave the impression that *Stettin* was in a kettle with boiling water.
>
> About 9.10am the fire was broken off, as the range quickly increased, owing to the low speed of the ship–the steam had temporarily fallen, so that only 15 knots could be made. I decided to firstly raise steam in all boilers and would go near Sellebrunnen buoy during this time, as meanwhile further gunfire was heard in the SW.

During this action *Stettin* received one hit on the starboard number 4 gun, whereby two men were killed and one was badly wounded. The intervention of *Stettin* had undoubtedly saved *V1* and *S13* from certain destruction, however the official history was critical of Korvettenkapitän Nerger's decision to return to Sellebrunnen Buoy to raise steam:

> The premature return of *Stettin* to Sellebrunnen buoy, whilst well founded on the desire to raise steam so as to keep pace with the enemy, must be deplored. The reason is that meanwhile the enemy had pushed onto the picket line consisting of the boats of the III Mine Sweeper Division, and proceeded to roll it up.[10]

The boats of the III Minesweeper Division, and their lead boat *D8*, had observed the fire fight between the V TBF and *Stettin* and the English forces. The Division Chief, Kapitänleutnant Wolfram, immediately took course on Helgoland but at 08.40hrs the English destroyers opened fire on *D8*. They achieved five hits on the obsolete German minesweeper, whose speed was rapidly reducing. The commander and eleven men were killed, and nineteen were wounded. The other boats of the III Mine Sweeper Flottille were likewise armed with only 5cm cannon and had a maximum speed of just 15 knots. It seemed they would be overwhelmed almost immediately. *T73* came under a heavy fire for 7 minutes before she could escape. *T33* was under fire for 35 minutes and suffered three hits, one of which caused flooding in the engine room. *T37* came under fire for 25 minutes, but remained unhit. The next boat, *T35*, was under fire for 10 minutes and suffered one hit whilst *T31* only came under fire for a short time. The three remaining boats, *T40*, *T29* and *T36* were able to retire without coming under fire. The boats were in danger of being annihilated and only the timely intervention of the small cruiser *Frauenlob* saved them from further destruction.

During the morning *Frauenlob* had taken up her picket position between the Jade River and Helgoland, and when cannon thunder was heard her commander, Fregattenkapitän Mommsen, quickly gave orders to steer toward the sound of the firing and sounded 'Clear ship for battle!' Fregattenkapitän Mommsen wrote in his war diary:[11]

> 8.58am: Run at highest speed to the thunder of guns, 'clear ship for battle' sounded. After a few moments we saw torpedoboats and minesweepers at highest speed. The boats of the Picket Line of the German Bight ran off in the direction of Helgoland. Soon thereon the impacts were observed in the vicinity of the boats, that must be from the enemy. Finally came the silhouette of a ship with 1 mast and 3 funnels, firing violently with course W by N, accompanied by approximately 6 destroyers, some travelling in the wake.
>
> Seemingly *Frauenlob* was sighted by the enemy and fire was directed on *Frauenlob*. Impacts landed in the vicinity of the ship and we moved from the bridge to the fore direction position in the conning tower, and the I Offizier went to the Leak Central (the Broadside Torpedo Room).

A short time later, at 09.08hrs *Frauenlob* returned fire on the cruiser, *Arethusa*. Commodore Tyrwhitt's flagship had many advantages over the German cruiser. *Arethusa* was a new ship, and was much more powerfully armed than her German opponent with a broadside weighing twice as much. She was also much better protected and had belt armour, whereas the old *Frauenlob* had no belt. On the other hand *Arethusa* had been rushed into service and had not properly worked up, but neither had *Frauenlob*. The German cruiser had been placed in reserve in January 1908 and had only been recommissioned on 2 August 1914, only 13 days before *Arethusa*, and *Frauenlob* was crewed by reservists. At first *Frauenlob* approached the English forces at an acute angle, quickly reducing the range, and only when some of *Arethusa*'s destroyers passed ahead of *Frauenlob* did she turn to port onto a WSW course. A violent firefight now ensued. Despite the rapid changes in range and course alterations, *Frauenlob* straddled the target with her third salvo and obtained a hit with her forth salvo, ranged at 45hm. At 09.15hrs a hit was observed adjacent to the third funnel. After that blows were traded freely, with *Arethusa* being struck by shells between 25 and 35 times, whilst *Frauenlob* was hit 10 times. On *Arethusa* a German shell exploded a cordite charge which set fire to her deck. All but a single 6-inch gun were knocked out and the hull was penetrated so that the engine room flooded to a depth of 3 feet, and the speed eventually fell to 10 knots. On the bridge the Signals Officer was killed whilst standing next to Commodore Tyrwhitt. The wireless was also put out of action. Sometime later *Arethusa* was forced to stop to effect repairs. According to Commodore Tyrwhitt[12] she had eleven killed and about sixteen wounded. As *Arethusa* began to suffer she turned away 8 points, or 90 degrees, to starboard onto a NW course. *Frauenlob* followed this course change and the range reduced to 32hm. The ships now fought it out on this course until *Arethusa* and the destroyers vanished into the haze. Surprisingly the destroyers had not launched any torpedo attacks. However, the half-hour battle was not entirely one sided and *Frauenlob* was hit ten times. Green-black and yellow explosions marked the bursting of the English shells, however, the Germans noted that many shells failed to detonate. Early in the battle a shell struck the forward port edge of the conning tower and splinters killed one man and wounded three others. However, contrary to later assertions, this in no way affected the fight. A further shell struck the forward crow's nest and wounded several men, and also shot through the wireless antenna. The aft artillery position was hit and an order transmitter was killed. Further hits struck the galley, the clothes store, aft funnel and several places on deck. Total losses were five men killed and thirty-two wounded. *Frauenlob*'s commander had praise for his men and wrote: 'they widely surpassed what could be expected after a short training period and during the pause in battle went quickly and dutifully about their work. Nowhere were wails or moans heard.'[13] The last was a reference to the many wounded.

Soon after the battle was broken off, in the direction in which the British forces had disappeared, a badly damaged vessel was seen. It was the hapless *T33*, in poor condition. At first *V3* took her in tow, but finally *Frauenlob* towed her to Helgoland. After seeing *T33* safely into harbour *Frauenlob* began the journey to Wilhelmshaven at about 11.30hrs, where the dead and wounded were landed. From the forgoing it can be seen that assertions by Commodore Tyrwhitt and other authors that *Arethusa* fought *Stettin* and *Frauenlob* concurrently are without foundation.

Whilst these actions were occurring, some of the British destroyers were engaging the V Torpedoboote Flottille Leader *V187*. After receiving the first contact report from *G194*, *V187* held course north for some 20 minutes and about 08.20hrs sighted two enemy vessels on a SE course. A short time later these vessels, which had been held for destroyers, were recognised as cruisers, and *V187* turned and ran before them at 24 knots. An ESE course was held until about 08.35hrs they were lost from view. At 09.00hrs these two cruisers were again sighted more to the north and with a turn to starboard of 2 points they were again avoided. Then at 09.25hrs four British destroyers were made out to port which opened fire on the German torpedoboat. Initially the range was

60hm and as it reduced to 48hm *V187* was able to make reply. Then suddenly at 09.45hrs two cruisers with four funnels and attendant destroyers appeared to starboard. It was *Nottingham* and *Lowestoft* blocking any escape for the German boat. *V187* now attempted to break through the destroyers to the north, but she was cut off and surrounded and soon began to suffer. The forward gun was put out of action and then the boilers and finally the forward turbine room received hits, so that steam poured from the hatches and deck lights. There was no hope of saving the boat and the Flottille Chief, Korvettenkapitän Wallis, ordered demolition charges to be exploded to scuttle the boat. Shortly after 10.00hrs *V187* slipped beneath the waves. On the British side the destroyer *Goshawk* was badly hit aft, in the wardroom. Then the destroyer *Defender* approached the sinking scene and launched boats to save the German survivors. However, now an unfortunate incident occurred. The cruiser *Stettin*, after raising stream in all her boilers, returned to the battle scene. At 10.01hrs a smoke cloud was sighted, and at 10.06hrs eight destroyers could be recognised. Korvettenkapitän Nerger did not hesitate to attack and wrote in his combat report:

> At 10.06am 8 destroyers that were close together but on several different courses, were made out and thereon a signal to the I BdA was given: 'Am in battle with Flotilla in 133 epsilon'. Turned to port and at 10.08am opened fire at 72hm. The first salvo landed square, so that quick salvo fire could be maintained. A great number of hits were observed with the following salvos.
> After about the fourth salvo the destroyers split from one another. Two boats went northerly, four boats somewhat to SW with highest speed; these were further pursued by *Stettin*, without the range decreasing. Two boats remained laying still, seemingly badly damaged. These and the boats going to the north now vanished from sight.
> About 10.13hrs the group pursued by *Stettin* was so difficult to make out that fire was broken off and I turned away to the NE, as the conditions were favourable for a torpedo attack, and a torpedo track was reported (supposedly an error).[14]

Under the prevailing conditions of poor visibility it is apparent that Korvettenkapitän Nerger had been unable to identify that one of the two boats remaining was the *V187* and that she was about to sink. The other was *Defender* going about rescue work. The British destroyer was forced to abandon the rescue boats but they were later sighted by the submarine *E4*, which closed on the boats and rescued the British sailors and three of the German survivors. The others, wounded and unwounded, were left in the boats to save themselves, but were rescued towards noon by the torpedoboats *G11* and *G9*.

The numerous destroyers had made an effective reply to the German cruiser, as Korvettenkapitän Nerger reveals:

The Battle in the Helgoland Bright, 28 August 1914   11

With the second battle *Stettin* received a hit through the FT antenna, whereby at 12hrs the FT Station was made unclear, and further a hit in the aft funnel (strong splinter effect), a hit near the starboard 3 gun, that struck the ready ammunition and in a short time the incendiary effect was extinguished with a pail of water. Further, an apparent short shot struck the ship in the height of the starboard engine under water, without causing damage.

The personnel losses were as follows: 2 dead, 1 badly wounded, 3 lightly wounded.[15]

With the first contact report the old cruiser *Hela* had rushed to support the other forces in the west, but at 11.15hrs, when she was 15 nautical miles SW of Helgoland she received a report from *Stettin* that the enemy forces had withdrawn to the west and therefore she went to a position on the northern picket line.

There was now a pause in the battle, and Commodore Tyrwhitt allowed *Arethusa* to lay stopped from 10.17hrs to 10.40hrs to effect repairs. Some of the armament was got back into working order, but two 4-inch guns remained unserviceable. To what extent other repairs took place remains unknown, but the British official history states: 'Meanwhile, as his crippled ship could only do 10 knots, he directed the *Fearless* to keep him in sight.'[16] Meanwhile Commodore Goodenough ordered *Nottingham* and *Lowestoft*, whom he had detached earlier, to join the battlecruiser force.

The first phase of the operation had been very disappointing for the British raiding force. The hoped-for rolling-up and destruction of the German picket line had not occurred, and just one torpedoboat had been destroyed. Of the others only *D8* and *T33* had suffered badly but they had both returned safely to harbour. The cruisers *Stettin* and *Frauenlob*, inferior in armament and speed, had carried the day, had saved the other picket forces from destruction and crippled the British flagship. However, the British fortunes were about to change in a big way.

Kontreadmiral Hipper, as BdA or Commander of Reconnaissance Forces, had responsibility for the security of the German Bight, including command of all torpedoboat and minesweeping forces. In hindsight it could be seen that this was too much workload for one command but it was not until 1918 that this command structure was changed. Therefore it was he who was responsible for counter moves to the British raid. His second in command was Kontreadmiral Maass, who was 2 Admiral of Reconnaissance Forces and also held the position of I Leader of Torpedoboats, or I FdT. The picket forces in the Bight were addressing most of their reports to him. On the morning of 28 August Kontreadmiral Maass was aboard his flagship, SMS *Cöln*, which lay in Wilhelmshaven coaling. Also in Wilhelmshaven were the cruisers *Straßburg*,

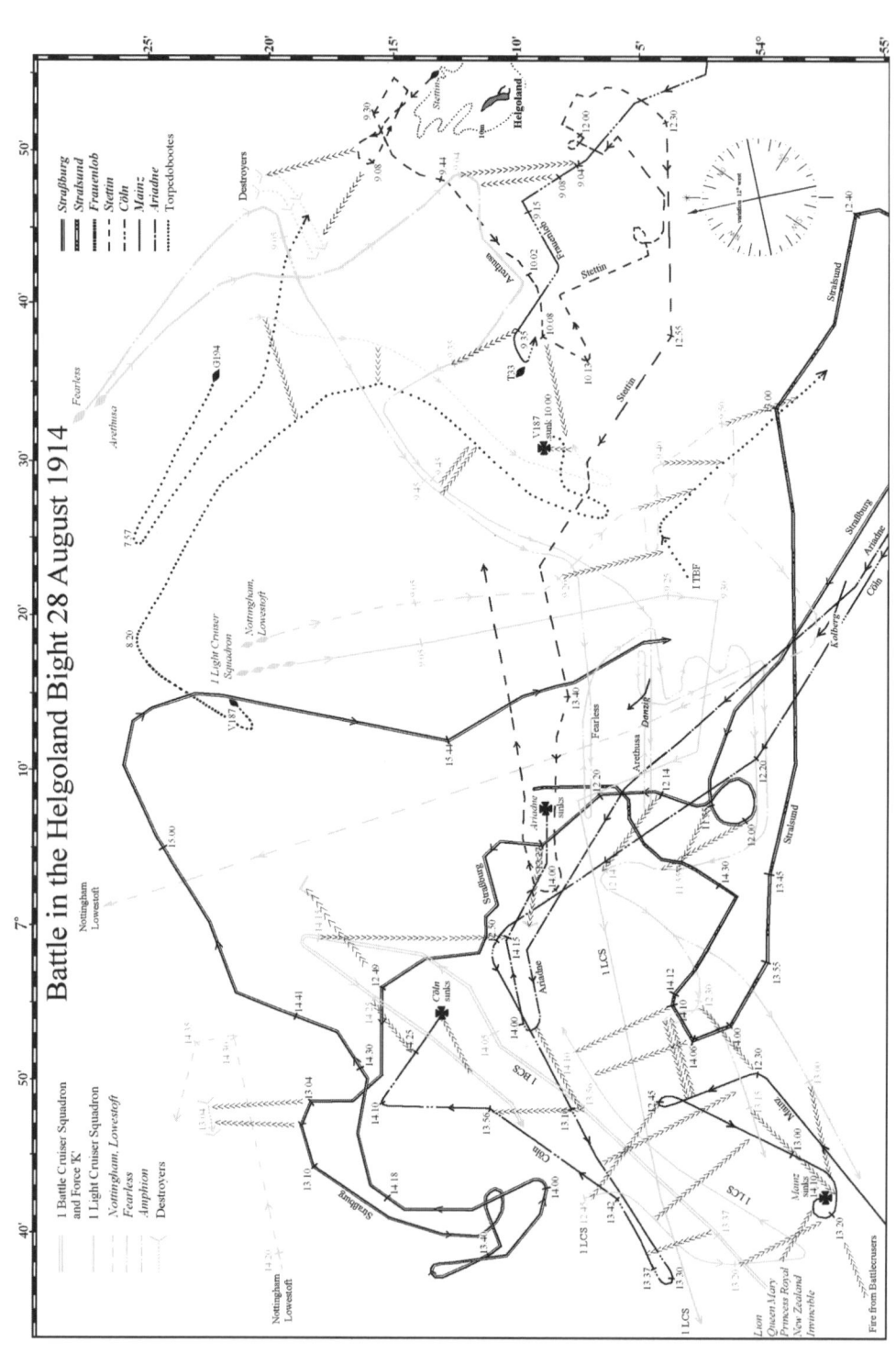

Stralsund and *Rostock*, whilst *Kolberg* lay on the roadstead. The cruisers *Danzig* and *München* lay in Brunsbüttel on their way back from the Baltic. When enemy cruisers were reported in the Bight *Cöln* and *Straßburg* immediately received orders to put to sea in support, whilst *Kolberg* was ordered to raise steam. *Stralsund* was ordered to the roadstead and *Danzig* and *München* were ordered to the Elbe river mouth to await further instructions. The cruiser *Mainz*, lying on the Ems River, was ordered to remain in readiness and shortly after to cut off the enemy from the rear. Accordingly at 09.10hrs *Straßburg* ran out of harbour, followed at 09.30hrs by *Cöln*. All haste had been ordered and unfortunately this meant that the cruisers arrived piecemeal in the Helgoland Bight. No explanation can be offered as to why Kontreadmiral Hipper did not allow his cruisers to concentrate before they entered the battle area, other than the desire to get to grips with the enemy as soon as possible, fearing he might escape before the cruisers could intervene, and also that he was unaware of the fog in the Bight and hence his forces were uncertain as to the composition and whereabouts of the enemy.

As early as 09.42hrs the High Sea Fleet Chief, Admiral Ingenhol, ordered the German *Panzerkreuzers*, as German battlecruisers were known at this time, to raise steam ready to put to sea. When questioned by Kontreadmiral Hipper whether they should run out as soon as they were ready, Admiral Ingenhol replied that this was at the discretion of Kontreadmiral Hipper, should the enemy 'still be there'. With the exception of *Blücher*, they lay on Wilhelmshaven Roads. However, the outer Jade bar had not been completely surveyed and as it was low tide the battlecruisers would not be able to cross this bar in complete safely until 12.00hrs at the earliest. Whilst *Moltke* and *von der Tann* were fully ready, *Seydlitz* was not completely combat-ready as the port main condenser was being fitted with new pipes and therefore only the starboard engine was serviceable. *Blücher* received orders to go to the roads. Although most of the battleships lay on Wilhelmshaven Roads, Admiral Ingenhol did not give them any preparatory orders, and acting independently only the commander of the II Squadron, Vizeadmiral Scheer, ordered his ships to be at one hour's readiness. On the other hand the commander of the U-boats in Helgoland, Kapitänleutnant Spindler, gave his boats orders to go to sea as soon as they could.

Under these circumstances a second riposte was conducted to cut off the British forces. SMS's *Cöln* and *Straßburg* were the first to take up the pursuit of the retreating British light forces and at 09.47hrs *Mainz* received orders to take the enemy forces in the rear. The German official history best conveys the prevailing mood:

> All cruisers were in wireless contact and from incoming reports it emerged that enemy light forces were in the German Bight in large numbers and that

Stettin and *Frauenlob* had already been in action several times with enemy cruisers and destroyers and that now the enemy forces were in retreat in a NW direction. This was the first time since the commencement of the war that the enemy had been within grasp of surface forces. Therefore there prevailed on the cruisers a martial spirit that filled the entire fleet, and the desire to help our *Armee* that already lay deep in enemy territory. This desire was supported by the feelings of wanting to bring help to the torpedoboats of the picket line, as there was no intelligence over their fate as yet. Therefore as the first cruisers ran out of the Jade and Elbe they did not lose time in taking up the pursuit, without waiting for later arrivals. The cruisers all steered separately with 'utmost speed' towards a likely meeting point with the retreating enemy, although they weren't warned about the conditions of changing and unfavourable visibility.[17]

At 11.31hrs Kontreadmiral Hipper could report to the Fleet Chief: '*Cöln, Straßburg, Stralsund* have run out. *Kolberg* follows. Our U-boats are under weigh. BdA.'

The first to make contact with the enemy was *Straßburg*. At 11.55hrs she sighted two cruisers 60° to starboard, accompanied by a large number of destroyers. Four destroyers immediately ran in to attack the German cruiser, which gave way to port, whilst opening fire on the leading cruiser at the same time at a range of 84hm. With the third straddling salvo a hit was seen on the stern of the enemy from which three brown smoke columns rose mast high. The British cruisers both returned the fire, whilst running off to the north. Because of the approaching enemy destroyers *Straßburg* gave way to port and just after 12 noon the enemy was lost to sight aft. *Straßburg* described a complete circle before resuming the pursuit. Her commander, Fregattenkapitän Retzmann, had no intension of breaking off contact and wrote in his war diary:

12.05hrs. *Straßburg* turns with port rudder towards the enemy destroyers and again sights the same at 12.14hrs to port ahead.

12.14hrs. Enemy destroyers in 320° approximately 80hm. Destroyers run to the attack. *Straßburg* turns slowly to starboard away from torpedoes. The destroyers were fired on between 54 and 78hm. Behind the destroyers, just in visible range, stood 2 light cruisers or scouts. One enemy torpedo ran to the port side past *Straßburg*. A second torpedo went behind the stern. Destroyers went from sight aft. The fire was answered from the destroyers.

Fregattenkapitän Retzmann wanted to catch these forces between himself and *Mainz* in the southwest, but this plan was suddenly interrupted when at

12.27hrs new enemy forces were sighted to port ahead. Enemy destroyers were sighted at a range of 90hm and they immediately opened fire on *Straßburg*. *Straßburg* returned the fire at ranges between 88hm and 64hm and slowly gave way to starboard as two torpedoes were observed approaching. At 12.36hrs the enemy was lost from view, but shortly afterwards at 12.49hrs several more destroyers were sighted, which attacked and once again *Straßburg* was forced to turn away.

In the meantime the cruiser *Mainz* had joined the battle.

On the morning of 28 August *Mainz*, under the command of Kapitän zur See Wilhelm Paschen, was anchored off the mouth of the Ems River as picket, having replaced *Kolberg* two days previously. An aircraft floatplane was moored astern. At 09.47hrs the order came for *Mainz* to cut off the enemy forces in the Bight and about 10.00hrs she ran out and dispatched the aircraft for reconnaissance ahead. At first course was taken in a northerly direction, but after contact reports from *Stettin, Frauenlob* and then *Straßburg* were received, it was altered to intercept the enemy, which was estimated would occur at about 12.30hrs. Then a message arrived from *Cöln* saying she would join the battle from the southeast. Meanwhile the aircraft returned without having sighted the enemy. Shortly afterwards *Mainz* ran into hazy weather so that visibility was reduced. This meant that the chances of being surprised were greatly increased and the lookouts in the forward crow's nest, one of which was Oberleutnant von Tirpitz, strained their eyes peering into the mist. At about 12.30hrs the enemy was sighted. Oberleutnant von Tirpitz continues:

> Meanwhile we drove on a northerly course with 'utmost power'. About a half hour later I called the commander again: 'We must at any moment meet the destroyers.' My *signalgast*,[18] Keese, and I were in suspense and keenly aware. We alternated between bare eyes and telescopes to scan the stretch before us. Then all at once, four points to starboard, dark vessels came out of the noon summer haze, that allowed a visibility of only 7,000 metres. Eight could be made out with certainty; on the green background they stood out like dark beetles. Immediately I passed to below; 'Enemy destroyers four points to starboard!' The destroyers were on a westerly course until we approached, and then at once turned off to the north. Through the speaking tube I could hear the artillery commands and saw how the barrels took their aim, with the exception of the starboard fifth, that apparently could not take aim as the target was too far ahead. Clearly the salvo bell sounded and immediately the first salvo went away. Now I had to call the correct fall of shot. It was unbelievably difficult to observe…The enemy shot now, but how! In the pause between our salvos the only enemy fall of shot I saw lay far off to starboard. Only the hisses through the air informed us of his wide shooting. So far the situation was not very dangerous for us.[19]

However, a short time before, when his 'crippled' *Arethusa* was engaged by *Straßburg*, Commodore Tyrwhitt had signalled Vice Admiral Beatty with an urgent appeal for help. Vice Admiral Beatty's response was to order Commodore Goodenough to dispatch two cruisers for the assistance of Commodore Tyrwhitt's sorely pressed forces. These forces now made their presence felt.

From 12.30hrs to 13.45hrs *Mainz* had taken up a NNW course and was engaged with *Arethusa* and her attendant destroyers. Then suddenly a new opponent emerged from the mist. Oberleutnant von Tirpitz wrote:

> While I had my eye to the telescope the *signalgast* nudged me; 'Herr Oberleutnant, cruisers to port!' I spun around and with the glass saw three cruisers of the *Town* class three points to port. Now there was no time to lose. I yelled down through the speaking tube; 'Three enemy cruisers three points to port!' With that immediately there were gun flashes over there already. We turned to starboard onto an opposite course. This was a different opponent one noticed immediately. The salvos lay close to our ship and with each fall of shot a sallow gas development showed itself. High water columns piled up. The deep buzzes through the air left no doubt as to the calibre–it was 15cm, which we could only counter with 10.5cm. Now the English were directly abaft. They follow us *en-echelon*. The first hit arrived; a steam pipe to the siren was hit and steam escaped in torrents with hisses. Blast! We were now being shot, but we were not yet lame. In my estimation the range astern remained constant. The range was low however, and we could not afford a further reduction. Our two aft guns bravely took up the battle. It was totally impossible to observe the fall of shot. Meanwhile we received several deck hits. One saw now the men falling, and being carried away, everything carried out in immaculate order.

The I Offizier, Kapitänleutnant Tholens, reported:

> About 12.45pm a smoke cloud was suddenly reported in the NW and a few minutes later three cruisers of the *Birmingham* class could be made out. *Mainz* immediately turned hard to starboard. However, whilst still in the turn the first enemy salvo fell nearby, and a little later *Mainz* received the first hit, on the poop and the middle deck. The fire of *Arethusa* and the destroyers, that now were seemingly out of sight, had been without result. Now our own fire was directed exclusively on the new opponent. This was reported by wireless at the same time. About 12.55pm the enemy cruisers could only be recognised by the flash of their guns. Shortly after this he also stopped firing and with that the impacts of enemy shells. *Mainz* went at 25 knots, course approximately SSE, towards the East Ems and developed thick smoke.[20]

The escape of *Mainz* was short lived. Now to port abeam another cruiser came in sight, at first taken to be of the *Town* class. It was however *Fearless*, preceded ahead by six destroyers. *Fearless* opened fire on *Mainz* and *Mainz* replied by opening fire on the destroyers as they manoeuvred to launch torpedoes. The firing of *Mainz* was very accurate and the destroyers soon began to suffer. The first to be hit was *Laurel*, which had just fired two torpedoes and was occupied with turning away when she was hit by a salvo from the German cruiser. Ready ammunition in the aft racks was hit and detonated, putting the aft gun out of action, and also damaged the aft funnel so that the ship was smothered in smoke. So concealed she was able to crawl away despite having damaged engines and boilers. *Laurel* had twenty-three casualties. The next destroyer in line, *Liberty*, was then hit forward. Her mast was brought down and her commander, Lieutenant-Commander Barttelot, was killed. *Mainz* missed the next in line, *Lysander*, but the last in line, *Laertes*, was struck by a salvo in which every shell hit. Her boilers were put out of action and she was brought to a standstill. Luckily there were only two dead and six wounded.

Mainz had repulsed the torpedo attack but soon began to suffer at the hands of the cruisers. A hit struck aft at about 13.00hrs and jammed the rudder at 10°. Sanitätsmaat (Medical Mate) Partzech wrote the following about this hit:

> I belonged to the aft dressing station. Our position was in the rudder room. There I stayed with two doctors and two litter bearers when we had run out of the river Ems. At approximately 12.15hrs the shooting began. We felt continuous strong vibrations from hits, amongst them two in our vicinity that struck against the hull side without penetrating. One seems to have hit the rudder. From above gases with a sharp smell penetrated through the ventilation shaft, which finally made breathing difficult. After some time we felt an especially strong vibration, which was apparently due to a torpedo hit. The electric lights extinguished and the steam, that we saw in the manometer of the compressor room, quickly fell.[21]

The next part of the action is best described by the I Offizier, Kapitänleutnant Tholens:

> The hereupon taken measures to restore the steering and repair the rudder arrangement of the ship remained without success. It was therefore taken that the underwater hit had jammed the rudder to starboard. The port engine was stopped. However, *Mainz* still slowly turned to starboard.
>
> At the same time a report arrived on the bridge that three guns and their entire crews had fallen out. Because of the unmanoeuvrability of the ship we now found ourselves also against the three *Town* cruisers as well as *Arethusa* and eight destroyers. Now the ship was overpowered by no fewer than five

cruisers and twenty destroyers. Now we could only expect success against the latter and our fire was directed exclusively in the destroyers' direction. In part they came near and a number of hits were observed on them. On *Mainz* seemingly one disaster followed another. Towards 1.20pm the greater part of the guns and their crews were out of action. The upper deck resembled a debris house. The ammunition supply was interrupted, and several positions below the armoured deck had to be evacuated because of smoke and gas danger. The starboard engine only gave revolutions for half speed.

About this time the ship received a torpedo hit to port amidships (probably in the IV boiler room). In the conning tower all means for transmitting orders, with the exception of the speaking tube to the central control position and torpedo room, had fallen out. Hereupon the commander ordered, 'Sink the ship. Crew clear for life jackets,' and he then left the conning tower, whereby he and the Navigation Offizier, Kapitänleutnant Freiherr Friedrich Karl von Maltzahn, were immediately killed. This order only went as far as the next battle station and accordingly was only partially carried out.

Because of the torpedo hit the gunfire had slackened. At this time only the I Artillerie Offizier, Kapitänleutnant Otto Niese, and the I Torpedo Offizier, Oberleutnant zur See Karl Pohle, were in the conning tower. Somewhat later I came on the bridge, however without knowledge of the commander's last order. On my order the gunfire was resumed and simultaneously a torpedo shot was attempted. This was practically chanceless because the ship lay entirely motionless and for the most part the enemy cruisers and destroyers were abaft or on the edge of the torpedo angle. The torpedoes were launched, one to port on a cruiser and two to starboard at a destroyer, and remained without success. Meanwhile the enemy gunfire had completely ceased, and there was a fire pause on *Mainz*. Moreover two or more enemy battlecruisers intervened in the battle. If they achieved a hit is not determined with certainty. However some men testified that a 34cm shell smashed into the middle deck, without exploding, while gigantic water columns erupted around the ship. On *Mainz* only two guns were in action. The gun crews were from the ammunition men from the *Zwischendeck*.

Meanwhile I had been informed about the last order of the commander. The order: 'Sink ship. Crew clear for life jackets,' was again given at 1.35pm. Although now the order was delivered over the whole ship to aft, it was later determined that some men below decks that still had to be evacuated, did not receive it. They only came up some ten minutes later, when the enemy ceased fire. The port engine room and port torpedo room made water and were previously abandoned.[22]

Mainz had been torpedoed by the destroyer *Lydiard*.

Oberleutnant von Tirpitz had a good overview from his lofty vantage point in the crow's nest. He wrote:

> A most terrible blow shook the whole ship, and in the crow's nest one was thrown high; the whole ship vibrated. That was a torpedo hit. From where and how it had come I had not observed. Previously I had seen several different torpedo tracks, however all had passed by us. As the giant water column of the torpedo hit climbed up almost to the height of the crow's nest, and then fell again, I could clearly feel that the engines had stopped. A glance below showed that we only made slow speed. The enemy had encircled us, with the most of them being to starboard. Our gun crews shot to all sides. The guns, in part at least, fired independently. I tried to count our opponents; there were at least twenty destroyers. For them it was a wonderful skeet shoot. We were no longer a danger to them. Then suddenly my neighbour said: 'It's time, Herr Oberleutnant, oh, these English, these accursed swine!' He had been hit and half held in his hands his gory innards. The poor chap had been hit in the stomach by a splinter. Although I covered him with a cloth, it amounted to nothing. Quickly my good Keese's strength faded and he slowly leaned over, and with the blood loss his colour faded.[23]

Mainz was now badly damaged. The two aft funnels were shot through and had fallen, as had the main mast. The electric lighting failed and the engines no longer made revolutions. The leak pendulum showed that the cruiser was slowly sinking by the bows but had no list. The guns had all fallen out. When *Mainz* fired no more the British destroyers quickly approached, and *Lurcher*, Commodore Keyes's flagship, came alongside aft and towards 14.00hrs took off the wounded. Towards 14.10hrs *Mainz* lay over to port and sank. Those survivors in the water gave three cheers for their ship. Of the crew, 89, including the commander, were killed, and 348 were taken captive.

Whilst *Fearless* and the 1st Cruiser Squadron were in combat with *Mainz*, the British light cruiser *Arethusa* was distracted by the appearance of a new combatant on the scene, the small cruiser SMS *Cöln*. *Cöln*, under the command of Fregattenkapitän Meidinger and flying the flag of Kontreadmiral Maass, had been coaling in Wilhelmshaven when the British raid into Helgoland Bight was first reported. As we have seen she departed Wilhelmshaven just behind the cruiser *Straßburg* and her course followed that of *Straßburg* to the NW across the Bight. At 11.55hrs when *Straßburg* entered into her first fight the sound of the guns was clearly audible aboard *Cöln*. After *Straßburg* described a full circle, *Cöln* was just 7 nautical miles behind her and from then until about 12.50hrs *Cöln* followed on the same NW course. At 13.05hrs *Cöln* relayed a signal to the BdA from *Mainz* saying she was in battle with enemy battlecruisers. At the same time *Cöln* made an 8-point turn to port onto course WSW towards *Mainz* and the sound of cannon thunder. After about 20 minutes *Cöln* sighted *Arethusa* and attendant destroyers to port ahead. As *Arethusa* was travelling at reduced speed it was easy for *Cöln* to catch her and at 13.30hrs she reported she was in battle with British destroyers, however the message abruptly ended before a position report could be given. The sole survivor from *Cöln*, Leading Stoker (Oberheizer) Neumann, wrote that the battle began at a longer range for that morning: 'I heard "78 hundred" called. At the same moment the fire bells sounded and the first salvo crashed out.'[24] However, shortly afterwards Vice Admiral Beatty's battlecruisers appeared to port ahead and opened a violent fire on *Cöln*. *Cöln* immediately turned through 16 points and reversed course, replying to the fire at 13.37hrs. At 13.42hrs Admiral Beatty altered course to port slightly to close the range, and *Cöln* likewise turned away to port. Now the German cruiser was beginning to suffer at the hands of her superior opponents:

> At first no enemy fire was heard, however, short shots were observed. The first hit was felt at about 4000m commanded range, apparently near the N°5 gun. A *Bootsmannsmaat* from the N°5 gun was heavily wounded and brought to the rudder room, the dressing station, and then came the information–apparently through a speaking tube–that the Admiral had fallen, the Commander was shot through one arm, and the Artillerie Offizier was shot through both legs–then a shot struck in compartment III–one from starboard–and all men in the compartment fell.[25]

At 13.56hrs *Cöln* turned further port onto a northerly course and as the battlecruisers were now distracted by the appearance of another small cruiser ahead of them they ceased fire. Although *Cöln* was in a bad way, with the hull shot through and the aft magazine flooded because of the danger from fires, there still remained a chance to save the ship. At 14.10hrs, a short time after the British battlecruisers had been lost from view, *Cöln* turned onto a SE course back towards Wilhelmshaven in an attempt to retire from the battle area. However, Vice Admiral Beatty was becoming concerned about his forces being scattered across the Bight and feared that heavier German forces would soon arrive and do to him what he had been doing to the German light forces. Therefore at 14.10hrs he gave the general order: 'Retire!' The British battlecruisers turned to port and, as luck would have it, a short time later at 14.25hrs *Cöln* came in sight ahead, steaming on a SE course across their bows. Had *Cöln* stood away to the north for a short time longer she would have been safe, but in turning onto a SE course her fate was sealed. The battlecruisers once again opened a deadly fire from which there was no escape. The fire of heavy cannon at close range quickly brought the small cruiser to a sinking condition. The order was now given for the men to assemble on deck, in preparation to abandon ship. Oberheizer Neumann wrote about the scene above which greeted his eyes:

Above my eye was met with a picture of indescribable devastation. The guns were completely destroyed, their barrels were smoke blackened, and their protective shields were perforated and bent. One gun was blown out of its mounting. The muzzle of the barrel hung steeply down. The gun crew lay tattered in their blood. The deck was rent apart and resembled a desolate debris field. Boat parts, davits, brackets, stairways, charred life vests, antennas, signal lines, ammunition, splinters and shrapnel all lay in a confused mess. The funnels were shot through. The bridge was totally destroyed. From masts hung shot through lines. Giant holes gaped in the hull side...Our ship did not have a list; but still floated on an even keel and had sunk only indiscernibly deeper. It was accepted that we would be sunk with a torpedo shot, and therefore the *offiziers* gave orders to provide all with life vests and to throw all floating objects such as empty munitions cases, hammocks and timber baulks, overboard. The badly wounded and non-swimmers were bound with two life vests. I found a half burnt life vest with which I later also jumped into the water.[26]

Deep inside the stricken cruiser the *Ingenieurs* set demolition charges to scuttle the doomed ship. At 14.25hrs, as the survivors in the water sang the anthem, *Cöln* slowly rolled over to port and sank. The German sailors swimming in the water expected to be picked up by their opponents, but it was a vain hope, only Oberheizer Neumann was picked up by his own comrades 72 hours later, all the others who had survived the sinking perished.

The cruiser that had distracted the British battlecruisers from their practice on *Cöln* was the late arrival *Ariadne*. At 11.33hrs *Ariadne*, the Leader Ship of the Jade-Weser Harbour Flottille, received the order from *Seydlitz*: 'Advance for support when possible.'[27] The order was also addressed to the small cruiser *Niobe* but she was coaling in Wilhelmshaven and thus was unable to immediately comply. *Ariadne* though was able to follow the fast disappearing *Cöln* for a time, before losing sight of this ship and proceeding on her own. However, *Ariadne* was not alone for long, as towards 13.40hrs *Stettin*, proceeding on the basis of the position reports given by the other cruisers, sighted her directly ahead at a range of approximately 5 nautical miles. Korvettenkapitän Nerger takes up the story:

About 1.40 SMS *Ariadne* came in sight ahead and at first was taken for an English mine cruiser. The exchange of recognition signal only came after a long time, when it at times became somewhat clearer. The visibility changed at this time very greatly.

At 1.45pm gunfire was heard ahead, which towards 1.55pm made the impression of heavy artillery. About 1.58pm strong muzzle flashes were also observed and thereon turned to starboard onto the opposite course. Still during the turn the heavy impacts were observed in the vicinity of *Ariadne*, likewise in the turn. Soon after followed the first hit on *Ariadne*.

In the turn SMS *Stettin* made out this new opponent as the newest battlecruiser type.

About 2.05 the forward battlecruiser also opened fire on *Stettin* which because of the unfavourable position of the enemy and being unable to target the muzzle flash, could not be replied to. The shots of the enemy lay very close to the ship (inside 500m) to both sides, ahead and aft, but were predominantly over. The visibility did not permit observation of the opponent. After about 10 shots he broke off the fire, however after a few minutes the fire was briefly taken up again. At 2.20 to starboard abeam (south) SMS *Danzig* was sighted on a western course, however likewise turned onto an easterly course on the searchlight message from *Stettin* that she was being chased by enemy battlecruisers. At the same time the enemy appeared to break off the pursuit.

Ariadne was not so lucky. Shortly before 14.00hrs two ships emerged from the fog directly ahead which did not answer the recognition signal. One ship was *Cöln*, under heavy fire, and the other was her adversary. When the British battlecruisers sighted *Ariadne* they immediately changed target to this hapless cruiser. This relieved *Cöln* for a short time and meanwhile *Ariadne* turned away to starboard and took course east at highest speed. *Ariadne* soon received a hit in the forward boiler room, which caused a bunker fire and the boiler room had to be evacuated because of smoke. Five boilers were put out of action and the speed was reduced to 15 knots. A second British battlecruiser joined the battle and the range reduced from 55hm to 40hm, and finally to 30hm, point blank range for the big ships. *Ariadne* nevertheless returned fire as she could. The commander of *Ariadne*, Fregattenkapitän Seebohm, described the course of the battle:

> *Ariadne* received many hits from heavy guns, including a whole series of hits in the aft ship, which was totally engulfed in flames. Of the personnel found there, it was only due to chance that some were rescued. The foreship also received a series of heavy hits, one of which penetrated the armoured deck and put the torpedo room out of action, a second hit the dressing station and killed all personnel there.
>
> Strangely the amidships and command bridge remained almost spared.
>
> How many hits were suffered in total is impossible to estimate. The antenna was destroyed by the explosions. Several shells were observed to strike the water and failed to explode. Many shots went past right and left, because *Ariadne* fled directly away from the enemy and offered only a narrow target.[28]

Obermaschinisten Schröder further detailed the damage:

> The port side passage from the *Zwischendeck* to compartment VII was not passable, so I proceeded on the *Oberdeck* and found that a heavy hit had penetrated the hull side approximately between the III and IV boiler rooms below the men's galley. The *Oberdeck* and the wall of the forward upper bunker were completely torn. Likewise the cofferdam was demolished and the burning cork of the cofferdam in association with the fast burning paint caused a very strong, biting dense smoke. With some other people I immediately threw away the ready ammunition that lay in the vicinity of the fire, partly overboard, partly to the side. I attempted to extinguish the fires with water standing on deck near the guns, whereby the smoke danger was almost entirely removed.[29]

A vivid description of what it was like to be caught below during and after the hail of shells is given by Obermaschinist Schottmann:

> I found myself in the forward boiler room as the *Maschinist* having the watch. The first disruption was the forward siren was shot through. Later it was taken down. A large hit in the bunker caused a violent vibration in the forward boiler room, so that the hand wheels of the valve linkages flew down. On the port III and IX boilers torrents of steam escaped from the steam collectors, through damage to the steam carrying parts. Both boilers were turned off, and the fires were extinguished. The escaping steam passed through the shot hole, so the boiler room was steam free. The boiler room filled with smoke. There was no improvement through the ventilation engine because the dense smoke did not go through the open fire doors and the funnel flaps themselves did not move, so it was supposed the funnel had been crushed. The dense smoke increased in such a way that the men could no longer see and breathing became difficult. The remaining boilers of the forward boiler room were stopped, the fires were extinguished and the room was evacuated. On the armoured hatch to boiler room III there lay several corpses. The armoured hatch could not be opened from below. The armoured grating of the emergency exit could be opened through the bunker bulkhead, against the air pressure, only so far that a slender person could creep through. The stairs to boiler room IV were pushed together and impassable. The corpses on the armoured hatch to boiler room III were removed and the stairway was passable. The aft 4 boiler, stair- and emergency exit were in order. The aft 4 boilers were reduced to 15kg pressure and fires extinguished. Hereby, on orders, I quit the boiler room watch.[30]

At around 14.15hrs the British fire ceased and *Ariadne* was able to creep away to the east. The ship was in a wretched condition, with fires fore and aft. The forward magazine had to be flooded to prevent an explosion. There were many men trapped in compartments I and II aft because a shell hit had bent a hatch to these compartments. The ready ammunition near the guns began to detonate and splinters were thrown all about the ship. The crew were assembled on the forecastle and preparations were made to abandon ship. Now some relief arrived as shortly before 15.00hrs *Danzig* approached and sent some boats across to *Ariadne*. The wounded were lowered into the boats whilst some men rescued themselves by swimming across to *Danzig*. Others went to *Stralsund*, which had also just arrived in the vicinity of sinking ship. At 16.25hrs *Ariadne* suddenly lay over and capsized, and the keel remained visible above the surface for some time.

Not all the German small cruisers that came into contact with the British battlecruisers came off the worse. When we left *Straßburg* at 12.49hrs she was in battle with British destroyers to starboard. Fregattenkapitän Retzmann turned away to port from these and at the beginning of *Ariadne*'s battle *Straßburg* was just 5 nautical miles to the northwest. Soon after, at 13.04hrs, two enemy cruisers and numerous destroyers came in sight to starboard ahead. The destroyers were taken under fire and both the cruisers and destroyers replied. *Straßburg* was hit once by a 6-inch shell aft above her armour and the shell smashed through the bulkhead between compartments I and II. There was slight flooding but little damage. The destroyers manoeuvred for a torpedo attack but *Straßburg* turned away to port. From 13.10hrs *Straßburg* attempted to make for the last reported position of *Mainz*, to render assistance, but failed to make contact. However, the sound of heavy cannon thunder could be heard to the southeast. Then at 14.00hrs apparent enemy armoured cruisers could be made out ahead. These were probably Commodore Goodenough's light cruisers. *Straßburg* turned away to the north but soon after, at 14.18hrs two cruisers of the *Town* class were sighted at a range of 80hm, to port on a parallel course. It was *Nottingham* and *Lowestoft*. Then suddenly, at 14.30hrs, to starboard 4 points ahead, four battlecruisers came in sight on the opposite course at a range of 80hm. Fregattenkapitän Retzmann wrote in his war diary:

> Apparently the enemy battlecruisers hold *Straßburg* as one of their own. To hold this perception as long as possible, *Straßburg* holds her course. An immediate course alteration would arouse suspicion. In addition such a course alteration to port would again put *Straßburg* in the area of the *Town* cruisers that had just gone from sight.[31]

The battlecruisers were passed 75hm abeam to starboard and only after passing did the British flagship make the recognition signal. At 14.42hrs the battlecruisers passed out of sight, and *Straßburg* had survived a narrow escape.

The Battle in the Helgoland Bright, 28 August 1914   25

The last small cruiser to come into contact with enemy forces on 28 August was SMS *Stralsund*, under the command of Kapitän zur See Harder. At 10.50hrs she had run out of the lock at Wilhelmshaven and at 11.00hrs she received the searchlight signal from *Seydlitz*: 'Immediately run out for the support of *Cöln*.' At first *Stralsund* tried to make for the reported position of the enemy forces but nothing was found, only a diving submarine which was fired on at 12.37hrs. Only at 13.40hrs was the sound of cannon thunder identified, and *Stralsund* made for this. Fifteen minutes later muzzle flashes could be seen and then at 14.05hrs three enemy light cruisers could be made out. A little ahead of them an enemy battlecruiser could be recognized. Kapitän zur See Harder wrote in his war diary:

> Battle course ENE taken and fire opened on the forward most cruiser at approximately 73hm in 280°, to relieve our own ship found on the other side. The visibility was very low. From the crow's nest no impacts could be observed.
>
> The fire was immediately answered by the enemy. It lay approximately 2/3 short and 1/3 over. The explosive shells exploded with clear yellow-green clouds. Numerous short and over shots lay close to the ship. With one of the first salvos the large wireless antenna was shot through. A further short shot penetrated the hull side in compartment IV. The shell did not explode. The ship made no water. Splinters of the short shells flew on deck and further damaged the ship and men. *Stralsund* was well covered and it is a wonder that it did not receive several more hits.[32]

At 14.15hrs *Stralsund* turned away from her opponents that outnumbered her three-to-one and gradually ran out of range. After that *Stralsund* returned to a northerly course and at 15.00hrs sighted *Danzig* and the badly damaged *Ariadne*. The commander of *Ariadne*, Fregattenkapitän Seebohm, six *Offiziers*, two *Fähnrich* and fifty men were rescued, some being fished out of the water. It proved impossible to go alongside the sinking cruiser as the munitions aboard the ship were continually exploding.

Of the other cruisers *Danzig* and *München* received orders at 12.25hrs to run out to support *Straßburg*. This order was later amended and at 14.06hrs *München* was ordered by the BdA to conduct reconnaissance in the direction of Amrum Bank. In conducting the advance to the west *Danzig* ended up in the vicinity of *Ariadne* at 14.09hrs, and in addition to the sound of heavy gunfire also observed the fall of some shot. *Danzig* turned onto a NW course to lend support and soon *Stettin* and then *Ariadne* came in sight. As related previously *Stettin* warned *Danzig* of the approach of British battlecruisers and *Danzig* turned to the east. Not long afterward *Ariadne* hoisted the flag signal: 'Have pressing need for assistance', and the commander of *Danzig*, Fregattenkapitän

Reiß, decided to come to the aid of this ship despite the presence of superior enemy ships in the vicinity. *Danzig* put out two cutters and began the work of rescuing the crew of *Ariadne*, and did not break off this work even after the arrival of the recall order. Kontreadmiral Hipper ordered: 'All small cruisers fall back on *Moltke* and *von der Tann*,' to which Fregattenkapitän Reiß gave the terse reply, 'Rescuing people from *Ariadne*.'[33]

The cruiser *Kolberg*, under the command of Fregattenkapitän Widenmann, also ran out to rendezvous with *Straßburg* but could only run at 22 knots. At 14.20hrs *Stralsund* came in sight and, because of the report from *Stettin* and *Straßburg* about enemy battlecruisers, *Kolberg* turned onto a parallel easterly course. After that *Kolberg* conducted reconnaissance to the northwest of the *Ariadne* group, to secure them during their rescue work. The cruiser *München* made reconnaissance to the northeast of Helgoland and *Hela* wisely remained to the east of Helgoland, as her armament was inferior to that of even the British destroyers.

The first report of the presence of British heavy forces in the Helgoland Bight had come from *Mainz* at 13.02hrs. Kontreadmiral Hipper responded by ordering the battlecruisers *von der Tann* and *Moltke* to run out to support the small cruisers at 13.10hrs. He advised that *Seydlitz* would follow them. Nevertheless, it was not until around 15.00hrs that these two battlecruisers, under the command of the 3rd Admiral of Reconnaissance Forces, Kontreadmiral Tapken, passed the outer Jade light vessel, almost 2 hours after the first report of enemy armoured cruisers. *Seydlitz* and *Blücher* were still to appear. At 15.25hrs *von der Tann* and *Moltke* arrived in the vicinity of the sinking *Ariadne*, however at 16.00hrs Kontreadmiral Hipper signalled them to proceed no further west until the arrival of *Seydlitz*, which duly occurred at 16.10hrs. After that Kontreadmiral Hipper undertook a brief advance to the northwest, but the German ships found nothing, and tragically turned back when the vanguard was just 4 nautical miles short of the sinking position of *Cöln*. Shortly before the heavy ships made the turn *Blücher* finally caught up. At 21.23hrs *Seydlitz* anchored on Wilhelmshaven Roadstead and Kontreadmiral Hipper went to the Fleet Chief to give a report. With that the day was at an end.

The question must be raised as to why heavier German cruiser support did not arrive sooner. The last signal from *Mainz* at 13.02hrs ran: 'Am pursued by enemy *Panzerkreuzer*', meaning battlecruisers. *Straßburg* reported the same at 14.00hrs, as did *Stettin* at 14.10hrs. Then at 14.35hrs *Straßburg* finally gave a position and course for the British battlecruisers. Up until 13.00hrs the German Fleet Chief, Admiral Ingenohl, believed that the German small cruisers were dominant and in the ascendancy. He believed that there were only two, or at most four, enemy light cruisers and perhaps two flotillas of destroyers present in the Bight, and that these had been repulsed by the German cruisers. Nevertheless, around 13.00hrs Admiral Ingenohl issued orders to recall the scattered small cruisers. Kontreadmiral Hipper did not order a recall of the small cruisers up until then as he believed they would fall back in the presence of superior forces, as indicated in the general tactical orders. These, however, did not take into account poor visibility. In any case a recall order would only have been effective had it been issued prior to 12.30hrs, and the presence of British battlecruisers had not been established at that time.

Regardless, it is difficult to understand why the German leaders did not allow supporting forces to run out in an organized way, and in a greater strength, not withstanding it being low water at the Jade bar. It is incomprehensible that they believed the British forces would not be supported by stronger units (although this was nearly the case) and should have undertaken more resolute steps to mount a secure, supported defence. The loss of three small cruisers and heavy loss of life were the results of the measures undertaken by the German leadership.

The outcome of the battle was a resounding British success, although almost by default. During the first phase of the battle the Germans had successfully repulsed the initial British attack, and inflicted heavy losses on them for the loss of one torpedoboat, to the point where Commodore Tyrwhitt signalled he was in pressing need of support. When this arrived the Germans lost three small cruisers in quick succession. Total casualties were 712 *Offiziers* and men killed, 381 taken prisoner and 149 wounded. Compared to this the British losses were extremely light, just 35 killed and about 40 wounded. Nevertheless the cruiser *Arethusa* had to be towed away by the cruiser *Hogue*, and the destroyer *Laurel* had to be towed back by *Amethyst*.

One reason offered by the German history for the piecemeal arrival of the small cruisers in the Bight was the attacking spirit of the individual cruiser commanders, who were allowed initiative and freedom to attack. Many of these commanders went on to give outstanding service later in the war; Kapitän zur See Harder commanded *Lützow*, Fregattenkapitän Mommsen commanded *Pillau*, Fregattenkapitän Reiß commanded *Wiesbaden* and Fregattenkapitän Nerger commanded the raider *Wolf*. Nevertheless, the free attack spirit met with disaster in the fog against the battlecruisers and concentrated 1st Light Cruiser Squadron on 28 August.

The immediate result for the Germans was the laying of protective mine barriers in the Helgoland Bight in September, as proposed by the BdA, and the implementation of his proposal to use aircraft and airships to provide long-range reconnaissance. A further suggestion to use U-boats in a picket line was not adopted as these were foreseen in a more offensive role.

Finally the accusation made by the English press and official history that German *Offiziers* aboard *Mainz* had shot their own men with pistols reflects poorly on the malicious authors and can be consigned to the realm of xenophobic fantasy.

Chapter 2

The Sea Battle at Coronel, 1 November 1914

At the end of the 19th Century, just as at the beginning of the 21st Century, China was an important trading partner for the European countries. In 1895 Germany was second only to Britain in the volume of goods moved between China and Europe and the Deutsch–Asiatische Bank had become financially very powerful. Germany was also important to China from a military perspective as German military instructors and experts were employed at the Chinese military academies at Tientsin and Canton. After the disastrous Sino–Japanese War of 1894–95 the German presence was intensified and a German language training school for Chinese officers was set up. A German company also obtained a contract to build one of China's first railways.

However, like all the other European countries, Germany did not hesitate to force China into granting a 99-year lease on Chinese territory so that she could establish a colony to protect her interests and to provide a stable base for further trade with China. For Germany the lease was granted on the Kiaochou Peninsula, and there they developed the city and port of Tsingtao. The British leased Weihaiwei and Hong Kong, the French Kwang-Chou-Wan, and the Russians Port Arthur. At the same time Germany legitimately bought the islands of Palau from Spain, and obtained many other island colonies throughout the Pacific. To defend this Asiatic Empire the Imperial Navy based an East Asiatic Squadron at Tsingtao, and developed harbour facilities to support this squadron.

In August 1914 the East Asiatic Squadron consisted of the armoured cruisers *Scharnhorst* and *Gneisenau* and the small cruisers *Emden*, *Nürnberg* and *Leipzig*. Several gunboats and torpedoboats also supported the squadron.

The commander of the East Asiatic Squadron was Vizeadmiral Maximilian Graf von Spee. Graf von Spee was born in Copenhagen on 22 June 1861 and joined the Imperial Navy in 1878. He commanded the small cruiser *Hela* and battleship *Wittelsbach* and spent time at the Reichs Marine Amt. He was promoted Kontreadmiral on 27 January 1910. He then served as 2nd Admiral of Reconnaissance Ships and the 2nd Admiral of the III Battle Squadron before being appointed to command the East Asiatic Cruiser Squadron in December 1912. He was due to be relieved by Kontreadmiral Gädeke in autumn 1914 but the onset of war prevented this change taking place. Graf von Spee was known for being bright and cheerful, efficient and disciplined, but cordial. He was hard working and a very talented leader of men. He was promoted to Vizeadmiral on 15 November 1913. A contemporary wrote of him:[1]

> He was respected by all his subordinates. He was also a favourite in the wardroom. He made everyone his friend by his invariable kindness, his unaffected and engaging nature and his dry sense of humour. I sat next to him for eighteen months and during that time I got to know him and appreciate him more every day...I believe I can say without exaggeration that none of us ever found even the smallest fault with Graf Spee.

Although the principle base for the squadron was Tsingtao, most of the cruisers spent time away visiting other colonies and visiting other countries to show the flag. This was the case when war broke out in Europe in August 1914, and of the cruisers only *Emden* remained in Tsingtao. *Scharnhorst* and *Gneisenau* were at Ponape (Pohnpei), where Graf von Spee had taken them after the murder of Archduke Ferdinand when war threatened, as there was a large coal store at the island. The small cruiser *Nürnberg* was *en-route* back from the west coast of the United States, where *Leipzig* had replaced her. On 6 August *Nürnberg* arrived in Pohnpei and on the same day the squadron departed to rendezvous with the remainder of the ships at Pagen Island, in the Marianas, and arrived there on 11 August. On 12 August the small cruiser *Emden* arrived at Pagan Island and the following day definite news arrived about the declaration of war by Japan. Graf von Spee therefore convened a meeting of staff and commanders aboard his flagship, *Scharnhorst*, to determine a further plan of action. The outcome was that he decided to hold his squadron together and seek a military solution. Only one commander dissented, Fregattenkapitän Karl Müller of *Emden*, and he was allowed to detach his ship to the Indian Ocean for cruiser warfare. The following day *Emden* was detached whilst the squadron proceeded to Eniwetok, in the Marshall Islands. From there *Nürnberg* was dispatched to Honolulu to collect mail and seek instructions from the Admiralstab about their intentions for the cruiser squadron. The squadron then went to Majuro before meeting *Nürnberg* off Washington Island, where it was learned that the Admiralstab had instructed the squadron to return home via South America.

During the long journey across the Pacific the German squadron carried out several raids against the Entente. On 7 September *Nürnberg* destroyed the wireless station at Fanning Island, depriving the allies of a valuable communication link between Australia and Canada. Shortly afterwards *Scharnhorst* and *Gneisenau* made a surprise attack on Samoa, which had just been occupied by New Zealand troops. The hope was to take any British or Australian warships there by surprise. The First Offizier of *Gneisenau*, Korvettenkapitän Hans Pochhammer, wrote: 'We rapidly went over in our minds the ships we might find there, from *Australia*, whose 12-inch guns inspired a certain respect, to the old light cruisers, which would not long be able to survive our appearance.'² This was a bold operation, and the readiness of Vizeadmiral Graf von Spee to engage the battlecruiser HMAS *Australia* shows his brave resolve to attack the enemy. Unfortunately for the Germans, Apia's roadstead lay empty. Finally, on 22 September the German squadron attacked the French colony of Papeete, where the French gunboat *Zélée* was taken under fire and sunk. The French defenders opened fire on the German ships, but as Korvettenkapitän Pochhammer explained: 'Our men refused to regard the few old shells from the forts as enemy fire,' and considered they still had yet to receive their baptism of fire.

The odyssey of the German squadron continued and on 12 October *Scharnhorst, Gneisenau* and *Nürnberg* arrived at the Easter Island rendezvous. Also on 12 October *Dresden* arrived at the rendezvous after cruising down the eastern side of South America *en-route* from her pre-war area of operations in the Caribbean. A few days later on 14 October *Leipzig* arrived from the west coast of the United States with three colliers, where she had been looking after German nationals and interests during the period of unrest in Mexico. Vizeadmiral Graf von Spee's squadron was now complete, but not yet ready to continue its voyage. On the first day at the islands a tender alongside *Nürnberg* accidentally twisted a blade of the port propeller and during the entire time at Easter Islands *Nürnberg* lay heeled over at an angle of 15° whilst divers repaired the damage, although at times the propeller came right out of the water in the heavy swell. In this position the cruiser loaded coal and stores.

After departing Easter Island on 18 October the squadron went to Juan Fernandez Islands and on the morning of Tuesday 26 October were approaching Mas a Fuera. On the evening 27 October the squadron departed Mas a Fuera to convoy two steamers, *Yorck* and *Göttingen*, and the auxiliary cruiser *Prinz Eitel Friedrich*, to the neutral waters of Chile.

On 30 October the squadron arrived off Valparaiso and the steamers were detached to neutral waters. On the evening of 31 October, after the steamers had safely arrived, Graf von Spee received a report that the previous evening an English cruiser had been anchored in the port of Coronel. This cruiser was *Glasgow* and, as she could not remain longer than 24 hours in a neutral port, Graf von Spee thought he could ambush her when she departed Coronel. However, *Glasgow* was not alone.

Rear Admiral Sir Christopher Cradock was born on 2 July 1862 in Yorkshire. He entered the Royal Navy in 1875 and had seen action in the Middle East and China. He was promoted Rear Admiral in 1910 and in August 1914 was in command of the 4th Cruiser Squadron, whose area of responsibility stretched from the St. Lawrence in Canada to Brazil. Rear Admiral Cradock was energetic, brave and loyal. He had demonstrated his personal bravery on many occasions, both before the guns of the enemy and in saving the lives of others. When the German coal steamers became active off the coast of Chile the British Admiralty thought that the Germans were resuming trade and ordered Rear Admiral Cradock to break up the trade and destroy the German cruisers. For this purpose his squadron consisted of his flagship, the armoured cruiser *Good Hope*, the armoured cruiser *Monmouth*, the light cruiser *Glasgow* and the auxiliary cruiser *Otranto*. Also attached was the pre-dreadnought battleship *Canopus*, but her low top speed precluded her from joint operations with the cruisers. On paper this inhomogeneous group was more powerful than the East Asiatic Squadron, but they would find it difficult to work together. The Admiralty also allocated the armoured cruiser *Defence* to Rear Admiral Cradock, but then failed to inform him when she was withdrawn. It is often stated that *Good Hope* and *Monmouth* were crewed to a large extent by reserve personnel, but it must also be remembered that in early 1914 almost half the *Offiziers* of *Scharnhorst* and *Gneisenau* were replaced, and just before the outbreak of war a large proportion of the crews were also returned to Germany to form the basis of the crew for SMS *Derfflinger*. The main problem for Rear Admiral Cradock was the unrealistic expectation placed upon him by the Admiralty, and their lack of support for him in materiel and planning.

Early on the morning of 1 November *Prinz Eitel Friedrich* and the colliers *Göttingen* and *Yorck* ran into Valparaiso, and at 02.50hrs *Göttingen* sent the wireless message: 'English light cruiser anchored on the roads of Coronel on 31 October at 7 in the evening.' With this news Vizeadmiral Graf von Spee determined to search down the coast when it became light, as he knew the English cruiser could not remain in the neutral harbour longer than 24 hours. At 03.00hrs the German squadron was steaming south at 14 knots. At 08.30hrs *Nürnberg* was dispatched to search just 10 miles off the coast. Then around 10.00hrs *Leipzig* stopped and searched a Chilean four-masted bark, loaded with wood:

> Then a cannon shot reaches our ears! A few hundred metres away *Leipzig* has put a shot across a spick and span four-masted bark, and has gone nearer to investigate. The latter now turned in a majestic curve and at the same moment the sunrays broke through the clouds and struck the sails, a snow white. Unfortunately we must let her go as she flies the Chilean flag and carries no contraband on board. With full sails set she vanishes in a northern direction.[3]

Aboard *Gneisenau* the last preparations were made for battle:

> The guns were inspected, all screws and bolts were tested to make sure they were really tight; a spot of fresh oil was put on the lock to prevent it sticking.

We made sure that the ammunition in readiness was watertight; the night glasses were fixed, and the apparatus for signalling and transmitting orders was worked. The chief engineer made a tour of his domain; the torpedo officer followed his example to ensure that his silver fish had enough air and that they were adjusted for the short distances at which they would be employed during the night. The doctors satisfied themselves that the armour protected dressing stations and the gangways leading to them were installed according to regulation, and the First Officer inspected the arrangements made for combating fire or an invasion of water, as well as the general order of things on the whole ship. Thus everybody on board, the officers and the chiefs of batteries and sections below them, strove to keep their units of combat, great or small, in constant readiness in order to give the enemy as good a reception as possible.[4]

During the afternoon *Dresden* moved nearer to *Nürnberg*, and then *Gneisenau* was ordered to go to the southern entrance of Arauco Bay. However, shortly after 16.00hrs *Leipzig* sighted a smoke column to starboard ahead, then at 16.17hrs a second smoke column was sighted to the west and at 16.25hrs a third ship was sighted 15 nautical miles away.

The sea off the coast of Chile on 1 November was rough. On his southerly course the waves broke over the bows of Vizeadmiral Graf von Spee's ships, making it difficult to work the lower casemate guns of the *Panzerkreuzer* and the exposed 10.5cm guns of the small cruisers. As the ships plunged into the increasingly heavy seas clouds of spray were thrown over the ships, and as they were tossed about observation of the enemy was difficult. Likewise, aboard the English ships the lower casemate guns of *Good Hope* and *Monmouth* were almost unworkable, whilst *Glasgow* suffered from the same difficulties as the German small cruisers.

At around 09.00hrs *Glasgow* had departed Coronel and headed west to rendezvous with Rear Admiral Cradock, bringing him telegrams and mail. The wireless airwaves had been filled with German *Funken Telegraphy* signals at close range, mostly carrying the call sign of SMS *Leipzig*, so that the English admiral decided to establish a broad search formation with course north up the Chilean coast. It was not long before at 15.56hrs the right wing ship of the search line, *Glasgow*, observed smoke to the northeast and turned to starboard to investigate. A short time later not only *Leipzig* was sighted, but also the armoured cruisers *Scharnhorst* and *Gneisenau*. At 16.17hrs *Glasgow* turned away to rejoin the other ships of her squadron, as after he learned of the German presence Rear Admiral Cradock ordered his ships to concentrate.

The two opposing battle lines were now formed. In the west Rear Admiral Cradock's flagship, *Good Hope*, under the command of Captain Francklin, led the line, followed by *Monmouth*, Captain Brandt, and *Glasgow*, Captain Luce, with the auxiliary cruiser *Otranto* bringing up the rear. The battleship *Canopus* was over 200 nautical miles to the south in company with the colliers *Benbrook* and *Langre*, proceeding northwards at 9 knots. To the east of the British line was the German East Asiatic Cruiser Squadron, with the flagship, *Scharnhorst*, Kapitän zur See Schultz, *Gneisenau*, Kapitän zur See Maerker, *Leipzig*, Fregattenkapitän Haun and *Dresden*, Fregattenkapitän Lüdecke. SMS *Nürnberg*, Kapitän zur See von Schönberg, was still over the horizon as the two battle lines converged. Aboard the German ships 'Clear ship for battle!' was sounded and the horns blew and drums rolled. Vizeadmiral von Spee steadily closed on the British line before turning onto an almost parallel southerly course at 17.32hrs. Now the lines only approached one another slowly and at 18.07hrs the range had reduced to 135hm. The German admiral gave the order: 'Fire distribution from the left'. This meant that the Germans would fight ship against ship, and *Gneisenau*'s direct opponent would be *Monmouth*. 'Our target was therefore the *Monmouth*, the second ship of the enemy line. Not long since, in February 1913, we had fraternized with her officers at Hong-Kong, and in all friendliness, drunk the health of our respective sovereigns at meals,'[5] wrote Korvettenkapitän Pochhammer.

At first observation of the British line was difficult: 'Almost indiscernibly the range reduces, and the enemy is clearly recognizable, although initially, with the light behind him the sunlight blinded us.'[6] The sun began to disappear below the horizon and at 18.20hrs Graf Spee allowed his squadron to turn one point towards the enemy. The range was 124hm, speed 16 knots. With the setting of the sun towards 18.25hrs the English ships were silhouetted against the western horizon, giving the German gunners a sharp target, compared to the indistinct outline of the German ships against the dull coastline and rain clouds of the eastern horizon:

> With each minute the sunlight moderated. While a moment ago our gunleaders were blinded, now conditions became more favourable for us. The enemy was sharply highlighted on the bright horizon. Behind us lay the grey mountainous land and against this we became less and less visible.[7]

The moon had risen towards 18.00hrs, but was frequently hidden as the clouds raced across the heavens. Both lines laboured against the wind and heavy swell and the German ships pitched strongly and rolled 5° to 10° to either side. Seas were hurled over the forecastle and conning tower, and swirled through every opening, making observation of the enemy, range finding and fire direction extremely difficult. As the range reduced to 104hm at 18.34hrs the signal 'Jot-Dora' was hoisted aboard the flagship, the signal to open fire. The German line opened fire, ship against ship. At 18.39hrs the German line turned a point to port and reduced speed to 12 knots, and at the same time *Scharnhorst*, with the third salvo, scored a hit against *Good Hope*, which struck between the bow 9.2-inch turret and the conning tower. A large flame and fire resulted. Likewise, with the third salvo from *Gneisenau* the *Monmouth* suffered a hit which struck the bow turret. The roof of the turret was rent off and flames and fires resulted.

As the range reduced to 92hm the British line opened fire and Rear Admiral Cradock altered course to port to further reduce the range. The heavy artillery of *Good Hope* fired a salvo every 50 seconds, whilst the medium artillery seemed to fire sporadically. The firing of *Monmouth* began very quickly and solidly, but the salvo fire soon fell away under the effect of numerous hits as her guns were forced out of action. When the German guns found the range and went into rapid fire, a salvo left the barrels every 15 seconds. This rate of fire could only be maintained until the range was lost and placed a great strain on the gun crews, and then salvo fire began again. *Scharnhorst* fired mostly high explosive shells, and *Gneisenau* fired mainly armoured piercing shell. The Spotting Offizier of *Scharnhorst*, Oberleutnant zur See Knoop, had an excellent view of the battle and related the following, as reproduced in the official history:

> Continual hits could be observed…Repeated hits were observed on the unarmoured parts of the ship…Twice I believed ready ammunition flared up…The forecastle armour of *Good Hope* received one hit, probable heavy [21cm] and distinguishable by a thick black explosion cloud. A hit on the upper bridge, one on the mast about 10 metres above deck level and one on the aft edge of the fore spar were observed, recognisable by glowing for seconds.
>
> In the midships *Good Hope* was hit repeatedly, with much fire resulting. A cartridge explosion as high as the third funnel occurred just aft of there. Here I also observed deck hits. The wireless antenna was torn asunder. *Good Hope* received more hits in the aft battery with resulting fires. The interior of this part of the ship was on fire, which could be seen through the portholes, shining brightly.
>
> Two hits entered the ship near the aft turret, probably striking its armour, and black explosion clouds were perceptible.
>
> Turret hits on *Good Hope* were not observed, though by chance I saw the forward 15cm turret of *Monmouth*. The explosion blew off the turret top and the turret glowed red hot. It gave the impression of a boiler with flames striking out from the inside. Here a cartridge explosion of terrible force must have taken place and swept from the turret down into the forecastle.
>
> A salvo with a whole number of hits struck the armoured lower part on the midships.[8]

The battle also raged further down the line. With the signal to inaugurate fire at 18.34hrs *Leipzig* opened fire on *Glasgow* and *Dresden* fired on *Otranto*. Good shooting in the prevailing heavy seas was impossible, and the task for *Glasgow* was even more difficult with spray sometimes being flung over her masts and funnels and the German ships difficult to discern against the dull, eastern horizon. With the third salvo from *Dresden* the auxiliary cruiser *Otranto* was observed to turn away and take up a zigzag course in the lee of the English line. Finally at about 19.00hrs she was observed to flee in a westerly direction. One hit was observed on *Otranto* by *Dresden* and a fire was observed on her promenade deck by *Leipzig*. At 18.49hrs *Glasgow* hit *Leipzig* on the base of the conning tower, however the shell did not detonate.

After the retirement of *Otranto*, *Dresden* also directed her fire against *Glasgow*. Towards 19.00hrs *Glasgow* could no longer make out the German small cruisers so fired her bow gun on *Scharnhorst* and aft gun on *Gneisenau*. She must have also used her 4-inch armament against *Scharnhorst* as an unexploded 4-inch shell was found in the *Panzerkreuzer*'s forecastle. In return *Glasgow* was hit five times, the most serious hit striking just above the port outer propeller, which rent an irregular hole about 2 metres in diameter.

The battle continued with great ferocity as the range between the two lines steadily reduced. At 18.53hrs the range was 60hm and at 19.05hrs was just 49hm. Already at 18.50hrs *Monmouth* had reduced speed and was hauling out to starboard, not following the flagship towards the German line. There were fires raging aboard her but towards 19.20hrs these had been put out. *Gneisenau* was now hit, and a shell penetrated compartment III on the *Zwischendeck*, beside the main dressing station. The shell struck the aft turret and exploded outside, setting fire to a store of life jackets. Huge volumes of smoke were produced before the fire was extinguished. Leutnant zur See Lietzmann continued:

> Our opponent *Monmouth* is now out of the battle. He drifts on the turbulent ocean like a shot through wreck. We let him off and join *Scharnhorst* in firing on the enemy flagship, which is still bravely fighting back. In consideration of his desperate situation Admiral Cradock turns towards us. He wants to reduce the range and conduct a torpedo attack. Graf Spee sees this intention and turns to port by the same amount, so that now we run parallel to the enemy on course SE at 60hm distance. With the gathering night *Good Hope* is no longer recognizable. However, her glowing fires shine glaringly. The sea of flames on the English flagship offers our gunleaders an excellent target. However, still her guns fire. A 23.4cm shell hits our hull side. However it does not penetrate the Krupp steel of the casemate armour. The explosion splatters the paint of the outer hull and vanishes into the ocean depths. Splinters from another shell drill through our funnel. On the gaff our proud flag gets an honourable spray.[9]

However, *Good Hope* continued to be hit and Oberleutnant zur See Knoop wrote:

> About 19.20hrs (19.23hrs) a hit, probably a heavy armoured explosive shell, struck the deck between the second and third funnels. The hit was likely on the deck to port and flew across the ship. Suddenly, on the starboard side a powerful column of smoke and flame climbed almost to mast height and was 20 to 30 metres broad. The column of flames appeared pale red in colour and was towards its edges paler still. Its base was coloured green like a rocket flash. The explosion carried a quantity of ships parts skywards. The noise was not perceivable. The smoke formation from this explosion was small. I must speak against the assumption of a boiler explosion as the funnel remained standing, undamaged.
>
> In all there were 30 to 40 hits counted, two cartridge fires and approximately 15 to 20 common fires. From time to time 3 or 4 fires could be seen at the same time.[10]

After the large explosion aboard her at 19.23hrs *Good Hope* ceased fire, with even the two port aft 6-inch cannon, which until then had fired intermittently, ceasing fire. A short time later at 19.28hrs the German cruisers also ceased fire. By 19.30hrs the German *Panzerkreuzers* had lost sight of their opponents. *Monmouth* had not followed the alteration of the flagship towards the German line at about 19.00hrs and had turned away to the west at about 19.35hrs and then north about 19.45hrs, to position her stern towards the weather as the bows were damaged and allowing much water to enter the ship. *Monmouth* communicated to *Glasgow* that she was intending to seek shelter under the coast. *Glasgow* stood in the wake of the crippled armoured cruiser but when the moon appeared from behind some clouds and German cruisers were distinguishable to the ESE *Glasgow* signal signalled 'The enemy follows us', and then stood off to the NW at high speed.

Between 19.30 to 19.37hrs Vizeadmiral Graf von Spee wirelessed his small cruisers to attack the enemy with torpedoes, whilst at 19.33hrs he increased speed with his *Panzerkreuzer* to 17 knots and stood off to the south so as not to impede them.

On the signal from the flagship *Leipzig* swung away from the cruisers on a WSW course and then increased speed to 18 knots and steered on a NW course. In this direction a faint light was perceived and Fregattenkapitän Haun assumed it originated from *Good Hope*. Now the sudden appearance of a rain squall reduced visibility and when the small cruiser reached the position of the presumed enemy nothing was to be seen. It was not until some days later that it was reported that some men on *Leipzig*'s middle deck engaged in throwing empty ammunition packing cases overboard observed an area of debris, including barrels, hammocks and also a body about 10 minutes after *Leipzig* had turned northwest and increased speed. The *Offiziers* on the bridge were looking out for a ship and did not observe the debris field, and therefore no rescue work was undertaken.

At 19.30hrs *Dresden* went onto a SW course to position herself off the enemy's bow, as they considered the British line to still be on a southerly course. About 20.00hrs *Dresden* sighted a vessel in the NW about 60hm off, which turned onto a NW course and was probably *Glasgow*. *Dresden* followed her to the NW but soon the ship was lost from view. After that *Dresden* and *Leipzig* approached one another and had mistaken each other for the enemy, and it was not until an exchange of recognition signals occurred that they recognised each other, *Dresden* by that stage being ready to launch a torpedo.

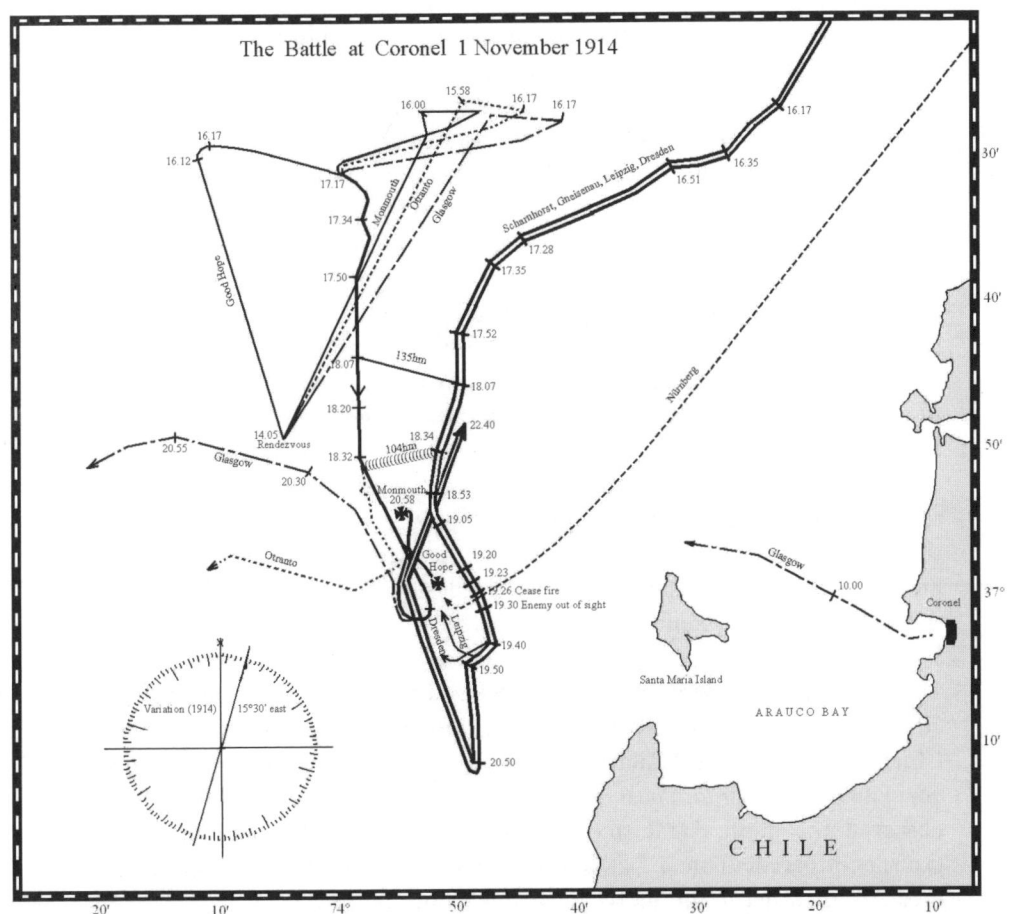

At 16.00hrs *Nürnberg* was approximately 25 nautical miles from the German main body. At 16.25hrs she received a message from the flagship to close with the squadron at high speed, which in *Nürnberg*'s case was 22 knots. However, *Nürnberg* lost contact towards 17.30hrs and only with the coming of dusk around 18.43hrs was the flash of gunfire observed to starboard ahead. *Nürnberg* gradually approached the battle lines and about 19.20hrs saw a violent explosion on the enemy line. About 20.05hrs *Nürnberg* sighted a smoke cloud to starboard ahead and this was followed with a NW course. Soon, 4 points to starboard a second smoke cloud was sighted. At first this was taken to be *Dresden* or *Leipzig*, but soon the vessel disappeared to the northwest. The second vessel was now challenged but made no reply. *Nürnberg* took a parallel course to this vessel whilst keeping a good lookout, should the other vessel return. The sighted vessel had three funnels and was listing over to port. This ship now increased speed and changed course to the NE. Although the repeatedly flashed recognition signal was not answered Kapitän zur See Schönberg feared he had a damaged German ship before him, therefore *Nürnberg* closed to close range and illuminated the ship with a searchlight. Immediately the English cruiser *Monmouth* was recognised with top flag set and missing fore turret. It appeared the ship was under weigh and she quickly turned away. Towards 20.50hrs the commander of *Nürnberg* allowed fire to be opened at a range of 6 to 10hm. A torpedo fired from the port torpedo tube of *Nürnberg* missed, which was probably because it ran too deep as the short range did not give sufficient time to set its depth. *Monmouth* did not return fire and therefore *Nürnberg* ceased fire and extinguished the searchlight. However, *Monmouth* did not lower her flag and began a turn towards *Nürnberg*, to either ram the German ship or else open fire with her starboard battery. Therefore Kapitän zur See Schönberg again opened fire and passed under the stern of *Monmouth* and engaged *Monmouth*'s starboard side. The fire was directed against the unarmoured hull and deck and *Monmouth* lay further and further over. At 20.58hrs *Monmouth* capsized and sank, her flag still flying. Because of the perceived proximity of other British ships, the rough seas and the fact that the boats had been filled with water before the battle, *Nürnberg* was not able to lower rescue boats. Two smoke clouds were also approaching and *Nürnberg* took them to be *Good Hope* and *Glasgow*. *Nürnberg* steered towards the approaching smoke clouds.

At 21.15hrs *Nürnberg* sent a signal, 'Have brought about sinking of enemy armoured cruiser,' to which Graf von Spee replied, 'Bravo *Nürnberg*. Squadron Chief.' Soon after, at 21.30hrs *Nürnberg* recognised the smoke columns as emanating from *Scharnhorst* and *Gneisenau*, which at about 20.50hrs had observed the gunfire and steered towards it. From 21.50hrs the German cruisers proceeded on a NNE course and at 22.00hrs the small cruisers received the order to form a reconnaissance line ahead.

The following morning the flagship assembled the small cruisers:

On the morning of the 2nd November the sun was shining in an azure sky. During the night the wind dropped and the sea had calmed down. Our ship gently rose and fell in the after swell. The atmosphere was clear, we could even see the distant coastline of Chile, and far and wide there was no ship which might have been dangerous to us. The light cruisers were therefore ordered to join the large ones, and wait for us in a line parallel with our course. As we steamed past them, their crews were lined up on the sides and gave three cheers in honour of the Admiral who had led them so splendidly.[11]

During the battle *Scharnhorst* was hit only twice and *Gneisenau* four times. *Scharnhorst* had no wounded, *Gneisenau* had two slightly wounded. On the small cruisers there were no wounded and no damaging hits.

On *Scharnhorst* a 4-inch shell had come through the starboard hull between decks and remained unexploded among crates in the forecastle. Another shell had passed through the upper part of the third funnel without detonating. The hull side was struck by splinters from three shells and a wire of the large antenna array was damaged along with a wire of the small array.

The first hit on *Gneisenau* penetrated the starboard hull side above the armoured belt and detonated, resulting in a fire. Part of the shell body penetrated several rooms without essentially causing much damage. A second shell struck the foremast on the starboard forward edge and splinters from this shell did local damage and wounded one man. A third shell struck the upper casemate armour of the starboard aft casemate without noticeable results. The fourth hit struck the aft 21cm turret and exploded between the turret and belt armour, starting a small fire at the base of the turret which produced much smoke. Some armour was displaced and jammed the turret for a short time.

However, the German *Panzerkreuzers* had used up roughly half their ammunition, and this was not replaceable in the immediate future. This would be a severe handicap when the German squadron met their next adversary, and it was inevitable that they would meet further opponents.

Nevertheless a great victory had been won. Within about 50 minutes the German cruisers had won an overwhelming victory against ships of comparable strength without suffering serious damage to themselves. The German ships victory had been achieved in atrocious conditions and was the result of a series of factors. The German squadron had been tactically well led, and the shooting of the artillery was the result of excellent training and battle drill, and good materiel. On the other hand some of the guns aboard the British armoured cruisers had not been fully utilizable.

Before the battle the German line manoeuvred to gain a position between the enemy and the coast, and to avoid the lee position and therefore smoke interference, and had delayed the beginning of the fight until sunset and favourable light conditions. Rear Admiral Cradock had attempted to manoeuvre to avoid this and had tried to close the range to force an earlier beginning to the battle, but to no avail. He had little choice about the battle on 1 November, being under the direction of the British Admiralty. When he heard of Cradock's actions, Vice Admiral Beatty, commanding the British battlecruisers at Rosyth in Scotland, bitterly reflected on where the blame rested:

> Poor old Kit Cradock has gone at Coronel. His death and the loss of the ships and the gallant lives in them can be laid at the door of the incompetency of the Admiralty. They have broken over and again the first principles of strategy.[12]

With the victory at Coronel Vizeadmiral Graf von Spee achieved the strategic aim of achieving sea mastery off the South American coast for a certain time, and could act without fear or reserve for the time being. He could defeat any British forces in the region and for the first time since the beginning of the war he could meet German diplomats and establish direct communication with the Admiralstab. He could also receive intelligence about the enemy. For the first time since the Napoleonic Wars the spectre of British invincibility had been broken and Graf Spee could justifiably be proud of his men and his ships.

Chapter 3

The Sea Battle Off Cape Sarych, Balaclava, 18 November 1914

At the beginning of the 20th Century the Ottoman Empire was in decline. On 29 September 1911 the Italians began a war with the Turkish Ottoman Empire to take the North African provinces of Tripolitania, Fezzan and Cyrenaica, what is now Libya, away from the Turks. This they succeeded in doing under the Treaty of Ouchy in October 1912. However, before this treaty was concluded, several Balkan states saw an opportunity to further weaken the Ottoman Empire. In 1912 Serbia, Bulgaria, Greece and Montenegro formed the Balkan League with the purpose of taking Macedonia away from Turkey whilst her attention was taken by the war with Italy. Montenegro began with a declaration of war on Turkey on 8 October 1912, and the other countries followed 10 days later on 18 October 1912. Things did not go well for the Turkish forces and a series of reverses followed.

The political situation was complex, but nevertheless Germany had close economic and military ties with Turkey. To protect these interests an Imperial Cabinet Order of 1 November 1912 determined to establish an Imperial Navy Mediterranean Division. The *Großer Kreuzer Goeben* was detached from the High Sea Fleet as flagship of the division, along with the small cruiser *Breslau*. The II Admiral of the I Battle Squadron, Kontreadmiral Trummler, was appointed commander of the division, and after fitting out in Kiel the division departed for the Mediterranean on 4 November 1912. During the journey from Wilhelmshaven to Malta *Goeben* achieved the outstanding average speed of 21.35 knots. On 15 November *Goeben* dropped anchor off the Turkish capital of Constantinople.

On 18 November *Goeben* landed 450 men as part of an international troop contingent, but a short time later, on 3 December, an armistice was arranged between Turkey and the Balkan League and the troops returned to their ships. A peace conference was begun in London, but after a *coup d'état* by the Young Turks in Constantinople in January 1913, war with the Ottoman Empire was resumed. Under a peace treaty signed in London on 30 May 1913, the Ottoman Empire lost almost all of its remaining European territory. In the event Bulgaria was unhappy about the result and a second Balkan War began on the night of 29/30 June 1913, when Bulgaria attacked Serbian and Greek forces in

Macedonia. The Bulgarians were defeated, however, and a peace treaty was signed between the combatants on 10 August 1913. Under the terms of the treaty Greece and Serbia divided up most of Macedonia between themselves, leaving Bulgaria with only a small part. Under these circumstances it was considered impossible for the Germans to disband their Mediterranean Division.

On 23 October 1913 Kontreadmiral Wilhelm Souchon replaced Kontreadmiral Trummler. Kontreadmiral Souchon was born in Leipzig on 2 June 1864 and entered the Navy in 1881. He was known to be cheerful and eventempered, and had good political sense. He served as Chief of Staff in the East Asiatic Cruiser Squadron from May 1904 to May 1906 and reached the rank of Kontreadmiral on 10 April 1911. His previous appointment was as 2 Admiral of the II Squadron from October 1912 until September 1913, before being sent to the Mediterranean Division, a post he held responsibly until September 1917.

Under the command of Kontreadmiral Souchon the Mediterranean Division continued to visit many ports around the periphery of the Mediterranean, and it was whilst showing the flag in Haifa, then part of the Ottoman Empire, that Kontreadmiral Souchon learned of the murder of Archduke Franz Ferdinand, the successor to the Austro-Hungarian throne, and his wife on 28 June 1914. His flagship was in poor condition and in need of major repairs to the boilers as she was only capable of 24 knots for brief periods and could not exceed 18 knots for long periods of time. Indeed *Goeben* was scheduled to be replaced by her sistership *Moltke* in October 1914. This now appeared impossible and the Reichs Marine Amt ordered the *Großer Kreuzer* to Pola, where she was to act in concert with the Austro-Hungarian fleet. However, the politically astute Kontreadmiral Souchon was more farsighted and insisted that the necessary 4,460 replacement boiler tubes be sent to Pola, where they were mostly replaced, before *Goeben* and *Breslau* slipped back out to sea. A bombardment of French North African ports followed.

After being defeated at sea during the 1st Balkan War, Turkey determined on the purchase of dreadnought-class battleships. To that end the Ministry of the Navy ordered a 27,500 ton ship from the British shipyard of Vickers. Then in 1913 a further battleship became available as there were doubts about whether Brazil would continue payments on a ship they had ordered. Turkey quickly bought this ship too and both were scheduled for delivery by mid-1914. However, the shipyards deliberately slowed construction, even though a Turkish crew went to Newcastle in July 1914 to take the first ship, named *Sultan Osman*, back to Turkey. On the afternoon of 1 August British troops evicted the Turkish crew and on 4 August the British Government declared that the two ships had been expropriated without compensation. In Constantinople Turkish War Minister Enver Pasha condemned this act as 'British treachery'.

Under these circumstances and with the following anti-British sentiment it is not surprising that Germany was able to affect a proposed sale of the Mediterranean Division to Turkey, a move that surprised and shocked all. The Turkish explained that they were replacements for the two confiscated battleships. In this way *Goeben* and her consort played no small part in involving Turkey in the war on the side of the Central Powers. Although the ships flew Turkish colours after that, the German crews remained, although some Turkish naval personnel were incorporated to undertake training. *Goeben* was renamed *Yavuz* and *Breslau* was renamed *Midilli*. To all intents and purposes the ships remained part of the Imperial Navy, but the Turkish population was intensely proud of them. Vizeadmiral Rebeur-Paschwitz later wrote that the ships 'embodied security and the strength of Turkey which comes from pride in a weapon in action under their own flag'.[1]

> All exploits and the destruction caused by famous cruisers, like *Alabama* and *Emden*, paled in comparison to the calamities caused by *Goeben*, which so decisively influenced the course of events not only in the Black Sea, but also the entire eastern theatre of military operations...The breakthrough of the German battlecruiser into the Black Sea caused confusion in the Russian Naval Command, although a similar course of events was forecast by the General Staff in 1907. The arrival of *Goeben*, having finally decided the Turkish-German union, which pushed Turkey into the war, broke the connection of Russia with the allies...The gloomy shallow of *Goeben* is cast over the defeat of the Dardanelles operation, and above all the defeat of Russia in 1915.[2]

The decision of First Lord of the Admiralty Churchill to take the Turkish battleships had certainly begun a chain of events which was to have disastrous consequences for the Entente allies.

On 29 October *Goeben* bombarded Sevastopol, which brought a declaration of war by Russia on 1 November. Britain and France pre-empted their declaration of war on Turkey on 5 November with a bombardment of the Turkish Dardanelles forts on 3 November. At the time of the declaration of war the Russian Black Sea Fleet was quite a homogenous unit. The battleship *Panteleimon*, the former *Potemkin*, was the prototype ship for the following *Evstafi* and *Ioann Zlatoust*, which incorporated lessons learned in the Russo-Japanese War. They all carried four 12-inch cannon, and the latter two carried four 8-inch guns also. These battleships were accompanied by the older *Rostislav*, with four 10-inch guns, and *Tri Sviatitelia* with four 12-inch pieces. There were two protected cruisers of the *Bogatyr* class, *Kagul* and *Pamiat Merkuria*, each with twelve 6-inch guns. The armed yacht *Almaz* was also used in the light cruiser role. The Black Sea Fleet also possessed four large new destroyers and thirteen torpedoboats. However, perhaps the best asset of the Black Sea Fleet was its leader, Admiral Andrei Eberhard. He was described as a gentleman, with a razor sharp mind and an iron will, with great tenacity. The son of a diplomat, he graduated from Naval Collage in 1879 and among other posts served as Chief of the Naval General Staff and commander of *Panteleimon*. Perhaps the best attribute Admiral Eberhard and Kontreadmiral Souchon shared is that they both wanted to fight.

On 15 November the Russian Black Sea Fleet departed Sevastopol to disrupt the Turkish coastal traffic along the eastern Anatolian coast. The Russian forces consisted of the cruisers *Pamiat Merkuria*, flagship of Rear Admiral Pokrov, *Kagul* and *Almaz*, under the command of Captain 1st Rank Zarin. The main body comprised the battleships *Evstafi*, under the command of Captain 1st Rank Galanin and acting as flagship for Admiral Eberhard; *Ioann Zlatoust*, Captain 1st Rank F.A. Winter; *Panteleimon*, commander Captain 1st Rank Kaskov and under the flag of the Chief of the Battleship Division, Vice Admiral Novitsky; *Tri Sviatitelia*, commander Capitan 1st Rank Lukin and under the flag of the Chief of the Second Brigade of Battleships, Rear Admiral Putyatin; and finally *Rostislav*, Captain 1st Rank Porembsky. The destroyers of the 1st, 2nd and 3rd Destroyer Divisions were under the command of the Chief of the Torpedoboat Brigade, Captain 1st Rank Sablin, and comprised three of the new, large, *Derzki*-type destroyers, and ten older boats. On the morning of 17 November the Russian force bombarded the Turkish port of Trabezond, which supported the Turkish troops fighting against the Russian Caucasian Army. After that Admiral Eberhard proceeded west along the Anatolian coast, searching in vain for Turkish transport vessels, before finally turning back towards the Crimea as he reached Giresun. Early on the morning of 18 November the accompanying minelayers *Konstantin* and *Kseniya* laid 123 mines off Trabezond, 77 mines off Platana, 100 mines off Unye and 100 mines off Samsun, with the purpose of further disrupting Turkish transport traffic.

When Kontreadmiral Souchon heard of the attack on Trabezond he determined to immediately put to sea to cut off the Russian forces. At 15.30hrs on 17 November *Goeben* and *Breslau* put to sea from the Bosporus and took course to the northeast, intending to intercept the Russians off the coast of the Crimea the following day. *Goeben*, under the command of Kapitän zur See Ackermann, and *Breslau*, under the command of Fregattenkapitän Kettner, maintained a speed of 15 knots and at noon the following day they were off the southern part of the Crimea, where Kontreadmiral Souchon ordered a search to be started, regardless of the fog that prevailed.

The Russians were unaware of the German presence and at 11.40hrs on 18 November were approximately 20 nautical miles off Cape Sarych, the southern tip of Crimea. The Russians did not expect to encounter any Germans and therefore Admiral Eberhard held the squadron in *en-route* formation in

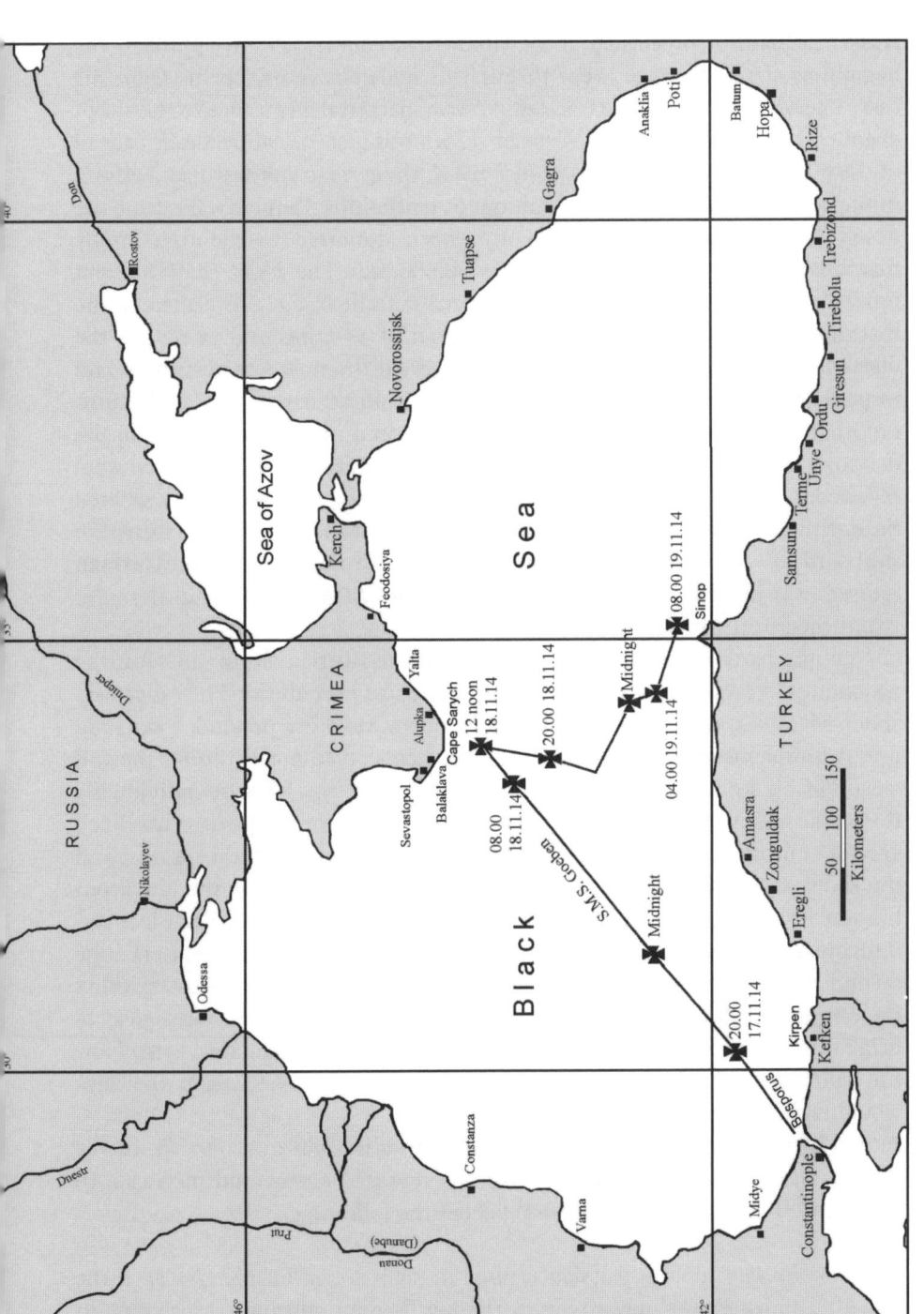

Movements of S.M.S. *Goeben* 17 to 19 November 1914.

single line ahead. The fog reduced visibility to just 5,500 to 7,400 metres as the Russian squadron proceeded at 14 knots with course 300° to approach the beginning of the channel swept through their defensive minefields from the east. The old coastal defence battleship *Sinop* marked the entrance to the swept channel. Because of the fog the cruiser screen was just 3½ nautical miles ahead of the main body, with *Kagul* to port, *Pamiat Merkuria* to starboard, and *Almaz* in the centre, ahead of the single column of battleships. In their wake came the destroyers in two columns. Suddenly *Almaz* reported to the flagship by searchlight signal that 'a large shadow' lay ahead. The Fleet Staff did not immediately believe the report and believed it to be *Sinop*. Nevertheless, the battleships were ordered to maintain a speed of 14 knots and to reduce the distance between them to 2.5 cable-lengths, or 500 metres. The destroyers and torpedoboats were ordered to close up. However, the rear two battleships reported they could not close the distance and therefore they, and the destroyers, remained far behind. Several minutes later *Breslau* and *Goeben* were revealed to *Almaz* through the fog and at 12.10hrs she reported 'I have sighted the enemy', and after obtaining an acknowledgement she immediately turned to starboard to join with the battleships. At this time the range to the German cruisers was just 6,500 metres. Shortly thereafter *Kagul* and *Pamiat Merkuria* also turned back towards the battleships.

Now the battle alarm was sounded aboard the Russian ships and soon the silhouettes of large ships appeared from the fog to port ahead. The range was about 85 cables, or 15,000 metres, but the poor visibility precluded opening fire. Admiral Eberhard ordered a turn in succession to port to bring the full weight of his squadron's broadside to bear on the enemy. Because individually the Russian ships were outgunned by *Goeben* they were using the centralized system of firing. Under this system all the battleships fired together as one, and the shots were spotted and the fire corrected as one; therefore, the line acted like one firing platform. This system was not unique to the Black Sea Fleet and destroyers in the Baltic are known to have used it against German cruisers. The second in line, *Ioann Zlatoust*, was to act as the master gunnery ship, ordering the range, deflection and corrections. Tactically, a turn to port was logical to bring the Germans to action, as it was towards their base in the Bosporus. Now the cruiser *Kagul* took station ahead of the Russian line, whilst *Pamiat Merkuria* would take station astern of the last ship.

At 12.05hrs *Breslau* reported a Russian cruiser in sight to starboard. It was *Almaz*. *Goeben* turned directly towards the reported enemy and increased to full speed. The log book of *Goeben* reported the following:

12.05: *Breslau* reports Russian cruiser in sight to starboard. *Goeben* turns with Utmost Power[3] towards it; in the fog thereon other warships come in sight to starboard. The Admiral orders to head straight for them. After a brief time 5 battleships come in sight from the fog between the 2 first sighted enemy ships. They travel in line ahead.[4]

At 12.15 *Goeben* ordered *Breslau* to take position in the fire lee because the 10.5cm guns of the small cruiser could play no part against the Russian battleships and it was safer to have the cruiser out of harm's way. At the same time *Goeben* observed that the Russian cruisers had likewise placed themselves ahead and astern of the Russian line. At 12.17hrs *Goeben* turned to starboard to bring the full broadside to bear against the Russian line. The new course for action was 135°, converging with the Russian line. The fog was patchy and making conditions difficult for both sides. The Russian Artillery Officer controlling the fire was Leitenant Smirnov, aboard *Ioann Zlatoust*, and he had determined the range as 11,100m, whereas it was actually approximately 7,400m. Time passed by, but the signal to inaugurate fire was not forthcoming from *Ioann Zlatoust*, and Admiral Eberhard was becoming anxious:

> 'He probably can't see the target…a fog patch is in the way', commented the Admiral. 'Range 40 cables', came the report from the range finder. 'We cannot wait any longer…This is not a training exercise…Open fire at once!' snapped the Admiral.[5]

At 12.20hrs the Senior Artillery Officer of *Evstafi*, Leitenant Nevinski, on the orders of the Fleet Commander, independently fired a two shot salvo on the German ship, one projectile from the forward turret, one from the aft turret. After just a few seconds flight time the fall of shot was observed, one shot over, and one a direct hit on *Goeben*. The 12-inch nose fused projectile contained black powder and it had struck the port N°3 15cm gun casemate. The effect was devastating. Kapitän zur See Ackermann explained:

> An enemy heavy shell struck SMS *Goeben* before we had opened fire (because of poor visibility). The impact of the enemy shell and its detonation were not perceived in most other ship's rooms or else were held to be our own guns firing. Nothing was noticed even in nearby casemate 2. Only in turret B and E, casemate 4 and magazine chamber 11 (double magazine for the 3 and 4 casemates to port) was it clear from the start about the fact it concerned a hit, as the fire and smoke and gases penetrated into their rooms. The commander of turret B, who had a view over casemate 3 from the upper deck, felt the hit and saw flames and smoke over the railing and seemingly also through 2 squeezed out coal hatches appearing over the upper deck.[6]

However, the shell only just penetrated the 15cm thick casemate armour, even at the low range of 65hm, and it broke up outside the armour. Several large fragments entered the casemate, along with the explosive flash flame. Three 15cm shells detonated, the only time during the entire war that German shells exploded as the result of an artillery hit, and a further sixteen 15cm cartridges of the ready ammunition burned. An intense fire in the casemate lasted for 5 minutes. Apparently the gun aperture and shot hole were not sufficient to dissipate the powerful gas pressure and flash flames, which found an escape route down the magazine elevator into magazine chamber 11, a 15cm shell and powder magazine. The flames scorched some beams and singed caps and hair, and then, searching for a path upwards, exited through the elevator that led to casemate 4. When the fire-extinguishing group arrived, the flames were gone. The casemate crew of twelve men were killed immediately through burns and splinters, but some were terribly mutilated. Later a Turkish sailor died from gas poisoning. It was a lucky escape, in as much as the flames entering the magazine did not cause a further explosion.

Two minutes later, at 12.22hrs, *Goeben*'s I Artillerie Offizier, Korvettenkapitän Arnold Knispel, opened fire with five gun salvos at a range of 70–72hm (38–39 cable lengths), firing one gun from each turret. The first salvo lay 30 metres over, however one shell struck *Evstafi* through the centre funnel. The 28cm projectile struck at the height of the mantel and tore out the opposite side. Splinters damaged the wireless antenna on the lee side, which was being used for the centralised fire control instructions from the directing ship, damaged a boat davit, the port searchlight and smashed a pulley block. Without causing serious damage this projectile had nevertheless deprived *Evstafi* of the main means of obtaining adjustments for laying fire, and subsequently she could only participate in the centralized fire by obtaining fire corrections with the aid of flags or semaphore.

The Senior Artillery Officer of *Evstafi*, Leitenant A. Nevinski, witnessed a rare phenomenon and wrote in his memoirs:

> Almost immediately after the fire of *Goeben* flames came from all five turrets (I clearly saw it through binoculars). Continuing to look through the binoculars, I saw some black dots. I wiped the binoculars with my handkerchief and again put them to my eyes; the same were visible, now higher. I realised that it was the enemy shells, numbering them–five pieces, and then they disappeared from sight, and at that moment I saw the fall of shells.[7]

The next salvo from *Goeben* was short, but the third German salvo also recorded two hits against the Russian flagship. One 28cm projectile struck the starboard forward casemate, at the joint of two armoured plates. One plate was destroyed and left lying near the 6-inch gun. Splinters entered the casemate and caused heavy damage, including tearing up the deck and buckling beams. All of the gun's serving crew were killed or wounded.

The Sea Battle Off Cape Sarych, Balaclava, 18 November 1914 49

The other shell from the third salvo to hit struck *Evstafi* on the casemate armour at approximately frame 54, piercing the 127mm thick armour and leaving an almost perfectly round hole. After penetrating the armour it struck 6-inch shells and cartridges, scattering the shells and igniting the cartridges. They were soon extinguished however. The shell then flew into the officers' galley where it exploded and caused great damage. The deck above was penetrated by splinters and the smith's below was also penetrated. Some splinters even penetrated to the boiler rooms below. The final shell to hit was from the fifth salvo which struck on or near the waterline at frame 22, probably just short of the hull side, which was riddled with holes. The infirmary longitudinal bulkhead was destroyed, as was part of the elevator for 75mm gun ammunition.

The losses in personnel were four officers killed and one died later of his wounds. A total of twenty-nine crew were killed immediately and a further twenty-four were wounded, nineteen of them badly, the majority of these dying later. The two casemate hits caused most of the casualties.

Goeben's logbook continued:

12.22hrs: *Goeben* stood abeam and answered the fire on the lead ship with heavy artillery. *Goeben* steers 135°.

The Russian salvos lay well, with the first salvo a heavy hit (30.5cm) in casemate III to port. The report comes to above: fire in casemate III.

Shooting range 62-60-65hm because the weather was very hazy under the coast, otherwise nothing was to be recognised.

The impact of the first salvo was observed wide. With that the range was reduced 2hm; the impact was then short. The spacing totals 160m. With the 1 salvo a hit obtained.[8]

At 12.24hrs *Goeben* turned away as the enemy could scarcely be made out in the fog, and continued to fire on the leading Russian ship with the aft heavy artillery at a range of 70–72hm.

After obtaining a hit with the first salvo the guns of *Evstafi* went into rapid fire. The bow turret could easily observe the target and fired evenly, whereas the aft turret reported several times that the target could not be seen because of the smoke and haze. The 8-inch and 6-inch batteries also joined in. In all sixteen shots were made from the heavy calibre battery, twelve from the bow turret and four from the aft turret, nineteen shells were fired from the 6-inch battery, and fourteen shells were fired by the 8-inch calibre battery.

The remaining Russian ships conducted fire only when they could see the enemy. When fire was inaugurated at 12.20hrs, the aft most two Russian ships, *Tri Sviatitelia* and *Rostislav,* had still not completed the turn in succession and were thus unable to immediately open fire. *Ioann Zlatoust* fired six projectiles of

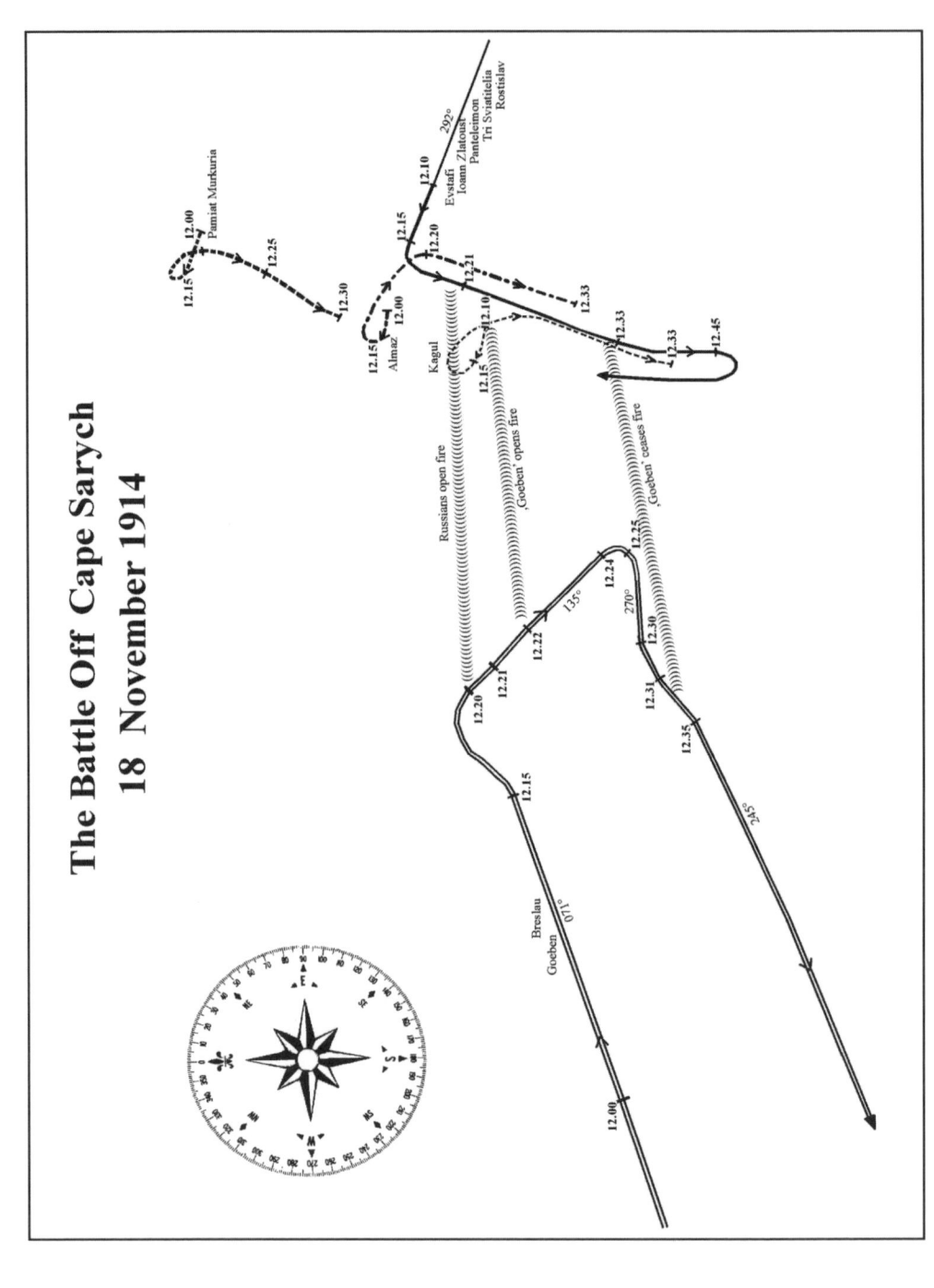

12-inch calibre at a range of 11,100m (60 cables). *Panteleimon* did not fire her main battery guns. *Tri Sviatitelia*, which did not turn until later, saw better than *Panteleimon* and made twelve shots at a range of 11,100m (60 cables), before the target passed from sight. *Rostislav* only fired at *Breslau* before this target vanished into the fog.

At 12.32hrs *Goeben* ceased fire and whilst the enemy was on the beam had fired twelve 28cm projectiles, and a further seven 28cm projectiles from the aft turrets after the turn away.

At 12.37hrs *Evstafi* altered course 20° to port in order to avoid a floating object suspected of being a mine, however she then resumed her course. Then at 12.45 hrs Admiral Eberhard ordered a turn in succession to starboard onto course north to reengage the enemy. However, the German cruisers had disappeared into the fog and soon after the Black Sea Fleet took course on the swept channel entrance that led to Sevastopol.

The two German cruisers did not retire to the Bosporus, as has sometimes been claimed, but rather headed south and then southeast to arrive off Cape Sinop at 08.00hrs the following morning. There they looked for Russians but found none. On Friday 20 November they returned to the Bosporus.

Kontreadmiral Souchon gives a much more interesting insight into his situation:

Wednesday the 18th of November: My reckoning has been right, today we cruised in hazy weather to the south coast of the Crimea, and into our arms ran the Russian main body: 5 battleships, 2 cruisers, and 5 torpedo boats, or rather we 2 ran into his arms. Like cheeky Oskar we cut loose and had a violent battle of about 15 minutes. We have quite damaged the Russian flagship, as far as we could observe and the bridge superstructure was shot through. Unfortunately, we ourselves were at first, shot by the Russians, a 30.5 cm shell hit through the casemate armour in the 3rd port 15cm casemate, and we lost 12 men, all immediately killed, dreadfully torn and mutilated, but so abruptly and fast an enviable heroic death. As we faced the line, I felt the desire to have a line of equivalent ships behind myself. What a hot trick this would have been, to shoot the high Russian ships together. The Russians shot badly, because after the first hit the battle lasted another ¼ of an hour. However, it was hazy, thus the smoke stuck very much and the ships were poorly made out. I allowed *Breslau* to remain outside the effective fire area, *Goeben* alone was not strongly superior enough, and therefore, we ran away bit by bit. Thus it will probably go on. If I had both old Turkish battleships behind me, so their destiny would have been sealed, because they had not been able to run away and still less would have been hit, for they are less protected than the Russians. The opponent always seems to want to hold his ships together, and this is quite clever of him. Against this I can make nothing and must limit myself to damage of his property. For the case that the opponent immediately did not run to Sevastopol I let the torpedo boats from the Bosporus come to attack them in a night attack. In total 2 boats had come out, from 8! These are the conditions of the Turkish Fleet. Always ¾ of the units are not ready for the front. About each damage the Turks feel an undisguised joy because then they then do not go out. Today I have been awarded the Iron Cross First Class. The fallen we have laid immediately on the battlefield in the chill sailor's grave. Then the music 'Fridericus Rex' blared and now one is further called to damage the enemy.

Thursday, 19 November: This morning we have hunted off Sinop for 5 clouds of smoke which evaporated, finally, like a cloud, then some unreliable observers wanted to have seen a submarine, but we had no contact with the enemy. Some people who have had their station yesterday near the hit have broken down tonight with smoke poisoning. However, the 3 doctors hope to get them healthy again. Tomorrow I want to run for a rest into the Bosporus to repair the different damages, moreover, I must save coal. Our stocks in Cardiff coal are now about 25,000 tonnes and will not stretch forever. The modern boilers cannot burn the Turkish coal which we always bring with the risk of hostile disturbance from the Black Sea coast. I let them mix, however, half of it with Cardiff coal, moreover, the cinders must burn through everywhere and loose heat value. Because I cannot be, however, everywhere with the German staff, this saving coal remains more desire than fact. Of course nothing at all could please the cowardly Turkish eyes better, than if the coal came to an end, then the ships need not go out anymore, and would be able, like before my time, to lie nicely in the Golden Horn and make *Keff*, or 'doze' in German.[9]

The short and vicious battle off Cape Sarych had lasted just 14 minutes according to Russian accounts. It was the first time a German capital ship had come into action during the First World War, and was the first and only time German ammunition had exploded in combat circumstances. Kontreadmiral Souchon had taken the fight to the Russian Black Sea Fleet, but then had been forced to concede. For the time being however the Black Sea remained a contested area, with neither side having sea mastery. For his part Admiral Eberhard was awarded the Order of the White Eagle, with Crossed Swords. Nevertheless he came in for unwarranted criticism from the Russian Supreme Headquarters, which accused him of lacking drive and energy, both unfounded claims.

The fight by the German cruisers in the Black Sea continued and whilst they could not dominate the sea they could dispute it. The Russians conducted their operations in full strength, raiding the 'coal coast', sinking Turkish coastal merchant shipping and appearing off the Bosporus. Individually their battleships were inferior to *Goeben*, but as long as they appeared as an integrated unit they could provide mutual protection. The first two Russian dreadnought battleships for the Black Sea Fleet were scheduled for completion in mid and late 1915, and then the tables could be turned on the precocious German *Großer Kreuzer*. Kontreadmiral Souchon, promoted to Vizeadmiral 27 January 1915, wanted to continue his sudden advances into the Black Sea, especially after the Entente invasion at Gallipoli, to damage the Russian sea forces and merchant traffic and to cause disquiet in the coastal areas. Therefore *Goeben* and *Breslau* repeatedly advanced into the Black Sea and appeared off the enemy and neutral coastlines. These operations continued throughout the spring. The Russians too continued their operations and from 2–5 May 1915 undertook a mission along the coal coast and appeared off the Bosporus. In turn the German ships, and the Turkish cruiser *Hamidie*, undertook an operation off the Crimean and Romanian coasts from 6–8 May.

On 7 May the Russian Black Sea Fleet again put to sea. Their operational plan called for attacks along the coal coast to destroy shipping and bombard ports, to boldly land a shore raiding party, and on the second day, 10 May, to use the battleships *Panteleimon* and *Tri Sviatitelia* to bombard the Bosporus forts. A submarine would occupy an ambush position off the Bosporus to attack any German or Turkish ships that might emerge.

On 9 May *Pamiat Merkuria* sank two Turkish steamers and twenty-seven Turkish sailing vessels in the Eregli area of the Anatolian coal coast. Nearby in the Kozlu area the destroyers *Derzki* and *Bespokoinyi* sank a steamer and a sailing vessel. Some Russian troops were put ashore at Eregli to destroy the power station there, and a fight developed with Turkish troops ashore. In Turkish Headquarters there was concern that further troops could be landed to destroy the colliery facilities. Therefore at 10.25hrs on 9 May *Goeben* received the following order by wireless: 'Go immediately as quickly as possible to Eregli, where Russian cruisers have dispatched boats to shore. Report when at sea. Fleet Chief not to travel with *Goeben*.'[10] The Fleet Chief, Vizeadmiral Souchon, was attending a conference with Turkish War Minister Enver Pascha and the German Generalfeldmarschall Freiherr von der Goltz, the head of the *Armee* in Turkey. The cruiser's turbines were still warm and could quickly be brought to full power, and at 13.00hrs *Goeben* put to sea. After passing the defensive mine barriers the cruiser steered a northerly course at a speed of 23 knots. *Goeben*'s commander, Kapitän zur See Ackermann, intended to be off Eregli at 18.00hrs, and towards 14.25hrs he received the following wireless message: 'At 10.40am the bombardment of Eregli was concluded. Cruiser and torpedoboat rejoined the battleship which came in sight, *Ioann Zlatoust*. Course north. *Goeben* should attempt to damage the enemy.'[11] At 14.48hrs *Goeben* sighted the Russian submarine *Nerpa*, which had been dispatched to the Bosporus, running on the surface. *Goeben* turned towards the submarine which immediately dived, but because he had been sighted Kapitän zur See Ackermann turned back towards the Bosporus in an attempt to deceive the submarine commander. Nevertheless by 18.00hrs the German cruiser was well out into the Black Sea but despite the clear conditions nothing was to be seen of the Russians. During the night *Goeben* ran along the latitude of Eregli with easterly and westerly courses at a speed of 12 knots to avoid potential Russian torpedoboat attacks. The night passed quietly.

At 04.00hrs on 10 May the Turkish torpedoboat *Numune*, under the command of the German Oberleutnant zur See Sommer, put to sea to screen off the Bosporus. At 05.15hrs the boat sighted a smoke cloud to the north and advanced towards it. At about 05.40hrs the Russian Black Sea Fleet could be made out: the battleships *Evstafi*, *Ioann Zlatoust*, *Panteleimon*, *Tri Sviatitelia*, and *Rostislav*, the seaplane tender *Aleksandr I* and minelayer *Kseniya*. Further, Russian minesweepers and torpedoboats came in sight. The Turkish torpedoboat reported by wireless: 'Seven Russian warships square 228, course southeast'. At 05.45hrs the Russians reached their designated 'Point A', and *Tri Sviatitelia, Panteleimon, Aleksandr I, Kseniya* and the transport *Svyatoi Nikolai* separated from the main body and proceeded towards the Bosporus to carry out their allotted tasks. At 06.35hrs *Numune* reported: 'Three enemy ships, one a cruiser, in square 228, twelve torpedoboats and minesweepers approach the Bosporus'. Then at 06.50hrs a Russian aircraft was observed to take off. At 07.10hrs, as the Russian minelayer approached water shallow enough to lay mines, *Numune* opened fire at a range of 75hm, whereon the Russian ship turned east. Then the two Russian battleships approached and took *Numune* under fire. However, soon the Russian battleships ceased fire, turned off to the northeast and made off; *Goeben* had arrived.

After receiving *Numune*'s wireless message *Goeben* quickly took course on the reported square and at 06.30hrs sighted a smoke cloud which was seen to be originating from a Russian cruiser. *Goeben* went to high speed and steered towards the Russian, which was the cruiser *Pamiat Merkuria*, whilst for her part the Russian cruiser made a contact report at 07.00hrs. Upon receipt of this Admiral Eberhard cancelled the bombardment and at 07.05hrs sent a wireless message to *Tri Sviatitelia* and *Panteleimon* to rejoin the main body, and he went towards them with his three ships. Because the Russian minesweepers had already deployed their sweeps it took a further 18 minutes for Rear Admiral Putyatin aboard *Tri Sviatitelia* to assemble and turn his unit. However, there was insufficient time for Admiral Eberhard to concentrate his forces as *Goeben* had seized the opportunity to engage the Russian forces whilst they were divided, and was approaching at high speed. Admiral Eberhard consecutively turned his ships towards the enemy and joined battle with the rapidly approaching *Goeben*, whilst Rear Admiral Putyatin's battleships still remained 2 miles behind. Course was taken to bring *Goeben* onto a relative bearing of 110° to starboard and at 07.53hrs when the range was 17,400 metres *Evstafi* and *Ioann Zlatoust* opened centralized fire with four-shot salvos. *Rostislav* did not open fire. *Goeben* lay on a converging course with a speed of 15 knots and, with the enemy on a bearing of 305°, the German *Großer Kreuzer* opened fire at almost the same instant as the Russians. The first salvos of *Goeben* fell well and *Evstafi* disappeared in a shower of water columns from impacting 28cm projectiles. On orders from Admiral Eberhard *Evstafi* took a zigzag course and varied her speed. The German short shells were making it difficult for the Artillery Officers aboard the Russian battleships to observe the fall of shot of their centralized fire. Nevertheless, in contrast to the battle off Cape Sarych, *Goeben* was unable to inflict any damage against the Russian flagship.

At around 08.00hrs *Goeben* was struck by a 12-inch shell which struck the forecastle from a relative bearing of 305°, and landed on the upper deck with a very steep trajectory. The shell broke through the upper deck and *Batteriedeck* before detonating on the *Zwischendeck*. From the thin-walled shell fragments it was determined that it was a high explosive projectile. There was damage to fittings and light structures and the port capstan was also damaged.

At 08.05hrs *Panteleimon* passed *Rostislav*, reaching a speed of 17½ knots, and opened fire on *Goeben*. The Senior Artillery Officer of *Panteleimon*, Leitenant Melchikovski, wrote that at 08.08hrs with the second salvo ranged at 18,500m *Goeben* was straddled and a hit was obtained amidships.[12] In actual fact the projectile struck 2 metres from the outer skin between frames 97 to 103 and detonated immediately after entering the water. Splinters were thrown upwards and damaged the net carrier and struck the bottom of the barrel of the port II casemate 15cm gun. The gun and crew were temporarily put out of action. The outer skin was dented below the armoured belt for a length of 6 metres and rivets were sprung, so that the wing passage between frames 100 and 104 temporarily filled with water. With the converging course the range had rapidly decreased to about 14,500m. Seeing that the Russians had again concentrated their forces and that *Goeben* was outgunned, Kapitän zur See Ackermann determined to increase speed and range and altered course to starboard. At 08.12hrs, as the range increased to 20,300m, fire was ceased. The battle had lasted 22 minutes. The German cruiser commander intended to draw the Black Sea Fleet away from the Bosporus and therefore steered a northerly course, and then later he could breakthrough back to the Bosporus utilizing his superior speed. At 08.18hrs two torpedo tracks were reported and *Goeben* avoided these with starboard rudder. The Russians followed *Goeben* until at 12.35hrs when they turned away to starboard and thereon *Goeben* followed. Then the Russians steered east and *Goeben* followed in their wake. Thereon the Russians made a turn back towards the German cruiser and *Goeben* increased speed to 26 knots and took course back towards the Bosporus. *Goeben* held the range at 18,000 to

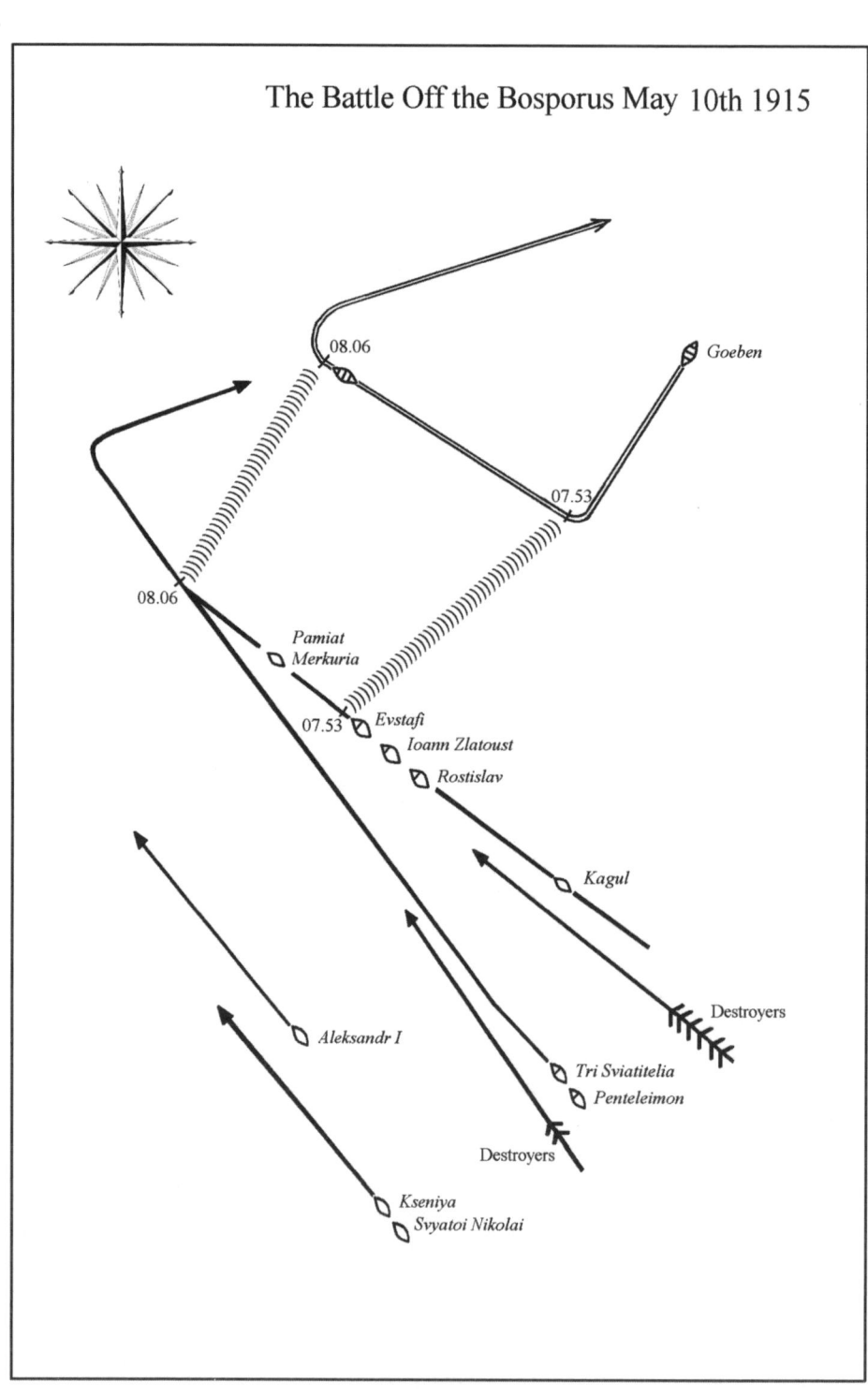

20,000 metres and the Russians maintained the pursuit until 14.10hrs when they turned away, and finally disappeared from sight at 14.50hrs.

During the action which lasted 22 minutes *Goeben* fired a total of 128 heavy calibre projectiles. The Russians noted that the German rate of fire was almost double their own rate. On the Russian side *Evstafi* fired fifty-eight 12-inch shells and three 8-inch shells, *Ioann Zlatoust* fired seventy-five 12-inch and four 8-inch shells, *Panteleimon* fired twenty-three 12-inch shells, and *Tri Sviatitelia* fired thirteen 12-inch shells, for a total of one hundred and sixty-nine 12-inch shells and thirty-six 8-inch shells. On this occasion the German shooting had not been successful, although many shells impacted close to *Evstafi* and the hull was strongly shaken by the near misses. Likewise Admiral Eberhard and his staff were drenched with water from the collapsing water columns caused by the exploding German projectiles. The German official history lamented this poor performance:

> Naturally enough *Goeben* had refused to join in a decisive battle with five enemy battleships with their twenty heavy guns against *Goeben*'s ten. The intention to draw the enemy away from the Bosporus was without doubt correct, and since *Goeben* was superior in speed she could manoeuvre at will and choose her own time to return to the Bosporus. It was regrettable, however, that in a battle lasting 22 minutes the Artillerie Offizier of *Goeben* could not more accurately strike the enemy. With the excellence of the materials, the excellent penetrative power of the German shells and their explosive result, a great success could have been expected against the old battleships. It was felt that an opportunity to reduce the Russian preponderance in the Black Sea had been lost.[13]

At the same time the often repeated cliché that HMS *Dreadnought*, and therefore the dreadnought type, had made all pre-dreadnought battleships obsolete was proved blatantly incorrect by Admiral Eberhard and his Black Sea Fleet.

Chapter 4

The Battle of the Falkland Islands, 8 December 1914

After the sea battle off Coronel the cruiser squadron of Graf von Spee stood away to the north during the night of 2 November. The wind of the previous evening abated, the swell eased, and the morning brought clear skies and good visibility. A reconnaissance line of small cruisers was no longer required and they concentrated with *Scharnhorst* and *Gneisenau*. As the ships assembled and the flagship passed each small cruiser they gave three cheers for Vizeadmiral Graf von Spee as a mark of respect for his leadership. During the afternoon the Admiral signalled that he intended to run into the port of Valparaiso the following day. As Chile was a neutral country only three warships of a belligerent country were allowed in port at the same time, and at that only for 24 hours. Therefore Graf von Spee determined that *Scharnhorst*, *Gneisenau* and *Nürnberg* would be the first to visit. The other two small cruisers, *Leipzig* and *Dresden*, would escort the squadron train and were to collect the colliers and take them to the island of Mas a Fuera, also known as Robinson Crusoe Island. There were many good reasons to take the cruisers to Valparaiso. The squadron had not been to a port city since departing Nagasaki on 22 June. Therefore Graf von Spee wanted to gain a clear picture of the overall war situation, instead of relying on second hand newspapers, and he would be able to communicate with the Admiralstab directly by telegram. This would allow him to determine the basis for further operations. The German squadron had also established sea mastery off the west coast of South America and he wanted to exploit and reaffirm this. It had to be demonstrated that the German ships had not suffered in battle. He also wanted to determine the fate of *Good Hope* and insist on her internment if she had reached a Chilean port in a damaged condition, as he did not learn definitely about her destruction until 4 November when the commander of *Leipzig* reported that his ship had passed through a debris field on the evening of 1 November. The ships would also be able to receive provisions and coal. In addition a further 127 reserves were recruited to the German squadron, coming from the local population and from German merchant vessels in harbour.

At dawn on Tuesday 3 November 1914 *Scharnhorst*, *Gneisenau* and *Nürnberg* entered the bay of Valparaiso. A pilot steamer came to meet them and showed them to their anchorage, where just after 11 o'clock they anchored. Vizeadmiral Graf von Spee and his adjutant went ashore and were met by the German Ambassador and Consul-General, and went about their official business; however, because of the brevity of the visit, just 24 hours, only *Offiziers* and *Deck-Offiziers* could be granted shore leave. After tending to official dispatches and other official tasks, the German party attended a dinner at the German Club before returning aboard their ships in the evening. Strictly adhering to international law, Graf von Spee weighed anchor at 10 o'clock on the morning of 4 November and departed Valparaiso.

At dawn on Friday 6 November *Scharnhorst*, *Gneisenau* and *Nürnberg* arrived at Mas a Fuera, where they could see *Leipzig* coaling from the newly acquired prize *Valentine*, a French four-masted bark. The next 4 days were spent coaling from captured prizes. On the evening of 10 November *Dresden* and *Leipzig* were detached to visit Valparaiso where they arrived early on 13 November. The remainder of the cruiser squadron remained at Mas a Fuera until 16.00hrs on Sunday 15 November, when they departed for St. Quentin Bay in the Gulf of Penas. At noon on 18 November *Dresden* and *Leipzig* rendezvoused with the squadron some 250 nautical miles west of Chiloe Island, and at dawn on 21 November the squadron anchored in the protected St. Quentin Bay in the northern part of the Gulf of Penas. The weather was uncertain but nevertheless coaling began immediately, and when the bunkers were full the cruisers filled sacks and stored them on the open decks. It would be a long journey around Cape Horn into the Atlantic Ocean and it was uncertain when the next opportunity to coal would come.

The reaction in England to the Battle of Coronel was one of disbelief and denial. However, after the initial shock the response was swift and decisive. Just 2 days before the battle, on 30 October, Admiral Fisher was reappointed First Sea Lord. On 4 November he ordered Admiral Jellicoe, commander of the Grand Fleet, to dispatch two battlecruisers, *Invincible* and *Inflexible*, to the South Atlantic to search for the German cruiser squadron. He also instructed Admiral Jellicoe to send the powerful battlecruiser *Princess Royal* to the Caribbean to block the exit from the Panama Canal. To command this squadron the Admiralty appointed the hitherto and recently sacked Chief of the War Staff, Vice Admiral Doveton Sturdee. Vice Admiral Sturdee was not having a good war. It was he who had denied the use of battlecruisers and the 1st Light Cruiser Squadron prior to the Battle of Helgoland Bight, and it was he who had countermanded orders to reinforce Rear Admiral Cradock's force with the armoured cruiser *Defence*. When Admiral Fisher was reappointed as First Sea Lord, one of his first actions was to have Vice Admiral Sturdee removed.

Vice Admiral Doveton Sturdee entered the Royal Navy in July 1871 at the age of twelve. After being promoted to midshipman he served in the Mediterranean Fleet, and after that in Australia and the Pacific. He was promoted Rear Admiral in 1910 and commanded the 1st Squadron of the Home Fleet, and then various cruiser squadrons. He was promoted Vice Admiral in 1913 and became Chief of the War Staff shortly before the outbreak of the First World War. Unlike Rear Admiral Cradock he was not known for his energy or flare, but more as someone who preferred to complete routine paperwork himself. On 9 November he joined the battlecruisers in Devonport, where they were fitting out for their long deployment, and hoisted his flag on *Invincible*. Two days later on 11 November *Invincible* and *Inflexible* sailed for the Falkland Islands. The unit coaled at St. Vincent in the Cape Verde Islands, before arriving at the prearranged rendezvous at Abrolhos Rocks on 26 November. There the ships coaled and replenished stores, whilst the commanders attended a conference. The British force assembled at Abrolhos Rocks consisted of the two battlecruisers, the armoured cruisers *Cornwall*, *Kent* and *Carnarvon*, and the light cruisers *Bristol* and *Glasgow*. On 28 November this formidable force departed for the Falkland Islands, which they reached at 10.30hrs on 7 December, the day before the German East Asiatic Squadron.

Before the beginning of the war Germany had attempted to solve the problem of lacking overseas bases by establishing the so-called *Etappe* system, where operational areas were divided into zones inside which an *Etappe Offizier* coordinated the supply of coal, water and provisions. The *Etappe* system had successfully provided Graf von Spee with coal and provisions by utilizing German merchant shipping operating from neutral ports. As an intelligence network was entirely absent, the *Etappe* system also tried to provide intelligence of enemy warship movements where and when it could. On 7 November a report arrived that the British armoured cruisers *Defence*, *Cornwall* and *Carnarvon*, and light cruisers *Bristol* and *Glasgow*, in addition to the battleship *Canopus*, were probably assembling at the Falkland Islands. There was news from San Francisco that powerful Japanese forces were off the west coast of North America. This force included the Japanese armoured cruiser *Idzumo*, the Australian battlecruiser *Australia*, which the British Admiralty had completely underutilized, and the light cruiser *Newcastle*. On 23 November a telegram was sent from San Francisco to Valparaiso quoting press reports that an English squadron of 10 ships had been sighted 300 nautical miles off Montevideo. It was urgently requested that the East Asiatic Squadron be informed, and also Punta Arenas, however it is unlikely that this message ever reached the squadron. Then on 20 November *Etappe* La Plata came into the possession of a report from Rio de Janeiro that the guns of *Canopus* had been mounted in the Falkland Islands as a fixed defence. Shortly afterwards, on 24 November, *Etappe* La Plata reported that the battlecruiser *Invincible* and armoured cruisers *Defence* and *Carnarvon* were at Abrolhos Rocks. Finally a message was sent from Punta Arenas to Valparaiso which could have influenced Graf von Spee. It stated that according to a report from an English steamer there were no

English warships at the Falklands, as they had gone to South Africa to help crush a revolt by the Boers. In Valparaiso they thought that this was a bluff and therefore did not forward the message to the cruiser squadron, however according to *Dresden* the message arrived in St. Quentin Bay but the Squadron Chief took no notice of it. Nevertheless the steamer *Amasis* was dispatched to Punta Arenas to determine if there was any truth to this rumour. After the departure of the squadron from Picton Island on 6 December *Amasis* reported by wireless that the rumour was very probable, as in mid-November there were no warships at the Falklands apart from *Canopus*, which was serving as a floating battery. However, it was also pointed out that this could be a deliberate ruse to draw the German cruiser squadron to the Falkland Islands.

The German squadron command was not sufficiently informed about the details of the political and military situation, and the dispatch of *Amasis* to check the details of a rumour indicates the uncertainty with which such reports were greeted. It is uncertain what effect, if any, the piecemeal reports had on the plans of Graf von Spee. It could be said therefore that the German Naval Intelligence Service had completely failed the cruiser squadron.

On the afternoon of 26 November the German East Asiatic Squadron departed St. Quentin Bay and the Penas Gulf in calm weather and took course south towards Cape Horn and the Atlantic Ocean. Soon a heavy swell came up from the southwest and the wind increased. Ropes were rigged all over the ships to help the men keep balance. The ships' boats and other heavy objects had to be double lashed to prevent them breaking away from their chains. Doors and portholes were secured closed. The temperature and barometer fell and the wind and swell increased, and whilst the large cruisers stood up to it quite well the small cruisers, which had taken on considerable deck cargoes of coal in sacks, began to roll violently. The waves came over the bows of the small cruisers, and swept over the bridges as far back as the middle decks and eventually they had to heave to and throw overboard some of their precious deck cargo to maintain stability. The further the squadron proceeded south the worse the weather became. On 2 December the German cruisers sighted Cape Horn, and shortly afterwards a huge iceberg at least 600 metres in length. As they rounded the Horn a three-masted sailing vessel was sighted to port. It was the Canadian *Drummuir*, carrying a cargo of 2,750 tonnes of Cardiff coal. *Leipzig* took the prize in tow and at 05.00hrs on 3 December the squadron anchored on the eastern side of Picton Island at the eastern end of the Beagle Channel. It had been a difficult journey but nevertheless work immediately began unloading the cargo of coal from *Drummuir* into the auxiliaries *Baden* and *Santa Isabel*, whilst the cruisers coaled from the auxiliary *Seydlitz*.

Vizeadmiral Graf von Spee did not want to remain at the Picton Island anchorage later than Sunday 6 December. The tedious work of coaling continued relentlessly, but there was time for some of the crews to go ashore and visit other ships during the evenings. On the morning of 6 December Graf von Spee convened a conference of commanders and staff aboard his flagship, SMS *Scharnhorst*. At the conference he outlined his plan to attack the Falkland Islands with the aim of destroying the facilities and burning the stocks of coal found there. Apparently he believed the information that the British forces had gone to South Africa, a view reinforced by the wireless message from *Amasis* received on the evening of 6 December. Despite this he still expected to encounter British forces at the Falklands, in the worst-case scenario meeting *Defence*, *Carnarvon*, *Cornwall*, *Glasgow* and *Bristol*, with *Canopus* as a floating battery. Therefore it seems that the *Etappe* at La Plata did not transmit by wireless the important information from 24 November about the appearance of *Invincible* at Abrolhos Rocks. Of those present, Vizeadmiral Graf von Spee, his Chief of Staff, Kapitän zur See Fielitz, and the commander of *Nürnberg*, Kapitän zur See Schönberg, were for the plan, whilst the commanders of *Gneisenau*, *Dresden* and *Leipzig* (Kapitäns zur See Maerker and Lüdecke and Fregattenkapitän Haun respectively) were against the operation. Fregattenkapitän Haun said that obviously the message about British forces going to South Africa was a ruse and he wanted to circumvent the Falkland Islands by 100 nautical miles and advance on La Plata, where merchant warfare could be productively carried out. Nevertheless those in favour of the operation held sway and the plan was carried. It would damage the enemy and provide a morale success.

At noon the German squadron weighed anchor. There was still a small amount of coal remaining aboard *Drummuir*, but the sailing ship was nevertheless scuttled just outside territorial waters. In fine, clear weather the squadron ran along the coast of Tierra del Fuego and gained the open sea. During the night *Leipzig* formed the vanguard, about 2 nautical miles ahead of the squadron. During the whole of Monday 7 December they steamed with a northeast course towards the Falkland Islands. *Gneisenau* and *Nürnberg* were delegated for the attack and aboard these two ships preparations were made for their landing parties. Small arms were broken out and field equipment was issued to the prospective landing parties.

The weather on the morning of 8 December was clear with good visibility, the sea was quiet and there was a light northwest wind. At 02.00hrs in the morning the dark masses of the Falkland Islands came in sight on the northern horizon. At 05.00hrs *Gneisenau* and *Nürnberg* detached from the squadron to carry out the projected operation and steered towards Cape Pembroke with 14 knots speed. Final preparations were undertaken aboard *Gneisenau* and the ship's boats were filled with water and a thin spray of water was cast across the deck, to prevent the spread of any fire. Towards 08.30hrs the wireless masts of Port Stanley came in sight and along with them the masts of several ships. Suddenly dense clouds of smoke climbed high from the harbour. Those aboard *Gneisenau* thought that the British were firing their stocks of coal, just as the

French had done at Tahiti, so that they would not fall into German hands. However, on the contrary, the smoke came from the British ships rapidly trying to raise steam. The two German cruisers had been sighted by a lookout on Sapper Hill, who had raised the alarm. From *Gneisenau* a smoke column was seen emerging from Port Stanley, but it quickly doubled back into harbour. It was the guard ship *Macedonia*, an armed auxiliary, whose place was rapidly taken by the armoured cruiser *Kent* and the light cruiser *Glasgow*. Aboard *Gneisenau* everyone was straining their eyes to discern their new opponents. Leutnant zur See Leitzmann wrote:

> From the spotting top we now received an insight into the harbour. There is an impenetrable wall of black smoke and a large number of mast tops! Then Oberleutnant Schwede imparts that he believes he has seen tripod masts! Tripod masts? With incredulous smiles we shake our heads. Only the most modern English big ships have such. We continued our journey disbelievingly.[1]

Gneisenau and *Nürnberg* increased speed to catch the emerging cruiser in the channel, when suddenly four giant water columns erupted between them and the coast. The grounded battleship *Canopus* had fired a salvo of indirect fire with her 12-inch gun battery. If the scene in the harbour had confused those aboard *Gneisenau*, further out to sea there was no such confusion aboard *Leipzig* and Kapitänleutnant Schiwig wrote:

> At 9.30hrs we could observe a cruiser of the *Cornwall* class appearing in the harbour entrance, followed by one of the *Glasgow* class. As the peninsula became lower, we could see the vessels putting on steam and running out to sea. I saw high straight funnels and a strange mast behind. My first thought was that they belonged to a special type of coal steamer as soon more of the funnels appeared. Almost at the same time the first *Steuermann* called what he saw through his rangefinder on the signal deck: 'That is a tripod mast.' Immediately I said to the commander, Fregattenkapitän Haun, 'Then it is *Australia*.' I thought to myself that she must have come from Australia via Coronel and Cape Horn to cut us off before we could gain the Atlantic. Soon after the shooting a message came from *Gneisenau*: 'Several ships, of the *Canopus* and *Cornwall* classes, in harbour.' Seemingly those on *Gneisenau* had still not recognized the tripod mast, because from their viewpoint they could not see the slowly moving battlecruiser.[2]

When *Gneisenau* reported the presence of up to six enemy warships in harbour Graf von Spee ordered the suspension of the operation and *Gneisenau* and *Nürnberg* to regroup with the main body. The speed indicator spheres on the foremasts of the cruisers climbed high to indicate utmost speed and the waves tumbled beneath the bows of the vigorously vibrating ships, as the German cruisers turned away to starboard to rejoin Graf von Spee:

> The Squadron Chief immediately wirelessed orders to us not to accept battle, but to rejoin the main body. Therefore we turned hard to starboard and ran at high speed to the east, to assemble with our three other cruisers on the open sea. Slowly the puzzling picture of the land became smaller. The ready ammunition was returned below. The men stood down from their battle stations and ascended the masts and superstructure, to ascertain a picture of the situation for themselves.[3]

At 10.45hrs the German squadron had reassembled and the three steamers of the fleet train, *Seydlitz*, *Baden* and *Santa Isabel*, were detached to the south to seek shelter amongst the islands near Cape Horn.

In Port Stanley the British ships were preparing to put to sea with all due haste. *Glasgow*, under the command of Captain Luce, was the first to get away and hurried after the German squadron. *Kent*, under Captain Allen, was next ready but had to await the other ships. Her captain wrote:

> No time was lost and at twenty minutes to nine, just under half an hour after the signal was received, the *Kent* was under way and steaming down the harbour past the flagship. A general signal had been made for all ships to raise steam for full speed. The flagship signalled to the *Kent* to proceed to the entrance to the harbour and wait there for further orders. From aloft we could now see over the land two cruisers approaching the harbour; one had four funnels and the other three funnels…Meanwhile, all our ships were busy getting clear of the colliers, raising steam and preparing for action. In the *Kent* we had prepared for action coming down the harbour, throwing overboard all spare wood, wetting the decks, and clearing away the guns.[4]

Soon after 10.00hrs *Invincible*, Captain Beamish, *Inflexible*, Captain Phillimore, followed by *Cornwall*, Captain Ellerton, and *Carnarvon*, Captain Skipwith and flagship of Vice Admiral Stoddart, all cleared harbour and began a stern chase of the German ships. The latecomers *Bristol*, Captain Fanshawe, and *Macedonia*, Captain Evans, were ordered by Vice Admiral Sturdee to pursue and destroy the German train. At 10.20hrs the signal was made for 'general chase' and all ships steamed their hardest. Soon the battlecruisers passed *Kent* at 25 knots speed and began gaining on the German ships.

Aboard *Gneisenau* a question mark still hung over the identity of the pursuers:

> Two vessels soon detached themselves from the number of our pursuers; they seemed much bigger and faster than the others, as their smoke was

thicker, wider and more massive. All glasses were turned inquisitively upon their hulls, which were almost completely enveloped by smoke. Were they Japanese?...There remained the possibility, even probability, that we were being chased by English battlecruisers, and this was a bitter pill for us to swallow...That meant a life and death struggle, or rather a fight ending in honourable death. 'Do not believe that everything will always go as well as at Coronel–things might turn out very differently.' The warning I had uttered vividly returned to my mind.[5]

At about 12.20hrs Vice Admiral Sturdee ordered the battlecruisers to push on ahead and attack and at 12.50hrs *Invincible* ordered *Inflexible* to take station 5 cable lengths (925 metres) astern of the flagship. It was to be the beginning of a very frustrating battle for *Inflexible* as she found herself severely hampered by the considerable volumes of smoke issuing from *Invincible*. A minute later, at 12.51hrs, Vice Admiral Sturdee allowed the signal to attack to be hoisted, and at 12.55hrs *Inflexible* opened fire on the last German ship, *Leipzig*, at a range of 140hm, followed one minute later by *Invincible*. It is often said that Vice Admiral Sturdee deliberately fought the battle at long range so as to remain outside the range of the German guns. This statement is just untrue. The 21cm guns mounted in turrets of *Scharnhorst* and *Gneisenau* had a range of 163hm, whilst the casemate mounted 21cm pieces were ranged to 124hm. The 15cm cannon could reach 137hm, in fact outranging the 21cm casemate guns. The Gunnery Officer of *Invincible*, Lieutenant Dannreuther, was stationed in the foremast foretop during the battle and wrote:

> The ranges were much longer than we had dreamt of. Our maximum range at the time was 16,000 yards (148hm) with the guns at extreme elevation. We intended to fight at 12,000 yards so as to be at a range compatible, we hoped, with good practice and at 12,000 yards our 6-inch side armour was likely to keep out the German 8.2-inch armour piercing shell.... The enemy turned to port and opened fire: much to our surprise they straddled us with their third salvo at 15,500 yards (143hm)...[6]

Therefore, the 21cm guns aboard the German *Panzerkreuzer* could outrange the British 12-inch pieces *at that time*.

The British battlecruisers continued to shoot at *Leipzig* for some time but the shooting was not good and *Leipzig* was not hit, however she was surrounded on all sides by high water spouts produced by the impacting projectiles. At around 13.20hrs a colourful signal was hoisted aboard *Scharnhorst*: 'Small cruisers detach. Attempt to escape.' The small cruisers turned away to the south and consequently, in accordance with their prearranged orders, *Kent* and *Cornwall* followed, and then at 13.33hrs also *Glasgow*.

Graf von Spee recognized that with the uncommon visibility conditions and clear weather there was no chance of escaping the British battlecruisers with their superior speed, and therefore he resolved to join battle with them under the most favourable conditions for the German line, whilst he hoped the small cruisers would be able to effect an escape. At 13.25hrs he turned his cruisers for a running battle on course NE, and therefore he claimed the lee position, which with the weak wind was more favourable for artillery fire. The wind would clear the powder smoke from the German ships quickly, whilst on the British ships it would drift downwind and foul the range, making observation difficult. The funnel smoke of the British ships would also be a hindrance. *Scharnhorst* signalled: 'Long range battle to port. Fire distribution from the right.' That meant *Scharnhorst* would fight against *Invincible* and *Gneisenau* would battle *Inflexible*. On the English side *Carnarvon* would remain unfired upon. At 13.30hrs the German cruisers opened fire on the battlecruisers and with a fire no less accurate than at Coronel *Invincible* was straddled by the third salvo aimed at her. Nevertheless, the British battlecruisers, with their supplemental oil firing, were veiled by a dense brown-yellow smoke, added to by the powder smoke from their guns, which drifted downwind. With the wind coming from port aft the smoke clung to the ships and made observation extremely difficult, especially for *Inflexible*. But observation was also difficult for the German ships as the British were frequently hidden from view. Aboard *Gneisenau* the revolution indicator showed 115rpm, giving a speed of 21 knots. The gun crews and ammunition transport crews worked quickly to maintain the highest rate of fire. Within a short time *Invincible* was hit twice and at 13.45hrs Vice Admiral Sturdee turned his ships 2 points away to port in an attempt to increase the range. This he achieved but at 14.00hrs with the range at 152hm the British line ceased fire, followed immediately afterwards by the German line. Graf von Spee did not follow the movement of the British line, but instead utilized the opportunity to distance himself from his superior opponent, turning abruptly away to the south at 14.05hrs. He had deftly outmanoeuvred his opponent and there was a 'battle pause' with a renewed possibility of escape.

During this first phase of the battle *Gneisenau* received two hits and a third near miss underwater. The first hit at 13.20hrs exploded against the aft edge of the aft funnel and splinters penetrated the 21cm and 15cm casemates below. 'A Deck *Offizier* had both his forearms torn off, an order transmitter was seriously wounded, other men suffered more lightly, and a stoker was killed in the corridor.'[7] The second hit struck the middle deck where it wrecked some cabins and damaged both cutters. A splinter from a short projectile penetrated the hull side to port aft and necessitated a magazine for the 8.8cm guns being flooded. Losses totalled one dead and ten wounded, who were removed to the dressing station during the battle pause. According to the observations of *Gneisenau* the flagship *Scharnhorst* remained unhit during this first phase of the battle.

Apparently the turn away by the German cruisers was not immediately recognized on the smoke-veiled battlecruisers. *Carnarvon* was the first to follow the German turn, followed a short time later by the battlecruisers, which again increased speed and renewed the pursuit. It was not until 14.45hrs that Vice Admiral Sturdee could again open fire at approximately 140hm and then he turned away one point to bring the full broadsides of six 12-inch pieces to bear. At 14.53 Graf von Spee turned onto an ENE course to reengage in a running battle at a range of 137hm. The British admiral quickly took up the same course and the battle recommenced under much the same conditions as the first battle phase. The respite had been brief and all recognized that under the prevailing conditions of fine weather and good visibility there would be no chance of the German *Panzerkreuzers* escaping from an enemy greatly superior in speed. Now the British gunfire became more effective. The German official history runs:

> The results of the British gunfire during this phase of the battle are given by the I Offizier of *Gneisenau*, Korvettenkapitän Pochhammer: 'At long battle ranges the ship presents a larger target area to plunging shells compared to just a silhouette of a medium to short range target. The steeply falling heavy projectiles easily penetrated the decks and casemates and caused much devastation inside the ship, and the side belt armour did little to protect the ship from these hits.'[8]

At this time a hit penetrated between the second and third funnels into the galley below, followed a short time later by another shell in the same area. A shell struck the casemate armour near the N°2 port 15cm gun, but did not penetrate the armour. Underwater hits caused the I and III boiler rooms to begin filling with water. The wireless room was wrecked. From his battle station in the central command position, deep in the ship, Leutnant zur See Lietzmann wrote:

> It became 3 o'clock. In quiet, monotonous tones the voices above could be heard. The compass rose showed course E.N.E. The Navigation Offizier stood at a map next to us, following the situation. The plug board of the Leak Countermeasures Engineer, Marineingenieur Meyer, gradually took on a colourful appearance [there was a large schematic board showing the watertight compartments, into which a red plug was inserted when that compartment flooded–hence the name plug board]. Here and there areas fell out or were flooded. However, the engines were still intact and the revolution indicators showed our highest speed.[9]

Furthermore:

By this time the buoyancy of the ship was considerably impaired, for the violent shocks which we felt at the central command position told us more quickly than the speaking tubes could have done that we had been hit below the water line by enemy shots. The middle stokehold filled so rapidly that all the men could not reach the emergency exit in time. Another soon followed, but it filled with water more slowly. Although all pumps were in action, the speed of the ship began to decrease, and in spite of attempts to redress the balance, we heeled over to starboard.[10]

During this time *Scharnhorst* also suffered heavily under the enemy fire. She had fires in several positions and her gunfire had become slower and deliberate. At around 15.15hrs the third funnel was shot away and for a short time *Scharnhorst* sheered out to starboard, probably after a hit to the rudder plant, but after a brief time regained her station.

The British battlecruisers were also being hit at this time, but no chronological order of their damage is available. Because of the interference from smoke the British ships made a turn to port at about 15.15hrs, in an attempt to clear the range. Graf von Spee did not wish to engage in a circular battle nor surrender the lee position, so at 15.27hrs he turned to starboard on to a south-westerly course. The German's targets were now reversed in order, with *Gneisenau* facing the flagship and *Scharnhorst* battling *Inflexible*. Vice Admiral Sturdee turned a complete circle and at 15.37hrs the battle recommenced on a WSW course at ranges between 90 and 110hm. During the turn the *Offiziers* aboard *Gneisenau* had a good opportunity to observe *Scharnhorst*. Her draught lay one metre deeper than normal and she listed slightly to port. There was a large hole in the port forward hull side and a large hole to starboard aft. There were also several raging fires, however, the starboard battery kept up a lively fire, including the 15cm guns. During this time *Gneisenau* was apparently obscured from view by smoke so that *Scharnhorst* had to endure the fire of both British battlecruisers. For a time Vice Admiral Sturdee again sought to increase the range to 140hm so that only the 21cm guns in turrets could fire, but as the underwater hits on the German ships were taking their toll and the German ships reduced speed the battlecruisers again began to overhaul them. As a result, at about 15.55hrs, Vice Admiral Sturdee again felt confident enough to allow the range to reduce.

During this time it was observed that the admiral's flag aboard *Scharnhorst* was not at the mast-head and Kapitän zur See Maerker, commander of *Gneisenau*, enquired: 'To *Scharnhorst*: Why is the Admiral's flag at half mast? Is he dead?' to which he received the reply: 'Admiral to Commander: I am still going well. Have you [seen] any hits?' 'Commander to Admiral: Owing to the smoke I have been unable to observe.' 'Admiral to Commander: You were right.' This last was a reference to Kapitän zur See Maerker's opposition to the proposed attack on the Falkland Islands.

Briefly before 16.00hrs Graf von Spee directed a further blinker signal to the commander of *Gneisenau*: 'If your engines are intact attempt to escape.' After that *Scharnhorst* turned 8 points towards the enemy, obviously in an attempt to launch a torpedo attack and bring relief to *Gneisenau*. *Scharnhorst* lay considerably deeper by the bows, with the 15cm casemates in the water and a conspicuous list to port. Steam and smoke came from beneath the bridge and the aft part of the ship, which was in flames. The bows were just 2 metres above the water as the bow turret continued to fire. Then at 16.17hrs *Scharnhorst* rolled over to port and sank, with battle flag still flying and the propellers still revolving. There was no attempt to rescue any of the survivors.

Gneisenau now began to suffer badly under the fire of the two British battlecruisers, and the armoured cruiser *Carnarvon* also joined in. Already at 15.30hrs the starboard engine room was heavily hit:

> At 3.30pm a shell penetrated the starboard engine. How it resembled a dying animal as the steel parts entangled themselves and then with a hellish sound the steam driven creature solidified, leaving *Gneisenau* with only two screws to work itself...With our two remaining engines the highest speed we could reach was 14 knots– and the enemy was running at almost 27![11]

An attempt to escape was impossible. At 15.45hrs a direct hit toppled the forward funnel and then at 16.00hrs the IV boiler room was put out of action. At the same time a hit wrecked the starboard side of the bridge. Then at 16.15hrs a shell passed right through the hull and out the port side without detonating, whilst another struck to starboard in the main dressing station, killing almost all the men there:

> In the port gangway on the *Zwischendeck* a hit scattered a pile of ready 8.8cm ammunition, which however did not explode. At the same moment a dull thud was felt aft. A direct hit had struck the main dressing station and relieved the suffering of the poor mutilated. Fate also caught up with their devoted guardians...Only a few survived, including Stabsarzt Dr. Claus.[12]

Nevertheless, things were not going entirely well for the British ships, and *Inflexible* was so smothered by the smoke of the flagship that she finally broke away in an attempt to come to windward of her. At around 16.20hrs *Inflexible* described a circle and took up a NE course for a passing battle with *Gneisenau*. However the movement was replicated by *Invincible*, which likewise steered to the NE before turning to starboard and resuming a westerly course and around 16.30hrs. *Inflexible* and *Carnarvon* dutifully fell into line once again behind the flagship before *Inflexible* again broke away to the southeast at around 16.50hrs.

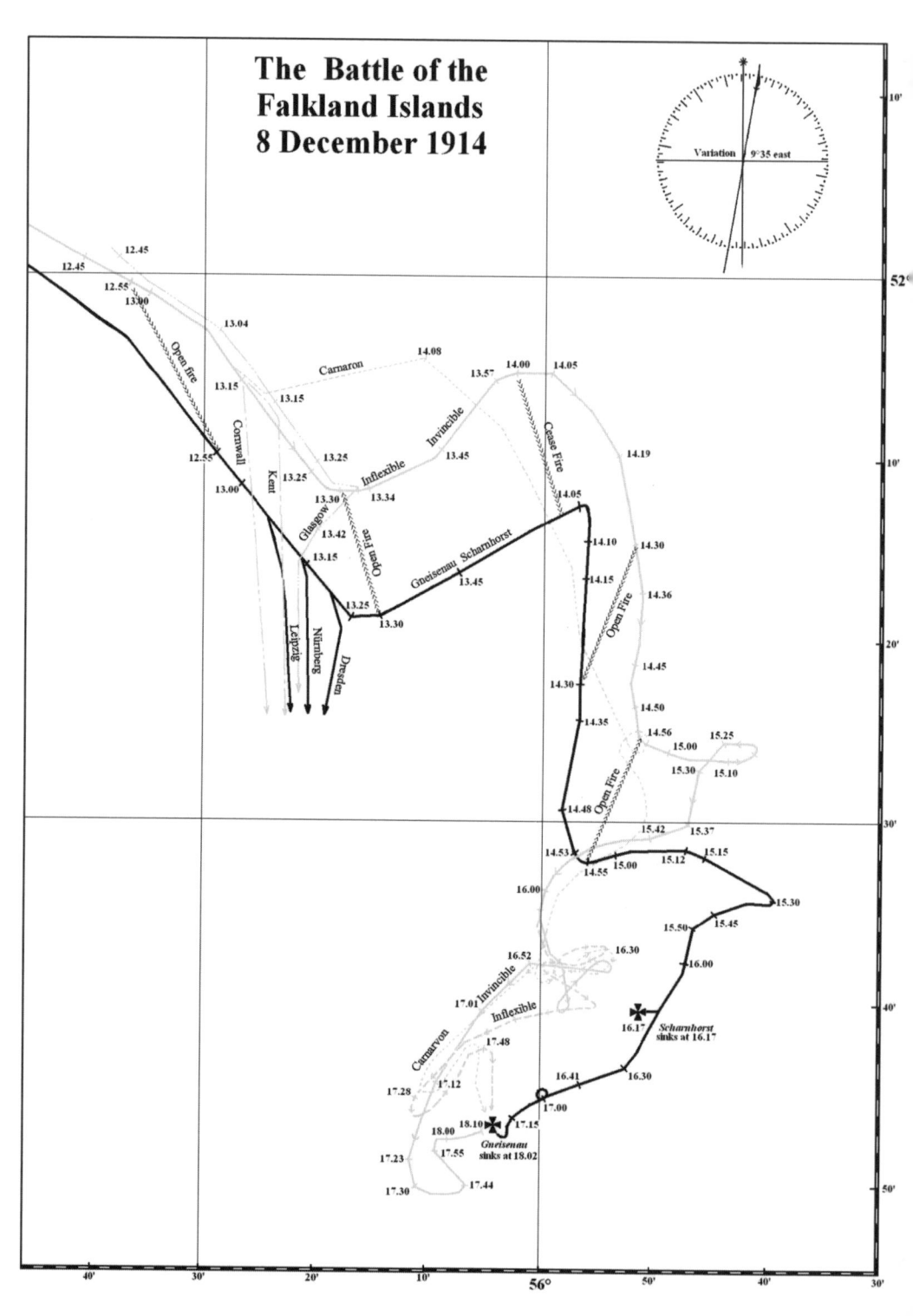

The I Offizier of *Gneisenau* wrote the following about this phase of the battle:

> The ship lost speed owing to damage to the boiler rooms and engines. The artillery also suffered heavily. A 30.5cm shell penetrated the top of the starboard forward 21cm gun casemate, burst over the base of the gun and killed the entire gun crew...The result of this hit also reached the port side 21cm casemate, and likewise the crew, bar two men, fell.
>
> Meanwhile *Carnarvon* ran closely past the sinking position of *Scharnhorst*, without stopping, and dashed headlong after us.
>
> About 4.30pm the battlecruisers turned further away as they came under a flood of our fire at 85hm and increased the range to 130hm.
>
> Towards 4.45pm *Inflexible* circled further behind us, seemingly to surround us. Whilst *Invincible*'s view of us was hindered by smoke and powder smoke, and the water spouts of short shots, *Gneisenau* attempted to turn at low speed with 10° rudder in a circle to starboard and so bring the port broadside to bear, after suffering rudder damage from shellfire coming from aft from *Carnarvon* and possibly *Inflexible*...The aft turret had for some time been jammed fast at 90°. This turret had run out of ammunition...Munitions supplies were brought from the casemate.[13]

After the ammunition was expended even the practice solid shot was fired, and after the battle Korvettenkapitän Pochhammer was shown one of these projectiles which had hit and remained lodged aboard *Invincible*.

The end was approaching for *Gneisenau* and she was being hit more and more frequently. At 17.15hrs there were two underwater hits on the starboard side and a third hit in the starboard 15cm gun casemate. By now all the crew there were dead and the cartridge fire had spread to a galley. Further hits followed. At around 17.35hrs the commander of *Gneisenau* ordered, 'All men on deck. Clear the ship for sinking!' This meant that explosive charges were to be detonated in the bottom of the ship, scuttling her. From all the intact corners of the ship the men now emerged, many blackened by either coal dust or powder smoke. As the hapless survivors collected on deck the forward turret loosed a final shell, contrary to orders. *Inflexible* released a retaliatory fire and a heavy shell struck the forward dressing station, saving many badly wounded from a slower death. Then about 17.42hrs it was reported that preparations for sinking the ship were complete and the explosive charges were immediately detonated. To hasten the sinking the torpedo room crew launched a torpedo and left the underwater door open. *Gneisenau* began to slowly capsize to starboard. Marineingenieur Meyer wrote:

> The commander brought out three cheers for His Majesty, whereon the crew abandoned ship. I slithered onto the outside hull by going down the port side

of the bridge, however came to the water to starboard as the ship quickly capsized. As I came to the surface I saw the keel of the fore part of the ship 25 metres away. On the torpedo launching tube I saw four men singing without ceremony. Soon they vanished as the ship disappeared forever, into the depths. I soon hung onto floating objects along with other men...[14]

It was 18.02hrs.

Scharnhorst and *Gneisenau* were gone. Incredibly, *Scharnhorst* had continued the battle for around 2¾ hours, but of her crew of 860 there were no survivors. The number of hits she sustained is unknown. *Gneisenau* held out much longer and during the 4½-hour battle with a vastly superior opponent she was definitely struck by heavy shells twenty-nine times. Of her crew 598 were lost, many from exposure after the sinking, but 187 men were saved.

Of the British ships *Invincible* was hit by shells twenty-two times. There were eleven hits on deck, four on the side armour, one below the water line, one on A turret and one on the fore mast. The officers' mess was hit and wrecked, as was the crew canteen. The dressing station was also hit along with a boat crane. The forward A turret was struck squarely between the guns, but the armour was luckily not penetrated. Surprisingly only one man was wounded. Lieutenant Dannreuther wrote:

> The *Invincible* was hit 22 times by 8.2 inch and 5.9 inch, mostly 8.2 inch, and suffered a good deal of damage, though fortunately the fighting equipment remained practically intact. Curiously enough the three 8.2 inch shells that did the most damage did not burst. One struck the armour forward and on the water line and flooded the two bow compartments. Another entered the side 10 feet below the water line below P turret and just below the side armour. This shell made a large hole and broke up against the internal armour around P handling room. The bunker was flooded and gave the ship a bit of a list. However, we came all the way back to Gibraltar with these compartments flooded.
>
> The third shell hit N°2 4 inch gun starboard, broke it in half and wrecked the mounting, then descended at a slope of 48 degrees through three decks and squashed all the 3 inch voice pipes from the foretop.[15]

Invincible was immediately released to go for repairs at Gibraltar, although she did reverse her course back to the south when it was rumoured there were German battlecruisers in the Atlantic. On 11 January 1915 she reached Gibraltar and was docked for repairs, and at the end of February 1915 she finally returned to Scapa Flow.

During the battle *Inflexible* received three hits which caused slight damage to the 4-inch guns on A and X turrets. She suffered one killed and three wounded. On 19 December she was ordered home but instead went to the Mediterranean for the Dardanelles operations.

After the small cruisers were detached from the squadron at about 13.25hrs they took up a SSE-by-S course at their highest speeds. They were pursued by the armoured cruisers *Kent* and *Cornwall*, and after a short time also by the light cruiser *Glasgow*. After the Coronel Battle *Glasgow* had docked in Rio de Janeiro for repairs to underwater damage and most probably had her bottom scraped, and therefore was superior in speed to the German small cruisers. With construction speeds of 23 knots *Kent* and *Cornwall* were faster than *Leipzig* and at least equal to *Nürnberg*. However, *Nürnberg*'s boilers were in poor condition, and *Leipzig*'s boilers and machinery were worn out and in need of overhaul after long service on the foreign station. *Dresden*, the turbine cruiser, was the fastest of the German group and it was not long before she began to outpace the British pursuers. Because *Dresden* had a high consumption of coal her commander, Kapitän zur See Lüdecke, determined to seek shelter among the islands of South America, rather than attempting to escape into the Atlantic. *Dresden* steadily pulled away and was able to escape destruction.

The commander of *Leipzig*, Fregattenkapitän Haun, at first attempted to edge his way towards the South American coast, hoping to vanish against the dark coastline with the approach of night. In this he was thwarted as *Glasgow* took station to starboard aft, coming between the cruiser and the coast. *Leipzig* maintained a speed of 21 knots and *Glasgow* was able to swiftly approach, so that at 14.40hrs she was able to open fire on *Leipzig* with her bow 6-inch cannon. When *Leipzig* saw that *Glasgow* had opened fire she immediately replied with her 10.5cm pieces at a range of 110hm. The Navigation Offizier of *Leipzig*, Kapitänleutnant Koehler, wrote the following:

> Towards 3pm, 20 minutes after the opening of fire, *Leipzig* received her first hit. A 15cm shell hit the superstructure in front of the third funnel. Splinters penetrated the speaking tubes to aft, the manual rudder position and wireless room. A large part of the shell went through the upper deck into the upper bunker, which was being used. Now for some time the forced draught to the III and IV boiler rooms was reduced as the air pressure escaped through the bunker and hole in the upper deck. With several joists and heavy baulks the hole was sufficiently closed.[16]

The range had dropped to 96hm:

> The commander allowed a turn to port to throw off the enemy's aim. Thereby the range gradually increased and the fire of both ships ceased, so that at 3 o'clock there was a pause in the battle, which was utilized to take the

dead and wounded to the forward dressing station. This pause lasted until about 3.10hrs.[17]

Then *Glasgow* closed the range and the battle began again, but now *Leipzig* turned a little to starboard to allow her full broadside to bear. Nevertheless *Leipzig* began to get hit and a shell splinter penetrated the conning tower and stunned Oberleutnant zur See Schiwig. He wrote:

> A very small splinter, about the size of a bent button, had entered through the door or a vision slit and struck my backbone, however without piercing the skin. Shortly afterwards a hit struck the starboard N°1 gun. The two men that stood unprotected by the gun shield fell, and of those from the port battery standing in the firelee of the conning tower, one suffered a shattered left arm. The linoleum between the two cannon caught fire and burnt well, threatening the ready ammunition. I believed this would explode, however the men immediately extinguished the fire with water. Immediately after this we were hit in the stern in the clothes store, which lay on the *Zwischendeck* under the cabins. This immediately caught fire and produced much smoke but this didn't hinder the aft battery as our speed caused the smoke to blow away to port. Nevertheless *Glasgow* was well covered by our salvos and hits were observed. The range totalled 8.6km.[18]

Leipzig hit *Glasgow* with two shells, one of which struck the foretop, killing one man and wounding four others, and the other damaged a boiler so that *Glasgow*'s speed was reduced to 23½ knots, still fast enough to keep pace with *Leipzig*. Now *Leipzig* was hit again, one shell striking the starboard aft upper bunker, another hit wrecking the wireless antenna. Nevertheless, the two hits on *Glasgow* had the effect that the British cruiser turned away to port at 16.27hrs to seek the protection of the armoured cruisers. Another brief battle pause began, during which the wounded were tended and the I Offizier attempted to fight the fire aft in the clothes store, however this fire burned until the ship sank. Due to the need to clean the boiler fires the speed of *Leipzig* reduced to 20 knots and soon the armoured cruisers came within range. When the range reduced to 110hm *Leipzig* opened fire on *Cornwall*, which immediately returned fire, and at 16.20hrs *Kent* came within range and opened fire from port aft for approximately 20 minutes. *Kent* obtained several hits, one of which penetrated an upper bunker and another which caused flooding so that between 17.00 and 18.00hrs the IV boiler room had to be given up. About 16.40hrs *Kent* suddenly turned away and ceased fire shortly afterwards as she took up the pursuit of *Nürnberg*.

As *Leipzig* began to suffer, her rudder failed due to an interruption between the conning tower and the tiller flat. From then on the ship had to be steered using the engines. The forward funnel also received a hit. As the IV boiler room gradually failed the speed reduced to 18 knots. The fires were a considerable worry and because many of the fire hoses had been shot through, and because of the shortage of men, they proved difficult to combat. However, *Leipzig*'s commander would not give up the fight and would continue until night came, or until the ammunition was used up. There was still some hope of escape as the heavens had become cloudy and a rain squall appeared ahead, which the cruiser would attempt to reach. Towards 18.00hrs the report arrived, 'The ammunition aft is expended, forward 200 shells are on hand.' Some men began transporting the ammunition to the aft guns. In the meantime, 'The poop and compartments hereunder were engulfed in flames and the personnel in the rudder room were trapped as water entered the forward rooms of compartment II, the path through the exits was blocked by fire, there being no possibility of escape. All the men here went down with the ship.'[19] Some of the *Offiziers* transporting the ammunition aft were killed on deck:

> During this last hour both *Ingenieurs* were killed on the upper deck. Then Leutnant Riediger fell on the poop while attempting to fight the fire in the hand rudder compartment. The fire was now at the base of the mainmast, covering the ammunition hoist. About 7 o'clock the last shell was fired and [I Artillerie Offizier, Oberleutnant zur See] Giseke notified the commander that the ammunition was exhausted. Shortly before *Cornwall* had been well covered and according to English statements had been hit several times. The range was approximately 7.5km. The ship did revolutions for 15 knots.[20]

At around 17.30hrs *Cornwall* was hit nine times in as many minutes with the range about 90hm, forcing her to turn away to starboard. During the course of the battle *Cornwall* was in fact hit eighteen times, although some of the shells failed to explode. One of these was displayed aboard HMS *Belfast*, but today is in the Imperial War Museum. The two most serious hits were below the water line, which bulged the armour inwards so that two bunkers leaked and filled on the port side and *Cornwall* took a considerable list to port. 'With the reception of the report from Giseke I said to the commander: "So, now my turn comes." The range was still too great for a torpedo shot in a running battle. I had the starboard tube readied and did my aiming calculations with my apparatus.' Towards 19.15hrs *Leipzig* fired three torpedoes, two at *Cornwall* and one against *Glasgow*, however, none found a target.

> Towards 7.20pm the commander gave the order: 'Sink the ship. All men on deck!' The sea-valves were all opened as was the starboard torpedo tube, which was jammed open by the *torpedo-maschinist*. Now the men poured on deck and the forecastle and middle deck quickly filled. Mostly they were the

technical personnel. Of the seamen the greater part had fallen and only a remnant of the gun crews and ammunition servers remained. It was proof of the protection that the armoured deck had offered! The aft ship burned to the forward edge of the poop, and the mainmast was glowing at its base and was cantered over to port, as the ship listed.[21]

The two British cruisers passed *Leipzig* to starboard at great range before coming across her bows. *Glasgow* was in the lead and delivered a Morse signal which could not be deciphered aboard *Leipzig*. Later it was learned they had enquired 'Do you surrender?' Aboard *Leipzig* the survivors thought the British ships had closed to rescue them, but as they approached to within 20 to 30hm they opened a withering fire on the defenceless German cruiser. 'The result was a shocking devastation and slaughter among the crew.'[22] The greatest carnage occurred when a cutter packed with wounded was turned into a bloodbath. The commander of *Glasgow*, Captain Luce, excused himself by saying he believed *Leipzig* had again opened fire. As reported in the San Francisco Examiner *Glasgow*'s gun crews refused to fire further on the survivors with the words: 'She is sinking now, that is sheer murder.' This incident caused bad blood between the surviving German sailors and Captain Luce, and they refused to acknowledge him when they disembarked the day after the battle.

When *Leipzig* was taken under fire again, many of the survivors leapt overboard, preferring to take their chances in the freezing water, which was just 3–4°C, and many of them died of exposure. The others waited on the forecastle with the commander for their ship to sink. It became fully dark and *Glasgow* finally sent a cutter towards the sinking ship. Towards 21.05hrs *Leipzig* finally lay over to port and sank with a loud hissing as the fires were at last extinguished. Fregattenkapitän Haun refused to leave his ship until she had sunk and was not amongst the survivors. Of *Leipzig*'s crew, eighteen *Offiziers* and men were rescued from the icy waters.

From the opening of fire to the sinking of *Leipzig* took a lengthy 6¾ hours, however, the battle of *Kent* and *Nürnberg* took just 2½ hours. After lunch the commander of *Nürnberg*, Kapitän zur See Schönberg, assembled his crew on deck and gave them his final address. He asked each man to fulfil his duty and persevere at his post. At about 16.40hrs the armoured cruiser *Kent* ceased fire on *Leipzig* and steered directly after *Nürnberg*. The weather had deteriorated and a light rain fell, making observation more difficult. During the pursuit several boilers aboard *Nürnberg* suffered broken boiler tubes and the cruiser's speed was reduced to 18 knots. The British armoured cruiser's engines gave a creditable performance and she quickly gained on *Nürnberg*, so that at 17.00hrs, according to British reports, *Nürnberg* was able to open fire with her two aft 10.5cm guns at the long range of 10.5hm. For the time being *Kent* was unable to make reply because her 6-inch pieces were outranged. The German commander manoeuvred his ship so that he could bring four guns of the port battery to bear. Between 10 and 30 minutes later *Kent* was able to reply and soon afterwards *Nürnberg* received her first hit, on the aft funnel. The aft damage control party extinguished the resulting fire and closed the hole in the funnel with mats. The next hit struck the middle deck near the N°3 gun and the crew were killed in part or else were wounded. As *Kent* had closed to within 50 to 60hm, Kapitän zur See Schönberg turned 8 points to port to bring all five guns of the port broadside to bear. This was soon reduced to four guns when multiple hits between the N°3 guns finished them both. Then the starboard N°5 gun was put out of action as the range reduced to between 32 and 28hm.

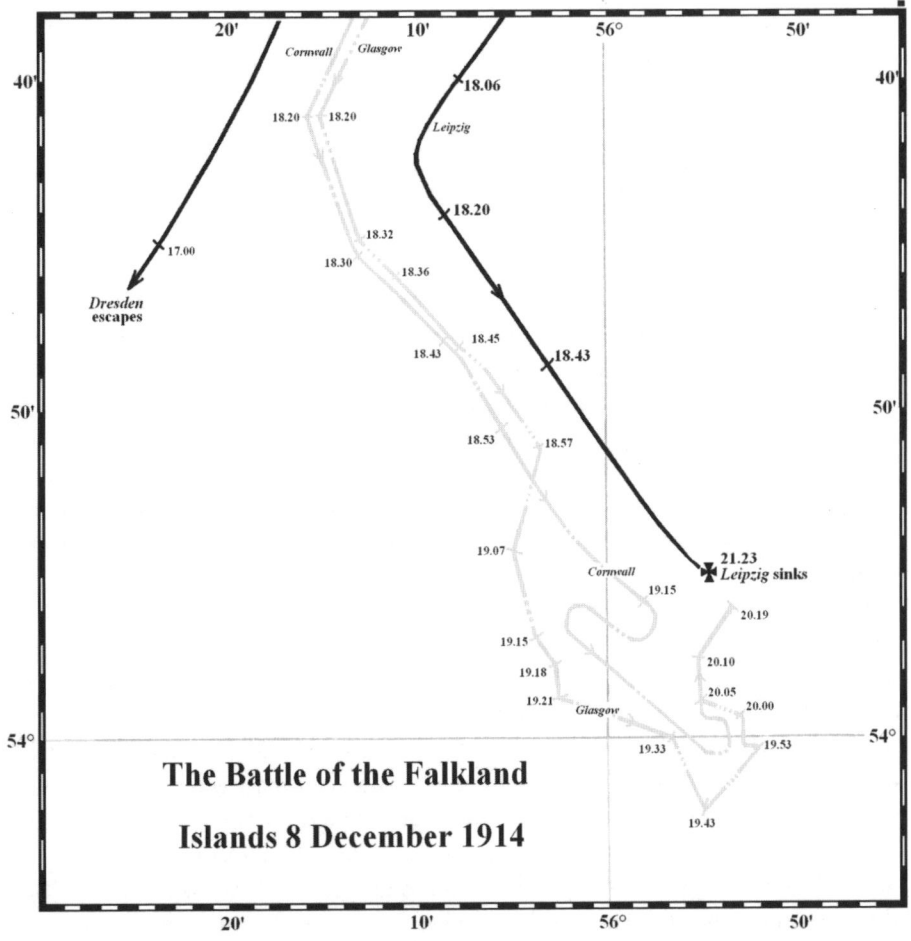

At 18.02hrs *Kent* passed across the bows of *Nürnberg* and took the starboard side under fire at relatively close range. The rudder room was hit and all the men there, with the exception of one, were killed. At the short range *Nürnberg* received hit after hit and many fires resulted. The boilers, engines and rudder had all been hit and the ship was almost unmanoeuvrable, precluding the chance of a torpedo shot. Towards 18.30hrs the commander gave orders to scuttle the ship. Now the men from below came on deck and prepared to abandon ship. *Kent* had ceased fire as the men assembled and began to go overboard. Now, just as in the case of *Leipzig*, the British cruiser reopened fire on the defenceless crew. Captain Allen justified his action as follows:

> We steamed slowly towards her, taking care to keep well before her beam, so that she could not hit us with a torpedo. As we got nearer to her we could see that her colours were still flying, and she showed no signs of sinking. We had to sink her: there could be no doubt about that, so at 6.45 we opened fire again. After five minutes, during which time she was repeatedly struck, she hauled down her colours. We immediately ceased firing. We could see now that she was sinking.[23]

About this time Kapitän zur See Schönberg was killed in the conning tower.

One of *Nürnberg* survivors, Stoker Räsch, wrote the following about the sinking:

> The I Offizier stood to the last by the railing near the starboard N°4 gun without his jacket and already ankle deep in water. From there he led three cheers for the Kaiser. Around *Nürnberg* all is now quiet and peaceful whilst those already stiff from cold in the water drifted about.
>
> Our ship suffered greatly from the English shells. The foremast is shot away at the height of the searchlights, the funnels were holed like a sieve, especially the fore most, the command bridge and chart house, just as the whole forecastle are in flames. There was only half the flag left on the cutter davit.[24]

Towards 19.27hrs *Nürnberg* capsized and sank. As the ship rolled over four men were seen on the upturned hull defiantly waving the battle flag. *Kent* sent two cutters to save who they could, but in the end only seven men were rescued.

The battle with *Nürnberg* was not entirely one-sided and *Kent* was hit a total of thirty-seven times by 10.5cm shells. The top-gallant mast was shot away and there were many hits on the hull and boat deck. The three funnels were riddled like a sieve. The most damaging hit was on the starboard 6-inch gun casemate A3. The exploding shell rent a large hole in the hull side and flash flames passed to the ammunition hoist, igniting a charge which was hooked onto the hoist. Flames

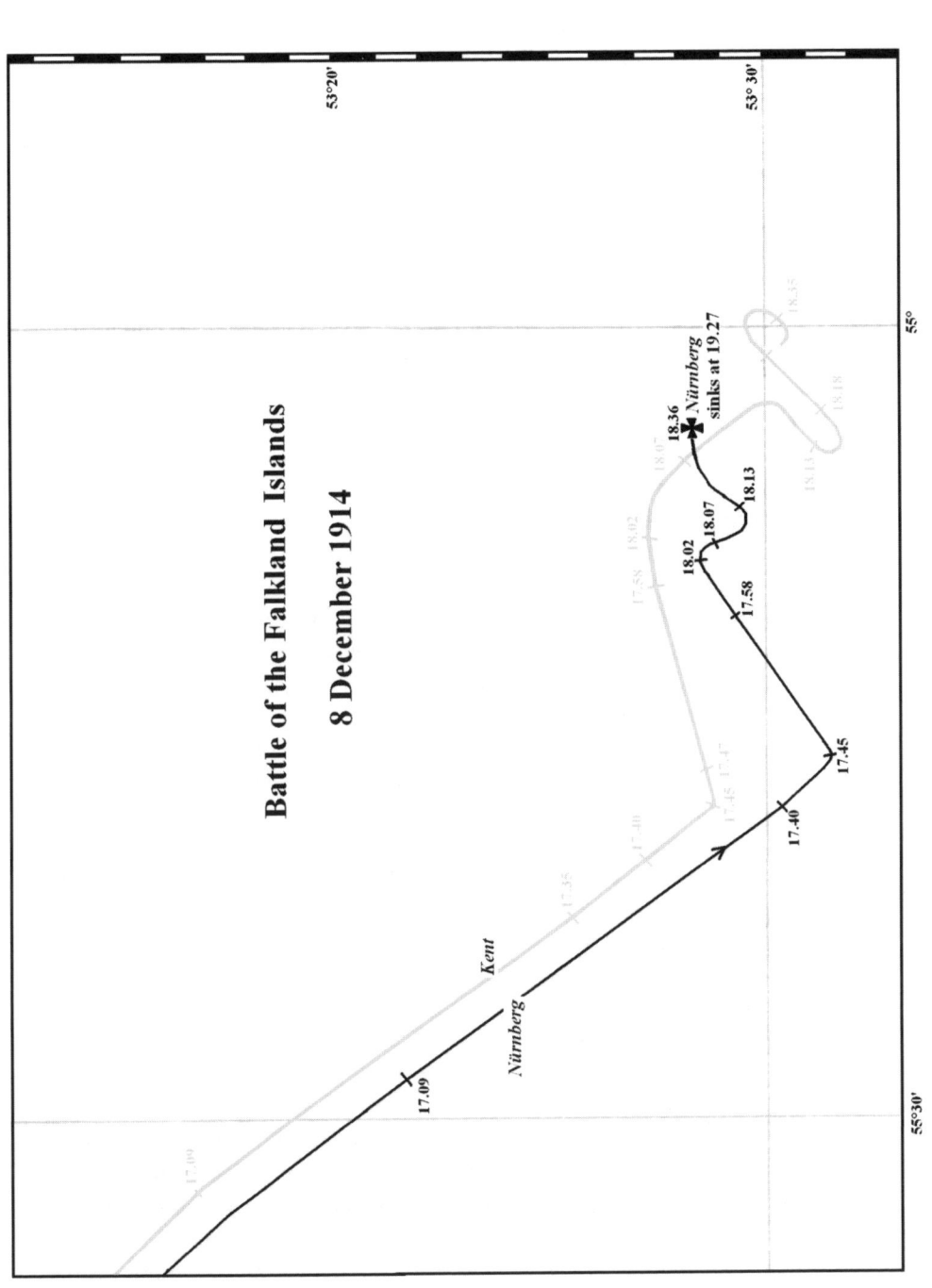

threatened to engulf the magazine, which would have doubtlessly caused the loss of the ship, but a marine closed the hoist scuttle and had the compartment flooded, in addition to extinguishing the flames. A further hit wrecked the wireless office putting the wireless transmitter out of action. Another shell holed the hull immediately below the aft shelter deck. *Kent*'s casualties amounted to sixteen men. Four died immediately, and two died later from injuries, and ten were wounded. Most of the dead died from burns suffered with the casemate hit.

At about 11.45hrs the cruiser *Bristol* departed Port Stanley harbour with orders to destroy Graf von Spee's fleet train. At 12.30hrs she was joined by the auxiliary *Macedonia* and they continued on a SE course. By about 15.30hrs they had *Baden* and *Santa Isabel* in sight and fired a warning shot to stop them. The German crews abandoned ship and were taken aboard *Macedonia*, whilst *Bristol* put twelve shots into *Santa Isabel*. *Macedonia* sank *Baden*, and then finished off *Santa Isabel* after *Bristol* made off around 19.00hrs. The auxiliary *Seydlitz* escaped, but during the night sighted a British cruiser abeam just 4 nautical miles away. She turned away to the south and made off. On 24 January 1915 *Seydlitz* was interned in Argentina.

The surviving warship from the Falklands Battle, SMS *Dresden*, made off to the southwest during the night of 8 December, and the following day rounded Cape Horn in a westerly direction. From there she went to Punta Arenas, arriving on 12 December, and took on 750 tonnes of coal from a German ship. The following day she departed and remained amongst the islands of South America until 14 February 1915 when she departed into the South Pacific. Although the Admiralstab wanted *Dresden* to return home, her commander determined that the coal situation was too uncertain to allow this and he headed his ship towards Mas a Tierra. On 27 February 1915 he captured the British merchant ship *Conway Castle* south of this island.

On 8 March *Dresden* sighted the armoured cruiser *Kent*, but escaped in the darkness. The following day the German cruiser anchored in Cumberland Bay at Mas a Tierra with just 80 tonnes of coal remaining. Time was running out for *Dresden* and on 14 March the British cruisers *Glasgow* and *Kent* and the auxiliary *Orama* arrived off Cumberland Bay. At around 08.50hrs *Glasgow* opened fire on the German cruiser even though she was anchored in neutral waters. It was not the first time such an illegal action had been undertaken as on 26 August 1914 the cruiser *Highflyer* had opened fire on the German auxiliary *Kaiser Wilhelm der Große* in Spanish territorial waters at Rio de Oro. The German ship was sunk after a battle lasting 1½ hours. Neither was this the last incident, as the minelayer *Albatroß* was shelled by Russian cruisers after she was put aground in Swedish territorial waters on 2 July 1915. Whilst it can be understood that military necessity was the overriding concern, these actions make the political protests of the Entente over similar incidents, such as the destruction of submarine *E13* in August 1915, both hypocritical and absurd.

The British cruisers rapidly approached *Dresden* and *Kent* joined in the firing, so that within a few minutes the four aft cannon and fire direction equipment of the German ship had been destroyed. *Dresden* quickly hoisted a white flag of truce to prevent further bloodshed and dispatched a steam pinnacle with a negotiator to *Glasgow*. Whilst these actions were underway *Dresden* was scuttled at 11.15hrs and sank to the depths. *Dresden* suffered a total of eight dead, fifteen badly wounded and fourteen lightly wounded. Most of the crew escaped ashore and were interned by the Chilean authorities.

The German East Asiatic Squadron had been destroyed. Graf von Spee had made his first mistake in deciding to attack the Falkland Islands. His second mistake was not to attack the British forces whilst they were still bottled up in Port Stanley. He could have quickly sunk *Kent* in the channel, perhaps blocking it, and expended the remainder of his ammunition on the British battlecruisers whilst they were confined in the harbour. However, the policy of flight is the age-old and tested first option for the cruiser commander. His final error was holding the small cruisers with him perhaps too long, although in the case of *Nürnberg* and *Leipzig* it made little difference as their speeds were scarcely faster than the *Panzerkreuzer*.

During the battle the tactics of Vice Admiral Sturdee and Captain Ellerton were in line with current Admiralty thinking. When superior in strength and speed the enemy was to be held at long range until he was reduced to a condition in which he could be closed and finished off without taking any risks at all. These tactics could only be adopted where time and space were not a consideration. Nevertheless they nearly resulted in the battlecruisers running out of ammunition. *Invincible* and *Inflexible* each carried 640 12-inch shells and 24 practice shells, and of these *Invincible* fired 513 and *Inflexible* fired 661. More importantly *Invincible*'s A turret only had six practice shots remaining in those magazines. On the other hand, before the battle *Scharnhorst* had just 360 21cm shells, and *Gneisenau* had 538 21cm shells remaining. The German *Panzerkreuzer* also proved exceedingly difficult to sink. Compared to this *Kent* closed to close range with *Nürnberg* almost immediately and this cruiser was defeated in a reasonably quick time. Granted this led to *Kent* sustaining a great number of hits, but only the hit on the casemate proved dangerous.

Graf von Spee was one of the best admirals of the First World War. He carried out his duty loyally, resolutely and skilfully until the end. His two sons also perished in his final battle.

Chapter 5

The Battle on the Dogger Bank, 24 January 1915

As the year 1914 came to a close it was becoming apparent to the German Naval Command that the British were not going to implement a close blockade of their coast, but were employing a more distant blockade. It also became apparent that the pre-war strategy of guerrilla warfare, whittling down the British forces by use of mine and torpedo, was not going to be effective. Therefore the Admiralstab determined on a more proactive policy of instituting raids on English coastal towns. There were many good reasons for undertaking this course of action. Firstly, it was hoped that raiding the coast would cause a reaction by part of the British Grand Fleet, who once lured out by the raid by German cruisers would be met and destroyed piecemeal by the German main body of the fleet, waiting in support at a distance behind the cruisers. Secondly there was the morale aspect on the British people who, it was hoped, would become disillusioned when the Grand Fleet was incapable of protecting them from bombardment. Thirdly, and most importantly, the coastal raids would serve as a cover and disguise the laying of mine barriers close off the coast, which was one of the aims of guerrilla warfare. The minelaying cruisers would have the protection of the battlecruisers of the I Reconnaissance Group, or I AG. The cruisers would be supported by the High Sea Fleet lying some distance behind.

The first coastal bombardment took place at Great Yarmouth on the morning of 3 November 1914. Although the results of the bombardment were meagre, the other objectives of a morale result and the laying of a mine barrier were successful. The next bombardment occurred on 16 December against Scarborough, Whitby and Hartlepool. This time the plan worked flawlessly. There was damage to the coastal towns, although this was secondary, and public opinion was incensed. The small cruiser *Kolberg* also successfully laid a mine barrier close to shore. Finally the isolated 2nd Battle Squadron and the 1st Battlecruiser Squadron were far out in the North Sea, unsupported. The British squadrons were between the coastal raiding I AG and the High Sea Fleet and it seemed that they could be engaged and destroyed. However, the German Fleet Chief, Admiral von Ingenohl, convinced himself he had been discovered and that he faced superior enemy forces, and inexplicably he reversed course prematurely and headed back to the German Bight. This left Kontreadmiral Hipper and the I AG exposed and they were lucky to evade the British forces. Admiral von Tirpitz said: 'On December 16th Ingenohl had the fate of Germany in the palm of his hand. I boil with inward emotion whenever I think of it.'[1] However, Admiral von Ingenohl had failed to take advantage of an opportunity presented to him on a plate. What is certain is that a perfect opportunity to achieve the aims of *Kleinkrieg*, or guerrilla warfare, in reducing the enemy forces piecemeal had been shamefully missed. At a conference about the operation on 22 December Kontreadmiral Hipper said there was much anger.[2]

On 27 December a further conference was convened and the main topic was another advance against the British coast, this time to lay mines off the Firth of Forth. The date set for this advance was 16 or 17 January, just after the new moon. However, on 5 January the fleet leadership announced that first a smaller operation to lay mines off the Humber River exits would be conducted around 11 or 12 January. Then on 7 January the Kaiser issued new instructions for the guidance of the High Sea Fleet. The new order ran in part:

> The High Sea Chief receives authorization to undertake at his own discretion frequent advances into the North Sea for operations with the goal of cutting off and attacking advanced enemy forces with a superior force. It should thereby be avoided if possible, to meet superior enemy forces and an unfavourably running sea battle…Intended large scale advances to the enemy coast should be previous reported to His Majesty the Kaiser.[3]

The fleet leadership was being given a freer hand in planning and conducting operations. However, on 9 January a period of wicked weather began, which lasted for several weeks.

Nevertheless, despite the restrictions of employment of the fleet being relaxed a little there was some concern about the coming large scale operation. Kontreadmiral Hipper was against the operation, and he wrote: 'The Fleet Chief called me today and heard in great detail my reasons, which I argued against the operation. The Chief of Staff has also become a bit more cautious. The expected success is just not in proportion to the effort.'[4] Meanwhile news arrived that the British were planning to blockade the river mouths and therefore the battleships and cruisers would be held back, and now only two small cruisers, *Straßburg* and *Stralsund*, would conduct the operation off the Humber. This barrier was duly laid on 15 January, despite continuing poor weather.

On 19 January a further conference about the operation against the Firth of Forth, or Operation 21, was conducted aboard the fleet flagship, *Friedrich der Große*. At around 13.00hrs the British 1st Battlecruiser Squadron was reported

100 nautical miles northwest of Helgoland and the German forces came to a state of increased readiness. Vice Admiral Beatty's squadron was supporting a reconnaissance sweep by the Harwich Force of light cruisers, and had withdrawn by the evening. A counter-sweep by German torpedoboats proved fruitless and found no trace of the British. Some thought it was the British blockade attempt but Kontreadmiral Hipper did not believe it so.

On 20 January the poor weather continued and the dispatch of the small cruisers for the beginning of Operation 21 was postponed. The wind was from the SW at strength 7 and this also precluded airship reconnaissance. 21 January brought even poorer weather so that Operation 21 was again postponed, whilst the wind came from the east at strength 6. On 22 January at a conference aboard the fleet flagship Operation 21 was postponed until at least 6 or 7 February and the next period of the new moon, a move welcomed by Kontreadmiral Hipper. Now the *Panzerkreuzer von der Tann* was sent for scheduled overhaul work, which would continue for 12 days, and the III Battle Squadron was detached to the Baltic for training. The Fleet Chief embarked aboard SMS *Deutschland*, allowing *Friedrich der Große* to also go to the Baltic. Nevertheless, the Admiralstab was pushing for more advances into the North Sea, a move which Kontreadmiral Hipper was strongly against.

The following day, 23 January, brought quieter weather and the Chief of Staff, Vizeadmiral Eckermann, did not want to let this opportunity pass without doing something, to make up for the time lost due to bad weather. Therefore he made the following proposal to the Fleet Chief:

> If tomorrow the weather is as today during the afternoon and evening, it would be desirable for the cruisers and *Flottilles* to make an advance to the Dogger Bank, in my opinion. Special preparations are not required, it is enough to give an order to the commander of Reconnaissance Forces early in the morning. Night out, morning there, evening back.[5]

At first Admiral Ingenohl was opposed to this proposal and wanted such an operation only if the fleet could go in support, but he nevertheless gave his consent. In addition to pressure from the Admiralstab to mount more operations, he gave the following reasons:

> The operation to the Dogger Bank was planned a long time ago. Up until now its implementation has been prevented by special circumstances. The aim was a torpedoboat advance with cruiser support, clear away the fishing vessels that are in the service of the enemy, and in a favourable case surprise the enemy light picket forces, just as the last advance to the east coast arrived at. For the first time in a while the weather is favourable and allows the partaking of torpedoboats. The English Fleet had briefly before shown itself

in the German Bight on January 19. It could therefore be taken that with their return the light forces will be coaling in harbour. Their dislocation seems likely according to the following intelligence: The battlecruisers are in Scapa Flow to prevent a breakout by German cruisers for merchant warfare, the heavy forces partly in Firth of Forth, partly in the Thames. Therefore a short advance by our quickest cruisers to the Dogger Bank without doubt seemed practicable. A short advance under these conditions did not seem to require the support of the main body, which was perhaps even dangerous because of the premature report to the enemy. A larger operation to bring part of the enemy fleet to battle was excluded, because the III Squadron had been sent to the Baltic.[6]

With that the die was cast and the following operational order was sent to Kontreadmiral Hipper on Schillig Roads, *by wireless* at about 10.25hrs on the morning of 23 January: 'I and II AG, I Leader of Torpedoboats (I FdT) and two *Flottilles* at discretion of BdA reconnoitre the Dogger Bank. Run out today in the evening during darkness; return following evening in the dark.'

Kontreadmiral Hipper still had reservations about this operation and he conveyed them to Admiral Ingenohl in a personal consultation. He gained the concession that he would arrange his advance so that with dawn his forces would be approaching the south-eastern edge of the Dogger Bank. This probably saved him from being cut off, as events turned out.

During the course of the afternoon of 23 January the following forces assembled on Schillig Roads: the I Reconnaissance Group, with *Seydlitz, Moltke, Derfflinger* and *Blücher*, and the II Reconnaissance Group with *Graudenz, Stralsund, Rostock* (the flagship of I Leader of Torpedoboats), and *Kolberg*. They were accompanied by the V Torpedoboote Flottille with nine boats, and the 15 and 18 Torpedoboote Half Flottilles, with together ten boats. At 17.45hrs the cruisers and torpedoboats put out to sea from Schillig Roads. It is often said that *Blücher* should not have accompanied the I AG, because she was slower and therefore a liability, but this was not the case. *Blücher* achieved 25.8 knots on trials and during the return from the bombardment of Yarmouth on 3 November 1914 *Blücher* had outstripped and passed *von der Tann*, who could not develop her maximum speed owing to poor quality coal. Therefore *Blücher* was easily able to maintain the highest unit speed.

Unknown to Kontreadmiral Hipper, or any other German commanders, the British were able to decipher their wireless signals and the orders wirelessed to Kontreadmiral Hipper at 10.25hrs on 23 January were in the hands of the British Admiralty approximately 1½ hours later.

At the beginning of the war in August 1914 the Detached Admiral of the Baltic, Kontreadmiral Behring, had undertaken a number of reconnaissance advances and on the night of 26 August he lost the small cruiser *Magdeburg*.[7]

When *Magdeburg* ran aground in thick fog and was unable to get clear, her commander ordered the forward magazine to be blown up, therefore scuttling the ship. Unfortunately this was done prematurely and there was tremendous confusion aboard the ship. Amongst this confusion the secret books and charts were not disposed of correctly and when the Russians arrived they were able to take possession of much secret information, including two examples of the signal book of the Imperial Navy. One copy, N°151, was supplied to the British and to this day remains in the National Archives at Kew. In October the British obtained a copy of the merchant ship code book and in November a copy of the code book used for communicating with attachés and warships overseas was recovered from a sunken torpedoboat. Armed with these three books the Director of Naval Intelligence set up 'Room 40', a department to intercept and decrypt German naval signals. A network of wireless direction finding stations was also set up to determine from where German wireless signals originated. By November Room 40 was reading everyday German wireless signals and passing them on to the Admiralty. They were helped by the German preference for sending even the most routine orders by wireless. This British ability to read German signals, combined with lax German wireless discipline, was to cost countless German sailors their lives, and cost the loss of many ships and U-boats. At least one German senior officer was suspicious, however, and on 19 February 1915 Großadmiral Prinz Heinrich wrote:

> The very searching legal inquiry into this matter has shown that at least certain naval charts in use…were lost; it must be assumed with virtual certainty that these charts were recovered by the Russians who came to the scene immediately afterwards. It is probable that the 'S.K.M.' key similarly fell into the hands of the Russians; finally the possibility must be envisaged that the Russians recovered one of the signal books from the clear and none too deep waters with divers. The War Diary was probably captured by the Russians…

Later, on 24 November 1915, the Großadmiral wrote to the Chief of the Admiralstab, saying that it had been observed that:

> with the beginning of German wireless traffic the Russian stations all grow silent. It could be assumed that the Russians are deciphering our wireless messages–perhaps with help from the books of SMS *Magdeburg* or one of the U-boats lost in the North Sea. It is not out of the question, and these aids would be helpful.[8]

With information about the composition and time of departure of Kontreadmiral Hipper's forces, the British were able to set a trap for them.

However, instead of the passing the information along to the fleet commanders to act on, those at the Admiralty instead gave Vice Admiral Beatty a position which he should reach at dawn on 24 January, and therefore the Germans were not cut off. Scarcely had the German cruisers quit the Jade when, at 19.00hrs, the British 1st Battlecruiser Squadron and newly-formed 2nd Battlecruiser Squadron, together with the 1st Light Cruiser Squadron, weighed anchor and put to sea from the Firth of Forth. At 21.30hrs the 3rd Battle Squadron put to sea to support Vice Admiral Beatty's battlecruisers to the north. The Harwich Force, of three light cruisers and numerous destroyers, would approach the British rendezvous on the Dogger Bank from the south. Finally the entire Grand Fleet under Admiral Jellicoe put to sea on the evening of 23 January to act as support. It was to be the first clash of dreadnought-type warships.

The British battlecruisers were commanded by Vice Admiral Beatty. He was born in Cheshire on 17 January 1871 and joined the Royal Navy in January 1884. After passing out he served in the Mediterranean and after service on various ships took part in the Khartoum campaign in 1898, where he commanded a gunboat. He saw further action in China during the Boxer Rebellion and was twice wounded. He was promoted Captain at age twenty-nine. Further shipboard appointments followed and in 1910 he was promoted Rear Admiral just short of his thirty-ninth birthday. A period on half pay followed and just when it looked like he would retire he was appointed secretary to the First Lord. In March 1913 he was appointed commander of the 1st Battlecruiser Squadron, a post he still held at the beginning of the war. Beatty was known to be intelligent and energetic, and was an aggressive leader.

His opponent at Dogger Bank was Kontreadmiral Hipper. He was born on 13 September 1863 in Weilheim, Bavaria. Like most German *Offiziers* he joined the Imperial Navy at the age of eighteen, in 1881. After passing out Hipper served aboard SMS *Leipzig* (the older vessel) during a two year world cruise, and then in the Mediterranean. He undertook courses in gunnery and torpedo training and served aboard SMS *Wörth* under Prinz Heinrich. He served aboard other battleships, and then commanded torpedoboats and cruisers, including *Leipzig* and *Gneisenau*. He was promoted Kontreadmiral on 27 January 1912 and in October 1913 was appointed Commander of Reconnaissance Forces (BdA). Kontreadmiral Hipper was known as energetic and hard working, and was liked by his subordinates. 'He was an active and quick man, who because of his cordial friendliness and personal modesty was much loved and admired by everyone.'[9] He was known to dislike paperwork and was happy to leave this task to his staff. For most of the war the BdA had responsibility for not only the I and II AG, but also the torpedoboats and minesweepers of the North Sea, and consequently was overworked with staff-work at a time when he should have been concentrating more on just the operations of his cruisers.

The night to 24 January 1915 was clear and overcast, with the quarter-moon setting at about 01.00hrs. There was a light easterly wind that freshened during the night. The German *Panzerkreuzers* ran at 13 knots. *Seydlitz*, commanded by Kapitän zur See Egidy, was leading the line, followed by *Moltke*, Kapitän zur See Levetzow, *Derfflinger*, Kapitän zur See von Reuter, and *Blücher*, Fregattenkapitän Erdmann. As vanguard 3 nautical miles ahead to starboard was *Graudenz*, commanded by Fregattenkapitän Püllen and serving as flagship of the leader of the II AG, Kontreadmiral Hebbinghaus, and to port *Stralsund*, Kapitän zur See Harder. The flank cover was formed to starboard by *Rostock*, serving as flagship of the I FdT, Kapitän zur See Hartog, and commanded by Fregattenkapitän Thilo von Trotha, and to port by *Kolberg*, under Kapitän zur See Widenmann. A Half-*Flottille* of torpedoboats accompanied each small cruiser. Early in the morning some enemy wireless traffic was observed and the lights of some trawlers were observed, which were given way to.

With the first rays of sunlight the wind freshened to strength 5 from the ENE. At around 08.00hrs the British 1st Light Cruiser Squadron under Commodore Goodenough, with the light cruisers *Southampton*, *Birmingham*, *Nottingham* and *Lowestoft*, reached the ordered rendezvous. About 5 nautical miles to the west of them steered the 1st and 2nd Battlecruiser Squadrons, the latter under the command of Rear Admiral Moore. These consisted of *Lion*, *Tiger*, *Princess Royal*, *New Zealand* and *Indomitable*, travelling in line ahead. To the south of them stood the Harwich Force under Commodore Tyrwhitt, comprising the light cruiser *Arethusa* with six destroyers, *Aurora* with fifteen destroyers of the 1st Flotilla, and *Undaunted* with thirteen destroyers of the 3rd Flotilla. The night had passed quietly for the British forces and just as Vice Admiral Beatty gave orders for the 1st LCS to reconnoitre to the NE by E gun flashes appeared in the SE.

At around 08.10hrs the cruiser *Aurora* sighted a three-funnelled cruiser and four destroyers, which her commander believed to be *Arethusa*. He turned towards the newcomer and signalled 'f u' by searchlight, the British recognition signal. A salvo of 10.5cm shells was the reply. The cruiser *Kolberg* on the western flank of the German line had also sighted *Aurora* about 08.10hrs and at 08.15hrs opened fire in a running battle to port.

> As the alarm was given the free watch were at breakfast, the stokers were still in the stokers' bathroom. On the guns the order had been given 'make guns clear for the day'. This exchange disrupted quick preparations, and above all the magazines were not fully manned. The transport of munitions only occurred as the ready ammunition was all fired.[10]

In the morning gloom range finding was difficult but nevertheless three hits on *Aurora* were observed at a range of 50hm. Then *Kolberg* turned away to

1. The funnel of the small cruiser *Stettin*, damaged by shellfire on 28 August 1914. Behind is her sistership *Stuttgart*.

2. The entrance hole of a shell hit on *Frauenlob* 28 August 1914, near the midships 10.5cm cannon.

3. Shell hit on *Frauenlob* that damaged the pinnace and destroyed the galley.

4. Crewmembers of *Frauenlob* inspect damage to the aft funnel in Wilhelmshaven. To the left is the small cruiser *Rostock*, which did not participate in the battle on 28 August 1914.

5. Sailors aboard a British light cruiser look on as *Mainz* burns just before sinking. The centre and aft funnel have been shot away, along with the main mast.

6. Another view of the German small cruiser *Mainz* shortly before sinking, seen from *Southampton*. *Mainz* is down by the bows, and smoke issues from amidships.

7. *Scharnhorst* in Manila, Philippines, in February 1914.

8. The small cruiser *Nürnberg* photographed from a British warship before the war.

9. *Scharnhorst* and *Gneisenau* on Valparaiso Roads on Tuesday 3 November 1914. The men over the side of *Scharnhorst* are repairing a light shell hit in the bow suffered during the Battle of Coronel.

10. The Russian battleship *Evstafi* moored to a buoy.

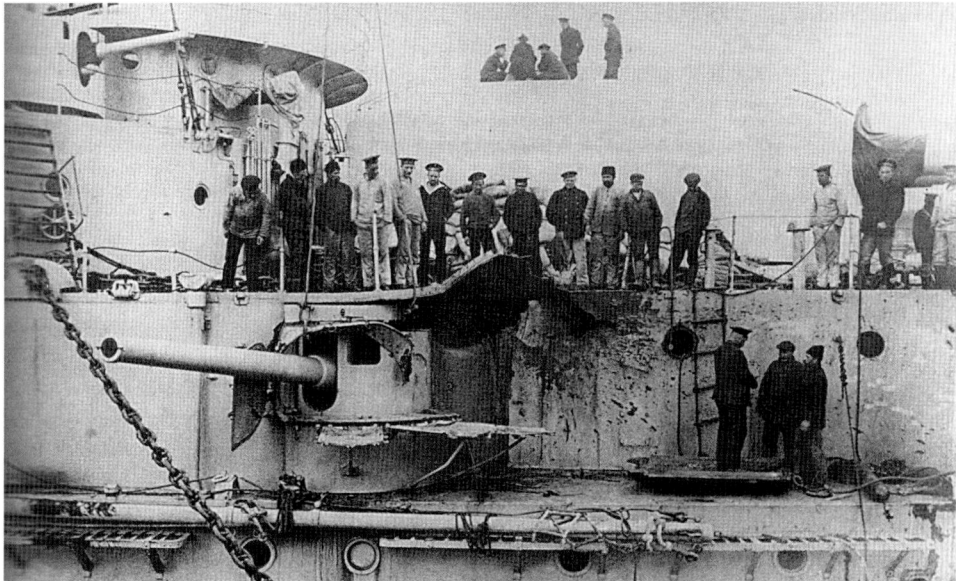

11. *Evstafi* showing damage caused by *Goeben* on 18 November 1914. This hit killed or wounded the serving crew of the 6-inch casemate gun.

12. The Russian battleships *Evstafi*, *Ioann Zlatoust* and *Rostislav* under fire from the German *Panzerkreuzer Goeben*. The photograph shows well the German ladder method of ranging salvos, with each projectile ranged 200 metres further apart.

13. The Russian shell hit on *Goeben*'s forecastle, 08.00hrs, 10 May 1915.

14. The German East Asiatic Squadron rounding Cape Horn in rough weather.

15. *Blücher*, with a tripod foremast, enters the III Entrance lock of Wilhelmshaven.

16. *Blücher* capsizes to port at 13.13hrs, 24 January 1915, taking with her 792 *Offiziers* and men as victims. Many shell holes and much damage can be seen on her hull and superstructure.

17. A pre-war view of the *Panzerkreuzer Seydlitz*, on Schillig Roads. *Seydlitz* was the flagship of the German Reconnaissance Forces for most of the war.

18. *Derfflinger* in a floating dock, almost cetainly after the Dogger Bank battle. Several shells impacted near to *Derfflinger* and caused some slight deformation to the propeller blades, as can be seen.

19. Pictured ahead of *Moltke* is *Seydlitz*, on the occasion of the visit by the Kaiser in Wilhelmshaven after the Dogger Bank Battle. The cannon have been removed from burnt out turrets C and D and the men of the crew are drawn up on the quay. *Seydlitz* flies the flag of Kontreadmiral Hipper.

20. A personal photograph taken aboard the *Panzerkreuzer Moltke* during her return from the Dogger Bank Battle, 24 January 1915. Collected on deck for later recycling are the brass powder cartridge cases for the 28cm heavy cannon. *Moltke* remained unhit during the battle.

21. The mine-layer cruiser *Albatroß* pictured in the Kaiser Wilhelm Canal.

22. *Albatroß* showing numerous shell hits in the hull and funnels on 2 July 1915. The faces of the 8.8cm gun shields have been painted red for the operation as a recognition device. The Swedish local population have come to the assistance of the cruiser in small boats to convey away the wounded.

23. The Russian armoured cruiser *Bayan* showing where she was struck amidships by a 21cm shell from *Roon* on 2 July 1915 at the battle off Östergarn.

24. The German armoured cruiser *Prinz Adalbert* enters Kiel Bay on 4 July 1915 after being torpedoed on 2 July by the British submarine *E1* and travelling 295 nautical miles with 2,000 tonnes of water in the ship.

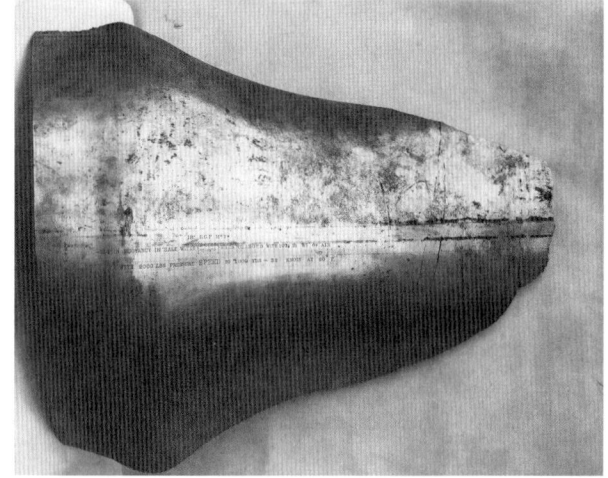

25. The commander of *Prinz Adalbert*, Kapitän zur See Michelsen, mentioned a 'still warm visiting card' from the British submarine, a fragment of the torpedo with English written specifications stamped on it.

26. The Russian cruiser *Zhemchug* was more heavily armed than *Emden*, but was caught by surprise and torpedoed twice.

27. The small cruiser *Emden* running trials in the Baltic in 1909. It is easy to see why she was later nicknamed 'the swan of the East'.

28. An aerial view of *Königsberg* at her final resting place in the Rufiji River, German East Africa. *Königsberg* was scuttled after sustaining heavy damage from British monitors on 11 July 1915.

29. *Lützow* pictured in the Baltic on 19 May 1916 during her final training exercise before the Skagerrak Battle.

30. *Lützow* running the measured mile on 19 May 1916. One of the *Offiziers* aboard reported that she achieved 27.9 knots on this day.

31. The *Panzerkreuzer Derfflinger* anchored on Schillig Roadstead. The aft funnel has been painted red for an impending operation, as has that of the small cruiser on the left, possibly *Hamburg* or *München*.

32. *Derfflinger* returns to Wilhelmshaven after the Skagerrak Battle. Many hits are visible and the anti-torpedo nets hang down in several places. At one stage during the battle *Derfflinger* had to stop completely whilst the nets were resecured, having threatened to foul the propellers.

33. *Seydlitz* returning from the Skagerrak Battle, looking aft along the port side. It can be seen that here *Seydlitz* is travelling stern ahead, due to being badly down by the bows.

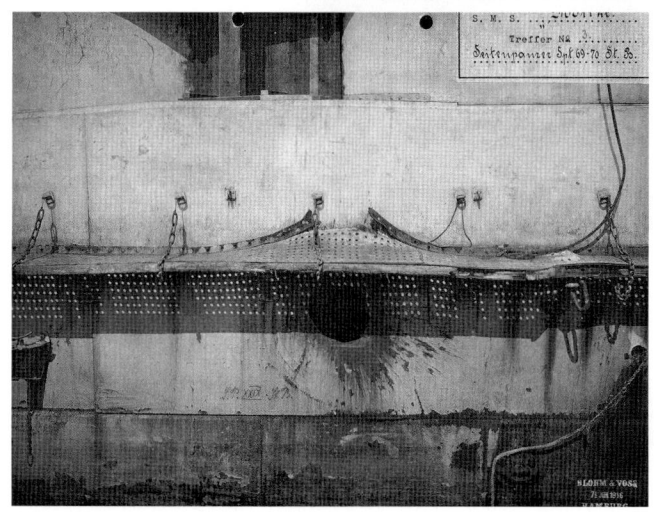

34. The hit on *Moltke* by a 15-inch shell at 17.17hrs beneath the V 15cm casemate penetrated the armour and detonated in the upper coal bunker, killing all 12 of the casemate gun crew and 4 stokers in the bunker.

35. A 15-inch shell hit to the aft conning tower of *von der Tann* completely destroyed surrounding light structures and killed several men inside the tower.

36. During the battle off Helgoland on 17 November 1917 the small cruiser *Königsberg* (II) was struck by a 15-inch projectile from *Repulse* which penetrated all three funnels and detonated in a bunker, setting fire to coal. Here she steams with smoke streaming from the bunker fire.

37. *Königsberg* pictured at 11.20hrs with smoke pouring from a bunker fire. *Königsberg* was the flagship of Kontreadmiral von Reuter, commander of the II Reconnaissance Group.

38. An aerial view of the small cruiser *Nürnberg*, sistership of *Königsberg*, which fought in the battle of 17 November 1917.

39. The small cruiser *Frankfurt* at anchor on Schillig Roads.

40. A photograph taken of *Frankfurt* during the height of the battle on 17 November 1917. Taken just after 10.00hrs it shows the impact of a heavy 15-inch shell close by the cruiser, whilst to the right the cruiser *Nürnberg* is also visible. *Frankfurt* is travelling at full speed.

41. A close-up view of the damage to the N°1 15cm cannon of *Pillau* caused by a 15-inch shell on 17 November 1917.

42. The small cruiser *Breslau* undergoing trials.

43. *Goeben* aground on Nagara Point, where she remained stuck for six days.

starboard to join the *Panzerkreuzers*, but kept up a lively fire until a range of 76hm was reached. *Aurora* only opened fire 3 minutes after the German cruiser. The result was two hits, a 6-inch and a 4-inch shell, on *Kolberg*. The two shells struck the hull side together between the N°2 and N°3 port cannon. They exploded in the crew's closet and splinters killed two of the N°3 gun crew. Other crew were tossed about by the gas pressure. Light structures were damaged and splinters penetrated the upper deck and forward funnel. Almost at the same time a 4-inch shell landed short in the water before the port N°2 gun, which had no protective shield. A 10.5cm cartridge was struck by a splinter and was immediately thrown overboard. A further short 4-inch shell damaged two blades of the port propeller. The Germans noted that the British fire was slow and deliberate, and that judging from fragments found aboard the ship the destroyers had also partaken in the battle. Fire was ceased about 08.25hrs.

On first contact *Kolberg* had reported 'Individual enemy force in 028 delta.' With this report, and with the first flashes of gunfire, Kontreadmiral Hipper went to full speed and turned *en-echelon* towards *Kolberg*. Then *Kolberg* reported further smoke clouds to the WSW and *Stralsund* the same to the NNW, and finally reported she that had recognized eight ships. Kontreadmiral Hipper followed the old cruiser rule and turned away from the enemy at 08.35hrs to obtain a clear overall picture before taking further action, however he had to reduce speed for some time to allow the small cruisers and torpedoboats to catch up and take station:

> With the naked eye only an indeterminable throng stood to port aft. However, with the glasses seven light cruisers and a great number of destroyers could clearly be made out. Their number increased with each new count. All involved in this count were of a cheerful disposition: *Offiziers* and bridge personnel. Finally the commander laughed and came to a decision on what I should encipher and send to *Seydlitz*: '9.19 morning. *Blücher* to *Seydlitz*: To BdA: in sight aft 7 enemy light cruisers and now 26 destroyers. Further smoke clouds behind. *Blücher*.'[11]

It was beginning to dawn on Kontreadmiral Hipper that he was facing a far superior enemy. He wrote:

> With so numerous forces nearby there was the likelihood that part of the English fleet was near, especially as from the wireless traffic the call signs were the same as those observed on 16 December, and therefore the II Battle Squadron must be close by. It was therefore communicated to the fleet the intension to seek the German Bight at high speed and only later seek contact with the enemy.[12]

As the German battlecruisers were only steaming at 18 to 20 knots to allow the small cruisers and torpedoboats to gain the head of the line, a small group of British destroyers were able to approach to port aft. At 09.00hrs the German units gradually increased speed to 23 knots and at 09.25hrs *Blücher* received permission to open fire on the destroyers on her own initiative. A few 21cm gun salvos at a range of 90 to 100hm were enough to make them turn off, however. Whilst *Blücher* was firing *Derfflinger*, the next ahead, manoeuvred out of line and requested permission to shoot. '*Derfflinger* puts herself out to the side of the line. Permission to fire reserved. Signal ZO[13], whereby we again sheer into the line.'[14] At this time five giant smoke columns came into sight to starboard aft, in the WNW. Soon the massive outlines of five British battlecruisers were discernable looming over the horizon, and from observed wireless traffic it was almost certain a squadron of enemy battleships was also in the vicinity. Kontreadmiral Hipper determined to maintain his present course for the coming battle. Although it was not favourable to fire downwind this was the quickest direct route to the German Bight, where he could expect support from German battleships, torpedoboats and U-boats.

With the increasing visibility at dawn, *Aurora* and *Undaunted*, which had made no attempt to join the battle, sighted more German light forces to the ESE and then German battlecruisers to the east. On the first report from *Aurora* Vice Admiral Beatty ordered the 1st Light Cruiser Squadron to reconnoitre to the south-by-east whilst the battlecruisers maintained their course until 08.35hrs, then after receiving further reports he turned SSE and increased to full speed. Now a long stern chase developed. By the Admiralty giving Vice Admiral Beatty a latitude and longitude to be at with dawn, and by Kontreadmiral Hipper showing caution by not arriving any further north until daylight, the Germans had not been cut off from their base, which could easily have been arranged. Instead, at 08.50hrs *Lion* sighted four large smoke columns 14 nautical miles away, on a day that gave unusually good visibility for the North Sea. At this time Admiral Jellicoe and the Grand Fleet were 150 nautical miles to the NNW and upon the battlecruisers' contact report he pushed to the south at 19 knots, at the same time dispatching the 2nd Light Cruiser Squadron at high speed to reinforce the 3rd Battle Squadron on the Dogger Bank, whilst the latter pushed ahead towards Helgoland.

The British battlecruisers quickly began to gain on the German ships, with Vice Admiral Beatty calling for higher and higher speeds, so that soon the last ship of the squadrons, *Indomitable*, began to fall behind. The battlecruisers were travelling so swiftly that the destroyers were unable to take station ahead of them, and after being taken under fire by *Blücher* and falling back, the fastest destroyers of the M-class fell back on *Arethusa* and the slower destroyers. The British battlecruisers had advanced so far that at 09.52hrs *Lion* fired her first shot at 200hm. At about 09.54hrs Vice Admiral Beatty allowed

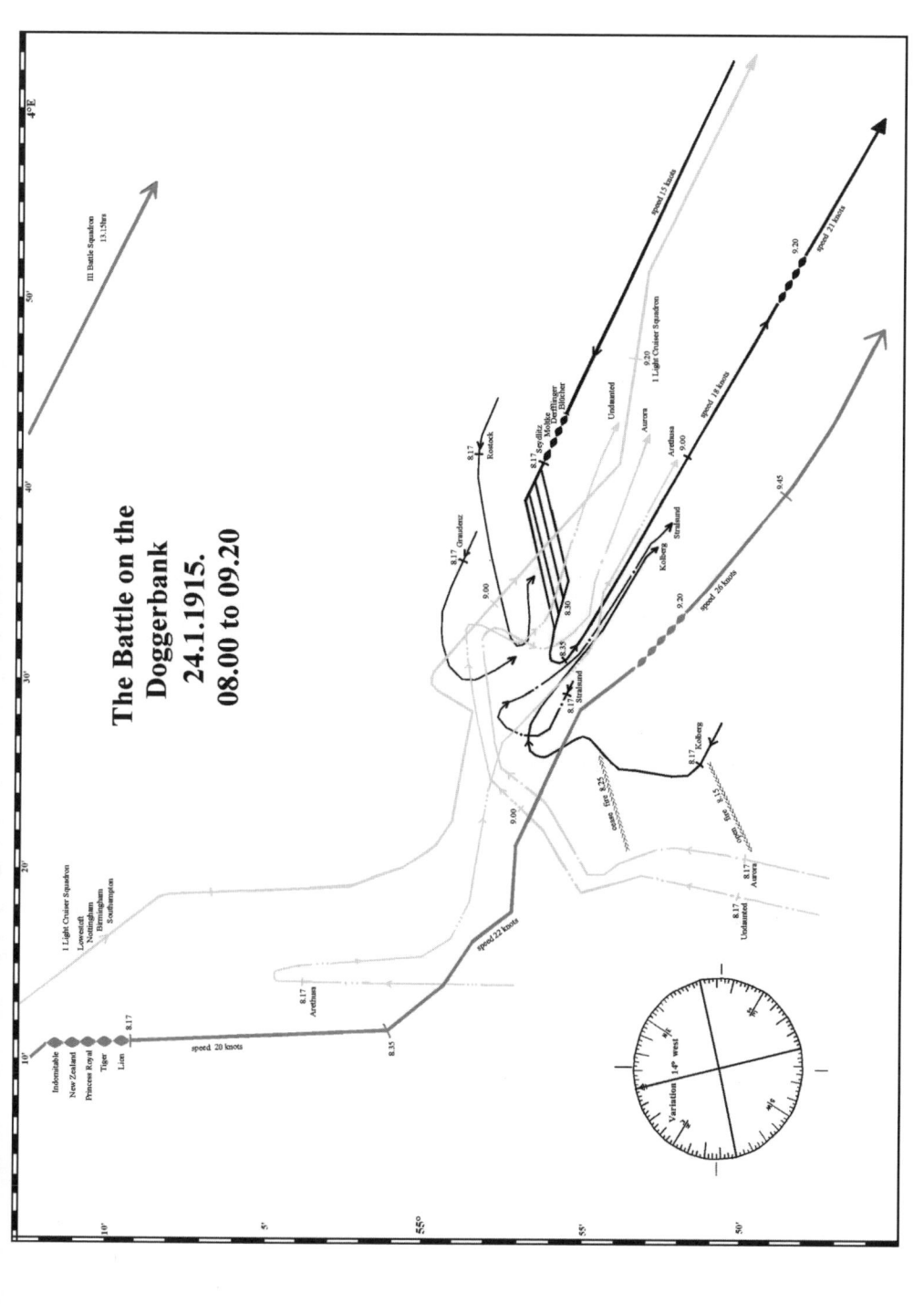

his ships to steer to port *en-echelon*, so that they could bring their broadsides to bear. At about 10.00hrs *Tiger* also began to fire deliberate shots as *Lion* gave the signal for a general 'open fire'. Now *Princess Royal* joined in, likewise firing on *Blücher*. From the German ships, which were arranged in line of bearing south on a SE course, nothing much could be seen of the British ships because of the dense funnel smoke being blown downwind from the German battlecruisers and light forces. All that could be seen of the enemy was the flash of their artillery and the high impact splashes 1,000 to 1,500 metres astern in the German's wake:

> There is a further dull, heavy detonation, and at the same time in the smoke of our ship approximately four points to aft and at a distance of 1,000 to 1,500 metres there is a heavy fall of shot in the water. For a moment a gigantic column of water stands up steeply in the air and then collapses on itself. We are being fired upon by an invisible opponent with guns of the heaviest calibre!
> 'To battle stations please, *Mein Herren*!'
> Laughing the Commandant says this and tips the peak of his cap with his finger, and then we others go forward to the conning tower and close the heavy armoured door behind us.[15]

Just as the British fire fell short, the Germans were unable to make reply, for at that time *Derfflinger*'s 30.5cm guns were ranged to 189hm, *Seydlitz* and *Moltke*'s 28cm guns could reach 181hm and surprisingly *Blücher*'s 21cm cannon were ranged to 191hm. In Germany it was considered that in the North Sea the upper limit of visibility would be 190hm, and that these conditions would be exceptional. The arrival of 13.5-inch shells from the British ships was clearly invalidating that conceptual theory. Nevertheless the British shells soon began impacting over, and at 10.10hrs *Seydlitz* hoisted the signal to open fire, with the addition 'Fire distribution from the left'. This last signal meant that the German ships would target their opposite numbers, ship against ship. For the moment only *Derfflinger* could open fire at 10.11hrs, but nevertheless on the first ship from the left, for the time being.

One minute later, at 10.12hrs, *Blücher* received her first hit on the forecastle between the anchor capstans, but little damage was done. However, after hitting *Blücher Lion* changed target at 10.14hrs to *Moltke*, whilst *Tiger* and *Princess Royal* continued against *Blücher*. At the same time Vice Admiral Beatty turned away slightly to allow his ships to bring their broadsides to bear. Soon *Blücher* could make reply:

> It is 10.18hrs as the salvo bell sounds. We stoop below the vision slits and rrrums! go the howling shells towards the enemy. Now finally I can see with

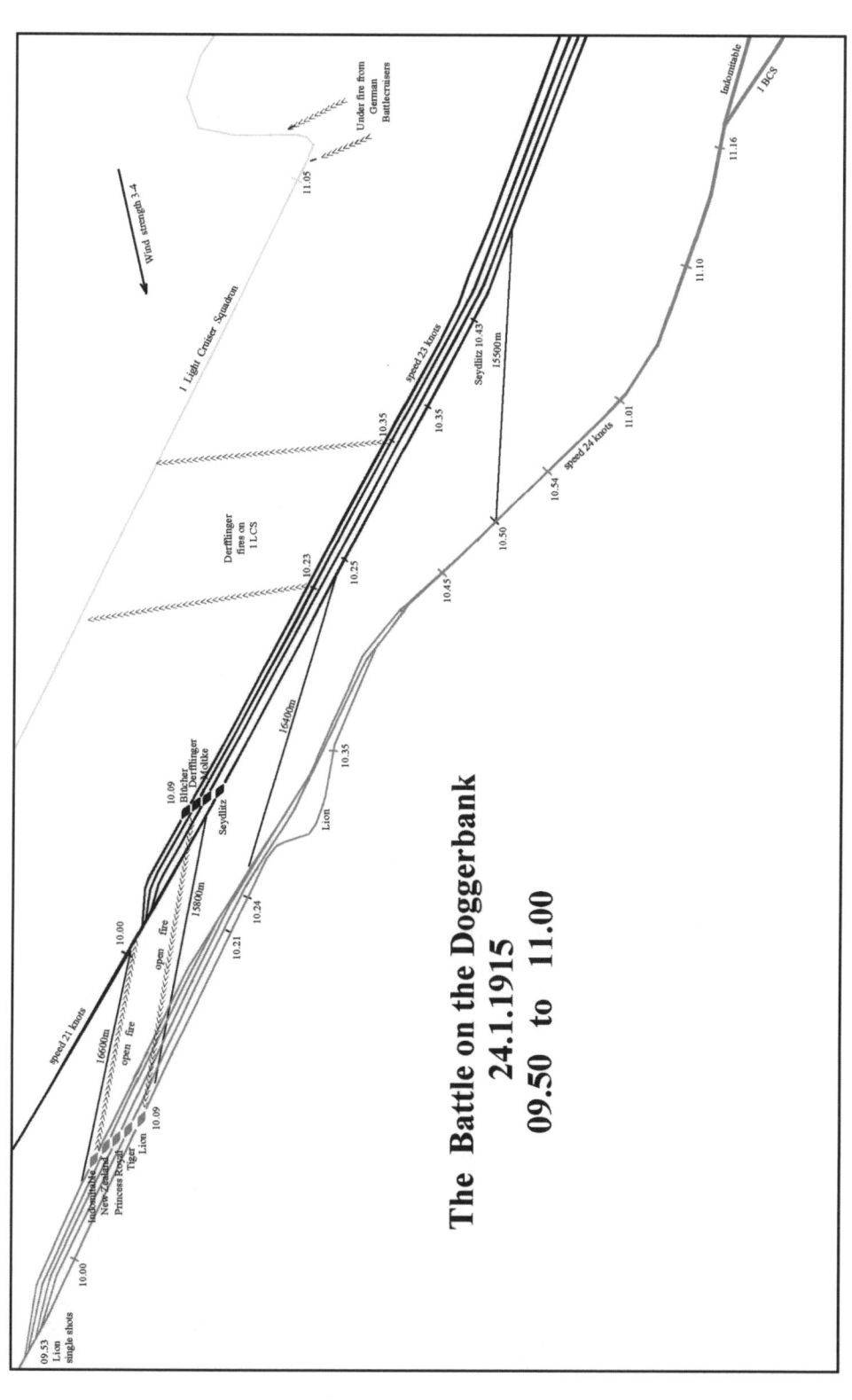

the glasses through a gap in the smoke veil two points to starboard aft. Unclear and indistinctively on the horizon are the silhouettes of five enemy ships. One can clearly see the muzzle flashes from their line. The fall of shot indicator sounds, but I cannot observe our fall of shot, all disappeared in the swirling smoke.[16]

Then *Seydlitz* joined in at 10.19hrs and *Moltke* at 10.20hrs. Because of the smoke conditions *Derfflinger* and *Seydlitz* took *Lion* under fire, whilst *Moltke* fired on *Tiger* from the beginning. At this time the range was 170hm and during the course of the battle it sank to 145hm, but when his ships began to be hit Vice Admiral Beatty increased range to an average of about 165hm. Therefore it became known to the Germans that although their opponents possessed superior speed they were unwilling to close for a fight to the finish. This was British tactical doctrine of the time. The Germans also noted that their opponents made frequent vigorous course changes, to throw off the German aim, but this also had the effect of making it difficult for their own fire. At around 10.35hrs *Derfflinger* changed target to *Tiger* and then briefly to *Princess Royal*, but in the main targets were chosen as visibility dictated. About 10.21hrs *Lion* received her first hit, below the waterline, which caused a compartment to flood. At 10.35hrs *Lion* appeared to temporarily sheer out of line. At 10.38hrs *Tiger* received a hit on the roof of Q turret, which put it out of action. In return *Seydlitz* received a hit in the forecastle about 10.25hrs. Also around 10.35hrs Vice Admiral Beatty ordered a change in fire distribution: 'Engage corresponding ship in line'. However, *Indomitable* had not yet caught up, but Captain Pelly of *Tiger* thought that she was present and would engage the fourth German ship, leaving the two ships at the head of the British line, himself and *Lion*, to fire on the leading German ship, whereas in fact he should have been firing against *Moltke*, the second in line. With *New Zealand* firing on *Blücher* and *Princess Royal* firing on *Derfflinger*, nobody was firing on *Moltke* who was left undisturbed firing salvo after salvo at *Lion*. According to *Southampton*, *Tiger* continually shot over her target.

Now the battle increased in intensity. At 10.28hrs shells impacting short shook *Derfflinger* and then at 10.43hrs further shells landing short, this time to starboard aft, again shook the ship. The propeller shaft in the outer shaft tunnel was bent slightly and rivets sprung in the ships side, so that the ship made water for a brief time. At the same moment *Seydlitz* received a hit with fateful consequences. A shell coming from 130° aft penetrated the quarter-deck and detonated against the 230mm thick barbette armour of D turret. Whilst the shell itself was kept out of the barbette, fragments and red-hot armour were broken off and entered the working chamber. There they set fire to main and fore charges on the loading rails. Flash flame shot upwards and downwards through the hoists and ignited charges on the turret turntable and in the handling room. Only those cartridges with their lids on did not ignite. With the first penetration of gases from burning cartridges the serving crew of the working chamber attempted to rescue themselves by quitting their room and passing into the corresponding room of turret C. To do this they had to pass through two doors, the first opened rearwards and the second forwards. When the aft door was opened the powder in the hoist room ignited and the flash passed forwards. Apparently the second door was carried away as if by gas pressure. Flash and flames penetrated into the working chamber of C turret, igniting charges there and passing up to the guns. In a few seconds 6,000kgs of powder had burnt and both turrets were ablaze. The aft of the ship was enveloped in flame and everyone believed that in a few seconds the detonation of shells would blow up the ship. Therefore the I Artillerie Offizier, Korvettenkapitän Foerster, who was directing fire from the aft conning tower and was therefore close to the devastation, ordered the guns into rapid fire to harm the enemy as much as possible before his ship blew up. Salvo after salvo left the guns, once every ten seconds.

A total of 165 men perished in the turret, working chambers and handling rooms of Dora and Caesar turrets, 161 immediately and the remainder on the following afternoon and the next day. The medical report read:

> One part of the turret crews were burned by the flash flame; for the greater part the corpses were in the position in which death had surprised them. Individual corpses were completely burned. Another part of the turret crew had succumbed to gas inhalation. Five were wounded with burns–three from turret C and two from turret D–and could be saved. One of them, a sailor, had 1st and 2nd degree burns to his entire body and succumbed to his injuries on the same afternoon on board.

All the compartments aft of the turret group were filled with poison gases and smoke, so that the rudder rooms had to be abandoned for the time being. On the bridge they expected the ship to blow up beneath them at any moment. The situation was critical and as news reached the Central Position, beneath the conning tower, the I Offizier, Korvettenkapitän Hagedorn, Obermaschistenmaat and 2nd Pumpenmeister Wilhelm Heidkamp, Feuerwerker Müller and the damage control group made their way aft to compartment III. The flooding valve of the magazines for the aft turrets was there and they pushed aft despite toxic gas and intolerable heat. The incredible heat singed the uniform, eyebrows, hair and hands of Pumpenmeister Heidkamp as he groped his way towards the flooding valves, the position of which he knew by heart. When he located the first valve it was glowing red hot, but selflessly he grasped and opened the valve, and had begun to open the second valve before he collapsed and had to be relieved by Feuerwerker Müller. The seawater quickly flooded in through the flooding valves, into the threatened magazine chambers. Then the turbo-fans of boiler rooms I and II degassed the room. Stabsarzt (Physician) Fischer and Marinepfarrer (Minister) Fenger assisted the two burned men. Heidkamp was the most badly hurt.

A catastrophe had been averted and the magazines flooded, but this caused the draught aft to increase to 10.5 metres, and together with the stern being sucked lower because of the high speed and the effect of being in shallow water, there was the danger that any further hits aft would cause more flooding.

About this time *Lion* also had a close call when a piece of shell wound up in a 4-inch magazine but failed to cause damage, the shell having failed to detonate. Then a 21cm shell from *Blücher* hit the roof of A turret and put the left gun out of action. About 10.54hrs Vice Admiral Beatty reduced speed for a time to allow the others to catch up as *Lion* and *Tiger* had pulled ahead. At 11.01hrs *Seydlitz* achieved hits number 5 and 6 on *Lion*. They penetrated below the waterline and caused flooding and salting of the boilers so that the starboard engine eventually had to be stopped. Both shells drove in the armoured plates and detonated inside the ship.

Vice Admiral Beatty now opened the range and the German ships were lost to view in the dense smoke. There was a battle pause, which Kontreadmiral Hipper utilized to take the 1st Light Cruiser Squadron under fire. At 11.04hrs the German battlecruisers opened fire on Commodore Goodenough's cruisers, which abruptly turned away to the north before resuming their old course at 11.16hrs, long after the Germans had ceased fire. Meanwhile Vice Admiral Beatty had increased speed to 26 knots and turned towards the Germans again. Scarcely had the Germans opened fire on them again when at 11.18hrs another two shells hit *Lion* together. One penetrated the 6-inch side armour and burst inboard, whilst the other struck the junction of the 6- and 9-inch armour and detonated inside, causing much damage.

At 11.30hrs *Blücher* received a fateful hit from *Princess Royal*. A 13.5-inch shell struck the ship amidships and penetrated down through the decks and unluckily found the munitions transport system for the forward wing turrets. Because of the boiler and engine arrangements of *Blücher* there was insufficient space for magazines below the forward wing turrets, B and F. They were served from the aft wing turret magazines by a transport system which consisted of two rubber conveyer belts, one for shells and one for cartridges, which ran for a good deal of the ships citadel. Each forward wing turret was supplied via an elevator from this so-called 'ammunition transport rail'. The shell penetrated the deck between the two forward turrets and ignited thirty-five to forty 21cm cartridges on the transport rails. Flash flames penetrated the two forward side turrets through the elevators and these were immediately engulfed in a sea of flames, just as on *Seydlitz*. Poisonous gases penetrated through the speaking tubes and ventilation shafts into the middle gangway, the central command position, the conning tower and numerous other compartments of the ship. All fire control apparatus, command elements and the rudder control shaft fell out with the blow. In addition a shell splinter penetrated the main steam pipe in the third boiler room, so that the steam pressure for the engines fell and reduced the maximum speed to 17 knots. Fähnrich zur See Paulssen described the scene below:

> A journey through the ship showed the devastation that was already directed in the interior of the ship. Boiler room III made much water, and had to be abandoned. In the middle gangway two men lay whimpering in a great pool of blood. One had both his legs severed off, the other had his back broken. They were taken to the dressing station by stretcher, cushioned by hammocks. The dressing station was packed with laid out badly wounded men. The Assistant Arzt [Physician] calmly dealt with these poor men, cutting and bandaging, working energetically to reduce the pain and agony. I proceeded further through the *Zwischendeck*. Boiler Room V had fallen out. It represented a horrifying picture: there were corpses, severed limbs, shell splinters and boiler parts lying amongst one another.[17]

Blücher was suffering badly, and now she was doomed by her fatal speed reduction.

Blücher needed to report the situation to the flagship but Wireless Offizier Leutnant zur See Gebeschus struggled with the signal:

> Immediately send to *Seydlitz* 'engines receive no steam.' The signal book does not give a group for this text. To avoid wasting time I will not send the signal word for word. After a brief consideration, the same could be said with a cipher group of three letters, and I allowed Pollin to give the signal: 'All engines unmanoeuvrable!'[18] At this moment, as the last letter is given, a wild vibration shakes us to the bones. Obviously a direct hit on the conning tower! 'Conning tower – *parole*?'
>
> 'Here all clear. Artillery direction has fallen out. Give to *Seydlitz*: *Blücher* can run at only 17 knots'.[19]

During this time the range had gradually increased so that by 11.30hrs only *Derfflinger* could fire at 190hm, and at 195hm seemingly the British line ceased fire. Therefore at 11.35hrs Vice Admiral Beatty allowed a turn of one point to port, then at 11.45hrs another point top port, and then at 11.47hrs he ordered his battlecruisers to close on the enemy and bring all guns to bear. However, scarcely had the range reduced than *Seydlitz* and *Moltke* unleashed a devastating fire on *Lion*. Between 11.35hrs and 11.50hrs no fewer than seven shell hits struck the British flagship. A 28cm shell wrecked the bakery, and another hit the 9-inch armour amidships but did not penetrate. The forward funnel was struck, and then the second funnel was hit twice. The forecastle deck was hit and then at 11.52hrs a 30.5cm shell from *Derfflinger* hit the lower 9-inch belt armour and pushed the plate 60cm inboard. The deck plates were ripped and the port feed tank was opened to the sea. The port engine room took on water and the port engine had to be stopped. The ship listed 10° to port and speed reduced to 15 knots. The last remaining dynamo shorted out and the ship was without power. *Lion* was out of action and as she sheered away out of line a shell struck the starboard side below the waterline. *Lion* had been hit by shell a total of seventeen times. The remaining British battlecruisers followed *Tiger* at irregular intervals.

Kontreadmiral Hipper now resolved to bring all assistance to the stricken *Blücher*. In his report he wrote:

> For some time *Blücher* had been falling behind, whilst the enemy was also being damaged (*Moltke* observed a hit on *Tiger* at 11.52hrs) so I determined to cover *Blücher* by energetically damaging the enemy and to go nearer him and put in a torpedoboat attack. At 11.58hrs the line that had been travelling SE by S, turned onto a new course. At 12.00hrs the signal was given for the torpedoboats to attack and at the same time the wireless signal 'Pennant Z'[20] and corresponding flag signal, a red pennant. The seldom-used wireless signal caused the FdT to question whether the torpedoboats should attack. At the same time the 'Z' pennant removed all doubt.[21]

At the same moment as the torpedoboats began to turn to the attack, the British battlecruisers turned away to port whilst the German line had turned south, and therefore there was the prospect of a circular battle. The reason for the turn was that Beatty had seen an imaginary U-boat, but because there was no power on his flagship he had to use signal flags to order the turn. This course also took him towards *Blücher*. This was not Beatty's intension and he wished to order Rear Admiral Moore to continue the fight with Kontreadmiral Hipper's main body. He therefore ordered 'Attack the rear of the enemy', but his Signal Officer, Lieutenant Seymour, hoisted the signal together with the previous signal, therefore the message read: 'Attack the rear of the enemy, course NE'. Rear Admiral Moore was unaware of the imagined U-boat and thought the turn to port was to engage *Blücher* more closely, and when the signal was read his conviction was reinforced and he took the remaining four battlecruisers towards the crippled *Blücher*. This was neither the first nor the last time Lieutenant Seymour had bungled his job, and at best he must be considered negligent; at worst, he should be seen as incompetent.

The British manocuvre had unwittingly thwarted the German torpedoboat attack and at 12.07hrs the torpedoboats were recalled. Kontreadmiral Hipper's instinctive reaction was to hurry to the assistance of *Blücher* and seek a circular battle, and to this end he ordered a S-by-W course. Then it was reported to him that turrets C and D had fallen out, that the aft ship was full of water and that only 200 shots remained for the other guns. Kontreadmiral Hipper wrote that the support of *Blücher* no longer came into the question as he was not supported by his main body, and a continuation of the battle would incur further heavy losses. He wrote:

> The support of SMS *Blücher* would involve the I AG in a circular battle between the English battlecruisers and the battleship unit that they had brought, supposedly behind them: as our own head gradually swung onto a northerly course it would be in an unfavourable position with regard to the enemy destroyers. In a running battle on a northern course it has to be considered that it had the same disadvantages with regard to the destroyers, who gathered in the north and went against *Blücher*. With the great distance to our coast any engine damage to other cruisers would mean their destruction without bringing help to *Blücher*. The battle of the battlecruisers takes place at high speed, but sometimes a ship is damaged, or in need of support, but this does not prevent the enemy, with a superiority in light cruisers and destroyers, from bringing that ship to action.
>
> The idea of helping *Blücher* with a Half-*Flottille* was also weighed. This was nevertheless rejected as perhaps from time to time the torpedoboats could force the enemy to turn away from *Blücher*, but the enemy light cruisers and destroyers could quickly finish her off, without the torpedoboats being able to help.[22]

At the beginning of the battle *Stralsund* had reported further smoke clouds in the NNW, but although the British 3rd Battle Squadron was approaching, according to British charts it was outside German visual range. Nevertheless Kontreadmiral Hipper suspected the presence of further British forces, in addition to those he had already encountered, and with due consideration he decided not to renew the battle after the British had broken off the action. At 12.12hrs Kontreadmiral Hipper turned away from the enemy with a heavy heart and resumed a south-westerly course.

Meanwhile *Blücher* was maintaining a stout resistance. Already shortly after 12.00hrs she forced the approaching 1st Light Cruiser Squadron to turn away to the north. Then four destroyers of the M-Class manoeuvred for a torpedo attack and at 12.20hrs *Meteor* was close enough to launch a torpedo. At that moment a 21cm shell from one of *Blücher*'s two remaining turrets struck the destroyer in the forward boiler room and caused a fuel oil fire which put her out of action. The other three destroyers launched torpedoes from a greater range, whilst *Arethusa* approached the near stationary German ship to within 23hm and fired two torpedoes. One hit under the forward turret, the other at the level of the engine rooms. Then the battlecruisers redirected their artillery fire on the hapless *Blücher*:

> The detonations of heavy shells had enormous force. You hear the howling arrival, smashing sound and then explosion. When standing one ducked involuntarily, and grasped one part or another of his body with his hands. Yet the Z-station was still completely untouched. A bright light in the room showed that the dynamos still worked. This is of great significance for us, as our turrets are electrically driven and still fire with undiminished speed. It was clear from the clang of light calibre shots between those of heavy calibre, that the light cruisers had already joined in, and their destroyers must be nearby...Then the howling, swirling sound arrives, then the clank, and heavy vibration that intermittently shakes the ship when it is hit...Sometimes the detonations are so powerful that I assume a torpedo hit. Many times I thought the ship had burst apart. The conning tower swings visibly here and there, yet continues to tower unperturbed above the smoking bent iron ruins that were formerly the bridge...In the main dressing station a direct hit caused horrible devastation. After the electric light failed only fires and explosions in the dark compartments showed the way through shell holes to the upper deck.[23]

Blücher fired several torpedoes, but none found a target. One after another the turrets grew silent, then the steering failed and the manual rudder position was manned, but the ship could only travel in a circle. The commander, Fregattenkapitän Erdmann, and I Offizier, Korvettenkapitän Roß, lay wounded in front of the conning tower:

> It was now 12.45 in the afternoon. Irresolutely I stood in the port direction position. Then a salvo struck the rubble of the bridge. A thunderous crash sounded outside in our vicinity. The entire conning tower shook. Biting, poisonous smoke, and also dirt and splinters flew through the vision slits and the hole in the tower hood, and the last part of the rangefinder position was torn off...Again the flying splinters wounded many and killed another one or two. The air pressure threw me in the corner...All that could be heard was the crash of exploding enemy shells and the whistle of splinters, together with the constant rush of blowing off steam and the crackle of flames and fires in the bridge rubble and on the middle deck. We lay into the wind and the fire and smoke went directly aft. There was nothing to see but smoke, flames, steam and between that burning rubble.
>
> I was only deeply remorseful over the fate of our ship and the misery around me, which I faced so powerlessly. We did what we could for the

wounded under the circumstances: the wounds were provisionally bound, and they were laid out clear of the debris, so they would not be dragged under when the ship capsized.

The list of the ship became more pronounced. People everywhere already jumped overboard. I advised my men to wait until the last possible moment, since that would give us the best chance of being picked up by the enemy after the sinking. A longer swimming in the icy cold water would mean certain death.

The list of the ship increased further. Now it could only be a few minutes before we capsized.[24]

Now *Arethusa* and her destroyers moved closer to pick up survivors, and suddenly at 13.13hrs *Blücher* suddenly lay over to port and capsized. After lying keel up for a short time she vanished beneath the waves. With the help of the destroyers 260 men were saved, but 792 *Offiziers* and men perished.

Now another one of those unfortunate incidents occurred, which seemed to have happened regularly during the war. The German aircraft *83* appeared overhead and dropped its bombs on the destroyers performing rescue work. The aircraft was immediately taken under fire and was hit, but made it back to Borkum. As the German official history related, it was a deeply regretted incident.

After Vice Admiral Beatty's flagship *Lion* was knocked out of the battle he boarded the destroyer *Attack* to transfer his command to another ship. *Attack* raced off after the battlecruisers but by the time Beatty had boarded *Princess Royal* at 13.20hrs it was too late to renew the battle, despite Vice Admiral Beatty's desire to do so.

During the course of the battle the other German battlecruisers were hardly touched. Apart from the barbette hit on *Seydlitz* she was hit just twice more, once in the forecastle and once on the armoured belt. *Derfflinger* was hit once, on the belt, but suffered some slight damage from near misses, as related previously. *Moltke* remained unhit. On the other hand *Blücher* was hit by around seventy shells and allegedly seven torpedoes.

The British ships suffered too. *Lion* was hit seventeen times and was knocked out of the battle. By 16.30hrs her speed had been reduced to 8 knots and when her engines failed completely she was taken in tow by *Indomitable* back to Rosyth. Casualties were just one dead and twenty wounded. Repairs were completed on 28 March. *Tiger* was hit seven times; Q turret was put out of action as related, a hit below the conning tower severely damaged light structures and caused casualties in the conning tower itself. A hit amidships damaged light structures whilst there were three other hits on the armoured belt. A 21cm shell from *Blücher* went through the aft funnel, but *Tiger*'s casualties were just ten dead and eleven wounded and repairs were complete on

8 February.

The first clash of dreadnought capital ships was over. The Royal Navy had been victorious and the press revelled in it, and the huge amounts spent on the fleet before the war seemed justified. However, there had been many mistakes made on both sides, but it was the Germans who took more away from the battle. The main concern was the damage to *Seydlitz*'s aft turret group and the huge fire that resulted, almost causing the loss of the ship. The commander of *Seydlitz*, Kapitän zur See von Egidy, wrote:

> Afterwards, a thorough examination showed that everything had been done in accordance with regulations. I told the gunnery officer: 'If we lose 190 men and almost the whole ship in accordance with regulations then they are somehow wrong.' Therefore we made technical improvements and changed our methods of training as well as the regulations.

In *Seydlitz* it was found that only fore and main charges still in their protective tins had not burnt, even though in some cases the intense heat had melted some of the zinc on the tins. It was also found that there were too many powder charges in the working chambers and in the turrets. Therefore in future the numbers of charges was strictly regulated and the charges were left inside their protective tins until they were required. The cartridge hoists (elevators) were also to be fitted with automatically closing doors. In future the connecting passage between the turrets was to be kept locked. On the other hand the German procedure of communicating orders by wireless was not changed. For their part in the operational planning Admiral Ingenhol and Vizeadmiral Eckermann were replaced.

The British did not learn any technical lessons. They were more concerned with castigating Captain Pelly for his decision to take *Seydlitz* under fire, and reprimanding Rear Admiral Moore for his interpretation of Vice Admiral Beatty's confusing signals. Rear Admiral Moore was transferred to a command in the Atlantic and Captain Pelly would be better criticized for his ship's failure to make a single hit during the battle, even though she was the only British ship fitted with the new director firing system. What concerned Admirals Jellicoe and Beatty was the German rate of fire, which they reckoned was in a ratio of 5:2 in favour of the Germans. More gunnery practice was required for the battlecruisers, they said. To attempt to improve the rate of fire the British crews began stockpiling their cordite charges, which unlike the German charges were only housed in a silk bag and therefore were not fire resistant, anywhere they could find space between the magazine and turret, in an effort to speed up the rate of supply. It was the exact opposite of what the Germans had done, and in the next clash between the battlecruisers it would cost them dearly.

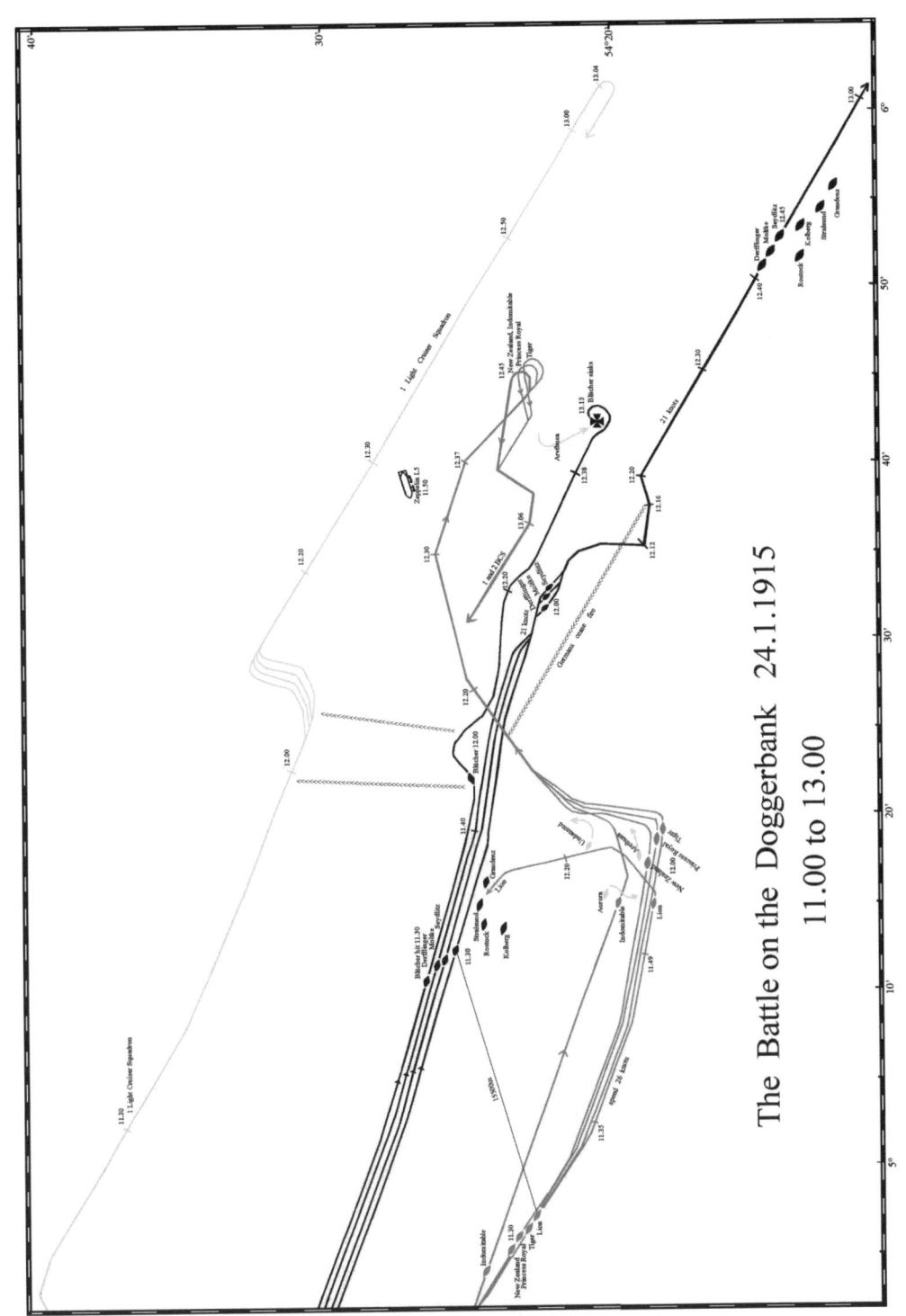

The Battle on the Doggerbank 24.1.1915
11.00 to 13.00

Chapter 6

The Sea Battle Off Östergarn, 2 July 1915

The German cruisers' war in the Baltic began with an unmitigated disaster that was to have a catastrophic effect on the war of the Imperial Navy for the remainder of the First World War. During a reconnaissance advance into the Finnish Gulf during the night of 25–26 August 1914 by the cruisers *Augsburg* and *Magdeburg*, a navigational error in fog by the commander of *Magdeburg* and a reluctance by him to alter course meant that *Magdeburg* ran aground on Odensholm Island at 00.37hrs on 26 August. The cruiser was hard aground just 300 metres from Odensholm lighthouse and could not be gotten free. The commander then compounded his mistake by failing to ensure the destruction of the secret code books and other material aboard the ship. Two *Signal Books of the Kaiserliche Marine* fell into Russian hands, and the Russians were gracious enough to forward one of the books, Number 151, on to their British allies. These books were the basis on which both the British and Russian code breaking services were based, and were directly responsible for the entrapment of many German ships and U-boats, and the loss of countless German sailors' lives.

Prior to the beginning of the war the art of naval intelligence had been greatly neglected by the Russian Imperial Navy. The General Staff of the Navy had virtually no intelligence agents and the only intelligence gathering organization was the Observation and Reporting Service, or S.N.I.S., which had stations along the coast and on many of the islands of the Baltic and was able to report enemy movements when such vessels passed within visual range. There was no such thing as a Wireless Intelligence Service in the Russian Navy before the war.

After the outbreak of war the Russians immediately began building a series of new wireless direction finding, or bearing finding, stations. These stations were able to measure the bearing of an incoming wireless transmission and by correlating three or more such bearings the location of the originator could be deduced. The head of the Intelligence Department aboard *Kretschet* was Captain 2nd Rank Rengarten.

The commander of the S.N.I.S. was Captain 1st Rank Nepenin and he and his staff had their headquarters in Reval. The S.N.I.S. and the Intelligence Department on *Kretschet* worked in parallel, but it was not until the capture of the secret material from aboard SMS *Magdeburg* in August 1914 that the work of these services became successful. When *Magdeburg* grounded within earshot of the S.N.I.S. station on Odensholm, Captain 1st Rank Nepenin was one of the first on the scene.

After the capture of the secret German code books the Russian Intelligence Service soon became able to read German wireless messages. Each intercepted German message was quickly deciphered and its contents were evaluated. Important signals were immediately reported to Captain 2nd Rank Rengarten or Captain 1st Rank Nepenin and could be in the hands of the Baltic Fleet commander almost as quickly as they were in those of the intended recipient. All information was collected on index cards, while the German ship movements were recorded on a large wall chart which was squared like the German sea charts or *Quadratkarte*. German movements were shown in red, Russian in blue.

Before each naval operation the admirals and commanders involved were usually briefed by Captain 1st Rank Nepenin or Captain 2nd Rank Rengarten, or a member of their staffs, about the situation with the Germans. Sometimes an intelligence officer was embarked aboard the flagship for the duration of the operation. One of the two senior officers would go to an advanced wireless station and pass on information gleaned from the German messages to the Russian sea forces. The system worked well and the fleet greatly appreciated 'Nepenin's Intelligence'. Given these circumstances it was inevitable that sooner or later a German advance would come to grief.

In June 1915 Captain 2nd Rank I. I. Rengarten and Leitenant A. A. Sakovich developed a plan to bombard a port on the German Baltic coast, partly in retaliation for the German bombardment of Windau on 28 June. Such bombardments were regarded by the Russian Naval Staff as 'strategic mischief', and rightly so, but nevertheless a reply was required. The plan was submitted to the newly appointed commander of the Baltic Fleet, Vice Admiral V. A. Kanin, who approved it. Originally the plan called for the bombardment of Kolberg, deep inside German territory, but then permission to use the newly-repaired powerful armoured cruiser *Rurik* was refused, and therefore an advance so deep into German waters was not to be considered. A meeting was convened on 30 June to discuss the final details for the bombardment. Vice Admiral Kanin was present, along with his Chief of Staff, Rear Admiral Kerber. Captain 2nd Rank Rengarten and Leitenant Sakovich presented the final details of their plan, however, Vice Admiral Kanin 'categorically refused to give *Rurik* for the operation',[1] and therefore the target for the bombardment was changed to Memel. Finally after 5 hours of discussion, at 2am the next morning, Captain 2nd Rank I. I. Rengarten lost his patience and gave a sharp retort to his commander. Thereon Vice Admiral Kanin replied: 'Well, well, when Ivan Ivanovich (Rengarten) becomes angry, then I shall give you *Rurik*.'[2] However the target of the operation was left as Memel and Leitenant Sakovich thought that this 'considerably lowered the integrity and importance of the operative plan'.[3] Vice Admiral Kanin was continuing the active operations of the rather weak Baltic Fleet begun under Admiral N.O. Essen. The new commander aspired to take advantage of the freedom granted to use the cruiser and minelaying forces granted to his predecessor by the Naval Staff and the command of the VI Army. The memoirs of the former Flag-Officer of Staff, Captain 1st Rank S.N. Timirev, said that a large demonstration in the German rear served to 'distract their attention and forces from the Riga Gulf, and this would give an opportunity to win time for defensive works at the entrance to the Riga Gulf.'[4] Rear Admiral Bakhirev, the Chief of the 1st Cruiser Brigade, was chosen to conduct the assignment. The bombardment of Memel would be conducted by the armoured cruiser *Rurik*, the cruisers *Oleg* and *Bogatyr*, the VI Torpedoboat Division and *Novik*. The following were assigned to support these attack forces: the battleships *Slava* and *Tsarevitch*, the cruisers *Bayan* and *Admiral Makarov*, the torpedoboats of the II Torpedoboat Division and some submarines.

Because the battleships lacked modern underwater protection they would remain in the rear. Despite this the 'attack on Memel' reflected the willingness to conduct a large-scale operation by the fleet in this theatre.

Rear Admiral Michael Koronatovich Bakhirev was better known to his colleagues as 'Crown'. Rear Admiral K.K. Pilkin wrote of him: 'He was a clever, simple and kind person. He was trusted, listened to the opinions of those older and more experienced in naval traditions, and was very popular in the fleet.'[5] Rear Admiral Bakhirev was born on 17 June 1868. He served with distinction during the Boxer Revolt and the Russo–Japanese War and was much decorated. He was considered as a fine professional, one of the bravest admirals of the Russian fleet. He began the First World War as commander of *Rurik*, the fleet flagship. In December 1914 he was promoted Rear Admiral and was given command of the 1st Cruiser Brigade.

The German 'Leader of Reconnaissance Forces in the Baltic'[6] in July 1915 was Kontreadmiral Albert Hopman. Under his guidance minefields had been laid to the north of Dagö Island in April and May 1915, in an attempt to impede the movements of the Russians with offensive minelaying operations. In June, after consultations with his staff, Kontreadmiral Hopman determined to step up the offensive minelaying program and to implement this he successfully applied for the transfer of two further minelayers to his command: the former railway ferry *Deutschland*, now converted to a minelayer, and the purpose built minelayer-cruiser *Albatroß*. Because the intended mine barriers lay so deep in Russian waters the minelayers would have to be escorted by cruisers, and Kontreadmiral Hopman's main concern was that his available ten torpedoboats were insufficient to screen his ships from Russian and English submarines. Yes, the English had transferred several submarines to the Baltic Sea and these were now giving the Germans cause for concern. From the beginning of May to the middle of June submarines fired approximately twenty torpedoes at the ships of the Reconnaissance Forces of the Baltic.

Seven minelaying operations were planned with the relatively faster, but lower mine capacity, *Albatroß* conducting the longer-range missions off the Finnish Gulf. On the evening of 20 June *Albatroß* carried out her first minelaying operation, numbered V, off the Finnish Gulf near the island of Bogskar. On this occasion the minelayer was escorted by the armoured cruisers *Prinz Adalbert, Roon* and *Prinz Heinrich* and departed from Neufahrwasser, and was also accompanied by the small cruisers *Augsburg* and *Lübeck* from Libau. By midnight on 22 June the armoured cruisers and *Albatroß* had returned to the Vistula River at Neufahrwasser. Because of the shortage of torpedoboats for an antisubmarine screen Kontreadmiral Hopman decided to cover the next two mining operations, VI and VII, each with half his ships. Operation VI would be covered by *Prinz Adalbert, Prinz Heinrich* and *Thetis*, and Operation VII by *Augsburg, Roon* and *Lübeck*, under the direction of the so-called 2nd Admiral, Kommodore and Kapitän zur See Johannes Karpf. Kontreadmiral Hopman though this was the only solution to provide his cruisers with an adequate screen against submarine attack. If Russian surface forces appeared, and this event was thought to be highly unlikely by the German High Command, then further German forces would be dispatched from harbour to join the battle.

On the morning of 25 June *Albatroß* took onboard 350 U-mines and that evening departed Neufahrwasser on a northerly course towards the Aland Islands to lay barrier VI. Ahead of her steamed *Prinz Adalbert* and *Prinz Heinrich*, whilst towards midday the following day *Thetis* took station about 4 nautical miles ahead of the main body and eight boats of the X Flottille formed an anti-submarine screen. By 23.00hrs on 26 June the mine barrier had been laid and the ships had returned safely to Neufahrwasser.

Two days later on 28 June the old coastal defence ship *Beowulf* bombarded the railway station at Windau. *Beowulf* fired thirteen 24cm shells but caused little damage. Meanwhile the small cruisers *Augsburg* and *Lübeck* skirmished with fifteen Russian destroyers off nearby Lyserort. At 1945hrs the Russian submarine *Okun* fired two torpedoes at *Augsburg* off Windau. The attack was from long range, some 1,500 to 2,000 metres, and the result was probably the best that could be achieved under the circumstances. Even if there were no material results the attack furthered the impression that the Germans could not venture far from harbour without encountering the submarine threat. The accompanying torpedoboats, *S149* and *S131*, took up the hunt for *Okun*, but their efforts were without success.

After a brief fire-fight the Russian destroyers withdrew into the Riga Gulf. It remains unknown if any hits were obtained on the Russians, while on *Lübeck* a 10cm shell shot through the flag and several splinters landed on deck. The fire of the Russian destroyers was highly respected and their salvos' spread was small. It appeared that several boats at a time were directing their fire together, apparently controlled with flag signals. The Germans were surprised at their good results.

After the conclusion of Operation VI, there remained only one mine barrier to be laid to complete the current mining program. On the evening of 29 June orders were issued to conduct this operation, which ran:

> With favourable conditions execute Operation VII on Thursday evening (July 1st). In case of drifting mines from mine barrier VI, lay the barrier at dusk. Advance to the west seems favourable in light of the latest submarine attack south of Bogskar. All arrangements should be via land telegraph or written.[7]

The last remark indicates that the Germans realized the need for secrecy and that frequent wireless transmissions compromised their plans, but they did not appreciate the extent to which the Russian Intelligence Service could read their wireless traffic, nor did they adhere strictly to maintaining wireless silence whilst at sea.

According to the prearranged plan Kommodore von Karpf would lead the operation. Therefore, on the evening of 30 June *Roon*, Fregattenkapitän Gygas, *Albatroß*, Fregattenkapitän West, and five torpedoboats quit the Vistula River in Danzig. The following morning *Augsburg*, *Lübeck* and two torpedoboats departed Libau. As the two groups approached the rendezvous to the northwest of Steinort they encountered fog which steadily thickened and prevented them contacting one another. The separate groups used searchlights and sirens, then detached torpedoboats and finally used their wirelesses but were still unable to locate one another. After being delayed for an hour the 2nd Admiral decided the groups should proceed independently and he ordered a rendezvous on the latitude of Faro. To complete the operation within its timetable framework the ships had to run at high speed, despite the dense, thick fog. Fortunately the new rendezvous was clear and at the determined hour the ships came in sight of one another.

After the order of march was arranged the unit took course on Gotska Sando to obtain a position fix. Towards 1800hrs that evening *Roon* and *Lübeck*, each escorted by a torpedoboat, swung away to the east; *Lübeck* was to guard the channel between the German minefields A and C, while *Roon* was to take position to the rear to support the small cruiser. *Augsburg* and *Albatroß* continued away to the north. The Germans were very conscious of the submarine threat and at one stage *Albatroß* believed she had a periscope in sight; in response she made the alarm and turned away. Actually she had sighted some drifting object. Likewise, later on *Lübeck* experienced a false alarm when one of the screening torpedoboats opened fire on the remnant of a drifting sea marker buoy.

The minelayer group continued towards Bogskar from the southwest and at 19.30hrs the island came in sight directly ahead. The flagship thereon steered away to the northwest and cruised between Svenska Bjorn light vessel and Bogskar, whilst Fregattenkapitän West laid 160 mines in two barriers to the northwest and northeast of Bogskar between 20.45hrs and 21.32hrs. During this time *Albatroß* repeatedly encountered drifting mines from barrier VI. After the last mine had fallen *Augsburg* and *Albatroß* began the return journey. Three hours later they met *Roon* and *Lübeck* at the appointed rendezvous, 35 nautical miles south of Bogskar. Then the 2nd Admiral made the following report by wireless: 'Operation VII completed without being sighted by the enemy. Position at 1am: Quadrant 020 epsilon, course 190°, speed 17 knots.' This message was to prove fateful.

The Russian plan was for the forces to put to sea in various groups from different bases, the Lum and Pipsher Roads and the Irben Straits, planned for 30 June or 1 July, and for the bombardment of Memel for 2 July. If the enemy was detected the plan for the group specified that if 'the situation appeared favourable...the cruisers should enter into battle'. Wireless-telegraphy arrangements for the operation were regulated by special instructions from Captain 2nd Rank I. I. Rengarten. From midnight on 1 July all wireless communication should be stopped. However, reception of wireless messages should be conducted cautiously. The operational plans were given to Rear Admiral Bakhirev on 30 June and the cruisers immediately began preparations to put to sea. Apart from the Chief of the Brigade, the purpose of the operation was only known to the authorized members of his flag staff, Starchi Leitenant Krykhanovsky and Leitenant Maksimov. Komflot directed that staff officers be sent aboard the ships from the beginning to the conclusion of the operation: Captain 2nd Rank Cherkasski arrived aboard Rear Admiral Bakhirev's *Admiral Makarov*, and the torpedoboat division from Moon Sound was joined by Leitenants Vinter and Sakovich. Rear Admiral Trukhachev went aboard the torpedoboat-destroyer *Kazanets* to give final instructions to the VI Division, which was under the command of Captain 1st Rank Patton. For the operation Captain 1st Rank Rengarten went to Kielkond on Ösel, where there was a wireless intelligence station.

With the consent of Komflot, Rear Admiral Bakhirev would take all five cruisers of the Cruiser Brigade to Memel, along with the VI Division and *Novik*. On the day before the force departed the submarines *Alligator*, *Krokodil* and *Kaiman* put to sea in the entrance to the Finnish Gulf. On the orders of Vice Admiral Kanin other submarines were directed to positions: *Makrel* to the west of Lyserort, *Okun* to Steinort, and the English submarine *E9*, which was covering Steinort, was ordered to transfer to Rixhoft, in the area where the German forces put to sea from the river Vistula. The battleships *Slava* and *Tsarevitch* lay in full readiness on Sevastopol roads, near the island of Ayr in the Finnish skerries.

At 01.00hrs on the morning of 1 July 1915, Rear Admiral Bakhirev weighed anchor on Pipsher Roads and put to sea with the cruisers *Admiral Makarov, Bayan, Bogatyr* and *Oleg*, escorted by the destroyers *Boevoi, Vnimatel'nyi, Vynoslivyi* and *Burnyi*, and took course to the south at a speed of 15.5 knots. At 02.00hrs the group arrived off Reval and were joined by *Rurik*, which travelled in the wake of *Oleg*. At the same time the commander dismissed the escorting destroyers. In the meantime Captain 1st Rank Patton's destroyers were leaving from Moon Sound, however *Novik* was delayed by fog and was compelled to anchor near Worms Island. At about 05.00hrs in the morning *Admiral Makarov* encountered fog. Rear Admiral Bakhirev made a decision to bombard Memel on the evening of 1 July, and in consideration of the fact that the VI Division could not catch up with the Cruiser Brigade he ordered them to turn back, and only the high speed *Novik* would continue with the plan. The latter, having received the course, speed and coordinates of the brigade, met the group at about 12.00hrs and pulled into the wake of *Rurik*.

Soon after midday on 1 July the German units must have passed to the right of the Russian cruisers at a distance of no more than 10–12 miles. Both the Russian and German ship groups had already entered into extensive wireless communication, but the Germans were not as advanced in wireless interception, and the leaders of both sides did not yet understand what was happening. At about 17.00hrs the Russian group entered an especially thick fog. During the next 10 minutes whilst manoeuvring to make a change in course towards Memel, *Rurik* and *Novik* became separated from the group. Despite the fact that the cruisers of the group had stern lights lit for those following in the wake and were using special horns, the commanders of *Rurik* and *Novik* were unable to rejoin the group. Rear Admiral Bakhirev, in turn, decided that it was too risky to attempt to approach Memel in the fog without a sure navigational fix, and therefore he postponed the bombardment until the morning of 2 July. Shortly before midnight *Admiral Makarov* obtained a secure fix and again tried to lead the brigade towards Memel.

Shortly afterwards the group not only again encountered fog, but also Rear Admiral Bakhirev received important information that caused him to change his plans. The wireless interception department of the fleet, under Rear Admiral Nepenin, intercepted some messages from German ships, and deciphered Kommodore Karpf's wireless message and transferred the information to the squared chart. At 00.45hrs two messages from Captain 2nd Rank Rengarten were received by *Admiral Makarov*: '18.06hrs *Augsburg* at appointed rendezvous with armoured cruiser in square 377' and 'Appointed rendezvous for cruisers at

08.45hrs square 339. Flag.'[8] Rear Admiral Bakhirev decided not to risk approaching Memel and not to await conditions of improved visibility, but instead to try to arrive in the probable area of the German cruisers. He changed course to NE 10° and gave the signal to the cruiser group: 'Wireless-telegraphy at low power'. By 02.00hrs it had to be accepted aboard the flagship that *Rurik* and *Novik* had completely disappeared in the fog.

Soon after 04.00hrs on 2 July Rear Admiral Bakhirev received the following message from the flag-officer: '...At 01.00hrs *Augsburg* was in the fourth quarter of square 357, course 190°, speed 17 knots.' Starchi-Leitenant Kryzhanovski calculated a course to intercept the enemy, NW 57° (303°). On this course *Admiral Makarov* emerged from the fog at 05.15hrs and the cruisers reformed their line ahead. Admiral Bakhirev ordered an increase in speed to 19 knots and to punch the battle alarm.

On the other hand Kommodore von Karpf had no inkling of the proximity of the powerful Russian force. Although several Russian wireless transmissions had been picked up at sufficient strength to suggest that ships were in the vicinity they were attributed to guard forces in the Irben Straits. At around 06.00hrs the 2nd Admiral detached *Roon* and *Lübeck*, together with four torpedoboats, to Libau via the swept channel off Steinort. *Augsburg*, *Albatroß* and the remaining three torpedoboats took course for the southern tip of Gotland from where they would proceed to Rixhoft. The two German groups soon lost sight of each other in the poor weather conditions, as visibility was no more than 5 nautical miles.

At 06.30hrs *Augsburg* sighted a heavy smoke column to the southeast and soon out of the gloom appeared a four-funnelled cruiser, followed quickly by another. The Russians swiftly altered course to port to take up a running battle. The 2nd Admiral ordered 'utmost power', or full steam ahead, and took course west, whilst at the same time urgently recalling *Roon* and *Lübeck* by wireless. Wireless Rating Wendt aboard SMS *Albatroß* wrote the following:

> From 4 o'clock in the morning FT Obergast Pleiser and I had FT Watch together. Around 6.45 we received a wireless message from *Augsburg*: 'four enemy cruisers in sight to port aft.' At the same time 'clear ship for battle', was ordered by flag signal. I could see the enemy armoured cruisers from my wireless booth. They appeared from a fog bank. The Russians went in line ahead with south-western course at a range, which I estimated at 13–14,000m.[9]

The Russian ships too observed the smoke of the enemy and at 06.30hrs *Bogatyr* saw smoke a little to port of directly ahead. The range to the enemy totalled no more than 50 cable-lengths (9,100m). At 06.35hrs *Admiral Makarov* identified the cruisers *Augsburg* and *Undine*.

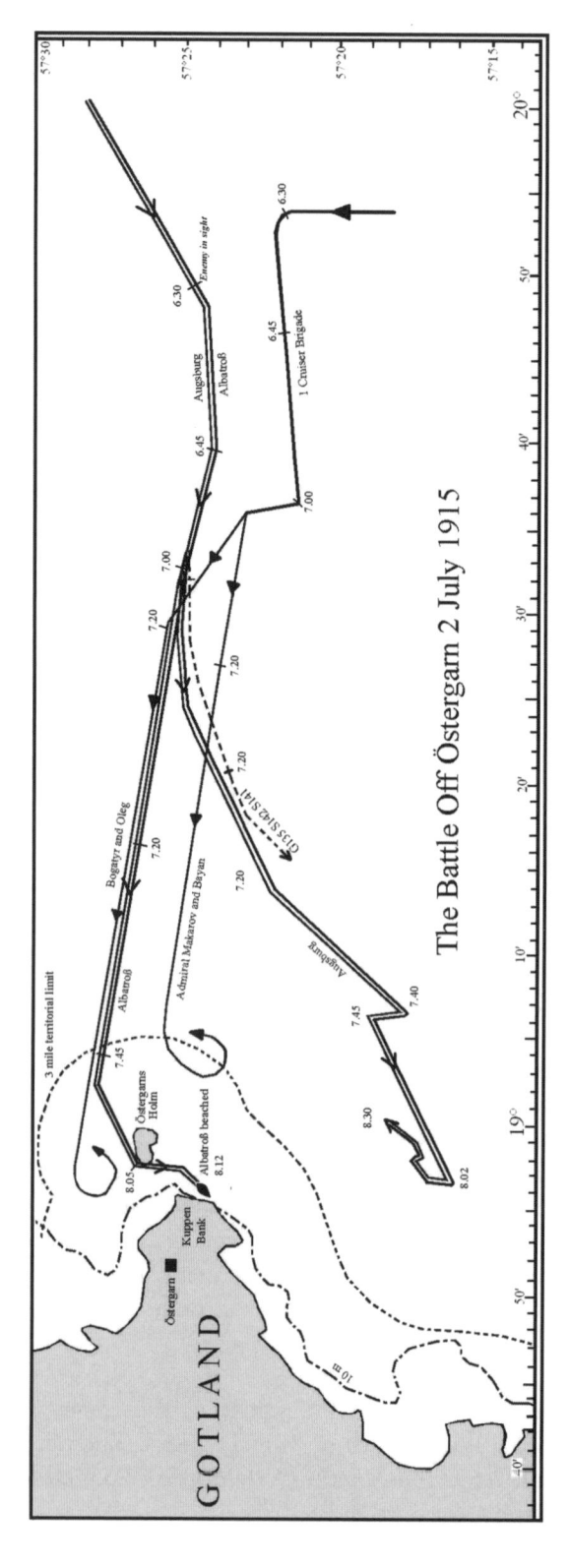

The flagship of Rear Admiral Bakhirev immediately turned to port, bringing the enemy on the starboard side 40° ahead. The battle flags were hoisted and fire was opened on *Augsburg* at a range of about 44 cables (8,000m). After 2 or 3 minutes *Bayan* followed this example. According to the instructions of the flag officer of the brigade for a meeting with two opponents, *Bayan* also fired on the lead ship. At 06.45hrs and 06.50hrs the cruisers *Bogatyr* and *Oleg* opened fire on the imagined *Undine*, which was actually *Albatroß*.

At 06.32hrs the Russians opened a lively fire and 6-inch gun salvos and single shots from the 8-inch pieces began falling around the two German cruisers. The Germans were immediately placed in a critical situation as their artillery was unable to make reply because the Russians were still shrouded in darkness and gloom and the rangefinders and gun layers telescopes were unable to locate them. Only the muzzle flashes of the Russian guns could be seen. Additionally, all of the Russian cruisers were superior in speed to the mine-cruiser. Rear Admiral Bakhirev had skilfully manoeuvred his squadron into a tactically excellent position as visibility to the northwest was much better and the Russian gun crews could easily make out their German targets. In an attempt to throw off the Russians aim both German ships made small, random alterations in course and *Augsburg* sprayed extra oil into her boilers which developed a thick, black smoke. None of these measures were completely successful, however, and both German ships remained under a heavy, accurate fire. Therefore, at 06.45hrs, the 2nd Admiral turned his ships away 2 points[10] to starboard but Rear Admiral Bakhirev did not alter course, seemingly content to let the range open slightly. Wireless Rating Wendt wrote:

> *Albatroß* went at 19 to 20 knots, and *Augsburg* and the boats ran at considerably more. The original course was maintained. The fire of the Russians was lively, however, very irregular. As far as could be observed, it was salvo fire. The individual salvos lay short or wide, and at first hits were not obtained, so that the enemy fire made a wretched impression.

Kommodore von Karpf now weighed the chances of conducting a successful torpedoboat attack. Nothing was in their favour. The battle was being fought at a range of 80 to 90hm and the sea was glassy smooth, while the three torpedoboats *G135*, *S142* and *S141* were equipped with the old C/03 type torpedo which had a maximum range of just 3,000 metres. The four Russian armoured cruisers had their entire secondary armaments, something like thirty-four 7.5cm guns, available to ward off the attack whilst *G135* could scarcely make 20 knots, with the other two boats being slightly faster. Under these circumstances a torpedo attack would appear to have little chance of success. Aboard the *Flottille* boat, *G135*, Korvettenkapitän Wieting and his Flag Leutnant, Kapitänleutnant Stratmann, made the same considerations and came to the same conclusion, whilst the battle reports of the other two commanders, Kapitänleutnant Menche aboard *S142* and Oberleutnant zur See von Prittwitz und Gaffron on *S141*, ran along similar lines. Nevertheless, Korvettenkapitän Wieting manoeuvred his boats for an attack and aboard *G135* the red pennant 'Z', meaning '*Ran*', or 'Attack the enemy!', was hoisted. The three boats closed into tight formation.

In the meantime Kommodore von Karpf decided to break through to the south across the head of the Russian squadron and at least attempt to save the cruiser and torpedoboats, and accordingly at 06.53hrs he swung away to port. *Albatroß* received orders to seek the protection of Swedish territorial waters and on the basis of these manoeuvres and the fact that the Russians had turned north at 07.00hrs the Flottille Chief abandoned his attack.

At 07.00hrs Admiral Bakhirev ordered the signal to be given: 'Operate at own discretion'. The commander of *Bogatyr*, Captain 1st Rank Verderevsky, immediately deviated to starboard to cut off the perceived *Undine* 'from the north'. Having described a turn *Bogatyr* and *Oleg* renewed fire on *Albatroß* from starboard at 07.10hrs, and soon the minelayer received heavy damage and loss of life. A short time earlier *Admiral Makarov* and *Bayan* had transferred fire to *Albatroß*.

Augsburg and the torpedoboats bore away more and more to the south and from time to time the Russian cruisers were lost from view in the smoke. At one stage, when the Russians reappeared from a smoke bank, the range was as low as 60 to 70hm and the torpedoboats were able to participate in the battle. *S141* believed she had observed a hit on the leading ship. From 07.20hrs to 07.33hrs *Augsburg* renewed her fire at long range. The Russians did not pursue *Augsburg* away to the south, however, and as a result by 07.35hrs the Germans were out of range and had vanished from view.

Meanwhile for *Albatroß* the situation was becoming graver. Her boilers and engines were working to the limits of their capacity in an effort to gain neutral territorial waters. By about 07.00hrs the range had reduced to the extent that *Albatroß* could commence returning fire with her 8.8cm guns. Fregattenkapitän West found himself in a desperate situation and he attempted to throw off the Russian aim by making rapid course alterations and in an attempt to force the Russian admiral to turn away he sent a plain, open German wireless signal to the 2nd Admiral: 'Please allow U-boat to attack.'

At 07.20hrs, some 45 minutes after the beginning of the battle, *Albatroß* received her first hit. Signal Rating Wendt wrote:

> Only after 40 minutes, during which we maintained the same course as *Augsburg* and the torpedoboats, which meanwhile vanished from sight, did *Albatroß* receive the first hit in the aft ship near the pinnace. I myself had not noticed the smashing of the shell, but only got to know of the hit as slightly

wounded soldiers came past my wireless booth. I could observe the effect of further shells hitting from my booth. As we later ascertained, the Russians shot 24cm and 15cm shells. Roughly towards 7 o'clock came a wireless message from *Augsburg*: 'Attempt to run into Swedish Territorial waters.' *Albatroß* immediately altered course and ran towards Gotland with a zigzag course northwest. The fact that we went with a zigzag course is memorable to me because the ship lay over. The Russians now likewise changed course so that now pursuing us were two ships to port and two ships to starboard. The distance between *Albatroß* and the Russian ships was estimated at approximately 6,000m at this time.[11]

As the range closed the small 8.8cm guns of *Albatroß* were able to make reply, but as Wireless Rating Wendt wrote:

Just as I heard the starboard side did not intervene in the fire, whilst on the port side the forward gun could not fire from the beginning because of the limited training angle, and the port aft gun fell out because of a broken cylinder pump, so that only two guns of the port side actually fired. I could observe nothing of the effect of our fire on the Russian armoured cruisers.

The commander of *Albatroß*, Fregattenkapitän West, wrote in his report:

About 7^{40} the ship was hit. The first struck on the deck, the second destroyed the steam pinnace, the third struck the room for the evaporator, the fourth struck the men's room (accommodation), the fifth destroyed the stern in a heavy manner, so that it seems incomprehensible that the rudder and propellers were not damaged. The order of the later hits cannot be ascertained exactly enough, they fell primarily in the foreship. The Russians now shot, and only the circumstance that a continuous zigzag course to the position of the salvos was taken to avoid the shots, is it to thank that only a few hit from the numerous shells impacting about the ship.

The fire of 4 ships concentrated on *Albatroß*. The two aft positioned Russian armoured cruisers altered course about 7^{35} to give their guns a better shot, and took us under effective longitudinal fire which covered us. According to estimates the Russian ships fired at least 3,000 shots on *Albatroß*.

The ship was usually straddled by the shots. At 70hm range the fire was answered by our guns on the forward armoured cruiser, and a few hits were irreproachably observed, one with flames and smoke effect. Munitions use approximately 500 cartridges. At 7^{35} the coast of the island of Gotland came in sight. In the further course of the battle the foremast was shot down and the forecastle literally shot through like a sieve. The Russians also utilized shrapnel. The forward conning tower fell out, the entire personnel were killed, and likewise the charthouse was shot up, the helmsman, there occupied, was torn into pieces. The conning tower rudder and engine telegraphs were destroyed, on the bridge, Oberleutnant zur See Löwenberg, fell near me, the Oberleutnant zur See Hähner received near me a heavy femoral shot, I myself was thrown to the deck with a left thigh wound and a slight knee wound, but could further continue command after I was picked up.

At 7⁴⁷ the ship received a hit in compartments 7 and 6, the number 2 mine room filled with water, the dry store made water. Fire broke out above the water in compartment 6, which was soon extinguished. In general the incendiary effect was not considerable from the small explosive part of the shell. Compartment 1 in the aft laying deck and the infirmary were likewise in flames, but they were soon extinguished. Compartment IV, about frame 57-64, received a direct hit, the aft longitudinal bunker, double bottom, cell 57/65, 65/71 all filled with water.[12]

Wireless Rating Wendt continued:

Around 8.15, the foremast was hit and fell down, so that the FT [wireless] also fell out. The enemy wireless traffic was monitored continuously until then, however, not a single signal was given. In the meantime *Augsburg* maintained further traffic. *Albatroß* had asked: 'May U-boat intervene?' *Augsburg* answered: 'U-boat should attack immediately.' While bringing out the reserve antenna I was wounded and soon thereon went to the battle dressing station, on the *Oberdeck*, starboard forward. There lay some badly wounded.[13]

At 07.45hrs *Albatroß* reached Swedish territorial waters off Östergarns Holme and ceased fire. The Russians however, did not stop firing but rather increased their rate of fire and it was only after the German mine cruiser had run through Östergarn Sound from the north that they ceased fire towards 08.07hrs. By this stage the German minelayer was in poor condition. She had developed a list to port and had increased her draught. The rudder room had been abandoned so that the manual rudder had had to be employed, however, this also became unusable so that the ship had to be steered using her engines. Surprisingly neither boilers nor engines had been hit and remained undamaged. As the list to port increased it was feared that she would capsize and therefore at 08.12hrs the ship's commander allowed *Albatroß* to be beached at slow speed. The Russian cruisers ceased fire between 07.30hrs (*Bayan*) and 08.07hrs (*Oleg*).

It was a wonder that *Albatroß* had survived. With her relatively weak broadside of four 8.8cm guns she had held off the entire Russian squadron for

1½ hours. The German *Offiziers* estimated that the Russians had fired over 3,000 shells, almost half of each ship's outfit. Of these, six 8-inch and twenty 6-inch shells had hit *Albatroß* and later four duds which had failed to detonate were found aboard the ship. Of the 11 *Offiziers* and 226 *Deckoffiziers*, *Unteroffiziers* and men crewing the ship, the Artillerie Offizier, Oberleutnant zur See Löwenberg and 26 men were killed. Four *Offiziers* and fifty-one men were wounded. *Albatroß* did not strike her flag and Fregattenkapitän West was able to state in his battle report: 'I have confidence, that the honour of the flag was upheld.' From the fire of *Albatroß* there was one 8.8cm shell hit on the cruiser *Admiral Makarov*. The splinters from this shell damaged a 75cm searchlight and wounded a seaman.

After *Albatroß* was beached near Östergarn the Russian 1st Cruiser Brigade turned away to the north and began to reassemble, whilst at the same time Kommodore von Karpf made to *Albatroß* by searchlight: 'Will fetch you later.' As the Russians could be seen withdrawing to the north *Augsburg* turned to follow at a respectable distance, outside artillery range. The 2nd Admiral felt it advisable to be cautious in consideration of the changing visibility conditions. The Russians, however, were now confronted with a new problem and had lost interest completely in the German flagship.

When the *Roon* group received the 2nd Admiral's urgent wireless message they immediately reversed course and closed at high speed, although through a slight discrepancy between the two groups' calculated positions and owing to poor visibility, reduced to 5 nautical miles at times, they were forced to march to the sound of the cannon thunder. At 08.20hrs *Lübeck*, Fregattenkapitän Halm, sighted two Russian cruisers and soon others could be made out to the north and east of Östergarns Holme. The Russians quickly regrouped and steamed away to the north. With *Lübeck* in the lead the German ships formed line ahead and gave chase, although the four torpedoboats of the 19th Half-Flottille were unable to obtain a position ahead of the Russians. Just after 09.00hrs *Roon*, Fregattenkapitän Gygas, had closed the range sufficiently to open fire with his 21cm guns on the last ship in the Russian line. The commander of *Bayan*, Captain 1st Rank A.K. Vejs immediately ordered the battle flags to be raised and the cruiser answered the opponent with salvos from the 8-inch guns at a range of 62–64 cables (11,500m). One of the first shells damaged the wireless antenna of *Roon* and deprived the German cruiser of wireless communication up until the end of the fight. According to the report of P.V. Lemishevski, formerly of *Bayan*, Captain 1st Rank Vejs, 'zigzagged at 90° all the time along the mean course, which greatly influenced the rate of change'.[14] However, one 21cm shell did hit *Bayan* on the hull side and mine deck in the middle part of the ship. Splinters from the shell damaged the second funnel, the crew's galley, the mounting of a 75mm gun of the battery and some other equipment and destroyed a cutter. Two men received slight wounds. Meanwhile *Bogatyr* and *Oleg* targeted *Lübeck*. Neither *Lübeck* nor her two opponents were straddled by any salvos as the range was scarcely less than 130hm.

The manner in which the battle was developing was beginning to concern Fregattenkapitän Gygas. He questioned why the Russians were content to conduct the battle on a northerly course when they clearly outnumbered the Germans two to one. He thought that perhaps they were trying to lure him into the arms of even stronger forces. The whereabouts of *Augsburg* also concerned him as, according to *Roon*'s estimations, the flagship should now have been in sight; however, unlike *Lübeck*, which had briefly sighted Östergarns Holme, *Roon*'s navigation remained slightly in error and hence the non-appearance of *Augsburg*. With these considerations in mind Fregattenkapitän Gygas determined to break off the action and reunite with the flagship, so at 09.22hrs the German armoured cruiser ceased fire and sheered away to starboard onto a south-westerly course. *Lübeck* followed soon after. Rear Admiral Bakhirev declined to continue the action and held his north-easterly course, citing his shortage of ammunition as the reason. *Admiral Makarov* had approximately ninety 8-inch shells remaining and only half her 6-inch ammunition. To cover his retirement he ordered the two battleships *Slava* and *Tsarevitch*, which lay on Oro Roads as a reserve, to put to sea to meet the Cruiser Brigade. He did, however, return briefly to a southerly course when the errant *Rurik* joined the battle.

When he began pursuing *Albatroß* Admiral Bakhirev wirelessed *Rurik*, which was to the southeast: 'Enter battle with the enemy, square 400 [at Östergarn].' The commander of *Rurik*, Captain 1st Rank A.M. Pyshnov, increased speed to 20 knots and took course to the reported position of the battle. He arrived on this position after approximately one hour, at 09.45hrs, and 'not seeing the enemy', Pyshnov assumed that 'the Brigade had driven to the north', and therefore he turned onto course 030°. The commander of *Novik*, Captain 2nd Rank Berens, lost *Rurik* in the fog on the morning of 2 July and thereafter operated independently, and after a fruitless search went to the Irben Straits where she anchored at midday.

At 09.30hrs, 5 minutes after turning onto a south-westerly course, *Lübeck* observed a smoke cloud to the east and immediately turned towards it to investigate. Soon after the indistinct form of a ship could be made out and *Lübeck* gave the recognition signal by searchlight. The stranger gave an incorrect reply and at first Fregattenkapitän Halm took her for *Novik*, because of her astonishingly thin masts. *Lübeck* held course towards the enemy but at 09.45hrs, as the range reduced to 110 to 112hm, the ship was recognized as *Rurik*. *Lübeck* was now in a critical situation as at this range the Russian heavy artillery could soon account for the German small cruiser. *Lübeck* quickly

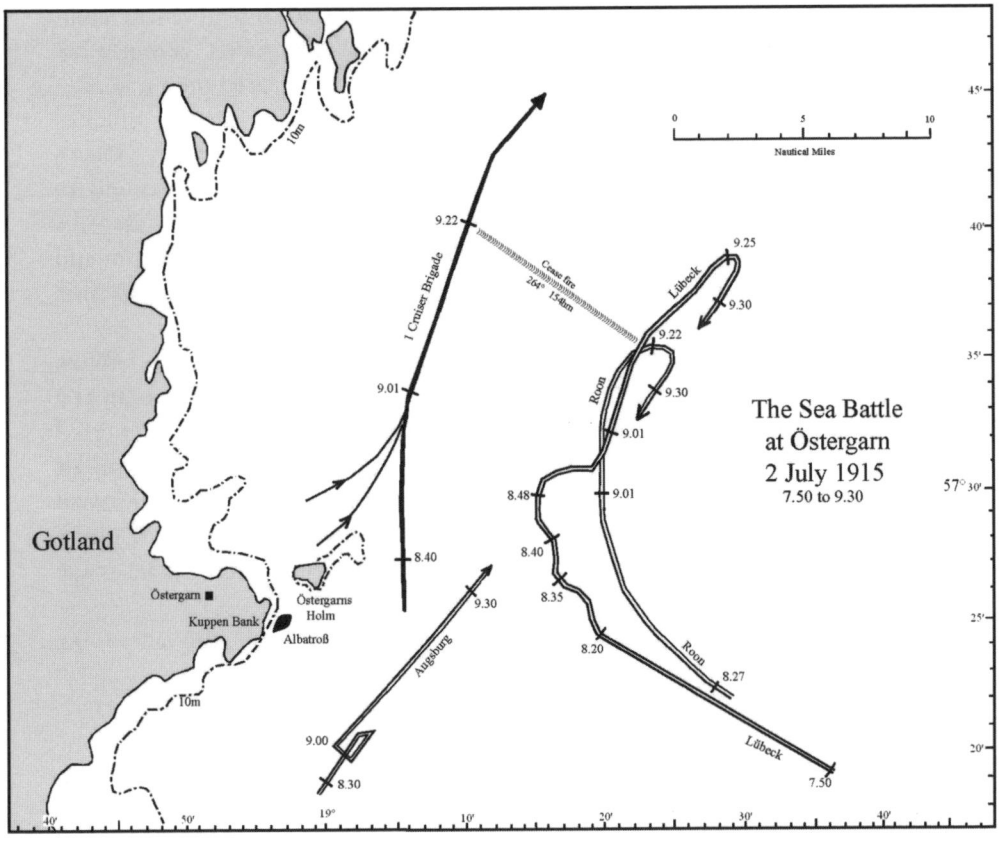

turned onto a south-westerly course whilst *Rurik* opened fire. Soon the 10-inch shells from *Rurik* were straddling the German cruiser but for some unexplained reason the medium calibre 8-inch shells almost without exception fell short. *Lübeck* replied to the Russian fire at once and her Artillerie Offizier, Oberleutnant zur See Kaupisch, ordered 'rapid fire' so that usually there were two or three salvos in the air at once. A total of five hits were observed on *Rurik*, one of which caused a fire, whilst *Lübeck* remained unhit, although splinters from near misses fell on deck. In actual fact the small cruiser's fire was more effective than she believed. One salvo landed close off *Rurik*'s bow and threw so much water over her decks that the rangefinder apparatus on the command bridge was damaged. A further hit started a fire in the forecastle. Then suddenly, 'A shower of small shells fell upon the deck and through the unarmoured hull side'. *Lübeck* made a total of ten hits on *Rurik* with 10.5cm shells, which damaged the deck, funnels and officers' cabins. These shells could not penetrate the areas protected by armour, but gases from the explosion of one of them caused poisoning of a 10-inch turret. It had to temporarily cease firing while the poison gases were removed, but the turret commander, Leitenant G. A. Aleksev, remained at his battle post and cleared the turret.

The battle between *Rurik* and *Lübeck* had continued for some 15 minutes before *Roon* had closed enough to open fire on the Russian opponent. *Roon*'s heavy artillery consisted of four 21cm pieces, equivalent to *Rurik*'s secondary battery, so on paper at least the German ship was at a severe disadvantage. A message was then flashed to *Lübeck* by searchlight to break off the action and steer through neutral waters towards home. *Lübeck* complied and at 10.04hrs fire between her and *Rurik* had ceased.

Meanwhile *Augsburg* had joined with *Roon* on a southerly course. When *Rurik* sighted them she turned a point to port and a running battle began at a range of 150 to 160hm. *Rurik* fired mainly on *Roon*, but the Germans reported no hits on either her nor *Augsburg*. *Rurik*, however, was soon hit on the aft conning tower and the adjacent superstructure was destroyed. The Russian commander made a slight course alteration to ensure his aft 10-inch turret could bear. The poor visibility and shell splashes from short shells made observation extremely difficult for both sides.

The commander of *Roon*, Kapitän zur See Gygas, wrote this about the second phase of the battle:

10.01am open fire on *Rurik*.
10.21am cease fire. The range is too great.
The observation during both battle phases was extraordinarily difficult, through uncertain weather and through the numerous short shots of the enemy. The fire of *Rurik* at the beginning gave the impression of very precise measurement, but later became inexact with great ammunition expenditure.
At the first, just as with the second battle a hit was irreproachably observed.
Range with the first battle 126–154hm.
Range with the second battle 140–160hm.
Fired munitions: 110–21cm explosive shells, 4–15cm explosive shells.
In addition to the previously mentioned damage to the wireless antenna, there was no other damage or disruption.
The men performed their duty quietly.[15]

Kommodore von Karpf did not desire to continue the fight against his more powerful opponent and as the range was too great for a torpedoboat attack, he decided to turn away slightly to starboard and unobtrusively slip away, especially as he expected the Cruiser Brigade to appear at any moment. At 10.20hrs both sides ceased fire with the final range at 160hm. At the same time the lookouts aboard *Rurik* erroneously reported a periscope so that the Russian

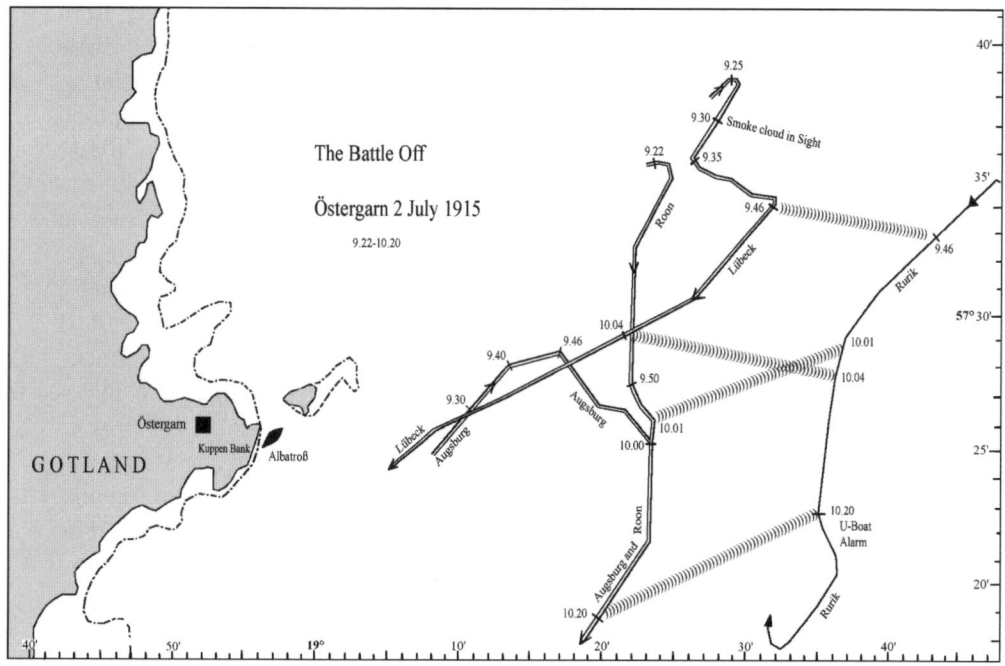

armoured cruiser quickly turned away. She continued in a southerly direction until at 10.50hrs Rear Admiral Bakhirev recalled her by wireless. The Germans did not maintain contact with her, which was to be expected as in all three phases of battle they had been faced by a greatly superior enemy, and at one stage had nearly been caught between two units. The 2nd Admiral decided to steer to Hoburg, obtain a position fix there and collect *Lübeck* and then continue to Rixhoft. His resolve was strengthened when a wireless message arrived from Kontreadmiral Hopman saying he had run out of Danzig at 10.00hrs with *Prinz Adalbert* and *Prinz Heinrich*. He determined to unite with this force before returning to Östergarn. He considered sending one or more torpedoboats to assist *Albatroß* but the distance from home, the uncertain weather and the likelihood of the Russians returning deterred him from this course of action. As observed from the flagship the minelayer lay aground and listing, however many small Swedish boats were putting out from shore so the wounded would surely be attended to. The air station at Libau received orders to dispatch an aircraft to *Albatroß* and to send a second to reconnoitre towards the enemy cruisers.

In the meantime the Russians had likewise begun the rear march. Rear Admiral Bakhirev was apparently influenced by his great ammunition expenditure, the approach of German reinforcements and the danger from U-boats. *Rurik* believed she had sighted a U-boat, and during the battle between the Cruiser Brigade and *Roon* at around 09.45hrs both *Admiral Makarov* and *Bayan* gave the submarine alarm and opened fire on a supposed periscope. What effect, if any, the open wireless message of *Albatroß* to 'please allow U-boat to attack' had is unknown.

To Kontreadmiral Hopman in Danzig, the events occurring to east of Gotland remained a total mystery. He had received the 2nd Admiral's report indicating the completion of mining Operation VII but then at 07.12hrs a message was picked up in open German: 'To armoured cruisers and II Squadron, enemy position Quadrant 003 Beta. Surround, cut off and attack.' This message was sent by *Augsburg* after *Albatroß*'s example. The mine-cruiser's signal was not picked up in Danzig. Then an order for *Albatroß* to shelter under the Swedish coast followed. Then at 07.48hrs a message was received from *Roon*: 'Position Quadrant 117 Epsilon, course W.N.W., 19 knots.' Kontreadmiral Hopman now ordered steam to be raised with all haste. The only torpedoboats available to form an anti-submarine screen were *S138* and *S139*, which were engaged in boiler cleaning, and they were ordered to prepare to put to sea as quickly as possible. Due to fine efforts by their crews the armoured cruisers *Prinz Adalbert* and *Prinz Heinrich* were able to cast off at about 10.00hrs and by 10.50hrs had put the shallow, narrow Vistula behind them, taking course north at 17 knots. The two torpedoboats caught them up at 12.00hrs. As the admiral advanced he ordered *V108* and *UA*, which were lying in Danzig, to proceed to Libau to reinforce the weak forces there. By this time a further report from the 2nd Admiral had been received and although it appeared that the immediate danger had passed Kontreadmiral Hopman intended to join with Kommodore von Karpf's unit and push to the north and, if possible, recover *Albatroß*.

After rounding Cape Hela the German unit encountered thick fog and seemingly the entire Baltic was shrouded on this day. The screening torpedoboats closed on the flagship but when the fog cleared half an hour later the screen was not renewed as another fog bank could be seen ahead. In addition, the ships were running at high speed in an area of enemy minefields and up until this time no Entente submarines had been detected in this area. Towards 13.00hrs Kontreadmiral Hopman retired to his cabin to rest, in the expectation that he would be on the bridge for most of the night, whilst his Chief of Staff and *Prinz Adalbert*'s commander, Kapitän zur See Michelsen, remained on the bridge. By 13.57hrs the Germans were 6 nautical miles northeast of Rixhoft; Kapitän zur See Michelsen described what happened next:

> We emerged from a fog bank and I was considering ordering the torpedoboats back to their screening positions–I had command of the ship

and was standing on the starboard wing of the command bridge–when suddenly a white spot appeared on the water's surface, direction 070°, range 300 to 400 metres. I commanded 'Submarine at 070°! All engines utmost power ahead!' The white fleck on the waters surface could only be the exhaust air from the launch of a torpedo from an English submarine. Thereon immediately followed the alarm which had still not died away when the dark line of a periscope of a submarine revealed itself in a slanting position, raised from the water approximately 1 metre and a further vortex appeared…The range and direction were correctly given to the guns, however, fire was not opened as at this moment a powerful detonation took place on the starboard side of the ship and all was veiled in darkness. From the sighting of the first firing vortex to the striking of the torpedo was just seconds–probably around fifteen.[16]

Kapitän zur See was Michelsen was a torpedo expert and had been Chief of Staff of the Torpedo Inspectorate and in the Torpedo Trials Commission prior to the war. He now stood staring at the torpedo tracks weighing the chances of a hit with a professional eye:

The second shot of the enemy was cause for concern. This torpedo ran accurately and must hit our broadside. In the clear Baltic waters I could clearly see the red upper side of this torpedo and saw it strike on the hull side close ahead of the bridge. At the moment it struck I pulled my head back behind the railing…the other torpedo went close to *S138*, that was still travelling behind us, and stuck the bottom where it detonated and covered the torpedoboat from top to bottom with mud, and the wireless, compass etceteras were put out of action. With praiseworthy swiftness the *S139*, Kapitänleutnant Menche, immediately steamed over the position of the enemies periscope and forced the enemy under water. At this time depth charges had not been invented, and it was truly a golden time for submarines.

The torpedo attack on *Prinz Adalbert* had been conducted by the English submarine *E9*, Commander Horton. She had departed Reval at 03.35hrs on 28 June to support the Russian cruiser raid on Memel. For the following 2 days she patrolled 40 nautical miles northwest of Steinort before shifting her patrol area to Rixhoft on 1 July, where the same day Commander Horton forewent attacking three merchant ships so as not to compromise his presence, preferring to await military targets. On 2 July at 13.45hrs *E9* sighted the F.d.A.d.O.'s unit at a range of 4 miles and Commander Horton immediately began an attack, pressing home to just 400 metres range to loose his torpedoes as he feared they would be easily spotted in the calm conditions. Commander Horton wrote:

Sighted enemy squadron coming up fast from eastwards proceeding westerly inshore of us. Distance when sighted approximately 4 miles. Squadron consisted of two heavy ships with destroyers. Turned to attack. Sea smooth. 3.00pm–Our position 400 yards 5 points on starboard bow of leading ship–a three funnelled battleship of either *Deutschland* or *Braunschweig* classes. Fired both bow torpedoes at her.

N°1 torpedo was heard and seen to strike her just before foremost funnel. Smoke and debris appeared to go as high as mast head. Immediately on firing enemy destroyer on starboard quarter of battleship turned to ram. So, observing her, I took my periscope off the battleship, but at correct interval after explosion of first torpedo the second was also heard to explode, though not actually seen…Destroyer just missed us. Struck bottom in 43 feet.[17]

After firing the two bow torpedo tubes *E9* turned to port to bring the beam torpedo tube to bear but the rapid intervention of *S139* meant that she was unable to fire and Commander Horton was only able to obtain one brief glimpse through his periscope during the following hour. That evening, at 18.00hrs, *E9* sighted the 2nd Admiral's three cruisers at a range of 3,000 metres but was unable to develop an attack. *E9* returned to Reval early on the morning of 4 July where Commander Horton reported the destruction of a three-funnelled battleship of the *Pommern* class and was awarded Russia's highest award for bravery, the order of St George. Luckily for the Germans he was wrong on both counts: the torpedoed ship was not a battleship and it did not sink. Nevertheless, the torpedoing of *Prinz Adalbert* sealed *Albatroß*'s fate and the minelayer cruiser was left to be interned by the Swedish authorities.

SMS *Prinz Adalbert* had been heavily hit, with the torpedo striking the aft part of the broadside torpedo room. Immediately the forward boiler room, the broadside torpedo room, the forward 8.8cm magazine and the central control position, or *zentral*, filled with water. Later the bow torpedo room, the workshop, the main gangway, 21cm magazine and several smaller compartments also filled with water that leaked through ventilation shafts, speaking tubes and leaky joints. In the forward boiler room and torpedo room two *Unteroffiziers* and eight men perished. All the command elements and artillery control apparatus failed. The ship had to be steered from the rudder room and all orders for steering had to be relayed over the deck. Soon after, a still-warm visiting card of the torpedo was found embedded in the wooden deck and was taken to the bridge. It was a large piece of an air flask that was marked with the construction details of the torpedo and as it was in English all doubts as to the identity of the assailant were removed. It was most satisfying, however, that although many of *Prinz Adalbert*'s torpedoes in the broadside room had been torn apart, and guncotton strewn about, none had detonated even though the pistols had been in place.

As the flagship turned towards the coast *S139* took up a screening position and *S138* took up the hunt for the submarine. *Prinz Heinrich*, Kapitän zur See von Krosigk, was detached to Danzig. At first it was likewise intended for *Prinz Adalbert* to retire to Neufahrwasser, but as the flagship approached the 20 metre line off Rixhoft and the flooding was finally stabilized, the draught forward had already increased to over 9 metres, somewhat too deep for the Vistula. Kontreadmiral Hopman therefore decided to travel along the coast to Swinemunde. At first the flagship travelled at 15 and then 12 knots, to distance herself from the submarine, but this speed could not be held as it put great strain on the shored-up bulkheads and hatchways. All pumps were working to capacity but the water always found new ways to leak into adjacent compartments. By 16.00hrs that afternoon there was already 1,200 tonnes of water in the ship. The circulation pump of the port engine was used to drain the bow torpedo room and as under these conditions there was insufficient water for the port condenser, the port engine could not be used. As *Prinz Adalbert* proceeded westwards at slow speed the bows gradually sank deeper so that the forward outer casemate decks were awash and began acting as a kind of diving plane, pushing the bows lower. On passing Leba at around 17.10hrs, *Indianola*, which was working on the Russian minefield there, received orders to recover her motorboats and follow *Prinz Adalbert*.

At 20.30hrs the armoured cruiser anchored off Stolpemunde and a life-and-death struggle to save the ship began. It was estimated that there was now 2,000 tonnes of water in the ship, while her reserve buoyancy was 2,500 tonnes. Throughout the night the crew, and especially the leak countermeasures personnel[18], worked desperately below in flooded, dark compartments under the personal direction of the First Offizier, Korvettenkapitän von Zerboni di Sposetti and Marinestabsingeneur[19] Gunther. Due to their efforts some compartments were drained and the draught was reduced slightly. When *Prinz Adalbert* got underway at 04.00hrs on 3 July, she travelled astern. It was doubtful if the armoured cruiser could enter Swinemunde, therefore it was decided to utilize the calm weather to travel direct to Kiel, where repair facilities were available. The work of the crew successfully reduced the draught to 11 metres, but two pump steamers failed to find *Prinz Adalbert* and continued to Swinemunde as they were not fitted with wireless. Nevertheless, despite encountering fog and mist, *Prinz Adalbert* passed the outer harbour barriers at Kiel at 14.00hrs on 4 July going ahead, and towards 15.00hrs she made fast at buoy 10A. His Highness Prinz Heinrich, the Commander in Chief of Baltic Forces, immediately went aboard and congratulated her commander and crew on an outstanding performance. The ship had been brought 295 nautical miles in a sinking condition, travelling 240 miles going astern.

Although the Russians had obtained a victory in that *Albatroß* was lost and *Prinz Adalbert* was out of action for several months, they had missed the opportunity of an even greater success. Their superiority in numbers, speed, armament and armour should have meant a resounding victory for them. The promise of the excellent ground work of their Intelligence Department had not been fulfilled by the Cruiser Brigade, and with only a little more initiative and aggression the high expectations of the Fleet Command for this operation could have been satisfied. Nevertheless, Rear Admiral Bakhirev had obtained a clear-cut victory at virtually no expense, notwithstanding their belief that the Germans had lost a battleship to *E9*. However, in Russia he was criticised. What is certain is that *Albatroß* and the twenty-seven dead, along with countless other German sailors, were the victims of the inept and criminally negligent performance off Odensholm Island on the foggy morning of 26 August 1914.

SMS *Albatroß* was moved away on 23 July by the Swedish salvage company Neptun after she was made watertight and makeshift repairs were completed. She was towed to Faro Sound and from there was transferred to Oskarshamn at the end of September. The German crew were allowed to return onboard but *Albatroß* remained in internment until the winter of 1918 when she finally returned to Germany.

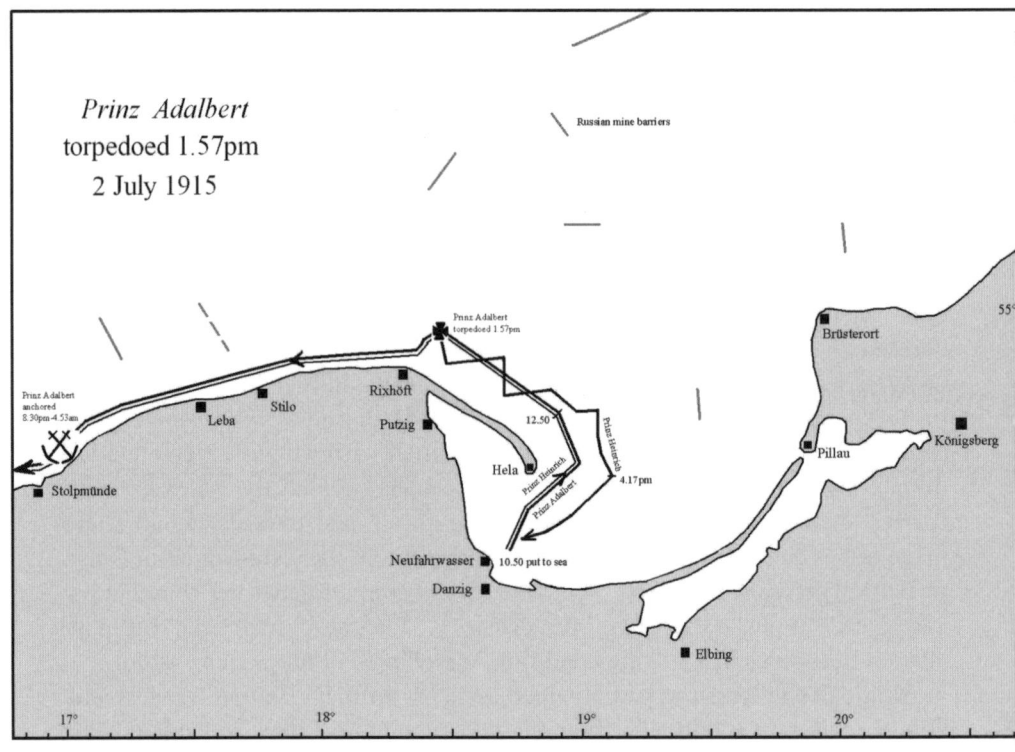

Chapter 7

The Battles of *Emden* and *Königsberg*

The short-lived careers of *Emden* and *Königsberg* during the First World War were remarkably similar. Both ships operated and found their fates in the Indian Ocean. Both ships shone brightly, if briefly, and boldly sailed into an enemy harbour to sink a cruiser opponent. Both ships were not sunk, but were destroyed and came to rest on the shallow bottom, where parts of them remain to this day.

At 11.00hrs on Thursday 13 August 1914 at Pagan Island aboard SMS *Scharnhorst*, the flagship of the East Asiatic Squadron, a commanders' conference was held where Vizeadmiral Graf von Spee made known his views about the situation and his plans for the future of the squadron. Because of the great coal consumption by *Gneisenau* and *Scharnhorst*, he had determined to sail for the west coast of South America, where it would be easier to obtain coal through the German *Etappe* supply organisation. The proposal of the commander of *Emden*, Fregattenkapitän von Müller, to dispatch at least one small cruiser to the Indian Ocean was considered. After the meeting was concluded all the cruisers were ordered to be ready for sea at 17.30hrs. At 15.00hrs *Emden* received orders to conduct cruiser warfare in the Indian Ocean and that evening at 18.00hrs the squadron put to sea. At 08.00hrs the following morning the flagship signalled *Emden*: '*Emden* detach, wish you good success', to which Fregattenkapitän von Müller replied: 'I thank Your Excellency for the confidence placed in me. I wish the cruiser squadron a safe voyage and good luck.'[1] After that *Emden* proceeded by the Palau Islands and the Lombok Strait into the Indian Ocean and the Bay of Bengal. There *Emden* intercepted and captured thirty steamers, of which she sank sixteen, and released seven neutral steamers. *Emden* also successfully bombarded the petroleum tanks at the port of Madras on the Indian coast and severely damaged them. Whilst conducting this commerce raiding the I Torpedo Offizier, Oberleutnant zur See Witthoeft, suggested a raid into the harbour at Penang, in Malaya. Whilst Fregattenkapitän von Müller was in favour of such an operation, he decided to shelve the idea until a later date. By late October he had determined to undertake this operation, and set the date as 28 October. He wrote: "As the next operation I had a surprise entry into Penang Harbour in my eye, with the object of destroying warships or merchant ships lying there. I hoped for a success to both disrupt enemy trade passing through Singapore, as well as diminish the prestige of England among the populations of India, Indochina and the Malay States."[2]

On 26 October the Russian light cruiser *Zhemchug*, under the command of Captain 2nd Rank Cherkasov, arrived in Penang. *Zhemchug* had been involved in the search for *Emden* under the overall command of the British Vice Admiral Jerram and had just finished an inspection of the Nicobar and Andaman Islands. She now needed to clean her boilers and Captain 2nd Rank Cherkasov requested Vice Admiral Jerram to conduct this work in Singapore, however this request was refused and the unprotected port of Penang had to be used. All the boilers except one were out of service which meant in particular that the ammunition hoists were unserviceable because of lack of power. The following day, 27 October, the wife of Captain 2nd Rank Cherkasov arrived in Penang aboard a steamer, and citing sickness he went ashore to a hotel on the coast. Firstly, however, he ordered all ammunition to be replaced into the magazines, as he feared that the high ambient temperatures would heat the projectiles; an order which the Senior Officer had rescinded to allow five ready projectiles to be stored near each gun, with a further shell loaded. Despite the fact that it was already the third month of the war all lighthouses and lead-in lights to Penang harbour shone as in peacetime, doubtlessly a risk to security.

During 27 October aboard *Emden* the last preparations were made for the raid. The sun-shade awning of sailcloth was taken down and the ship was cleaned. At 17.00hrs the commander ordered all men aft and explained his plan to attack Penang and destroy any warships found there. To deceive the enemy and prevent premature recognition of *Emden* a fourth funnel was rigged from wood and sailcloth to represent the appearance of an Allied cruiser, as both the British and Japanese had four-funnelled cruisers in the region, the *Yarmouth* and *Chikuma*. Although steam was up in all boilers *Emden* travelled at 18 then 17 knots, to arrange her arrival in Penang at just before dawn. At 04.30hrs the buoy of the northern channel was made out and passed to starboard and by 04.50hrs *Emden* was approaching the warship anchorage. The brightly burning navigation lights made entry to the harbour easy for *Emden*, and she passed the picket vessel, the French torpedoboat *Mousquet*, and the harbour pilot vessel apparently without being observed. At 05.04hrs, one hour before sunrise, the stern light of a warship could be made out 1,200m ahead to starboard. At 800m this ship could be made out as the Russian cruiser *Zhemchug*. As *Emden* closed she was seen from *Zhemchug*, but it was already too late to counter the German cruiser. Fregattenkapitän Müller wrote:

> The torpedo tubes were already made ready beforehand. I turned with hard rudder away to port, to increase the passing range with regard to the running depth of the torpedo shot, then back hard to starboard and at 5.18am gave the Torpedo Offizier, Oberleutnant zur See Witthöft, permission for the

torpedo armament to fire. The shooting distance was 300–350m. Even as the torpedo quit the tube I gave the Artillerie Offizier, Kapitänleutnant Gaede, orders for the artillery to open fire. The torpedo struck *Zhemchug* about the level of the aft funnel. The stern of the Russian cruiser lifted somewhat as a result of the detonation and soon dropped away. At the same time the forecastle, and then also the mid and aft ship were taken under a devastating fire, so that the hull side was soon holed like a sieve.[3]

In the torpedo room we could see nothing, and naturally wished to be kept in touch with the progress of the attack. At 5.05am we received the order from above: 'Clear starboard tube.' We waited with suspense for the order to release the torpedo. At 5.18am there appeared on the torpedo room telegraph the illuminated word 'Fire!' The torpedo was out and away. There followed some

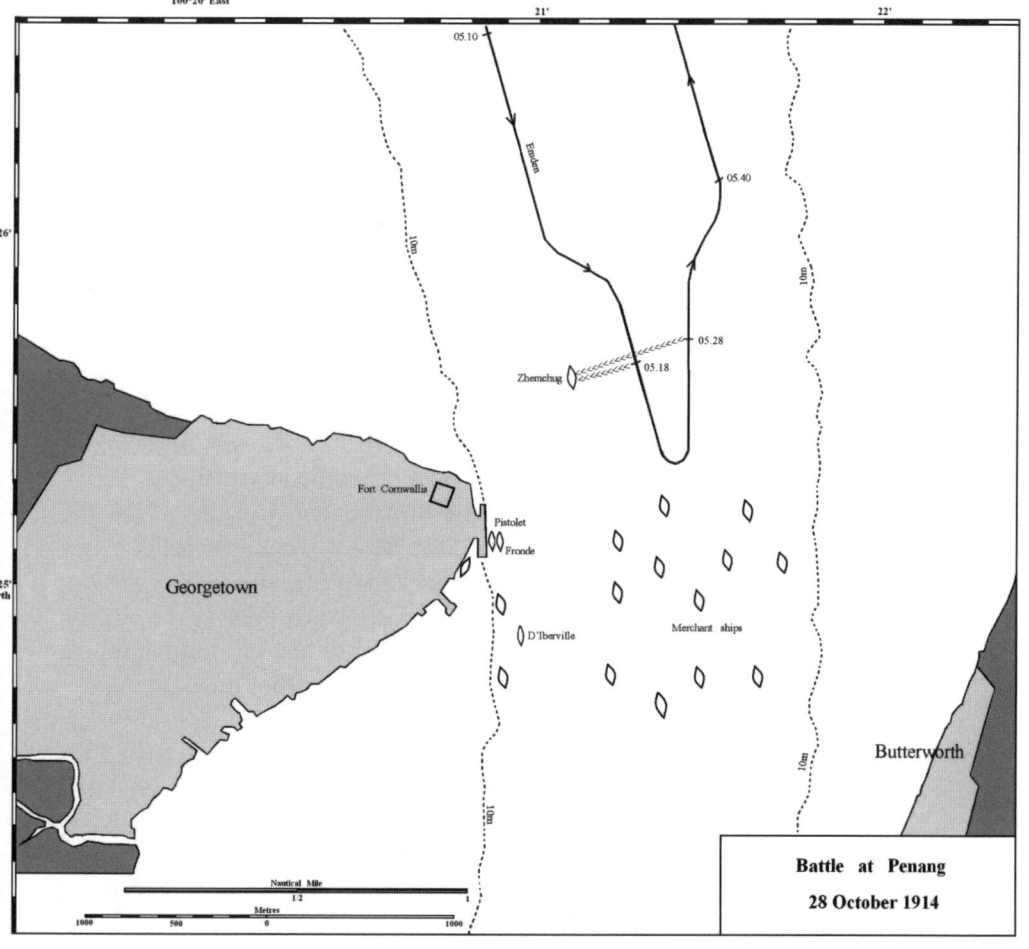

seconds of suspense and breathless listening. Then there was a dull report. There were cheers and general congratulations in the torpedo room.[4]

The Russian cruiser was heavily damaged by the torpedo and the aft boiler room, aft engine room, aft magazines, infirmary and commanders cabin were destroyed, and two guns were disabled. However, although *Zhemchug*'s powerful broadside of five 120mm cannon had been reduced she still had the capacity to seriously damage *Emden*.

> Onboard *Zhemchug* panic broke out and part of the crew rushed outside. Senior Officer Kulibin and Artillery Officer Rybaltovski knew how to restore relative order, but the men who came up to man the guns had no projectiles as the elevators did not supply them.
>
> Leitenant Rybaltovski himself opened fire from the stern gun and after several shots the indications were that two projectiles hit *Emden*. Michman Sipailov opened fire from the bow cannon and according to the recollections of the crew he attained a first shot hit which caused a fire. The second shot coincided with the direct hit of a German projectile which destroyed the gun and all the people located near it.[5]

Fregattenkapitän von Müller wrote:

> As soon as *Emden* had passed the enemy cruiser I turned the ship close ahead of the position of a steamer lying in the harbour. During this time *Emden* was fired upon by the bow gun of *Zhemchug* and apparently from another position that was not recognized in the gloom. *Emden* was not hit, the shells of *Zhemchug* went over the ship and some in part struck a merchant steamer.
>
> As it did not appear that *Zhemchug* would sink after the first torpedo hit, and it was not impossible for him to utilize his torpedo armament, I gave orders to fire a second torpedo after the turnabout was made. Whilst the artillery of the port side fired further at 5.28am a second torpedo struck *Zhemchug* under the command bridge. It resulted in a tremendous explosion, that totally ripped the ship apart and part was thrown high in the air, the entire cruiser was veiled in thick smoke. As this cleared away nothing was to be seen of the enemy ship other than a mast towering from the water.[6]
>
> We quickly reloaded the starboard tube and immediately came the order: 'Clear port tube'. The electric firing gear was connected and we waited for the order to fire. The *Emden* canted to one side, from which we inferred that we were turning. The electric signals showed: 'Ready!' We signalled back: 'Everything ready!' Shortly afterwards followed the order: 'Fire!' The torpedo rushed hissing from the tube. At once there was a fearful crash which also gave the *Emden* a considerable shock.

Rejoicing in the torpedo room! We greeted the noise and shock as proof that this shot had got home, probably in the magazine or torpedo room of the Russian, as the tremendous explosion was not otherwise explicable.[7]

Zhemchug was gone, taking with her 81 dead, and leaving 129 wounded, 7 of whom later died. During the battle *Emden* was also fired upon by several other vessels in the harbour, the French torpedoboat-destroyers *D'Iberville* and *Fronde*. According to reports their fire was inaccurate and in part their shells landed amongst the merchant ships. Nevertheless, Fregattenkapitän von Müller decided to be content with his success, citing a number of reasons. He was uncertain as to the position of the enemy torpedoboats, and would find it difficult to manoeuvre in the crowded harbour should they launch torpedoes at him. Although there were plenty of merchantmen present he would find it difficult to inspect each one before he ordered their crews to disembark if sinking was warranted. He was also uncertain if any superior forces were nearby, and should *Emden* come to grief the impression created by sinking *Zhemchug* would be greatly diminished. Therefore he steamed off to the north, but as it was becoming lighter he sighted the French *D'Iberville* in the harbour and decided to take her under fire. Before this could be accomplished, however, a vessel was sighted to the north of the harbour, approaching at high speed. Apparently atmospheric refraction caused the vessel to appear larger than it was and *Emden* opened fire at 50hm but after a few salvos the vessel turned away and was then recognised as a British Government boat. Fire was thereon ceased, but nevertheless she was already hit in the funnel.

Immediately thereafter a large ship was sighted to the north which because of the refraction was taken as a cruiser, however she turned out to be a merchant steamer. The newcomer was stopped near the navigation buoy and a cutter was sent across with a prize command to inspect her. It was the British steamer *Glen Turret*, which was detained from 06.50 to 07.00hrs. However scarcely was the cutter alongside than a new warship was sighted in a NNW direction, so that Fregattenkapitän von Müller released *Glen Turret* with nothing more than an apology to the crew of the Government vessel for firing on them, with the explanation that they were mistaken for a warship.

As the newly sighted vessel quickly approached she was made out as a French torpedoboat-destroyer, *Mousquet*. As the range reduced to 43hm the order to open fire was given. *Mousquet* turned away, but this only made her an easier target for *Emden*. The third salvo hit either a boiler or a steam pipe and around the middle of the boat there were great torrents of steam. *Mousquet* returned fire with a single gun and fired a torpedo, which however passed 400 to 600m ahead of *Emden*. As *Mousquet* began to sink by the bow, Fregattenkapitän von Müller ordered his gun crews to cease fire and then approached the boat from aft. Meanwhile the torpedoboat stood on its bow, seemingly standing on the bottom, and then disappeared beneath the waves. *Emden* sent two cutters to rescue the survivors but at first some of the French swam away, fearing for their lives. Allied propaganda had told them the Germans murdered their prisoners. Nevertheless one officer and thirty-five men were saved, of which twenty-five were wounded. Forty-two crew, including the brave captain, went down with the ship. Just after 08.00hr the cutters were hoisted aboard *Emden* and course was taken NW. Whilst *Emden* had been rescuing the French sailors the torpedoboat-destroyer *Fronde* had appeared, but held at great range. Now she followed *Emden* so that the latter increased speed to 21 knots, but the Frenchman tenaciously held contact until at around 09.00hrs *Emden* could make good her escape in a rainsquall. When towards 11.00hrs the weather again cleared nothing was to be seen of the torpedoboat-destroyer.

In September 1915 Captain 2nd Rank Cherkasov and Leitenant Kulibin faced a court martial charged with dereliction of duty. In sentencing them their flawless service records and awards from the Russo-Japanese War were taken into account, but they were still deprived of their rank, medals and insignia and were barred from naval service, forfeiting all rights and privileges. Cherkasov received a 3½ year sentence and Kulibin 1½ years, which were both commuted to service at the front. Both men distinguished themselves and were later restored in rank and awarded the St. George Cross. At a visit in 2003 President V. Putin reminded the Malaysians of the destruction of the Russian ship, and sacrifice of Russian lives.

After *Emden* departed Penang she went to the Nicobar Islands, where time was taken to bury some French sailors who had passed away from their wounds, with military honours. On 30 September *Emden* stopped the British freighter *Newburn*, to which the French prisoners were transferred before the steamer was released. *Emden* then spent some time coaling before checking on the Sunda Straits, however no merchant steamers were found. Fregattenkapitän von Müller now determined on a raid on the Cocos Islands group in the Indian Ocean. His reasons for this raid were the temporary interruption of telegraphic communications between Australia, Britain, India and South Africa; the destruction of the wireless station; a general unrest among the shipping to and from Australia; and a diversion to draw off the forces hunting *Emden* so as she could move her area of operations to the Gulf of Aden. Originally the raid was intended for 8 November, but unusual hourly messages were picked up between a warship and the shore station so the raid was postponed for a day. The ship was the armoured cruiser *Minotaur*, which had been called to the Cape of Good Hope as a revolt by Boers had broken out. Fregattenkapitän von Müller debated whether to delay a further day but decided that the British warship was far enough away, judging from the strength of her signals. The commander of *Emden* was also concerned about coaling and if conditions were suitable planned to coal at the Cocos Islands. A little after 06.00hrs on

9 November *Emden* anchored in Port Refuge, off Direction Island. No enemy ships were sighted and as soon as anchor was dropped the landing party went ashore under the direction of the I Offizier, Kapitänleutnant Mücke. They quickly set about their destructive work. The collier *Buresk* was also summoned to the island.

When *Buresk* was signalled by wireless the island wireless station asked, 'What code? What ship is that?' *Emden* did not answer and soon afterwards the station began to transmit the message, 'Strange ship off entrance,' which *Emden* immediately tried to jam. The message was repeated, this time preceded by an S.O.S. Then there was silence. A short time later a warship whose signal identification letters *Emden* had not previously heard called the island, but there was no answer as the landing party had destroyed the wireless station.

As chance would have it the great ANZAC convoy was just 50 nautical miles from the Cocos Islands early on the morning of 9 November. The convoy was transporting 1 Australian Imperial Force to the Middle East in twenty-eight transports, whilst ten other ships carried the New Zealand contingent, altogether a total of 20,000 men and 7,500 horses. The convoy was escorted by the British armoured cruiser *Minotaur*, the Australian light cruisers *Melbourne* and *Sydney*, and the Japanese armoured cruiser *Ibuki*, which mounted 12-inch cannon. On 8 November *Minotaur* was ordered to South Africa, leaving *Melbourne* in charge of the convoy. Upon receipt of the signal from the Cocos wireless station *Melbourne* increased speed and turned sharply towards the island, however her captain remembered his responsibility for the safety of the convoy and therefore resumed his station ahead of the transports. He then ordered *Sydney*, the escort nearest the islands, to raise steam and run to Cocos Islands. Although *Sydney* was an Australian warship, she was commanded by the Royal Naval officer Captain Glossop, who had been appointed Captain in the Royal Australian Navy in March 1913. By 07.00hrs *Sydney* had departed the convoy and was making 20 knots towards the island. At 09.15hrs she sighted *Emden* off South Keeling Island and, knowing he had a faster ship, Captain Glossop slowed to allow final preparations to be completed for the coming battle.

Meanwhile the Germans continued their work. Towards 09.00hrs a smoke cloud was sighted to the northwards, however it was presumed to come from *Buresk*. The crow's nest also incorrectly identified the approaching ship, which made much smoke. As towards 09.15hrs the landing party had showed no sign of returning Fregattenkapitän von Müller signalled them to hasten their work, and soon after the approaching ship was recognised as a warship.

> What followed now happened extraordinarily quickly, as the enemy warship was coming on at high speed–20 to 25 knots. I ordered steam up in all the boilers and repeated several times the recall for the landing party: then I gave

the orders 'Up anchor', 'Clear ship for battle', and 'Get up steam immediately to put on all possible speed.' By this time it was seen that the enemy ship had four funnels, and we guessed it was the English cruiser *Newcastle*; only in the afternoon did we discover that she was the Australian cruiser *Sydney*, a ship of a very similar type...

About 9.30 a.m. the landing party began to re-embark, but, with the enemy quickly approaching, it was seen to be impossible to get them on board before the battle began. Therefore, as soon as the anchor was weighed, I ordered full steam ahead and set the ship on a N.N.W. course so as to improve still further our favourable position with regard to the wind until the actual beginning of the battle. My object was to attempt to inflict on the enemy such damage by gunfire that her speed would be seriously lessened, and I might be able to bring on a torpedo action with some chance of success.[8]

As *Emden* took up a NNW course *Sydney*, which had been steering towards South Keeling Island, changed course to starboard and came straight at *Emden*. When the range had reduced to 11,900m *Sydney* again changed course to starboard to steer a slightly converging course. At about 09.40hrs as the range decreased to 90hm Fregattenkapitän von Müller ordered fire to be inaugurated. The first salvo went over and left of the target, the second went over, and the next two were short, but after that *Emden* began to hit *Sydney*.

That first salvo was excellently ranged along a rather extended line, but every shot fell within two hundred yards of *Sydney*. The next was better still, and for ten minutes *Sydney* moved through a hail of shell, though, just because of the narrow target she presented to shell arriving from so high an angle, only fifteen hits were actually made on her, and of those only five burst. It was during these early minutes that all her casualties occurred. Two shells from a closely bunched salvo hit the after control platform, and wounded all engaged there. Almost simultaneously a shell hit the rangefinder on the upper fore bridge, killing the operator and wrecking the instrument; if it had burst, it would probably have killed Captain Glossop and two more officers, but it passed harmlessly on through the screen and over the side. Other shells bursting inboard killed or wounded some of the crews of guns on the disengaged side, and set fire to some cordite charges lying near those guns; this fire was quickly extinguished. A shell that pierced the forecastle deck and exploded in the boys mess-deck caused some inconvenience but no loss of life.[9]

By 09.45hrs *Emden* was firing a salvo every ten seconds in an attempt to overwhelm *Sydney* before her superior armament could take effect.

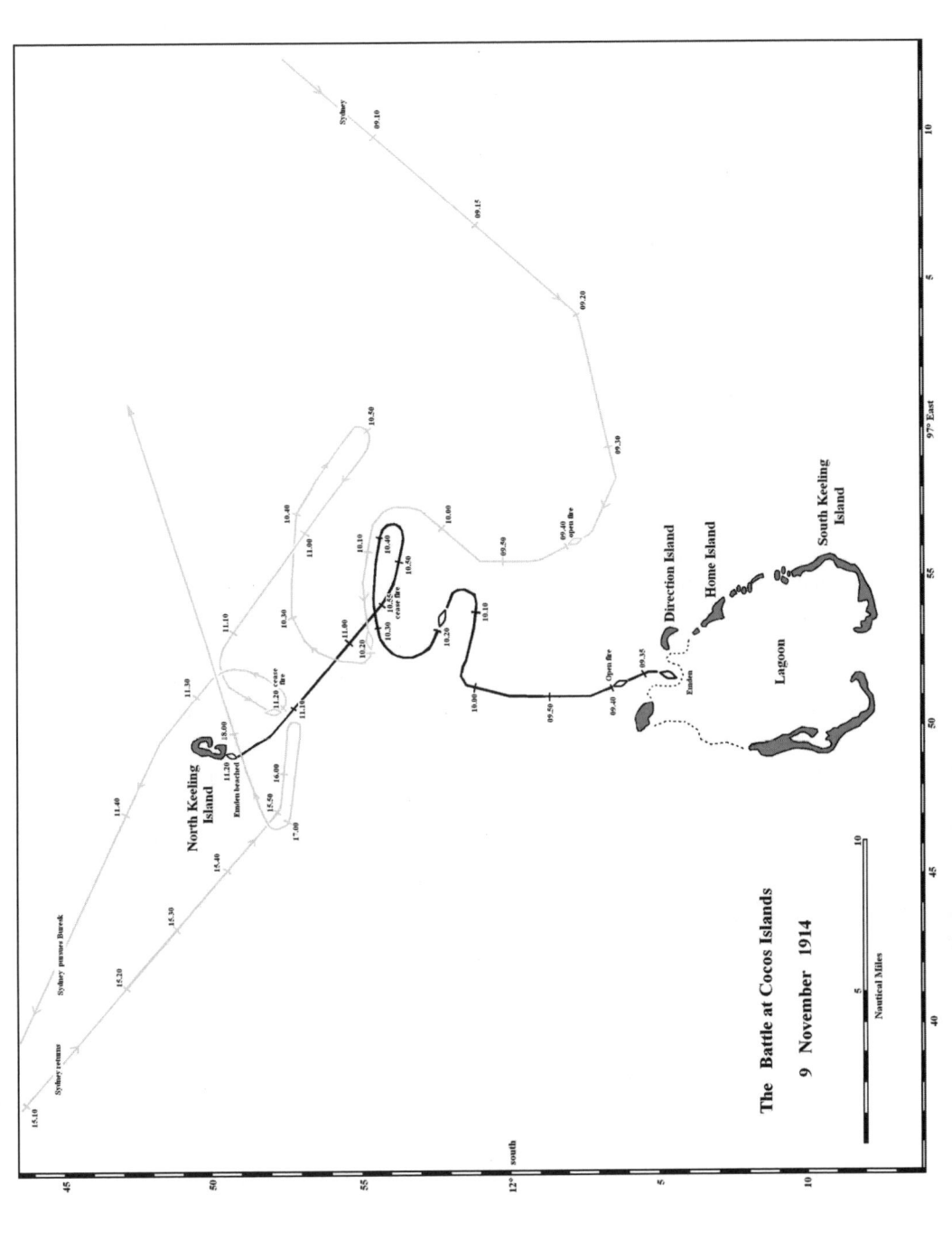

A short time after the beginning of the fight a strong flare-up was noticed on the *Sydney*'s main deck, probably the result of a lucky hit on some cordite which it set on fire.

The *Sydney* opened fire immediately after the *Emden*, having shortly before set her course parallel. At first she shot far over the *Emden*, and it was quite a long time before she got our range. I have since learnt the reason. With the second salvo of the *Emden* two very lucky hits were scored; one shell, which unfortunately did not explode, hit the forward range-finder station, destroyed the rangefinder, and killed the operator. A second shell burst in the after control station and wounded all its crew, an officer amongst them.[10]

Soon after fire was opened *Emden* altered course 2 points towards *Sydney*, to close the range, but *Sydney* altered away. Nevertheless once *Sydney* had got the range on *Emden* the German cruiser was quickly damaged and soon *Sydney* had gained fire superiority. The explosive effect of the British 6-inch shells was considerably more than the German 10.5cm shells, a fact that would cost the Germans dearly during the course of the war. *Sydney* also had 2-inch belt armour, whereas *Emden* had none, and as hits were registered the damage quickly began to accumulate. At 09.50hrs a shell destroyed *Emden*'s wireless room and then one exploded just ahead of the conning tower, putting the crew of the N°1 gun out of action and also some men in the lee of the conning tower. Then the electric command transmitter to the guns failed and with that all orders had to be transmitted through speaking tubes. This was therefore affected by the noise of battle and affected the rate of fire and spread of salvos. Then the steering gear in the conning tower failed as well as the helm telegraph and eventually the ship had to be steered using the engines. At 10.04hrs the forward funnel went over to port, affecting the draught to the boilers.

At 09.55hrs *Emden* had again turned towards the enemy. Around 10.00hrs it was learned that the hand steering had been jammed by a direct hit. A further hit near the N°4 gun ignited ammunition which started a strong fire under the poop deck. Because of the steering failure the ship meanwhile swung 8 points (90°) to starboard before the turn was checked using the screws. The port battery now came into action.

During this phase of the fight the range-finders failed. The fire of the port battery soon weakened also, probably because of the lack of ammunition and the serious casualties among the gun-crews and ammunition-carriers. The *Offizier*-in-charge of the range-finders and a Gunners *Maat*, who had been engaged in transmitting orders, were sent aft to help the guns, as they were of no further use in the conning-tower. Both of these men were killed later in the course of the fight. From the torpedo-room came the report that the torpedo-air-compressor was now out of action.[11]

As the artillery battle was going more and more against *Emden* Fregattenkapitän von Müller decided to again attempt a torpedo attack and therefore turned to port and reduced the range to 45hm. At this time the fire of *Sydney* was ragged and it was not possible for her to bring all her guns to bear at once, and she fired using independent fire instead of salvo fire. At 10.20hrs *Sydney* fired a torpedo which nevertheless failed to run the distance to *Emden*. Then *Sydney* altered course to starboard and opened the range and increased speed.

The fire of *Emden* had by now slackened and orders to the engines had to be passed over the deck and called down through the engine room skylight. Therefore manoeuvring became more difficult. Nevertheless *Emden* attempted to again close on *Sydney* but could get no closer than 50 to 55hm. The engines could only make revolutions for 19½ knots because two funnels had been shot away and one or two boilers had also failed. There was now no hope of causing *Sydney* further damage as meanwhile *Emden*'s gunfire had fallen away, and therefore to avoid further useless bloodshed Fregattenkapitän von Müller determined to put *Emden* aground on North Keeling Island. At 11.15hrs *Emden* was run up onto the reef as thoroughly as possible. Then the fires were drawn and the engine and boiler rooms were flooded, along with muntions rooms.

When *Emden* gave up her second attempt to gain torpedo range *Sydney* made a turn to starboard and followed *Emden* in a running battle to the northwest. By the time Captain Glossop realized *Emden*'s intention to beach herself it was too late to do anything about it, although he turned 8 points towards *Emden* and maintained a vigorous fire until after *Emden* was beached. Then *Sydney* described a complete circle and headed off to pursue the collier *Buresk*. When the collier was caught she was dutifully scuttled.

Meanwhile aboard *Emden* the cannon were rendered useless by throwing the breech-blocks overboard, the sights were destroyed and torpedo aiming gear was thrown overboard. All the remaining secret papers and signal books were destroyed and the torpedo room was flooded. The wounded were tended as well as was possible.

> About 4 p.m. the *Sydney* was again sighted to the westward. As she had two boats in tow, we imagined that she intended taking the survivors on board. When a fairly long distance from the *Emden* the boats were cast loose, and the *Sydney* steamed past the *Emden*'s stern at a distance of about 4,000m, As she had international signals flying I sent a Morse message by flag: 'No signal-book aboard', for our signal-books had been burnt. When the *Sydney* had passed our stern and lay aft on our starboard quarter, she opened fire again unexpectedly with several salvoes, by which several of my men were killed or wounded, and fresh fires were started. I again gave the crew leave to abandon ship if they could swim and wanted to, as I did not know how long the *Sydney* would go on firing, and this seemed to be the only possibility of escape. A

number of the crew went overboard; some reached the island, some were drowned in the attempt, some were afterwards dragged back on board. As the *Emden* was now incapable of fighting, and lay a helpless wreck on a coral reef, I ordered a white flag to be shown in token that the rest of the crew surrendered, and at the same time had the ensign, which was still flying at our main-mast head, hauled down and burnt. Thereupon the *Sydney* ceased fire.[12]

Captain Glossop excused himself by saying that he twice questioned *Emden* 'Do you surrender?' to which no satisfactory answer was received and therefore he opened fire, killing twenty men in the process. 'I can, I think, say that in his place I should not have behaved so, but that I should have sent a boat to the *Emden*, probably under a flag of truce. I had also the impression that the whole transaction was later on very painful to Captain Glossop himself, and that he had let himself be persuaded into the affair mainly by his first officer.'[13] Apparently Glossop did show some remorse: 'It makes me feel almost like a murderer', he said.[14]

During the battle *Sydney* had lost three men killed and thirteen wounded. *Emden*'s losses were: killed, drowned or succumbed later to wounds, 134 men, and a further 65 wounded. During her three-month cruise her engines had made 10 million revolutions for 30,000 nautical miles. She had destroyed 16 merchant ships for a total of 70,825 gross registered tonnes, but more importantly had severely disrupted vital sea communications. *Sydney* had used the approved tactics of the day: to stand off using superior speed and use a superior armament to reduce the enemy before closing. Even though *Emden* had been within effective range her inferior armament had been insufficient to cause decisive damage against a more powerful and more modern opponent. Under these circumstances the meritorious and brave performance of her crew could do little to save her.

It was not until 11.40hrs the following day that *Sydney* returned to *Emden* and began embarking the survivors. Many men, both aboard the German cruiser and on North Keeling Island, had died during the night. The wounded were eventually landed in Colombo, Ceylon, where they were taken to hospital. The wounded were eventually interned in Australia, whilst the unwounded were taken to a prison camp in Malta, being repatriated only in 1920. The wreck of *Emden* remained on the reef at North Keeling Island, and was partly dismantled and salvaged in the 1950's. Many parts of the wreck still remain on the reef today.

The landing party under command of the I Offizier was able to make their escape from Direction Island in the schooner *Ayesha*, and eventually made their way through the Middle East and back to Germany.

Unlike *Emden*, the small cruiser *Königsberg* did not immediately go to service abroad after being commissioned, but served with the Reconnaissance Forces of the High Sea Fleet. In the spring of 1914 the Admiralstab issued instructions for fitting out *Königsberg* as Station Ship for the waters of German East Africa, to replace the gunboat *Geier*, which was sent to southern seas. The commander,

Fregattenkapitän Looff, hoisted his flag and pennant on 1 April. On 28 April she ran out of Wilhelmshaven and after stopping at several Mediterranean ports and a brief co-operation with the Mediterranean Division she went via Suez and Aden to arrive in Dar-es-Salam on 5 June, where the commander took over business as Station Senior Offizier.

So as not to be blockaded in the capital, Fregattenkapitän Looff took *Königsberg* to sea before the declaration of war and on 5 August around 22.00hrs he received a report from the wireless station at Dar-es-Salam about the declaration of war by Great Britain on the German Reich. The following day *Königsberg* captured the British steamer *City of Winchester* in the Gulf of Aden, which was later scuttled on 11 August.

Whilst the British sea forces initially supposed that *Königsberg* was on the coast of German East Africa and therefore searched the bays and harbours there, the sojourn in the Gulf of Aden had paralysed navigation and had delayed the transfer of an expeditionary corps from India against the German colony, and had allowed time for the mobilization of Imperial colonial troops on the northern border in defensive positions. The cessation of merchant traffic and the shortage of coal, however, now forced *Königsberg* to move her theatre of operations. Fregattenkapitän Looff determined to search the waters off Madagascar as there was insufficient coal to travel to South African waters, but neither a steamer with coal nor a military target could be found. After coaling from the auxiliary *Somali* the cruiser ran into one of the reaches of the river Rufiji, which had been surveyed briefly before by the survey ship *Möwe*, for necessary overhaul work. On 3 September *Königsberg* ran into the Kikunja arm, whose bar was only passable at spring tide. They anchored 10 nautical miles upstream of the Government Station at Ssalala. By 18 September *Königsberg* had enough supplies and coal for another appearance in the Indian Ocean. On Saturday 19 September the coast watch station south of Dar-es-Salam reported smoke off Zanzibar and as this cruiser had continually been sighted along the coast during the previous two weeks, it would now probably be at anchor off Zanzibar for material replenishment.

The British protected cruiser *Pegasus*, under the command of Commander Ingles, along with the cruisers *Hyacinth* and *Astraea*, formed the British Cape of Good Hope squadron under Rear Admiral King-Hall, which had been searching for *Königsberg* since 31 July when they had lost the German ship in the dark and rain squalls off Dar-es-Salam. Now *Pegasus* lay at anchor off Zanzibar for boiler cleaning and engine repairs.

During the afternoon of 19 September *Königsberg* negotiated the mouth of the Rufiji at high water and during the night set course for the southern entrance to Zanzibar harbour. The commander of *Somali*, Oberleutnant zur See der Reserve Herm, was seconded for duty as pilot. Off the southern entrance an armed auxiliary was encountered and passed just 600m distant without the German cruiser being observed. Although all the light buoys and lights off Zanzibar were extinguished *Königsberg* successfully found and negotiated the southern entrance and passed close to the guard ship, an armed tender, formerly the German *Helmuth*, without the latter raising the alarm.

Fregattenkapitän Looff wrote:

> Although we are through the entrance to Zanzibar there are many invisible reefs and strong currents which at night are extremely difficult to navigate, but *Königsberg* still manages to arrive south of the roadstead in darkness.
>
> Soon the rays of light enable us to distinguish an English two funnelled cruiser at anchor under the land next to Ras Shangami. In the weak light she looks like *Astraea* but as the light grows stronger I perceive her as *Pegasus*.[15]

Pegasus lay 200 metres off shore at anchor, with no steam in her boilers and was completely surprised. *Königsberg* lay under the cover of darkness against the western heavens.

At 05.10hrs *Königsberg* raised her flag and opened fire at a range of 70hm. After a short time *Pegasus* replied, and thick black smoke was seen emitting from both funnels as the British cruiser tried to rapidly get steam up. Nevertheless after three salvos *Königsberg* had the range of her adversary and began scoring hits. Soon a large explosion was observed on *Pegasus*'s forecastle, whist another hit broke off the forward funnel and the ship was on fire in several places. The forward 4-inch gun was wrecked and most of the gun crew were killed. Although it is reported that *Pegasus* fired for only 8 minutes, *Königsberg* continued the battle for 40 minutes with one pause:

> This pause was when the battery commander, Oberleutnant zur See Apel, reported the enemy were showing a white flag, which he had seen through the artillery rangefinder. Due to dense smoke covering the flag and the calmness of the day I am unable to see the white flag and decide to give the order for further firing. A South African newspaper article later confirmed that the white flag had been raised.[16]

When *Königsberg* ceased fire *Pegasus* did not immediately sink, but lay with a strong list over to port. Of her crew of 234 officers and men 35 were immediately killed, and 10 died subsequently, and there were 59 wounded. During an attempt to tow her to be beached she sank, leaving just the masts showing above water.

Fregattenkapitän Looff wrote:

> The rescue of *Pegasus*'s wounded could not be accomplished by *Königsberg*, which I still regret to this day. However after we ceased fire numerous small boats could be seen setting out from shore for *Pegasus*, so that the wounded would not go down with the ship. It was also well known that there was a large hospital in Zanzibar.[17]

During the battle *Königsberg* was not hit, however she did suffer splinter damage but suffered no casualties.

After ceasing fire on *Pegasus*, *Königsberg* drew close inshore and turned to starboard, whereby fire was opened on the new wireless station. Two of the four masts were brought down and there were casualties amongst the Askari soldiers. Then *Königsberg* began retracing her steps out the southern entrance of the harbour. As the German cruiser withdrew barrels were thrown over the stern to simulate laying mines. *Königsberg* then steered to Dar-es-Salam and from there back to the Rufiji River. With the afternoon tide she passed over the bar, which was impassable at low water. Luckily she caught the spring tide, otherwise she would have had to wait another 12 days outside the Rufiji River, in a completely exposed position. *Königsberg* had also suffered engine damage. A crosshead of one of the main engines was broken and would need to be removed and taken to workshops in Dar-es-Salam for repair. Transport of the engine parts overland and back would be difficult and require time. In the meantime the Germans fortified some of the river entrances on the Rufiji delta.

Once *Pegasus* was sunk in Zanzibar harbour the British conducted a systematic search of the coastal areas of the German colony. They also brought in the powerful, modern light cruisers *Chatham*, *Weymouth* and *Dartmouth* to search for and destroy *Königsberg*. On 19 October *Chatham* discovered the German East African Line steamer *Präsident* in the harbour of Lindi and a search of her revealed documents referring to the dispatch of coal to the Rufiji Delta. On 30 October a landing party from this cruiser found the berth of *Königsberg* and *Somali* by recognising the tips of their masts.

The British cruisers conducted a bombardment of *Königsberg* on 3 November but the only result was a hit on the auxiliary *Somali*, which caused a fire necessitating scuttling the collier 4 days later. The bombardment forced a precautionary move. After a short stay a few thousand metres upriver, on 5 November *Königsberg* moved further upstream and anchored in the Ssimba-Uranga arm. A new 'Section Delta' was set up on the river mouth coastal post and was fitted out with a 6cm cannon, machineguns and light arms. They would attempt to hamper the approach of the enemy. A torpedo tube of *Königsberg* was mounted on the Kikunja arm.

Fregattenkapitän Looff recognised that there was no chance of breaking through the blockade line. Thus it only remained to tie down as many enemy naval forces as possible. On 10 November the British tried in vain to blockade the Ssimba-Uranga-Arm by sinking the coal steamer *Newbridge* there. On 18 December *Königsberg* moved still further upstream along the Komboni and Bumba arms and on 14 April 1915 moved for the last time to the upper reach of the Kikunja arm. The numerous attacks by the British warships on *Königsberg* and 'Section Delta' had so far been unsuccessful, and the draughts of the large warships did not allow them to penetrate into the delta arms.

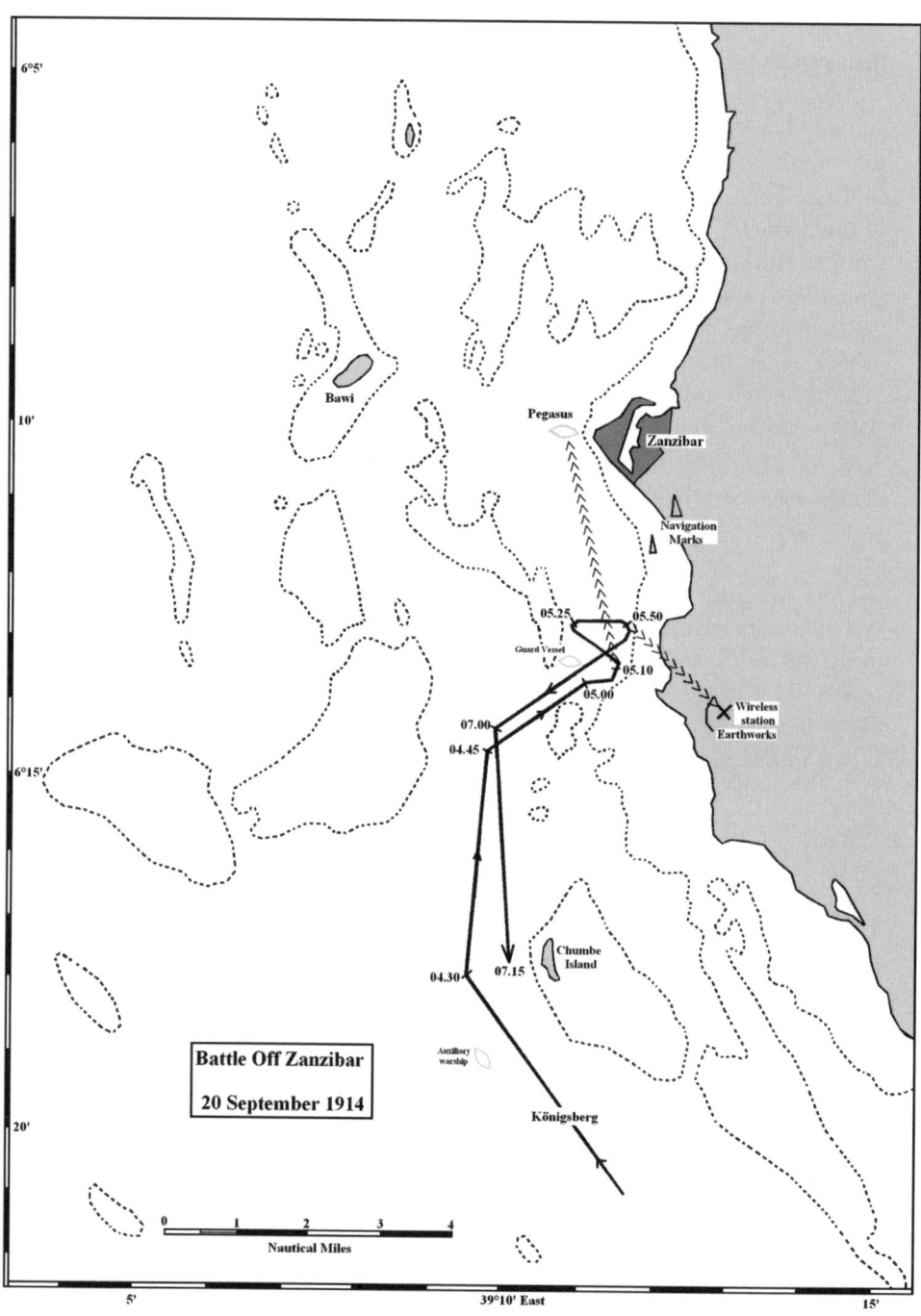

Meanwhile the supply ship *Rubens* was dispatched from Germany on 18 February, and reached Mansa Bay on 14 April 1915. Once again the shadow of *Magdeburg* was cast over proceedings. The British had incepted and decoded wireless messages about the arrival of *Rubens* and the cruiser *Hyacinth* intercepted her 2 miles off the entrance to Mansa Bay, at Tanga in German East Africa. The commander of *Rubens*, Oberleutnant zur See der Reserve Christiansen, was determined that his ship and her valuable supplies would not fall into Allied hands and he made a run into the bay without a pilot. *Hyacinth* opened fire and hit *Rubens* three times. Oberleutnant zur See d. R. Christiansen opened the sea valves to scuttle the ship and set the deck cargo of lumber on fire. An attempt to board *Rubens* was repulsed by machinegun fire from ashore, and this is perhaps the reason that *Hyacinth* opened fire on the life-boats of *Rubens* as they fled, wounding Oberleutnant zur See der Reserve Christiansen and two men. The cargo of supplies and munitions was not destroyed, but was later recovered, however this came too late to resupply *Königsberg*.

On the 4/5 June the small Government steamer *Wami*, which had been fitted with a torpedo tube from *Königsberg*, failed in a perilous mission against the British ships anchored near Mafia Island, and became stuck fast in the shallows. Beginning in May British aircraft had begun to drop bombs and direct artillery fire, but aboard *Königsberg* two guns were provisionally converted for antiaircraft use. Despite having only thirty shrapnel shells to employ, on 5 May an aircraft was shot down.

In mid-June 1915 the monitors *Severn* and *Mersey* arrived in East Africa, where with their small draughts and better combat capabilities they could be used more effectively against *Königsberg*. On 6 July a combined attack was mounted on *Königsberg*. It came as no surprise and all the Germans, both ashore and aboard *Königsberg*, who had meanwhile reduced her crew to bolster colonial troops, were relieved that the time of suspense was over. At 04.15hrs on 6 July the monitors *Severn* and *Mersey* weighed anchor and proceeded over the bar into the Kikunja arm of the Rufiji River. The monitors were anchored bow and stern and at 06.30hrs opened fire on *Königsberg*. The monitors were engaged by the shore posts and returned the fire. At 06.30hrs *Weymouth* attempted to pass over the bar but stuck fast for a time and was taken under small arms fire. One of the attendant whalers was hit by a shell fired from a 37mm revolver cannon. After getting free *Weymouth* anchored a short time later. The light cruiser *Pyramus*, a sistership of *Pegasus*, followed in her wake. *Weymouth* supported the monitors by taking the German observation position on Pemba Hill under fire with her 6-inch cannon. Meanwhile the light cruiser *Hyacinth* and the Australian light cruiser *Pioneer*, also a sistership of *Pegasus*, took the shore positions of the Ssimba-Uranga mouth under fire.

To make *Königsberg* difficult to observe Fregattenkapitän Looff had camouflaged her by painting her and hanging green fabric and bushes over the ship. The appearance of the monitors came as a surprise to the Germans as they had not previously been sighted, and Fregattenkapitän Looff noted that their appearance greatly increased the British chances of success. Nevertheless, at 07.40hrs, *Königsberg* achieved a hit on the forward 6-inch gun of *Mersey*, putting it out of action and setting fire to some ammunition. However, the ship was saved when crewmen threw the burning munitions overboard. After the monitors had opened fire their fall of shot had been impossible to spot from the aircraft carrying out observation duty, but nevertheless towards 08.00hrs they achieved their first direct hit on *Königsberg*, forward to starboard on the protective shield of a forward gun, which killed two men. A second hit struck the starboard side of the command bridge and put the large rangefinder and its crew out of action. Splinters from this shell wounded those on the command bridge, including the commander, navigation *Offizier* and signal rating. The third hit struck the *Offiziers*' galley, destroying it. A fourth shell struck the middle deck without essentially causing damage. The direction of *Königsberg*'s artillery was difficult, and several times there were interruptions, once when the telephone connection to the observation station was cut by shellfire.

Meanwhile, at 12.30hrs, the monitor *Severn* was signalled to proceed further upstream, and at 12.50hrs was rewarded with the sight of *Königsberg*'s topmast. Towards 15.30hrs the monitors were ordered to retire and at 18.00hrs joined the flagship near Koma Island. During the rear-march the vessels were again taken under fire from ashore but safely crossed the bar and retired. On *Mersey* there were four dead and four wounded, and the bow 6-inch gun was put out of action. *Severn* was not hit and suffered no losses. The losses of *Königsberg* amounted to four dead and ten badly wounded, and one slightly wounded. Approximately 800 projectiles had landed in the immediate vicinity of *Königsberg*, and many others had impacted up to 2,000m away. On the other hand *Königsberg* had restricted her fire to that of just two cannon for some time, to preserve ammunition. Although the ship remained fully seaworthy and combat ready, the reduction of crew and blockade meant that she would not be going anywhere in a hurry.

Five days later on Sunday 11 July, the monitors renewed their attack to the same plan. At 11.45hrs the monitors, with reinforced crews, crossed the bar and proceeded upriver. *Weymouth* and *Pyramus* followed them into the river, *Pyramus* moving 3 miles upriver, whilst *Hyacinth* and *Pioneer* again took the Ssimba-Uranga mouth under fire.

The monitors approached 900m closer than on 6 July, hoping for a more effective fire. At 12.00hrs *Königsberg* opened fire on them as they came into range, the fire being under the direction of the observers on Pemba Hill. At 12.15hrs the two monitors replied, their fire being directed once again by two aircraft. On this day the British fire was better and within 10 minutes *Königsberg* lay in a hail of shells. At 12.52hrs a shell landed forward of the conning tower and put both forward guns and their crews out of action. Another shell detonated immediately behind the conning tower and splinters

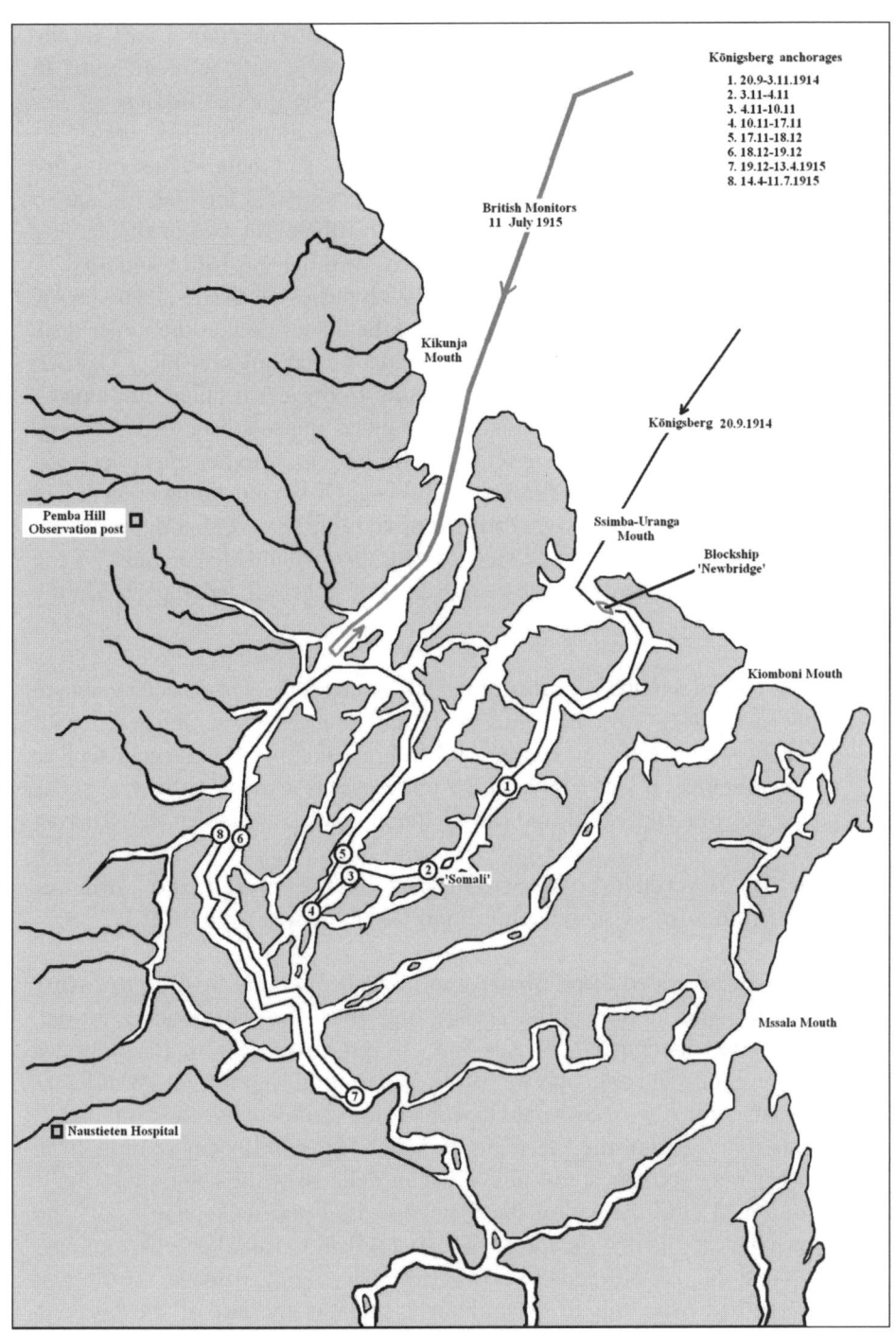

Battle on the Rufiji Delta 11 July 1915

entering the conning tower badly wounded Fregattenkapitän Looff in the stomach, upper arm and forearms. Soon there were only three aft guns in action, however their munitions chamber had to be flooded because of fire danger. Burning ammunition caused heavy losses amongst their crews. At 12.52hrs the centre funnel was struck and went over and there was a serious fire aft. One the last acts of one of the 10.5cm guns converted for Flak use was to shoot down one of the British aircraft. Shortly afterwards two of the serving crew were torn apart by a 6-inch shell, whilst the other was badly wounded.

Towards 13.40hrs *Königsberg* ceased fire. With the loss of almost all gun crews, the strong fire aft, the flooded magazine and the devastation on the upper deck further battle was impossible. The commander's final order to the I Offizier, Kapitänleutnant Koch, was to scuttle the ship to prevent it falling into enemy hands. Firstly the crew evacuated all the wounded and then two torpedo heads were detonated so that *Königsberg* settled on the bottom, with her upper deck still above water and her flag and pennant still flying. Of the remaining crew of 230 men, 19 had been killed, 21 were badly wounded and 24 were slightly wounded.

On this day *Mersey* was hit twice, causing two wounded. For most of the battle *Königsberg* concentrated on *Severn* and one of her officers reported in the Times newspaper:

> For seventeen minutes we came under *Königsberg*'s fire without being able to reply. *Königsberg* soon had our range and our deck was showered with splinters, so that each and every man had himself a piece of German shell as a remembrance. It was a wonder no-one was seriously hurt. Several shells penetrated our upper deck and caused much devastation so that the situation was critical. With but a few more hits and in all probability it was finished with us. Nevertheless we were helped by the aircraft and with our seventeenth salvo we scored a hit. Soon we had scored twelve hits.[18]

After *Königsberg* ceased firing *Mersey* approached closer and fired up to twenty salvos at the hull of the sunken cruiser, and after that the monitors retired. *Severn*'s officer continued: 'Towards 8pm we returned to Tirene Bay. It was a beautiful evening, and although we had laid a beautiful ship to ruin, in different circumstances the *Königsberg* would have made mincemeat of us in five minutes.'[19]

It was not over for the Germans though. The ten 10.5cm cannon from *Königsberg* were recovered and put to use in defence of the colony, a struggle that continued until the end of the war. Likewise Fregattenkapitän Looff and his surviving crew joined the forces of General Paul Lettow-Vorbeck, and only surrendered on 23 November 1918. Although engine damage meant that *Königsberg* had been run to ground early, she was the last of the German cruisers on foreign stations to be accounted for. The wreck survived and despite being partially salvaged between 1960 and 1963 the remains still survive in the mud of the Rufiji River. Many of her guns decorate parts of East Africa.

Chapter 8

The Skagerrak Battle, 31 May to 1 June 1916

From late on 31 May 1916 to early on 1 June 1916 what was then the greatest sea battle in history occurred in the sea area off the Skagerrak, off the coast of Jutland in Denmark. To the Germans it was the Skagerrak Battle, to the British the Battle of Jutland. After initially conceding defeat the British claimed that they did not lose the Battle of Jutland, whereas the Germans claimed victory in the Skagerrak Battle. After all, the two countries were engaged in a life and death struggle and we could not expect them to agree on anything, even the name of the battle.

After the defeat in the Battle on the Dogger Bank on 24 January 1915, the commander of the High Sea Fleet, Admiral von Ingenohl, and his Chief of Staff, Vizeadmiral Eckermann, were transferred to positions of less responsibility. In February 1915 Admiral von Ingenohl was appointed to the staff of the Baltic Naval Station, and at the same time commander of Kiel fortress, positions from which he retired in August 1915. Vizeadmiral Eckermann was appointed chief of the I Battle Squadron. Admiral von Ingenohl's successor was Admiral von Pohl. Throughout the remainder of 1915 the High Sea Fleet carried numerous sweeps into the North Sea but the coastal raids of 1914 were not repeated and there was no contact with British forces. In August the I Battle Squadron and I and II Reconnaissance Groups went to the Baltic to carry out an assault on the Russian held Gulf of Riga. During this operation the cruiser *Moltke* was torpedoed by the British submarine *E1*, and was under repair until 20 September 1915.

On 8 January 1916 Admiral von Pohl was taken seriously ill and was admitted to hospital in Berlin. There he was diagnosed with cancer and he passed away on 23 February 1916. He was replaced as commander of the High Sea Fleet by the hitherto commander of the III Squadron, Vizeadmiral Reinhard Scheer, on 18 January. Vizeadmiral Scheer was a more aggressive commander than his predecessor and he immediately began drawing up plans for future strategies and operations. Vizeadmiral Scheer's program called for more aggressive advances by the High Sea Fleet, with coordinated U-boat operations, attacks on military targets in Britain by airships and unrestricted U-boat warfare. The first offensive operation took place on the night of 10–11 February 1916 when

German torpedoboats advanced to the Dogger Bank and sank the British minesweeper sloop *Arabis*. At a conference on 23 February the Kaiser approved and endorsed Vizeadmiral Scheer's program but reserved approval for unrestricted U-boat warfare, giving as his reason that the effect on America and her possible entry to the war needed to be given further consideration. The next operation was an advance by the I and II AG in the Hoofden, the sea area between Holland and the English coast, with the objective of trapping the British sea forces that were frequently sighted there. Unfortunately there was no enemy contact during this operation.

The next operation of this Spring campaign was the bombardment of Yarmouth and Lowestoft on 25 April. This raid was practically a repeat of the operation of November 1914 and once again the small cruiser *Stralsund* would lay mines off the coast. The intention of the bombardment was to force a counter action by the British naval forces whereby the German forces would have an opportunity to attack them. On this occasion Vizeadmiral Hipper was on sick leave because he was suffering from sciatica, and leadership of the I Reconnaissance Group (I AG) was entrusted to Kontreadmiral Boedicker, who was normally commander of the II AG.

At 10.50hrs on 24 April the I AG weighed anchor and steered down the Jade. The weather was clear with bright sunshine and a light south-easterly breeze. The group headed west and then took a northerly diversion around the area the British had mined in 1915. However, in spite of this precaution at 15.48hrs the flagship *Seydlitz* ran onto a mine. There was a powerful vibration and a 15 metre high column of water rose into the sky. The explosion was on the starboard side at the level of the broadside torpedo room and compartments XIV to XVI below the armoured deck filled with water, but luckily no torpedo warheads detonated even though three were rent apart. A total of 1,600 tonnes of water flooded into the ship and the draught was increased by 1.6 metres. The area struck was unfortunately not protected by the torpedo bulkhead, but the ship's speed could be maintained. *Seydlitz* at first took course west, then south and finally east and circumnavigated the dangerous area before returning to Wilhelmshaven. Vizeadmiral Scheer signalled the cruisers to continue the operation and therefore Kontreadmiral Boedicker and his staff transferred from *Seydlitz* to the relatively new cruiser *Lützow*. At 05.13hrs on 25 April the German battlecruisers opened fire on Lowestoft and then Yarmouth and ceased fire at 05.44hrs. Meanwhile Commodore Tyrwhitt's cruisers *Conquest*, *Cleopatra* and *Penelope* had approached Lowestoft from the south and they were taken under fire at 05.50hrs by *Lützow* and *Derfflinger*. In 6 minutes *Lützow* fired ten salvos and a total of thirty-three shells of 30.5cm calibre. *Conquest* was hit five times and was severely damaged with hits on the superstructure and a funnel, suffering in total twenty-three dead and thirteen wounded. Despite having her speed reduced to 20 knots she was able to escape to the south. Later that day

Penelope was hit by a torpedo from the U-boat *UB18* and was badly damaged, so that two out of three of Tyrwhitt's cruisers were put out of action. After that *UB18*, under the command of Oberleutnant zur See Steinbrinck, sank the British submarine *E22*. The German cruisers retired back to Wilhelmshaven and at 19.30hrs the I AG anchored on Wilhelmshaven Roads.

As Vizeadmiral Scheer returned from the Lowestoft raid he received a telegram informing him of the German government's decision to continue U-boat warfare according to 'prize regulations', and not to the unlimited format that he desired. Vizeadmiral Scheer would not allow his U-boats to operate under these restrictions and he decided that instead of conducting merchant warfare the U-boats should be used to support the fleet undertakings. The next operation was to be against the coastal town of Sunderland, which was only a short distance from Vice Admiral Beatty's battlecruiser base at Rosyth. The operational order ran in part: 'The bombardment of Sunderland by our cruisers is intended to compel the enemy to send forces against us. For the attack on the advancing enemy the High Sea Fleet forces to be south of Dogger Bank, and the U-boats to be stationed for attack off the East coast of England.'[1] The plan called for U-boats to be stationed off the British bases and for extensive aerial reconnaissance by airships. It would also await the completion of repairs to *Seydlitz*. The operation was tentatively planned for 17–18 May 1916.

Now a series of setbacks occurred that delayed the implementation of the operation. On 23 May *Seydlitz* underwent a flooding test which revealed that the repairs to the mine hit of 24 April were not water-tight. The transverse and wing passage bulkheads leaked so much that it was necessary for the cruiser to return to the dockyard for further work, which would continue until 28 May. On 28 May Vizeadmiral Hipper wrote:

> Today the weather is so bad, no air reconnaissance, that the fleet must still wait for their operation. Tomorrow or the day after tomorrow is the last date that the U-boats could support the operation, since they have been on their stations since 22 and should return on 31. One of the main purposes of our cruisers in the North Sea is to get the English fleet to run out of their various harbours across our positioned U-boats which should bring about an attack. Whether this is successful is another question.[2]

Towards midday on 29 May *Seydlitz* reported she was again combat ready; however, the following day the wind turned north-easterly, precluding airship reconnaissance and was expected to remain thus for several days. Therefore Vizeadmiral Scheer decided to employ an alternate plan that did not rely on aerial reconnaissance. On 31 May the cruisers would harass merchant shipping off the Skagerrak, hopefully luring out parts of the British Grand Fleet, where they could be attacked by U-boats and be caught piecemeal by the High Sea Fleet, which would follow and support the cruisers.

For this operation a group of young German *Offiziers*, Wireless *Offiziers* and *Offiziers* of the Commander of Reconnaissance Forces's staff, devised a brilliant deception. They put forward the suggestion that the fleet flagship, SMS *Friedrich der Große*, and the wireless station of the III Entrance to Wilhelmshaven exchange call signs and that wireless messages to and from the flagship be passed through the III Entrance station. This would induce the British to believe the main body of the High Sea Fleet had remained in Wilhelmshaven and would facilitate Vizeadmiral Scheer springing his trap on any detached portion of the Grand Fleet. Any wireless direction bearings taken would also locate the call sign in Wilhelmshaven. This deception worked perfectly and when questioned British Naval Intelligence gave the location of the German flagship as in the Jade. The first Admiral Jellicoe knew of the presence of the High Sea Fleet was when *Southampton* reported them during the battle. Had Admiral Jellicoe known of the presence of the German main body the battle could have progressed differently.

At 02.00hrs on 31 May 1916 the weather was unsettled. There was a NNE wind, it was cloudy with rain showers and there was a moderate swell. The I Reconnaissance Group weighed anchor and ran out to sea in accordance with Secret Order Gg 2490/0 of 28 May. The group proceeded down the Jade in the following order: *Lützow*, Kapitän zur See Harder, *Derfflinger*, Kapitän zur See Hartog, *Seydlitz*, Kapitän zur See Egidy, *Moltke*, Kapitän zur See von Karpf, and *von der Tann*, Kapitän zur See Zenker. The I AG was preceded by the II AG under Kontreadmiral Boedicker, with *Frankfurt*, *Pillau*, *Elbing* and *Wiesbaden*, and was escorted by the II, VI and IX Torpedoboote Flottilles, led by II FdT Kommodore Heinrich aboard *Regensburg*. About 1½ hours later they were followed by the main body of the High Sea Fleet, the III Battle Squadron and the I Battle Squadron, which were joined from the Elbe River by the II Battle Squadron that consisted of the older pre-dreadnought battleships. The main body was escorted by the IV AG under the command of Kommodore von Reuter and consisting of the small cruisers *Stettin*, *München*, *Frauenlob*, and *Stuttgart* and with *Hamburg* attached. The torpedoboat forces were under command of the I FdT Kommodore Michelsen aboard *Rostock*, and consisted of the 1 TBHF, III Flottille, V Flottille and VII Flottille. Therefore the German forces comprised 16 modern battleships, 6 old pre-dreadnought battleships, 5 *Große Kreuzer* (battlecruisers), 11 small cruisers and 61 torpedoboats. Against these German forces was arranged the powerful Grand Fleet with 29 dreadnought-type battleships, 9 battlecruisers, 8 armoured cruisers, 26 light cruisers and 79 destroyers and flotilla leaders.

The British were aware of the increased U-boat activity in the North Sea and on the evening of 30 May intercepted the wireless signal for operation

'Gg 2490' (Completely Secret 2490). The Admiralty consequently knew an operation was about to occur, although not the magnitude, and ordered the Grand Fleet and Battlecruiser Fleet to rendezvous off the Skagerrak entrance. Therefore at 23.30hrs on 30 May, or 00.30hrs on 31 May according to middle European time, and 2½ hours before the Germans, the Grand Fleet put to sea and proceeded towards their ordered rendezvous. Some of the U-boats sighted various battlecruisers and battleships putting to sea but no successful attacks were carried out and the value of the intelligence was not appreciated by Vizeadmiral Scheer and his staff. He therefore did not alter his plan and thought that it would be possible to bring a part of the enemy fleet to action. For their part the British thought that Vizeadmiral Scheer remained in Wilhelmshaven, as that is where the call sign for *Friedrich der Große*, 'DZ', was located.

During the course of the day the German cruisers advanced to the north, steering to the west of Helgoland and passing Horns Reef light vessel 22 nautical miles to the east at noon. Both the British and the Germans continued their advances and at 15.15hrs Vice Admiral Beatty turned onto a northerly course to approach his rendezvous and would have missed the Germans if fate had not now intervened. A small Danish steamer appeared between the two opposing forces and the Germans sent the torpedoboats *B109* and *B110* to investigate, whilst the British light cruisers *Galatea* and *Phaeton*, on the eastern wing of Beatty's screen, also altered course towards her. At about 15.20hrs *Galatea* gave a contact report and at the same time opened fire on the German boats. The small cruiser *Elbing* went to support the torpedoboats.

> The vessels that appeared under the smoke clouds appeared to be battlecruisers, that at first steered east, then they soon turned onto a northern course and were now irreproachably made out as two light cruisers. The first enemy shell strikes at quite a large distance from the ship. *Elbing* opens fire at 15.32hrs at a range of 130–140hm in the brief passing battle, with the enemy bearing to starboard ahead. The enemy turns away to the west after the first straddling salvo. His number has meanwhile grown to 4 light cruisers.[3]

Elbing quickly hit *Galatea* below the bridge and the British cruiser turned away, however the greatest fleet battle ever had begun. In our story we shall describe the battlecruiser actions first.

Soon after the first report from *Elbing* was received at 15.26hrs, Vizeadmiral Hipper turned his ships to course WSW and went to full speed to close on the light cruisers as quickly as possible. At 15.34hrs aboard *Lützow* the order was given for clear ship for battle. This order brought great delight and Kapitänleutnant Jung, commander of A turret, wrote:

On 'Clear for action', drums and horns sounded through the decks. Those who have heard the call from the drums and horns will never forget how serious it was, but also the magic of the moment. In a few moments the last preparations are met, and the battle stations announce: 'Clear!' Solemn silence surrounds those in their rushing colossus. There are no longer men to be seen on the upper deck.[4]

At 15.35hrs *Lützow* reported to the High Sea Chief: 'Several smoke clouds of enemy forces in sight in 164 gamma'. At 16.20hrs speed was increased to 25 knots to chase the enemy light cruisers, but then large warships came in sight to port.

At 16.20hrs the German battlecruisers sighted, in the WSW, the two columns of quickly approaching dreadnoughts, and at about 16.22hrs, at a range of 15nm two battlecruisers with tripod masts, the 2nd BCS, were clearly sighted from *Seydlitz*. At 16.25hrs *Princess Royal* made out five smoke clouds in the east by north. Whether the British ships were easier to make out against the clearer western horizon, or if the German measuring and observation gear was better, or the light grey colour of the German ships was more favourable, as reason for the earlier German observation of the English ships remains unknown. In any case the German side continued to observe the composition and course of the sighted forces for some time.[5]

Leutnant zur See Kienast was on the staff of Vizeadmiral Hipper and later wrote: 'High tension dominates with all the crew, as after scarcely one hour after sighting British light forces smoke clouds and heavy masts of ships climb over the horizon. I hear more, as Admiral Hipper up the Admiral's bridge said to his Chief of Staff, in his Bavarian dialect: "Raeder, I'll eat my broomstick if that is not Beatty again!"'[6]

Korvettenkapitän Paschen, the I Artillerie Offizier of *Lützow*, wrote: 'With the sighting of the enemy heavy forces I could already see with certainty battleships behind the battlecruisers which were at least 26 kilometres distant, evidence of the excellent visibility to the west. When the battlecruisers took up a southern course these ships continued peacefully further to the north, whereby they found themselves in a position 10 nautical miles behind the battlecruisers, and at first could not interfere.'[7] *Lützow* now signalled for a speed of 18 knots and a distance between ships of 700 metres as the German line was now assembling into battle formation to begin the action on a northerly course. Vizeadmiral Hipper then signalled fire distribution from the right. This order meant that the German battlecruiser line would each take their opposite number under fire, ship against ship, beginning with *Lützow* taking the leading enemy ship as target. Vizeadmiral Hipper was happily beginning the battle against a superior enemy on a northerly course. *Der Krieg zur See* explains further:

Only this remained certain: the newly sighted force, including six dreadnoughts, steered north, and it was decided to choose this as a combat course. Indeed a battle on a northern course, away from the German main body, in no way agreed with the German operational plan, but nevertheless, Admiral Hipper determined to use this direction for battle. This course would also bring him closer to the II AG, and therefore he ordered fire distribution from the right. However, around 16.29hrs an enemy course alteration could be recognized.

About this time Admiral Beatty swung onto an easterly course, ordered 'action stations', and ordered the 2nd Light Cruiser Squadron, along with the 9th and 13th Flotillas, to take station at the head, and the 2nd Battlecruiser Squadron to follow the 1st Battlecruiser Squadron on ESE course in battle line. At the same time the 5th Battle Squadron, that at this time was 8nm WNW, received an order to push east at high speed. The visibility was good, the sun in the rear, the wind WNW. Vizeadmiral Hipper remained on his hitherto course and the enemy stood between him and his bases. Whether he received support or not, Vice Admiral Beatty's ships were of the same class and he would remain in contact and give battle, so long as the enemy numbers were not greatly superior. It appeared to him that he had a great opportunity, tactically and strategically, and the decision did not seem in doubt.[8]

The powerful 5th Battle Squadron did not follow this turn by Vice Admiral Beatty. Vice Admiral J. Harper explained why:

When *Lion* flew a general flag signal ordering the battlecruiser fleet to steer south of east to counter the reported danger, the very nature of the formation meant that the slower 5th Battle Squadron would be placed five miles astern of the battlecruisers.

The signal flags, scarlet, deep blue, yellow and white, flung out into the 22 knots breeze...were lost to sight in the palls of grey-black funnel smoke...reappeared for an instant...

Lion passed the signal to *Princess Royal*, who relayed it to *Queen Mary*; she in turn passed it to *Tiger*. 'Change course! Follow the *Lion*!'

The signal hoist came streaming down. *Lion*'s helm went over, the ships astern turned after her in column.

But the 5th Battle Squadron? Minutes passed by, and still Evan-Thomas had not turned, but stood to the northward, until the five mile gap between *Lion* and *Barham* had become six miles, seven, eight...It had been *Tiger*'s duty to relay the signal to Admiral Evan-Thomas, and *Tiger* had failed to do so. Once more the British Battlecruisers' signal organization had failed at a critical moment.[9]

Eight minutes passed before Admiral Evan-Thomas turned on his own initiative; the signal was never received. Scarcely was the turn of the British battlecruisers onto an easterly course in line of bearing formation observed from the German side, when at about 16.33hrs Vizeadmiral Hipper turned to starboard and onto a southerly course. 'A new movement of the enemy brought his deployment on a southerly course, which was immediately followed through a turn onto a south-easterly course, since this gave the opportunity of drawing the enemy forces onto our own main body, which was particularly welcome.'[10] At the same time he reduced speed from 23 knots to 18 knots, to allow the ships of the II AG, which were 10 nautical miles behind, to catch up. Vizeadmiral Hipper now ordered fire distribution from the left, speed 18 knots, and a distance between ships of 500 metres. American author Commander H.H. Frost sums up:

> Beatty's claim that he was 'between the enemy and his base' was not correct as far as the German battlecruisers were concerned. In fact, the line of bearing between Hipper and Beatty was very nearly at right angles to the bearing of Horns Reefs light vessel. It is true that Beatty might have been able to cut off the line of retreat of the II AG. This fact might have, in some measure, induced Hipper to offer battle to his superior foe but, if so, it was certainly only a contributory cause. The facts demonstrate that Hipper was fighting of his own volition. He had prepared for a fight on the unfavourable North-westerly course. Then, after counter-marching, he had deliberately slowed to 18 knots as early as 16.40. Five minutes later he had headed sharply toward the enemy. Not only did he wish to fight, but he intended to do so at decisive ranges. Our hats are off to Hipper![11]

The preliminaries were now over and at 16.48hrs finally the long awaited signal was given from *Lützow*: 'Jot Dora!' Open fire. When the Germans opened fire first, despite the British ships having longer-ranged pieces, Vice Admiral Beatty's ships were still deploying into battle line. The first four ships of the German line fired against their opposite numbers, whilst the rear ship, *von der Tann*, engaged the rear British ship, *Indefatigable*. The British battlecruisers returned the fire a minute later, however Beatty's ships had again messed up their fire distribution, just as at Dogger Bank. *Lion* and *Princess Royal* fired on *Lützow*, which was correct, but *Queen Mary* engaged the third German ship, *Seydlitz*, leaving *Derfflinger* unfired upon, whilst *Tiger* and *New Zealand* both fired on *Moltke* and *Indefatigable* duelled it out with *von der Tann*. The German fire was immediately effective and the British ships began to suffer. *Lion* was hit at 16.51 and 16.52hrs, with hits near the first and second funnels, whilst at 17.00hrs Q turret was struck and put out of action. This semi-armoured piercing shell struck at the junction of the turret face and roof, penetrated and exploded over the left 13.5-inch gun. The flash from the explosion reached the cordite in the main cages and penetrated to the handling room below, but the magazine doors were closed and this prevented the firing of the magazine and thus prevented the loss of the ship. All those in the gunhouse were killed. The mortally wounded turret officer ordered the magazine to be flooded, which was fortunate as at 17.28hrs a further flash fire ignited and passed down the hoist to the handling room and up as high as the mast head. This killed those remaining in the handling room. *Lützow* hit *Lion* nine times during this early part of the battle. At 17.00hrs *Lützow* received her first hit on the forecastle, followed closely by a second nearby. At 16.57hrs Vice Admiral Beatty turned his ships away 2 points to increase the range. Two minutes later Vizeadmiral Hipper also turned away, 1 point to port.

The second ship in the British line, *Princess Royal*, was hit at least eight times by *Derfflinger* during the first part of the battle. Initially *Derfflinger* overestimated the range but after 10 minutes secured her first hit on *Princess Royal*, with a shell that pierced the 6-inch belt armour below B turret and detonated inboard, causing the flooding of a coal bunker. Then a shell struck the deck below the bridge and together with the shock of the first hit caused the fire direction to fall out for some time. At 17.00hrs a shell exploded just aft of B turret and killed eight men and wounded thirty-eight more. Further hits followed with the right gun of Q turret being struck and a shell holing the second funnel. A further shell struck the base of the forward funnel, and another hit the junction of the 6- and 9-inch armour in line with the fore funnel which was holed. During the first 10 minutes of the action *Derfflinger* remained unfired upon.

During the first part of the battle *Queen Mary* was engaged in a one-on-one battle with *Seydlitz*. *Queen Mary* was hit at least twice early on, once in the aft 4-inch gun battery and also on the right gun of Q turret. In return *Seydlitz* was hit four times. One shell struck in compartment XIII in the electrical switch room at 16.55hrs. The next struck the working chamber of C turret at 17.10hrs. The hit on C barbette was practically a repeat of the fateful hit at the Dogger Bank Battle. A neat hole was punched in the armour and this piece of armour, together with splinters and flash flame, entered the working chamber and ignited two main and two fore charges found there. Turret C was immediately wrapped in a large, yellow smoke cloud. All crew in the working chamber were killed along with some men in the turret. The flash passed down the hoist to the ammunition room but the charges there did not ignite. The men of the magazine put on their gas masks and flooded the ammunition chambers of C turret. The turret was put out of action but the catastrophe of the Dogger Bank had been averted by the new precautions put into place.

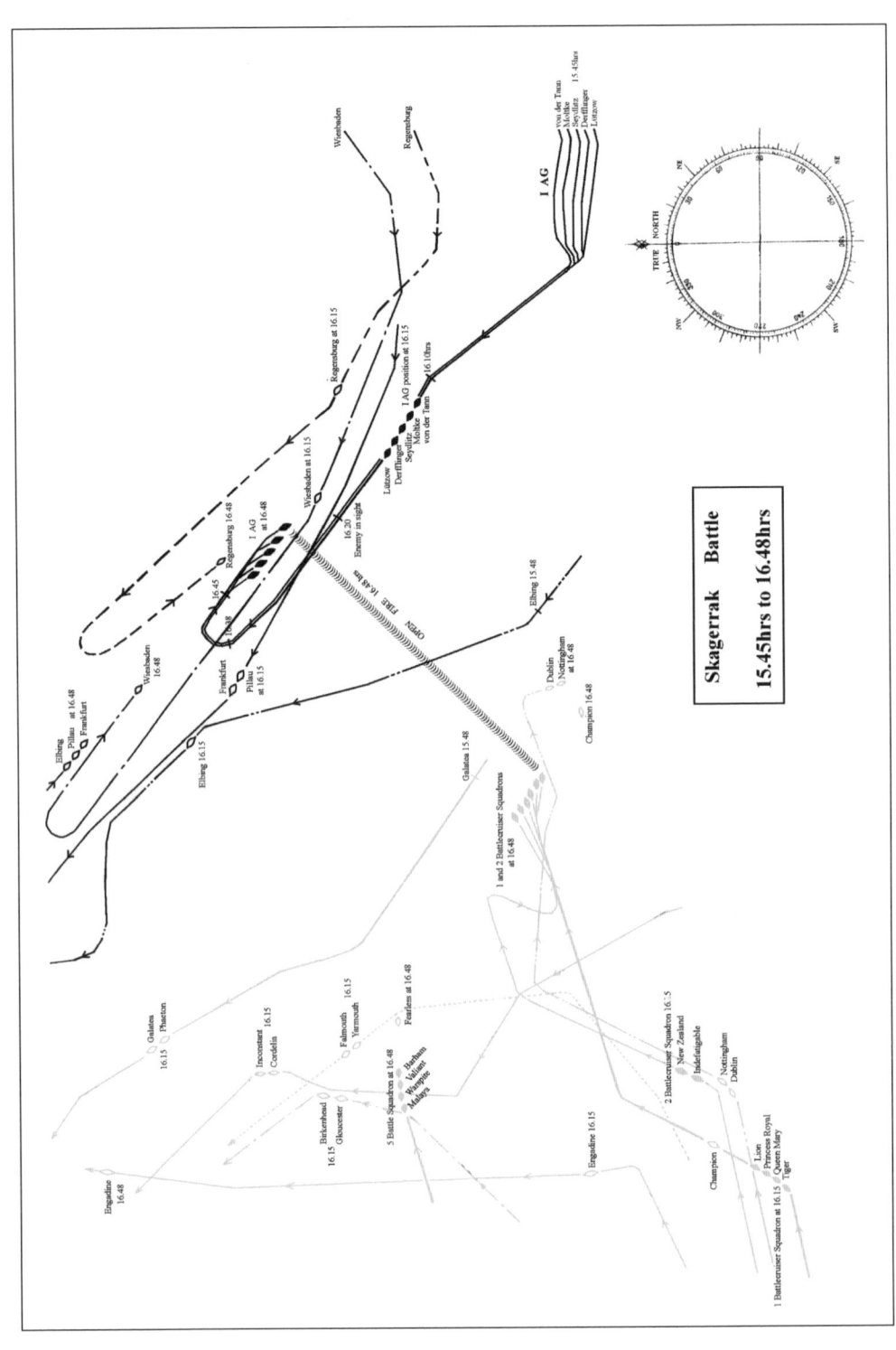

Then, approximately ten minutes after the opening of fire, Habler reported to me by telephone, 'Turret Caesar does not give any answer; from the speaking tube of turret Caesar smoke is penetrating the *Artillerie Zentral*.' This was exactly the same report that I had received on January 24 on the Dogger Bank, also at the beginning of the battle. I therefore knew what this report signified. The cartridges were in flames, and the turret was put out of action. Almost mechanically I gave the order: 'Flood magazine of turret C.'[12]

A further shell impacted short abeam turret B whilst the next hit at 17.15hrs struck the starboard VI 15cm cannon casemate. This hit killed all sixteen men of the gun crew, with the exception of the Squadron Minister, Pfarrer Fenger, and put the gun out of action.

The next ship in the British line was *Tiger*, and she was under a particularly pernicious fire from *Moltke*, even though *Moltke* was being fired on by *New Zealand* as well. *Tiger* was struck fourteen times by 28cm shells, although one hit is credited to *Seydlitz*. At 16.54hrs both Q and X turrets were hit. Q turret was struck on the roof and was put out of action for some time, whilst X turret's barbette armour of 9-inch thickness was penetrated and the shell entered the turret, although luckily it did not detonate correctly and just burned. However the turret was temporarily put out of action. Another shell struck A turret's barbette and displaced the armour whilst other hits did considerable damage to light structures and ignited some 6-inch gun charges. *Moltke* was not hit by either *Tiger* or *New Zealand*.

At the end of the respective lines were *Indefatigable* and *von der Tann*. Whilst the fire of *Indefatigable* was over and wide, that of *von der Tann* was up to the normal German standard with a straddle and hit with the third or fourth salvo. The I Artillerie Offizier of *von der Tann*, Kapitänleutnant Mahrholz wrote:

14 minutes after the beginning of the battle fate overtakes him. In my telescope of my Direction Pointer I see that briefly after the impact of a salvo, a giant explosion occurs in the aft gun turret of the enemy, flash flames come from the roof of the turret, broadening with rapidly increasing speed over the aft deck, and something black whirls high through the air, probably the turret roof. However the next salvo is already underway, and impacts forward, and thick, black smoke climbs from the mid ships, seemingly an oil bunker is hit and in flames, and soon all that is to be seen of *Indefatigable* is a thick, dark smoke cloud, which climbs several hundred metres into the sky. The auxiliary observation *Offizier* in the foremast jubilantly calls: 'Herr Kapitän, they are gone!' However, I am sceptical, since I know from experience how easy it is to make mistakes under these great circumstances.[13]

At 17.03hrs it was observed that *Indefatigable* was struck by two or three shells from one salvo around the aft gun turret. A small explosion occurred and *Indefatigable* swung out of line to starboard, probably to throw off the German aim. She appeared to be settling by the stern when two projectiles from the next salvo struck her, one on the forecastle and one on the forward A turret. After a further thirty seconds there was a tremendous explosion forward and the ship lay over to port and capsized. It is thought that the aft magazines of X turret exploded and then the forward magazines of A turret. A total of 57 officers and 960 men perished with the explosion, whilst 2 survivors were later picked up by a German torpedoboat. During the engagement *von der Tann* fired fifty-two 28cm shells and thirty-eight 15cm shells at ranges of 162 to 123hm.

So far Vice Admiral Beatty's battlecruisers were having a difficult time of it. By 17.10hrs *Lion* had been hit nine times, with Q turret being blown apart, *Princess Royal* had been battered, *Tiger* had been hit fourteen times and *Indefatigable* had blown up. At 17.06hrs the British line turned away a further point, but Vizeadmiral Hipper turned 2 points towards the enemy. Meanwhile *Moltke* had launched four torpedoes towards the British and at 17.11hrs *Lion* sighted a torpedo track in her wake whilst *Princess Royal* reported a torpedo passed underneath her. A third torpedo passed between *Tiger* and *New Zealand*. Vizeadmiral Hipper wanted to press his advantage and at the same time as he turned towards the enemy he increased speed to 23 knots. Around this time *Lion* sheered out of line to starboard and was lost to view from *Lützow* and she changed target to *Princess Royal*, and likewise *Derfflinger* changed target to *Queen Mary*. At 17.10hrs however, there was some relief for the British battlecruisers.

After the 5th Battle Squadron failed to receive the signal to follow the battlecruisers Rear Admiral Evan-Thomas turned of his volition and at 16.57hrs was 7 nautical miles astern of the battlecruisers when he sighted the ships of the German II AG, which he took under fire. By 17.06hrs the German battlecruisers had come in sight and within range and *Barham* opened fire on the last ship in line, *von der Tann*, at a range of 174hm. Soon *Valiant*, *Warspite* and *Malaya* also joined in, concentrating on *Moltke* and *von der Tann*. Now Vizeadmiral Hipper's ships were outnumbered two-to-one and his 28cm and 30.5cm pieces were pitted against 34.5cm and 38cm pieces; he was therefore at a severe disadvantage. The German *Große Kreuzer* were designed with the view that once battle was joined with the enemy they should join the battle line and be capable of fighting the enemy's battleships, but to face the most modern and powerful battleships armed with 15-inch cannon, and to be outnumbered two-to-one, would surely test them to the limit.

The battleships of the 5th Battle Squadron remained unfired on and could lob salvo after salvo at the last two German ships undisturbed. *Von der Tann* was surrounded by high water columns from the impact of shells of the heaviest calibre and at 17.09hrs she suffered her first heavy hit. A 15-inch shell struck the ship to starboard aft on the joint between two armoured plates and detonated during penetration. Several pieces of broken armour penetrated the ship and several rooms flooded. 'With the powerful impact of this shell the hull vibrated violently lengthwise, and the ship's end whipped up and down 5 to 6 times. After a brief interruption the rudder worked again without further disruption, but the rudder engine ran hot owing to the trim of the rudder spindle.'[14] In total 600 tonnes of water entered the ship, but there were no casualties. At 17.20hrs a 15-inch shell penetrated the barbette of A turret and put the turret out of action, and then at 17.23hrs a shell penetrated the battery deck and struck the barbette of turret C, causing this turret to jam for the time being. A serious danger was caused by this hit as the torpedo net was torn loose and hung over the side, threatening to foul the propellers until secured.

Nevertheless *von der Tann* was hitting back, and at 16.23hrs she struck *New Zealand*, her target since *Indefatigable* blew up, with a 28cm shell which punched out a large piece of armour from X turret's barbette. This turret was consequently jammed for some time. Then at 17.30hrs *von der Tann* changed targets to the 5th Battle Squadron, although only her midship turrets, B and D, were operable at that time. With their restricted training arc target had to be changed back to the battlecruisers at 17.37hrs, but just prior to this at 17.35hrs both guns of B turret failed to run out so that *von der Tann* had only one serviceable turret.

The *Panzerkreuzer Moltke* also came under heavy fire from the British 5th Battle Squadron. At 17.16hrs a shell struck the citadel armour below the V casemate and penetrated into the upper coal bunker, where it detonated. The explosion put the V casemate 15cm cannon out of action and killed the twelve serving crew. Four stokers in the coal bunker were killed and one man in the ammunition chamber below was wounded and died a few days later. At 17.23hrs a 15-inch shell struck near the water line beneath the forward funnel and detonated on the side armour. Although the armour was not penetrated a plate was displaced and the hull skin below the waterline was torn so that some wing passage and protective bunker compartments were flooded. A few minutes later at 17.26hrs there was an underwater hit aft which passed transversely across the ship before detonating and causing further flooding right aft. Finally at 17.27hrs a 15-inch shell detonated on the armoured belt below the aft superstructure and caused some flooding in the wing passage and protective bunker. As a result of these hits 1,000 tonnes of water entered the ship and she took a 3° list to starboard but was brought back to an even keel with counter-flooding.

Around this time *Derfflinger* was still holding *Queen Mary* as a target after *Lion* had disappeared from view. *Derfflinger* was firing at a range of 132hm whilst *Queen Mary*'s opposite number, *Seydlitz*, was firing at her at 135hm. At 17.26hrs three projectiles of a four shell salvo were seen to strike *Queen Mary* but the only result appeared to be a small smoke and dust cloud, and then from another salvo of four shells two struck the ship. A tremendous yellow flame erupted and the ship disappeared in a huge smoke cloud. Witnesses reported some of the hits struck near Q turret and this is substantiated by a survivor, Midshipman Storey:

> The fire was maintained with great rapidity till 5.20, and during this time we were only slightly damaged by the enemy's fire. At 5.20 a big shell hit Q turret and put the right gun out of action, but the left gun continued firing. At 5.24 a terrific explosion took place which smashed up Q turret and started a big fire in the working chamber and the gun house was filled with smoke and gas. The Officer on the turret, Lieutenant Commander Street, gave the order to evacuate the turret. All the unwounded in the gun house got clear and, as they did so, another terrific explosion took place and all were thrown into the water.[15]

There was also a huge explosion forward, thought to be from B turret magazine. The I Artillerie Offizier of *Derfflinger*, Korvettenkapitän Hase, wrote:

> First of all a vivid red flame shot up from her forepart. Then came an explosion forward which was followed by a much heavier explosion amidships, black debris of the ship flew into the air, and immediately afterwards the whole ship blew up with a terrific explosion. A gigantic cloud of smoke rose, the masts collapsed inwards, the smoke-cloud hid everything, and rose higher and higher. Finally nothing but a thick, black cloud of smoke remained where the ship had been.[16]

Queen Mary broke in two and the aft part was still afloat bottom-up as *New Zealand* passed. A total of eighteen survivors were picked up by the destroyers *Laurel* and *Petard* and two were saved by the German torpedoboat *V28*, whilst 1,266 men perished.

Just after *Indefatigable* had been destroyed Vice Admiral Beatty had ordered an attack by his destroyers of the 13th Flotilla, but it was not until towards 17.30hrs that they broke through the British line and advanced to the attack. On seeing this, the II Leader of Torpedoboats (II FdT), Kommodore Heinrich, aboard the small cruiser *Regensburg*, ordered a counter attack by the IX TBF. At 17.26hrs on *Regensburg* the red pennant 'Z' was hoisted, the signal for the torpedoboats to attack, and at the same time the optical signal was given: 'IX Flottille *Ran!*' The word *Ran* simply means attack, or go at it, and was used frequently in battle. As the British destroyers approached Vizeadmiral Hipper altered course away to the southeast and reduced speed. A violent destroyer versus torpedoboat fight ensued between the lines.

After the British torpedoes had been successfully avoided Vizeadmiral Hipper turned SSE at 17.38hrs and at 17.41hrs turned S-by-W to again close with the opponent, despite the fact the German cruisers were still outnumbered two-to-one. Soon after the smoke cloud of the High Sea Fleet was sighted and the support that had been absent on 16 December 1914 and at the Dogger Bank was close at hand. The British light cruiser *Southampton* signalled the sighting to Vice Admiral Beatty, who was surprised as up until now he had supposed the German Fleet to be on the Jade. Nevertheless he sent a contact report to Admiral Jellicoe and the Grand Fleet and hoisted the recall for his destroyers. At 17.46hrs the British battlecruisers turned north at high speed to close on their own battle fleet. However, Beatty once again failed to inform Rear Admiral Evan-Thomas until he passed on the opposite course so that the 5th Battle Squadron did not turn north until 17.54hrs. At 17.44hrs Vizeadmiral Hipper ordered his ships to change target to the battleships and 2 minutes later *Valiant* was heavily shaken by a near miss, and at the same time *Barham* received a hit from *Lützow* adjacent to the aft conning tower which caused much damage to light structures. At 17.51hrs and again at 17.55hrs Vizeadmiral Hipper signalled for course north. As his cruisers turned *Seydlitz* was hit at 17.57hrs by a torpedo fired by one of the British destroyers, either *Petard* or *Turbulent*. Aboard *Seydlitz* they had observed two torpedoes approaching and only one could be avoided. The torpedo struck in compartment XIII, directly below the turret A in the bow. A large hole was torn in the hull below the armoured belt but, although bowed, the torpedo bulkhead held firm and only the wing passage and protective bunker filled with water. For the damage control personnel it was a repeat performance of the events of 23 April, and *Seydlitz* could hold her place in the line at the unit speed.

The turn to the north ended the first part of the Skagerrak Battle. Vizeadmiral Hipper's cruisers could be justifiably proud of themselves: they had achieved around forty-six hits of heavy calibre on their opponents and had destroyed two of his large ships, despite being outnumbered by more than two-to-one. In return they had received just seventeen hits and all ships were still capable of action. However, the battle continued without respite.

At 17.55hrs *Lützow*, *Derfflinger* and *Seydlitz* renewed their fire on the British battlecruisers, which were now also being fired upon by the leading German battleships. *Lützow* made three hits on *Lion*, one starting a cordite fire in the aft 4-inch gun battery. *Seydlitz* struck *Tiger* once. It is believed that *Derfflinger* was actually firing on *Barham* at this time and made four telling hits. At 17.58hrs a shell penetrated the upper deck and exploded on the main deck, sending fragments into the 6-inch magazine. The flash passed up to the N°2 gun and caused a cordite fire. This was an extremely dangerous hit. At 17.01hrs a shell exploded in the aft superstructure behind the main mast. At 17.08hrs a shell

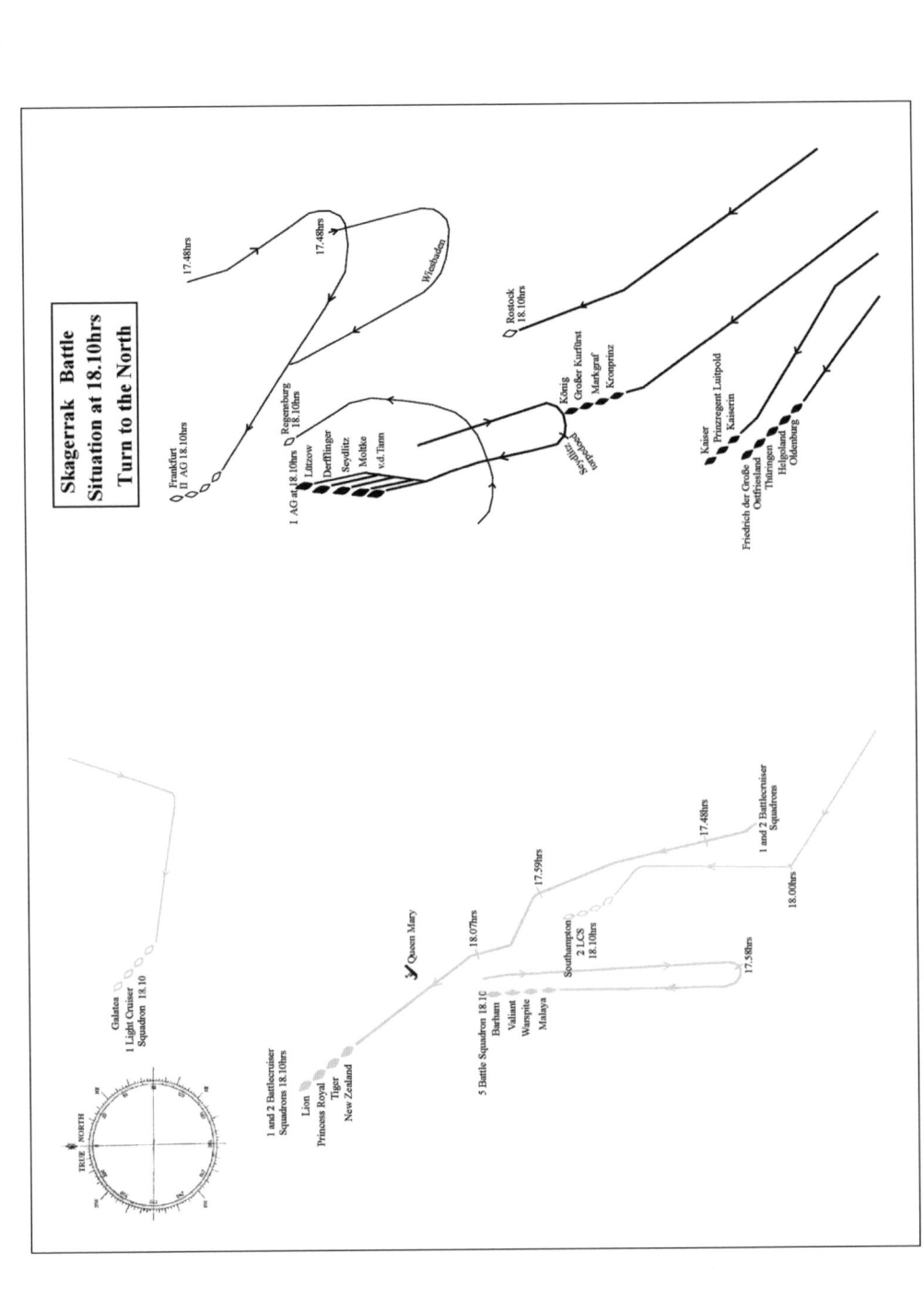

penetrated the side plating aft, severely damaging the decks and cabins. Then at 17.10hrs a projectile struck near the N°1 starboard 6-inch gun.

Soon however the British battlecruisers disappeared into the smoke and haze:

> Gradually the visibility becomes worse. The sun becomes a hindrance and occasionally also artificial smoke. In the north salvos come from the grey on grey, however, no glasses or cannon can hold the muzzle flashes (as targets). There is nothing to be seen of the enemy![17]

By 18.10hrs the British battlecruisers were outside effective gun range. Therefore the I AG changed target to the battleships of the 5th Battle Squadron, *Lützow* against *Barham*, *Derfflinger* fired on *Valiant*, *Seydlitz* against *Warspite*, *Moltke* firing on *Malaya* and *von der Tann* firing at *Valiant*. *Seydlitz* hit *Warspite* twice, once near Y turret barbette and once through the forward funnel. The hits on *Malaya*, which nearly caused the loss of the ship, must be credited to the German battleships. In the meantime the return fire of the British battleships was becoming effective. It must be remembered that although German design philosophy dictated that their *Panzerkreuzer* be capable of participating in battle between the battle lines, the cruisers of the I AG were now in a toe-to-toe slugging match with the most modern British battleships that were armed with cannon of the heaviest calibre.

Lützow was hit at 18.13hrs by a 15-inch shell on the belt on the waterline below the N°1 casemate gun. Although the ship was shaken only 85 tonnes of water entered. At 18.25hrs two shells, most probably of 15-inch calibre, struck *Lützow* between the funnels and destroyed the main and reserve wireless rooms, thereby severing Vizeadmiral Hipper's connection with the High Sea Fleet Chief and forcing him to rely on blinker signals. At 18.30hrs *Valiant* struck *Lützow* with a 15-inch shell between the N°4 and N°5 casemates:

> A *Deckoffizier*, who had the task of supervising damage control, appeared in the casemate to ascertain the effect of the reported hit on our cannon. We opened the manhole cover and I climbed down into the coal bunker beneath our gun. From above I had already seen the beam of light emanating from the large hole in the belt armour and the water in the coal bunker. When I stepped down onto the coal I immediately slipped into the water. After I returned to the casemate and made my report to the *Deckoffizier* I was admired by my comrades, as by slipping into the water I was wet through and was as black as coal in every sense of the word.[18]

Then at 18.45hrs, from out of the haze, *Princess Royal* struck *Lützow* with a shell below the conning tower.

At 18.19hrs *Derfflinger* was also hit on the hull forward, and then at 18.55hrs a hit detached two 100mm armoured plates far forward in the bows. This allowed some flooding. *Seydlitz* fared the worst of the German cruisers, and was struck by the 5th Battle Squadron's 15-inch shells a total of six times. At 18.06 and 18.08hrs shells struck the forecastle, and at 18.10hrs the right cheek of turret Berta was hit. Although one man was killed in the turret it continued in action. Two further hits at 18.55hrs struck the side armour forward and the port windlass. The final shell, which struck at an undetermined time, hit below the waterline near frame 114 to port. *Moltke* and *von der Tann* remained unhit, however at 18.18hrs on the latter the barrels of D turret failed to run out shortly after one another. With that *von der Tann* had no heavy artillery in action, but Kapitän zur See Zenker held his ship in line so the opponents would not concentrate their fire on the other cruisers.

The German cruisers, and their battle line, were in an unfavourable position as with the low-lying sun and haze observation and fire direction were practically impossible. Vice Admiral Beatty and his forces gradually swung north then NNE to come across the head of the German line. For this reason Vizeadmiral Scheer ordered Vizeadmiral Hipper to pursue Beatty and report his position as he was out of sight. Because *Lützow*'s wireless had been destroyed Vizeadmiral Hipper did not receive this message until 18.26hrs whereon he turned NW, however he was then forced back onto course NE.

Towards 19.00hrs Vice Admiral Beatty was approaching Admiral Jellicoe's Grand Fleet and he began to turn more to the east, so that at 18.55hrs Vizeadmiral Hipper gave the order for his ships to turn to the east. In addition Jellicoe had sent the 3rd Battlecruiser Squadron on ahead of the fleet to support Beatty, but because of differences in the position estimates of the two main British forces Vice Admiral Hood's 3rd Battlecruiser Squadron had steered to the east of the approaching German and British forces. However, the 3rd Battlecruiser Squadron was drawn into the fight between the II AG and British light cruisers and this unexpected appearance on the battle field also forced Vizeadmiral Hipper to turn east, just at the very moment he needed to be pressing ahead to the north to discover the Grand Fleet. To relieve the situation Vizeadmiral Hipper sent some of his torpedoboats to attack the 3rd BCS at 18.58hrs, and then at 18.59hrs he ordered his I AG to make a battle turn to starboard on to the opposite course. The reason for this manoeuvre was that once again the German battlecruisers had come under heavy fire from both Vice Admiral Beatty's battlecruisers as well as those of Vice Admiral Hood, with *Seydlitz* and *Derfflinger* both hit at 18.55hrs as related. Furthermore, British destroyers and light cruisers were sighted to the north, and they were obviously manoeuvring for a torpedo attack. Therefore Vizeadmiral Hipper determined to remove his unit from the enemy fire and also to close with his main body. Nevertheless *Lützow* hit *Lion* again at 19.05hrs on the starboard hull-plating forward of A barbette with a shell which detonated on the port side. As the leading division of the High Sea Fleet approached, Vizeadmiral Hipper made a further battle turn to starboard on to the opposite course and took station at the head of the German line, which stretched out 8 miles to the south. As the German ships again approached the British destroyers fired torpedoes, and during this part of the battle *Lützow* put *Onslow* out of action with three 15cm shells.

As the British Grand Fleet was deploying into its battle-line Vice Admiral Beatty appeared from the southwest and steamed across ahead of it, in-between the fleet and its cruiser screen. At the same time the 3rd Battlecruiser Squadron was approaching from the east, whilst the Germans were approaching from the south, all towards one giant collision. At 19.05hrs the 1st Cruiser Squadron, under Rear Admiral Arbuthnot, opened fire on *Wiesbaden* and at 19.15hrs passed across the bows of *Lion*, forcing her to swing out to port. Rear Admiral Arbuthnot was vigorously pursuing the German small cruiser when suddenly the German I AG and III Battle Squadron emerged from the smoke. At 19.16hrs *Lützow* opened fire on *Defence*, which along with *Warrior* was also under fire from the III Squadron. It was the first clear target the Germans had had for some time. I Artillerie Offizier Paschen wrote:

> Then something unexpected happens. From right to left a ship passes through the field of vision of my periscope, improbably large and near. From the first glance I make out an older English armoured cruiser and give the necessary commands. Someone pulls me by the arm: 'Don't shot, that is the *Rostock*!' But I see clearly the turrets on the forecastle and stern.–'Passing battle. Armoured cruiser, 4 funnels. Bow left. Left 30. Measurement! 76hm, salvo!' Five salvoes fall in swift succession, of them three straddle, then the sight seen with the battlecruisers was repeated, and the ship blew up in full view of both fleets. The English main body also at this time has *Defence* in sight, although to us they are invisible and remain so.–Behind him comes a second such ship, but we leave him for our next astern, as the English battlecruisers require our entire attention.[19]

Derfflinger did not open fire, but the other German ships damaged *Warrior* to the extent she sank the following day. Of the battlecruisers which 'required attention' *Lion* hit *Lützow* twice at 19.19hrs, one shell striking the forecastle the other behind B turret, starting a fire. Then at 19.20hrs *Lützow* put the destroyer *Acasta* out of action with two 15cm shells.

At 19.20hrs Vizeadmiral Hipper ordered a turn onto course SE as he was being forced away from the encircling and tightening ring of enemy capital ships, of which he could scarcely see anything. The German battlecruisers, with *Lützow* at their head, were clearly visible to the English battlecruisers of the 1st and 3rd BCS and now they covered *Lützow* with a hail of fire that left a lasting impression on those who endured it:

> To the front of the German head, from the NW to the NE, there was suddenly an unbroken line of muzzle flashes of heavy ships, firing salvo after salvo with powerful results and which the German ships could scarcely answer to, as not one British dreadnought could be recognized in the battle smoke. SMS *Lützow* and *König* came under an especially heavy fire. It seemed as though several ships were firing at them at once.[20]

Korvettenkapitän Paschen described it thus:

> The English battlecruisers required our entire attention. They stand to port aft, as we have swung onto an easterly course, 130hm away, for us barely recognizable. And then it began, which made all previous look like a game. Whilst the target of our guns was hidden from me by smoke, I gave the direction to the aft position, when suddenly a hail of hits struck from port aft and port ahead. There was nothing to see other than red flashes, not the shadow of one ship. Our turrets were directed hard aft to port and fired as well as was possible on our old friends, the battlecruisers of Admiral Beatty.[21]

Lützow was hit repeatedly to port during this period. All eight hits were from the 3rd BCS, *Invincible* and *Inflexible*. The most devastating of these hits were two 12-inch shells that struck the forward broadside torpedo room and two 12-inch shells that struck the bow torpedo room. One shell struck below the armour in the broadside room and the other struck the lower edge of the 100mm thick forward belt. Both penetrated the broadside room. The two other shells struck the bow torpedo room below the water line. Korvettenkapitän Paschen accurately described what occurred:

> The fateful red flash from port ahead came from the British 3rd Battlecruiser Squadron, which was ahead of the enemy main body, and had steered towards the gun flashes and had arrived within effective gun range unseen. Seemingly at this moment we had already received a fatal wound from them, as it later transpired.–Every ship has a weak point and our Achilles heel was the broadside torpedo room, situated before A turret. Here unfortunately, out of considerations for space, the torpedo bulkhead had been omitted; this incomparable protection against underwater hits, that distinguished the German ships so advantageously against all from abroad. And so two enemy heavy shells successfully penetrated here beneath the armoured belt and their explosive result was so thorough, that the entire forecastle ahead of turret A practically immediately filled.[22]

Derfflinger was also hit at this time, once on the belt between turrets C and D and once on the belt below D barbette at 19.30hrs. Neither hit caused much damage but a near miss around the same time caused some flooding. At 18.34hrs *Seydlitz* was hit on the belt below C barbette and the ship was severely shaken. These hits were likewise thought to have come from Rear Admiral Hood's 3rd BCS.

However, the Germans were hitting back when they could and at 19.19 to 19.22hrs *Princess Royal* was hit twice by a battleship, one shell putting X turret out of action, the other penetrating the armour a little ahead of X turret. A total of eleven men were killed and thirty-one were wounded by these shells. *Tiger* was hit by a 15cm shell. Also at 19.30hrs *Lützow* hit the light cruiser *Falmouth* with a 15cm shell. Then suddenly at 19.30hrs, just as the I AG was swinging away to the south to escape the deadly cannonade, one of the tormentors of the German cruisers suddenly became visible.

> Meanwhile we had turned onto a southerly course, and suddenly an English battlecruiser of the *Invincible* type appeared out of the haze clearly and relatively near 4 points to port astern. I cannot fully say, what satisfaction I have felt, to finally have this pest available before my eyes, and as quick as lightning the commands were given out. But already a dark object slides between my periscope and the opponent, the corner of the Admiral's bridge, which limits the angle of vision of my periscope object lens. 'Has the aft position measured?' –'*Jawohl*! 100hm!' – 'Direction aft position!' Kapitänleutnant Bode gives brief and clear orders, and to the inexpressible joy of the whole ship, 15 seconds later our guns crash out again. I heard everything myself through the headphones; what Bode and the artillery transmitting station said, and now also saw the opponents again. 'Over! 4 down, salvo! Straddle! Salvo!' As the sound of the fall of shot indicator screeched the columns flickered out of the water around the enemy and again the beautiful and unmistakable dark red flames flared up.[23]

Invincible had been struck on Q turret and the shell had detonated inside, blowing off the turret roof. A great explosion followed almost immediately as the magazine exploded and the ship broke in two and sank within ten to fifteen seconds. The magazine of A turret also exploded. The two halves of the ship came to rest on the bottom and were conspicuous above the water for some time. The time of the explosion was 19.32hrs. It had taken *Lützow* just 2 minutes from sighting her opponent to destroying her. One of the six survivors of *Invincible* was her Gunnery Officer, Commander Dannreuther.

At 19.36hrs the flagship *Friedrich der Große* ordered: 'Battle turn to starboard'. Vizeadmiral Scheer had decided that he was at a great tactical disadvantage and determined, after due deliberation and consultation with his staff, to execute a battle turn onto the opposite course. This manoeuvre was extremely difficult to accomplish, so much so that other navies would not even attempt it, and it had never been performed under heavy fire. However, Vizeadmiral Scheer had confidence in his men and ships and gave the corresponding order, thus extricating his fleet from a very dangerous situation. Aboard *Lützow* speed had to be reduced because of the flooding forward, and this, in conjunction with the fact *Lützow* had no wireless, made Vizeadmiral Hipper decide to change flagships. At first he thought he would go to *Seydlitz*, but finally decided on *Moltke*. Nevertheless it took him several hours to complete the transfer.

At 19.55hrs Vizeadmiral Scheer ordered another battle turn, back towards the English line. He believed that the British still had time before the arrival of darkness to force another action upon him and perhaps cut his line of withdrawal. He wrote:

> There was only one way of avoiding this: to deal the enemy a second blow by again advancing regardless of consequences, and to bring all the torpedoboats to the attack. This manoeuvre would necessarily have the effect of surprising the enemy, upsetting his plans for the rest of the day, and, if the attack was powerful enough, of facilitating our extricating ourselves for the night. In addition, this afforded us the opportunity of making a final effort to succour the hard pressed *Wiesbaden*, or at least rescue her crew.[24]

Commander H. Frost later commented on the spirit that was behind this last thought:

> Despite the terrible propaganda that was directed against the German Navy during the war by its enemies, there was a spirit of loyal comradeship among its *Offiziers* and sailors that is worthy of the highest praise. Despite the often-repeated claim that the German offiziers, ashore and at sea, were only too willing to drive their men into useless slaughter, the plain facts of Jutland show a remarkable spirit of loyalty, cohesion and self sacrifice. Time and time again commanders and captains came to the assistance of their threatened comrades with magnificent courage.[25]

About this time Vizeadmiral Hipper disembarked from *Lützow* and boarded the torpedoboat *G39* to transfer to another battlecruiser. Leutnant zur See Kienast recorded a friendly farewell:

> *G39* came alongside. With the BdA and his staff we quit *Lützow*, which had been hit 24 times in a cauldron of heavy shells. Conscientiously the Staff writer even took his battered typewriter across to the torpedoboat! With a 'Hail the forester', Admiral Hipper and the *Lützow*'s commander parted, just as old hunting companions."[26]

Vizeadmiral Hipper also gave Kapitän zur See Harder permission to sink his ship if the damage became too great.

After the turn to the east at 19.55hrs the German line quickly approached the centre of Grand Fleet line. The leading ships were coming under a rapid fire from a line that was invisible and stretched from the NNE in a great arc through the east to the SE. Before long the entire British line of at least twenty battleships had opened fire, although their formation was somewhat disjointed.

The High Sea Fleet had placed itself in a situation that was very hazardous and rapidly becoming critical. As *Lützow* had been badly damaged and had steered away to the south at reduced speed, her sistership *Derfflinger*, under the command of Kapitän zur See Hartog, was leading the entire German line on an easterly course into the maelstrom. The I AG as well as the leading battleships were coming under increasingly heavy fire. Vizeadmiral Scheer now came under tremendous pressure to do something to extricate his ships from their imperilled situation. His immediate reaction was to use the *Panzerkreuzer* and torpedoboats to cover a third battle turn away by his fleet and at 20.13hrs he gave the signal: '*Große Kreuzer Gefechtswendung rein in den Feind! Ran!*'–'Large cruisers battle turn to the enemy! Attack!' However, only one minute later at 20.14hrs he amended this order to 'Large cruisers operate against the enemy head'. Vizeadmiral Scheer had realized that his initial reaction to send the battlecruisers against the entire enemy line was a mistake, which he had quickly rectified. This order has often been the cause of much comment, and frequent misunderstanding. The term *Ran* does not mean ram the enemy, rather it was a term used to mean attack the enemy and was used frequently during the day by the German leaders, usually to order the torpedoboats to attack. There is no question of torpedoboats ramming the enemy and it is an absurd proposition. Likewise the folklore myth about a 'death ride' of the German *Panzerkreuzer*. Vizeadmiral Scheer had his battlecruisers attacking the enemy for less than a minute, before the order was countermanded, and during this time they would have travelled approximately 600 metres, which is not much of a ride. By 20.15hrs Kapitän zur See Hartog had swung around to a southerly course and signalled for an increase in speed to 23 knots. At 20.21hrs Vizeadmiral Scheer ordered his torpedoboats to the attack, and *Rostock* signalled: 'Attack the enemy', '*Ran an den Feind*'.

Nevertheless the German cruisers were heavily hit during this time, mainly because the range was relatively short, whilst they themselves had difficulty discerning any targets. *Derfflinger* was hit fourteen times, *Seydlitz* was hit five times and *von der Tann* once. Even *Lützow*, which was bearing away to the south, was struck five times. By far the most destructive hits on *Derfflinger* were the two from *Revenge* at 20.14hrs and 20.16hrs which put turrets C and D out of action. Turret D was struck first on the roof between the slanting and horizontal plates and the shell detonated over the right cartridge hoist, igniting a total of seven main and thirteen fore charges in the hoist and handling room. All equipment of the right gun was damaged but the splinter bulkhead between the two guns was not penetrated. The charges of the left gun did not burn but the entire crew immediately perished with the exception of two men, one of whom later died, making a total of seventy-four. Two minutes later a 15-inch projectile from *Revenge* penetrated the barbette armour of C turret between the two guns. The shell detonated between the two gun cradles and fourteen powder charges burnt,

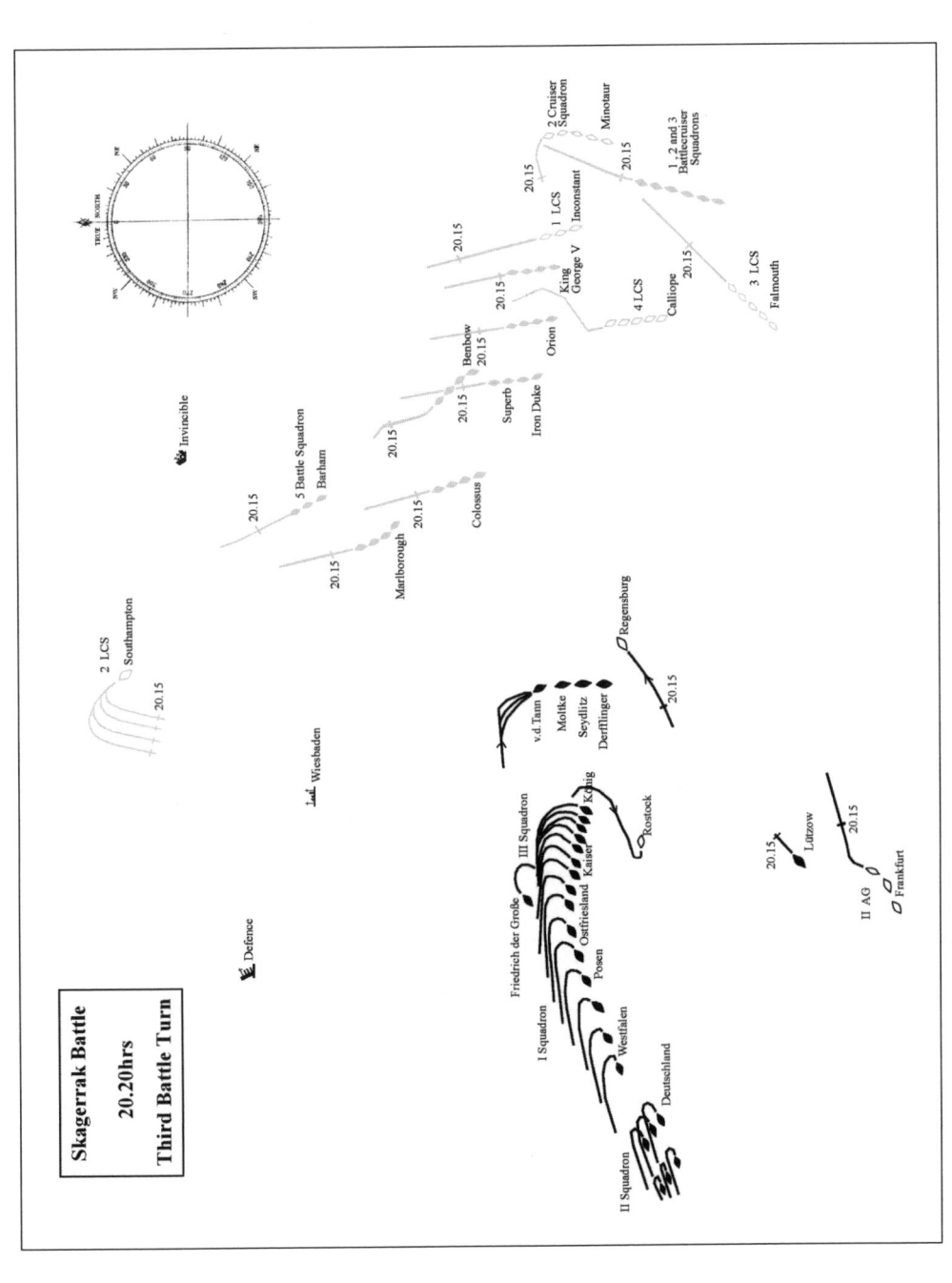

the turret being wrecked. A total of sixty-eight men died but there were five survivors. There were various other hits on the belt armour, decks and through the funnels but damage was only made to light structures. Even the hit on the conning tower about 20.22hrs only had the effect of a heavy vibration.

> Suddenly we seemed to hear the crack of doom. A terrific roar, a tremendous explosion and then darkness, in which we felt a colossal blow. The whole conning tower seemed to be hurled into the air as though by hands of some portentous giant, and then flutter into its former position. A heavy shell had struck the fore-control about 50cm in front of me. The shell exploded but failed to pierce the thick armour.[27]

Seydlitz was hit by four 12-inch shells from the British battleships between 20.14 and 20.20hrs. One wrecked an aft searchlight and another hit near the port N°3 15cm casemate gun causing slight damage. A further hit struck the hull below the bridge whilst the last struck the burnt out C turret. A 15-inch shell from *Royal Oak* at 20.27hrs hit the right gun of E turret, the port wing turret, and damaged the barrel so that it was of no further use. Today this barrel stands outside the Naval Museum at Wilhelmshaven. SMS *von der Tann* was hit once by a shell credited to *Revenge* which struck just below the aft conning tower. The ventilation shaft there was destroyed but although the conning tower remained intact splinters entering through the vision slits killed four men and wounded the others, whilst smoke and gas penetrated as far below as the engine room.

At this time only *Colossus* was hit in return. Two shells from *Seydlitz* struck at 20.16hrs, one hitting the bridge and the other the forward superstructure, which caused some 4-inch ammunition to burn. Two other shells impacted nearby and caused heavy vibrations.

Even the hapless *Lützow*, manoeuvring off to the south, came under a heavy fire between 20.15 and 20.18hrs. The battleships *Monarch* and *Orion* managed to hit this cruiser five times at a range of around 170hm. One shell struck the 250mm thick armour of the side of turret B. The shell struck the starboard side as the turret was trained to port, hard aft. The shell was kept out but fragments of armour penetrated inside:

> The right side wall was penetrated in the aft, lower part, leaving a ¼ square metre hole. The piece of plating punched out was found on the right cartridge cradle but the shell itself was not found in the turret. The loading facilities and the right upper hoist were destroyed, and the men stationed in the rear of the right gun were killed.[28]

The next shell from port struck the right barrel of A turret just outside the gunport, and the gun was disabled. A further hit struck the starboard belt armour below B barbette and resulted in flooding in the N°1 starboard 15cm magazine, then another shell struck the 15cm casemate armour of the N°4 starboard casemate and exploded, but the gun was not put out of action. The last hit at this time struck between C and D turrets and devastated the Main Dressing Station, where there were many wounded. An orderly wrote:

> The Stabsarzt [Staff Physician], to my surprise, was still alive, however his head was badly wounded. He succumbed to this wound some days later in the Wilhelmshaven Naval Hospital.²⁹ From this time, it was said throughout the ship, as he could not particularly stand well, he said: 'The wounded should be brought to the ships infirmary, so the Stabsarzt can concern himself with them.'
>
> I was amazed to hear that he was still alive. At the same time I say he was in a bad way, and only his extraordinary will to perform his military and professional duty, and his feelings of human sympathy, kept him going.³⁰

Between 20.16 and 20.18hrs, as the German line was turning away, the torpedoboats were advancing to the attack. From about 20.18hrs the British battleships began changing target to the torpedoboats and as the first torpedoes began to approach the line Admiral Jellicoe ordered a turn away to port of 2 points, although some ships turned 6 points. The battle turn by the German Fleet and the distraction of the torpedoboats meant that contact was broken and the action ceased for the time being. However, still around 100 minutes of daylight remained at this time of year and Admiral Jellicoe hoped he could renew contact with the German ships. In this he was disappointed and only at 21.18hrs did Vice Admiral Beatty sight the German battlecruisers to the northwest, along with some other three-funnelled ships. Beatty altered course to port to bring his broadside to bear, and from 21.20hrs *Inflexible*, *Princess Royal* and *New Zealand* opened fire at 75 to 119hm, and *Lion* and *Indomitable* joined in at 21.23hrs. The German cruisers were taken by surprise but immediately returned fire. At 21.32hrs *Lion* and *Princess Royal* were hit, but little damage was done. On the German ships *Derfflinger* was hit on A barbette whilst *Seydlitz* was struck five times. The N°4 port casemate was hit and put out of action and the belt was hit twice. The roof of D turret was struck but the most damaging hit struck in the lee of the conning tower and killed the signal personnel who were sheltering there, and wounded the Adjutant and Navigation Offizier. By 21.30hrs the German I AG had turned away at high speed. Assistance now came from an unexpected direction as the II Battle Squadron of pre-dreadnought ships intervened. In conditions of poor visibility they opened fire on Vice Admiral Beatty's battlecruisers but for their trouble *Schleswig-Holstein* and *Pommern* were both hit. Kontreadmiral Mauve now decided to disengage and turned 90° away to the west to draw the British towards his main body, but the British did not follow and by 21.40hrs battle had ceased. There would be no further action between capital ships mainly because Admiral Jellicoe did not wish to fight:

> But putting aside the question of attack by destroyers, the result of night actions between heavy ships must always be very largely a matter of chance, as there is little opportunity for skill on either side. Such an action must be fought at very close range, the decision depending on the course of events in the first few minutes. It is, therefore, an undesirable procedure on these general grounds.[31]

It seems the example of Aboukir Bay had been forgotten. Vizeadmiral Scheer expected to renew battle at dawn on 1 June, but with the coming of daylight nothing was to be seen of the enemy and so at 04.24hrs he ordered the I AG to run in to the Jade.

During the night the cruisers of the I AG were separated and *Derfflinger* and *von der Tann* joined the end of the long German line, whilst *Moltke*, now with Vizeadmiral Hipper aboard, and *Seydlitz* made their way independently towards the Horns Reef rendezvous. The I AG had no battle contact during the short night although *Seydlitz* had a narrow escape. Between 12.40 and 12.45hrs on 1 June the shadowy shapes of three large warships were observed to port:

> Temporarily reduce to 7 knots, course SW, for extinguishing a fire on the forecastle. Then again to course SE. To port abeam approximately 1500m distant 3 *Malaya*'s on course south. English recognition signal shown and turn away to the north. Enemy disappears from sight in our own smoke. FT signal from Z Station to *Friedrich der Große* and *Moltke*: 4 enemy Battlecruisers Grid 093 alpha, steering SSE.[32]

In fact it was the British 2nd Battle Squadron. *Seydlitz* made as much smoke as she could by use of supplemental oil firing in her boilers. Similarly *Moltke* sighted enemy battleships several times during the night but also turned away from them.

After *Lützow*'s last contact with the British, escorting torpedoboats drew a veiling smoke screen around the damaged cruiser and there was some respite, however a life-and-death struggle began to save the ship. By 21.13hrs there was 1,038 tonnes of water in the ship and at 22.15hrs there were 2,395 tonnes. At first *Lützow* ran at 13 knots but speed had to be reduced to 7 knots because of water pressure on the forward bulkheads.

Towards 01.00hrs the pumps began to lose further ground in the fight against flooding. The forward drainage group of pumps had failed, and the midships group were unable to cope with the vast quantities of water that were flooding

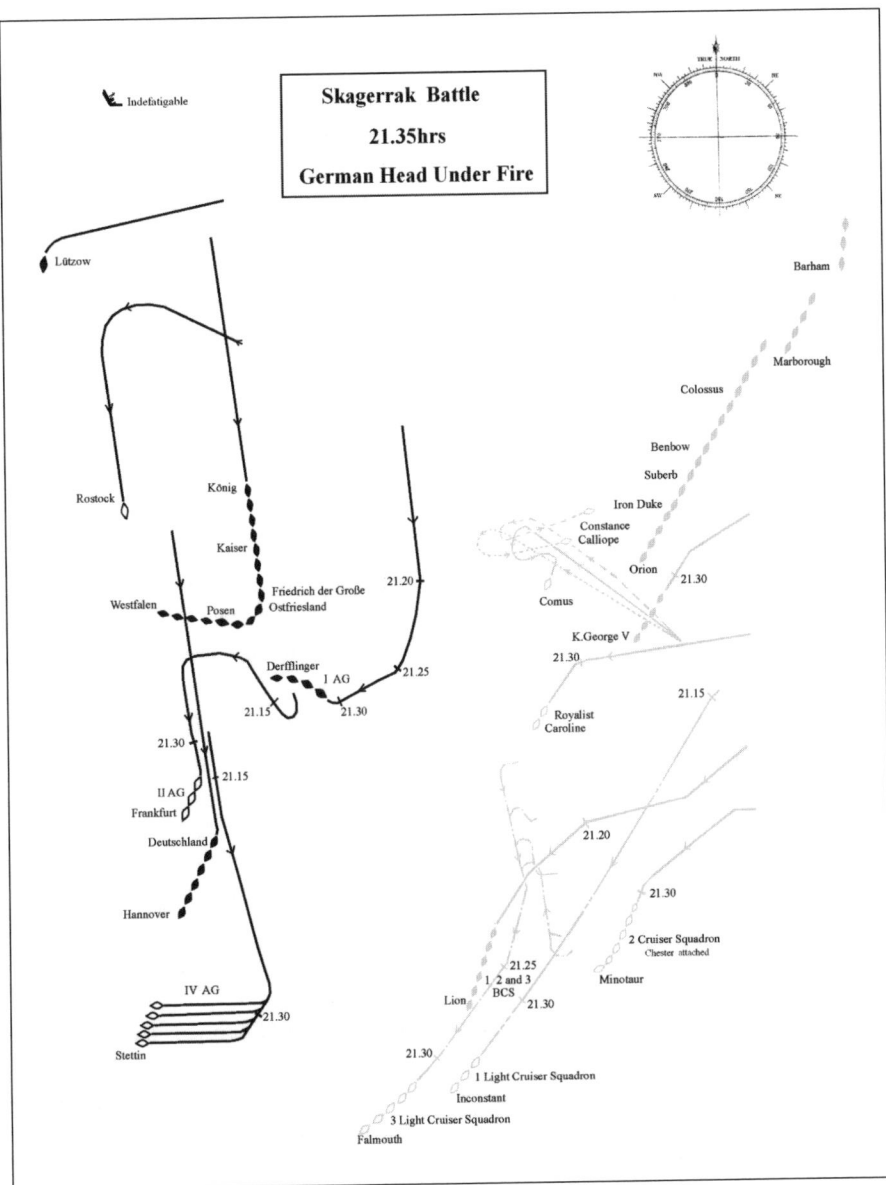

into the ship. Water began to penetrate the forward (N° VI) oil fired boiler room. 'The forecastle, the fore part of the ship, was rent apart by several hits and showed holes which a railway locomotive could comfortably have driven through.'[33] There were four gaping holes below the armoured belt and now the huge holes in the forecastle deck were admitting vast amounts of water above the armoured deck, which was freely flooding. At 02.00hrs Korvettenkapitän Paschen relates that the battle to save the ship was slowly being lost:

> I still held out hope for the ship, but as about 2am in the morning the Commander called the senior offiziers to a conference, and the First Offizier reported 7,500 tonnes of water in the ship, and gave his view that at the longest we could remain afloat until 8am in the morning. The news was a bitter blow. Our beautiful ship! However, it must be so; the forecastle was now 2 metres under water, so that through the open casemates entered the battery in streams, and poured through the ragged deck into the Between Deck. The large forward oil boiler room had to be abandoned, to save the men.[34]

The last figures from damage control indicated that there were 4,209 tonnes of water below the armoured deck, and 4,142 tonnes above, giving a total of 8,351 tonnes, but this was still increasing. Shortly after 02.00hrs an attempt was made to steer the ship stern first, but this failed because the propellers were already too far out of the water. Likewise an attempt to tow the battlecruiser with torpedoboats was abandoned. Kapitän zur See Harder ordered 'Fires out' and gave the order to abandon ship.

The four torpedoboats that had remained with *Lützow*, *G40*, *G38*, *V45* and *G37*, were now called alongside. Three lay contiguously aft to starboard.

> The survivors assembled on the quarter-deck. Above them fluttered the battle flag, shot to pieces by the enemy shells. Where there was no longer any *Offiziers*, the senior *Unteroffizier* took command. Still it was a black night. Only in the east the hesitating twilight appeared heralding the new day. The address of the Commander was short and concise. He concluded with the request that we be proud of SMS *Lützow* and her crew today for their selfless and extraordinary service for the Fatherland. Then three cheers were carried for the ship and the Supreme Warlord.
> 'And now go to the boats!' The last words of the Commander were almost paternal, sounding out of the dark. They touched the deepest senses of all of his subordinates.[35]

Kapitän zur See Harder was the last to leave the ship.

On the orders of the commander the torpedoboat *G38* fired a torpedo to scuttle the cruiser, but the draught aft was reduced and the torpedo ran under the sinking ship; a second struck amidships and the great cruiser lay slowly over to starboard and capsized at 02.47hrs.

A similar struggle was being played out aboard *Seydlitz*. At dawn on 1 June she found herself alone on the sea and found Horns Reef by scraping over it with her bottom. All navigation means had been destroyed, and the charts were soaked in blood, so the small cruiser *Pillau* was dispatched to pilot *Seydlitz* back to the Jade. The bows were shot through and leaked badly, only the airtight broadside torpedo room acted as a buoyancy chamber and kept the bows, and ship, afloat. Despite plugging as many holes as possible water continually found new ways to enter the ship. The damage control personnel and even the crew used buckets to help keep the rising water at bay.

Despite all the strenuous efforts the ship's hull gradually sank lower and deeper. As the list increased water penetrated into the casemates. Here the men again formed bucket chains to scoop out the water. The more water that entered the casemates the more the list increased. For a long, long time it seemed that the water was gaining but after many anxious hours the large ship's pendulum showed a gradual improvement. That evening the long awaited pump steamer from the dockyard made fast alongside and her large suction hoses were put to work in the casemates. It was a wonder that *Seydlitz* was still afloat with almost 5,300 tonnes of water aboard.[36]

On 2 June *Seydlitz* anchored off the Jade and early on 3 June was off Wilhelmshaven locks, where she was welcomed by hurrahs from the crews of the battleships anchored there.

On the afternoon of 31 May the II AG were being employed as the vanguard of Vizeadmiral Hipper's I AG. Ahead went *Frankfurt* under the command of Kapitän zur See Thilo von Trotha and flagship of Leader of II AG, Kontreadmiral Boedicker; to port was *Pillau*, Fregattenkapitän Mommsen, and further on the port flank *Elbing*, Fregattenkapitän Madlung. To starboard ran *Wiesbaden*, Fregattenkapitän Reiß, and on the starboard flank *Regensburg*, Fregattenkapitän Heuberer, and flagship of the II Leader of Torpedoboats (FdT), Kommodore Heinrich. The I and II FdT held equal authority. Missing from the II AG were *Graudenz*, undergoing repairs after mine damage, and *Stralsund*, undergoing dockyard overhaul and having 15cm cannon mounted.

Towards 15.00hrs the port wing cruiser of the German screen, *Elbing*, sighted the Danish ship *U-Fjord* and sent the torpedoboats *B109* and *B110* to investigate, but they were taken under fire by the British light cruiser *Galatea*, which was likewise investigating the neutral steamer together with *Phaeton*. *Elbing* hurried to support the torpedoboats and 15.32hrs opened fire on the two British cruisers in a passing battle at 130 to 140hm. Despite the high converging speed *Elbing* obtained a hit under the bridge of *Galatea*, Commodore Sinclair's flagship, however the shell failed to detonate. At 15.39hrs *Galatea* and *Phaeton* turned away to the northwest but were pursued by *Elbing* and were taken under fire again from 15.48hrs to 16.07hrs. With the first contact report from *Elbing*, *Frankfurt* and *Pillau* quickly hurried to her support, whilst six more British light cruisers of the 1st and 3rd Light Cruiser Squadrons moved to support *Galatea*. At 16.12hrs *Frankfurt* opened fire at extreme range on *Galatea* for a brief time as the British light cruisers withdrew to the west. Then at 16.30hrs both *Frankfurt* and *Pillau* opened fire on the reconnaissance aircraft launched from the aircraft tender *Engadine*. Also at 16.29hrs Vizeadmiral Hipper ordered the II AG to assemble on the I AG as heavy enemy forces had been sighted. Therefore the small cruisers made a turn onto course SW at 16.32hrs and ceased pursuing the British 1st and 3rd Light Cruiser Squadrons. Three minutes later the battleships of the 5th Battle Squadron were sighted. The British 5th Battle Squadron also sighted the II AG and at 16.58hrs heavy impacts arrived 300m from *Frankfurt*:

> The heavy impacts from the English battleships now lie continuously in the vicinity of the ships, somewhat short 80 to 100m, therefore artificial fog apparatus employed. The impacts in the vicinity of the ship cease after a short time; it was then observed that the impacts started in the vicinity of a smoke buoy thrown by *Frankfurt*. Therefore during this battle phase the artificial fog apparatus has served to allow the withdrawal of the 3 small cruisers from the well laying fire of the heaviest artillery of the enemy battleships.[37]

During the further run to the south the II AG remained to the disengaged side of the I AG.

As the battlecruisers run to the south continued *Regensburg* was able to position herself and the IX TBF ahead of the I AG. When the British destroyers advanced to the attack, the II FdT, Kommodore Heinrich, ordered the IX Flottille to repulse them. At 17.26hrs *Regensburg* gave the signal 'IX Flottille *ran!*', and hoisted the red 'Z' pennant, attack! In the following mêlée, in which the torpedoboats *V27* and *V29* were sunk, *Regensburg* supported the boats and engaged the enemy. Around this time the High Sea Fleet approached and the I and II AG reversed course and turned north. With this the small cruiser *Rostock* arrived and opened fire to cover the rescue of the crews of *V27* and *V29*, hitting the British destroyer *Obdurate* twice at 17.48hrs, and *Nestor* once at 17.53hrs.

At the beginning of the battle when Vice Admiral Beatty gave his contact report, Admiral Jellicoe dispatched the 3rd Battlecruiser Squadron ahead to support him at 17.15hrs. Because of discrepancies in the dead reckoning positions of Beatty and Jellicoe, the 3rd BCS under Rear Admiral Hood advanced to the east of the approaching British and German battlecruisers. Although their appearance in the east surprised and diverted the Germans' attention, it was by good fortune rather than good tactics.

As the 3rd BCS pushed 25 nautical miles southeast of the Grand Fleet one of the screening light cruisers, *Chester,* heard cannon thunder to the southwest at 18.27hrs. Visibility in this direction varied between 130 and 50hm but at 18.36hrs *Chester* could make out a cruiser with three funnels. Apparently *Chester* believed this to be one of Beatty's cruisers, a conception encouraged by the Germans' use of the British recognition signal that had been broadcast to the High Sea Fleet by *B109* after the first contact earlier. The II AG allowed *Chester* to approach to within 64hm when at 18.38hrs *Frankfurt* opened fire, followed by *Pillau, Elbing* and *Wiesbaden.* The surprise was complete and *Chester* did not reply until after the third salvo was fired at her. It was to be the only salvo *Chester* got away. The third German salvo hit and *Chester* began to suffer heavy damage, and she immediately turned away to the northeast. Three 5.5-inch guns were disabled and the crews of others were killed, there were three holes in the armoured belt and boilers A1 and A2 were slightly damaged. The aft rangefinder position was completely wrecked, the funnels were riddled and there was much damage from the 17 shell hits with a total of 35 men killed and 42 wounded. *Chester*'s engines remained intact, however, and she was able to make good her escape, and at the same time lead the II AG into the arms of the 3rd BCS. After a short time *Wiesbaden* and *Elbing* were ordered to cease fire to make observation easier, and *Frankfurt* and *Pillau* ceased fire on *Chester* at 18.51hrs.

At 18.40hrs the 3rd Battlecruiser Squadron observed the flash of gunfire in *Chester*'s direction and immediately altered course towards this fire. At 18.55hrs *Invincible, Inflexible* and *Indomitable* opened fire with their 12-inch guns on the cruisers of the II AG at a range of 73hm. '18.55hrs. Impacts lay very near. 18.56hrs. *Frankfurt* turns away to starboard, I have swung to avoid this turning point, so that the enemy cannot shoot on the turning point. *Wiesbaden* has seemingly not made the turn, but holds north, and is running into the fire of the heavy ships.'[38] At 18.58hrs *Pillau* was hit by a 12-inch projectile which struck from port as she turned and detonated in the *Offiziers*' wash room below the bridge. Initially a lubricating oil fire and damage to the boiler room flues caused the six forward coal fired boilers to be closed down, and then an auxiliary condenser was found salted so that *Pillau*'s speed was temporarily reduced to 24 knots, however later the boilers could be relit. The chart house, upper and lower bridges were wrecked and four men were killed.

The II AG was also under fire from the northwest. At 18.47hrs the advanced guard of the Grand Fleet, Rear Admiral Arbuthnot's 1st Cruiser Squadron, sighted the II AG and after opening fire on *Wiesbaden* at 18.50hrs he turned towards the German cruisers with his cruisers *Defence* and *Warrior* as his salvos had fallen short. However, it is generally thought that either *Indomitable* or *Invincible* hit *Wiesbaden* and disabled her engines so that at 19.01hrs she reported 'Both engines unclear, am unmanoeuvrable.'[39] Therefore she did not follow Kontreadmiral Boedicker's turn away to the south under the cover of a smoke screen.

Likewise *Regensburg* and accompanying *Flottilles* were distracted by the sudden appearance of British forces to the east. The German force had been steaming for the head of the German line but now turned ESE and from 19.04hrs to 19.08hrs *Regensburg* took the destroyer *Shark* under fire at 68 to 26hm and which she hit. The VI and II Flottilles also joined battle and fired torpedoes. When the light cruiser *Canterbury* attempted to bring relief to *Shark* and the newly-arrived *Acasta* she was hit by a shell from *Regensburg* that struck just abaft the stern 6-inch gun and passed through two bulkheads, the main deck and penetrated the fresh water tank without exploding.

Kontreadmiral Boedicker had escaped a dangerous trap, but he had never clearly made out his assailants and now made a bad error in reporting them as battleships and perhaps leading Admirals Scheer and Hipper to incorrect conclusions:

> The unimportant loss to the British here bore no relation to the gains. The surprise appearance of the 3rd Battlecruiser Squadron on the free flank of the German forces raised the possibility that they were either a separate unit or part of the main battle fleet. The diversion of the *Flottilles* from their prospective attack against Beatty and the likely discovery of the wing columns of the Grand Fleet were important results. Now the German I AG and III Battle Squadron were heading into the deploying enemy fleet...However owing to Beatty's overlapping the Germans were already in a tactically untenable position.[40]

The II AG was far to the lee side of the High Sea Fleet when at 19.20hrs the lone light cruiser *Canterbury* came in sight again to the ESE. At 19.23hrs the German cruisers reengaged as *Canterbury* turned north, and at the same time Kontreadmiral Boedicker turned to the south when he observed the I AG turning to the SE, to place himself at their head. As *Frankfurt* turned she was hit four times on the port side, with three shells impacting near the aft mast and one shell striking far forward. Kontreadmiral Boedicker did not pursue the single opponent but instead held to the south of the German Battle Squadrons running in circles and took no further part in the day battle, a performance for which he was later criticized.

Meanwhile the fourth member of the II AG, *Wiesbaden*, was having a difficult time of it. She had been disabled by a heavy shell from the 3rd BCS at 16.57hrs and lay stranded between the approaching battleships. The armoured cruisers *Defence* and *Warrior* had briefly engaged *Wiesbaden* before they were put out of action and then battleship after battleship took her as a target. *Wiesbaden* was also hit by a torpedo from *Onslow* some time about 19.20hrs which struck beneath the conning tower. There was only one survivor from *Wiesbaden*, Oberheizer Zenne, and after the commander, Fregattenkapitän Reiß, was killed, the wounded I Offizier, Kapitänleutnant Berger, asked Zenne to conduct an inspection of the ship and report. This is not unusual as the stokers of the off duty watch mainly made up the damage control parties on German ships.

> Our ships...came closer, then again turned away. A torpedoboat Morsed to us, however, we could give no answer. The enemy was in a semicircle around us, and then moved in the direction of our ships...Meanwhile it had become dark. Now we unwounded (approximately 30 men) bandaged our badly wounded, including the I Offizier, who was badly wounded in the head, and laid him on a hammock on the starboard side (The Commander and the remaining *Offiziers* and *Ingenieurs* were dead). Then we got dry clothes and something to eat, and two bottles of wine for the wounded. About midnight I went below deck, to see how it was there. Under the forecastle in compartment XIII it was quite unscathed. In compartment XIV and XV the hull side was shot through, with torn up sacks in the holes. The bulkhead to compartment XVI was penetrated and there was some water on deck. The armoured hatch to the munitions chamber was closed. In compartment XIII there was two holes in the hull side. I could only get to compartment XII with effort. The hull side was holed from the deck to above. The water went through several holes in the armoured deck to the official hold. The hatch of the torpedo loading arrangements was missing. In the torpedo room was some water, however the torpedoes could still be recognized. The way to compartment XI was blocked. I stopped up the lowest hole in the stoker's bathroom with some sacks and a wedged board. Then I went on the *Oberdeck* and in the ventilation shaft down into compartment X. Compartment X was not damaged, in the boiler room the water only stood door high...In compartment IX a hit that had gone through the bunker and through the air shaft and all was torn. A second hit went through the funnel neck. Also the drying room was full of water to door height. Bulkhead 46 was bent. In compartment VII and VIII were several hits, several holes in the hull side, in the bunker and air shaft, which were totally destroyed. In the boiler room the water was somewhat over door height. The bunker lid to the chute was closed, coal lay on the *Zwischendeck*. In compartment VI was fire, there I could only look...Of the funnels the first was holed, the second and third were completely shot away. The masts still stood, the flag flew...About 3 o'clock in the morning SMS *Wiesbaden* lay somewhat more over to starboard. Floats were let down aft. It was quite light. A cruiser and a destroyer each with 4 funnels came in sight, but took no notice of us. The ship lay deeper more and more. Then we all went aft and down onto the float, the badly

wounded had to be left behind. In total quiet *Wiesbaden* suddenly vanished beneath the waves with flying flag.[41]

During the day battle the IV Reconnaissance Group, under Kommodore von Reuter, was positioned to the rear of the High Sea Fleet and confined itself to rescuing survivors of sunken ships. However as day turned to evening and the German Fleet assumed a southerly course the IV AG found itself at the head of the entire line. Towards 21.10hrs the German forces were on southerly course with the IV AG leading, the II AG just aft of them to port, and the pre-dreadnoughts of II Battle Squadron following. The battle line was abaft the II AG in reverse order, that is with *Westfalen* leading the I Battle Squadron, followed by the III Battle Squadron. The British Grand Fleet lay to the east, on a converging course. At 21.26hrs the 4th Light Cruiser Squadron came under fire from German battleships and *Calliope* was hit five times. Whilst this action was taking place further action occurred to the south. The British 3rd Light Cruiser Squadron was just 4 nautical miles west of Vice Admiral Beatty's battlecruisers when at 21.14hrs *Falmouth* sighted five German small cruisers directly ahead on course south. Rear Admiral Napier immediately turned his light cruisers onto a parallel course and assembled them into battle line. The sighted cruisers were the II and IV AG's and at 21.17hrs these sighted the 3rd LCS on course SW. Whilst Kontreadmiral Boedicker turned his II AG away to starboard, Kommodore von Reuter turned his IV AG towards what was a superior opponent, and a violent fire fight ensued at a range of 87 to 54hm, in which the British had the advantage of better visibility. The Germans stood out clearly against the bright western horizon. Only *Stettin* and *München* could make an effective reply, whilst *München* was soon hit twice by 6-inch shells. One shell struck the upper part of the third funnel and rent a large hole and interrupted the forced draught to the aft four boilers, so that steam pressure could only be held with difficulty. The other shell detonated in the port aft cutter, killing four men and wrecking the N°3 searchlight. With their superior speed of 25 knots the British cruisers began to overhaul the IV AG so that the latter had to bear away to starboard and eventually turn away at 21.30hrs. At the same time as this action the British 1st Battlecruiser Squadron engaged the I AG and II Battle Squadron, as related earlier.

At 23.00hrs the German line with *Westfalen* at the head was heading SE at 16 knots. To port almost abeam some 8 miles distant were the battleships of the Grand Fleet, whilst to starboard ahead at 6 miles were the three British Battlecruiser Squadrons. To port abeam at 4 miles were the II AG and IV AG, between the two fleets, and between them and *Westfalen* were *Moltke* and *Seydlitz*, trying to gain position ahead of the line. Because of a leaky port condenser suffered at around 20.15hrs *Elbing* could run at only 20 knots and therefore was ordered to join the IV AG, to which *Rostock* had also attached.

At around 23.02hrs the II AG ran onto the 11th Destroyer Flotilla, under Commodore Hawksley aboard the light cruiser *Castor*. Kontreadmiral Boedicker erroneously believed he had five light cruisers before him and therefore after *Frankfurt* and *Pillau* had each launched a torpedo he turned away to the west. The commander of *Pillau*, Fregattenkapitän Mommsen, revealed a veiled criticism of his chief about his reluctance to offer battle when he wrote:

> Follow the flagship; until 23.17am several cruisers avoided. Course and speed varied. Enemy destroyers call several times with their own recognition signal, however despite the unclear night were clearly recognized because of their construction type, and the II Flottille stood to the south. In the course of the night *Pillau* avoided 7 to 10 torpedoes fired by cruisers and destroyers, and this was easy as in the moment of firing a small blue flame flashed. I have looked to the flagship of the II AG for guidance of my behaviour with the repeated meetings with enemy light forces during the night. The file *Frankfurt–Pillau* has by about 12.30am, the time point of the dividing of the two ships, met enemy light forces about five times, just as *Pillau* has recognized, in all cases a light cruiser or flotilla leader with 5 or 6 boats. *Frankfurt* has in all cases avoided them without illuminating (searchlights) or firing, and in one case has imparted to *Pillau* with Morse message: '*Achtung*, torpedoes were fired on port.' I have supposed the leader of the II AG has chosen this behaviour, not using searchlights or gunfire, so as not to draw the enemy light forces that were in the sector ESE–SSW onto the general course of the main body by artillery fire or searchlight illumination.[42]

Soon after at 23.05hrs *Castor* sighted three or more cruisers to starboard. *Castor* was challenged with the correct recognition signal and, uncertain whether they were friend or foe, *Castor* replied. Then *Elbing* illuminated a searchlight and *Hamburg*, *Elbing* and *Rostock* opened a rapid fire. *Castor* replied and on *Hamburg* the aft funnel was shot through whilst another hit struck the hull near the port N°3 gun, wounding five men. Aboard *Castor* a hit set fire to her motorboat and illuminated her and she was hit another nine times. A large hole was made beneath the N°2 4-inch gun, four shells struck the hull side, three shells struck the fore bridge and another exploded in the forecastle. A total of twelve men were killed and twenty-three were wounded. *Castor* and accompanying destroyer *Magic* each fired a torpedo as they turned away, and *Castor*'s passed beneath *Elbing* as she turned away. After that contact was lost.

A short time later, at 23.35hrs, the *Panzerkreuzers Moltke* and *Seydlitz* were steaming to gain the head of the German line and passed directly ahead of *Stettin* and the IV AG. To avoid a collision *München*, *Frauenlob* and *Stuttgart* sheered away to port and immediately the four *Town*-class cruisers of the

2nd Light Cruiser Squadron came in sight 30hm to port aft on a converging course. As the two sides approached *Dublin* and *Southampton* illuminated their searchlights and opened fire at ranges as little as 700 metres. The German small cruisers likewise switched on their searchlights and opened fire, however because the third and fourth British ships, *Nottingham* and *Birmingham*, did not light their searchlights they remained unfired upon, whilst they themselves made an effective fire. The range was extremely short and hardly a shot could miss in a battle of vehement violence. *Stettin* and *München*, *Frauenlob* and *Stuttgart* concentrated their fire on the two leading cruisers and after the first salvo *Southampton* and *Dublin* were on fire in several positions. *Stettin* turned to fire a torpedo but was hit twice. One shell hit the aft sponson gun shield, which was deeply indented, putting the gun out of action. The second struck the hull side just behind the port N°2 gun and detonated inboard. *München* was hit once through the second funnel, whilst two short shells caused splinter damage. On *Hamburg* a shell struck the fore funnel and showered the bridge area with splinters, killing ten men. *Elbing* was hit once by a shell in the wireless room, where four men were killed and fourteen were wounded. Suddenly there was a tremendous explosion that drowned all else out. At the beginning of the action, before opening fire, *Southampton* had launched a torpedo which now struck *Frauenlob* in the port auxiliary machinery room. Obermaschinist Max Müller wrote:

> Towards 12[40] the engines made revolutions for 15 knots when a violent explosion occurred in the aft ship, in the auxiliary engine room, (a crash and a cracking) which due to my recollections of SMS *Danzig*[43] could only come from a torpedo hit. At the same moment the engines stopped, probably as a result of bending the propeller shafts, the lights extinguished and through the bulkhead to the port auxiliary engine room a violent rushing of penetrating water could be heard. This rushing could be heard through the speaking tube in the starboard engine room.[44]

Another survivor, Fähnrich Stolzmann, wrote:

> Then the ship lifted, as if from a powerful impact…a vibration went through the entire hull…the lights went out, the searchlights extinguished…the engines stood still.
> That was a torpedo hit!
> Immediately the ship took up a list to port. I went further aft. From the stairways and openings of the aft ship smoke and steam climbed up…
> Meanwhile the port engine room leaked like a sieve. Thick water jets poured into the room….in the water they attempted to locate the leak…in vain, the water was rising too quickly! 'Attempt to hold the engine room by

draining with pumps!' instructed Oberingenieur Hahn, our Leading *Ingenieur*. All hands moved...Nevertheless, it was too late! The Auxiliary Engine room, which the deadly torpedo had hit, was already full of water. All the generators were submerged.

I came to the aft bridge. *Frauenlob* already lay heavily over to the side. The sea already washed about the approximately seven metre high deck. One felt that from second to second the ship lay over more and more, and the capsizing motion became ever quicker...The aft ship was a place of devastation. A savage heap of rubble; shot-down searchlight positions, ventilator heads and iron parts that were no longer recognizable...The fast capsizing moment of the ship becomes even faster.

From the funnels comes the hiss of air escaping from the interior of the ship. The last vestiges of the ship disappear in the deep. Our lively, valiant, brave *Frauenlob*. People are swimming all around.[45]

The commander Fregattenkapitän Hoffmann and 319 others perished with the sinking and there were only eight survivors. The next astern, *Stuttgart* under the command of Fregattenkapitän Hagedorn, sheered out to starboard to avoid the sinking ship. He lost contact with the IV AG and took station on the I Battle Squadron. *Hamburg* also turned away, to avoid *Moltke*, and *Elbing* and *Rostock* followed her, before attempting to reunite with *Stettin* and *München*. *Seydlitz* lost sight of *Moltke* and these two proceeded independently.

Likewise the British 2nd LCS turned away. *Southampton* had been badly damaged and hit up to fifteen times. There were many hits on the hull plating, some of which penetrated, and all four funnels were perforated. Only one 6-inch and one 3-inch cannon were damaged but three other starboard guns were put out of action because of losses to their crews. There were three cordite fires and both aft searchlights were wrecked, along with the one forward one. There were thirty-five dead and forty-one wounded crew. *Dublin* was hit by five 15cm shells from *Elbing* and eight 10.5cm shells from the other small cruisers. Seven hits were on the hull side, whilst the chart house was wrecked as were other light structures. *Dublin* became separated from the 2nd LCS and could only rejoin them after daybreak.

As 31 May turned to 1 June the night was dark, somewhat hazy and the visibility was poor. The German line was proceeding SSE at 16 knots, on a converging course with the rear units of the Grand Fleet and Vizeadmiral Scheer had given the order to hold course regardless of events. Everyone expected the battle to recommence at dawn and Scheer wanted to do this in the waters off Horns Reef. Admiral Jellicoe had assembled his destroyers at the rear of his battle fleet, whilst Vizeadmiral Scheer had sent his off to find and attack the British battleships. Ironically the German *Flottilles* failed to locate any targets, whilst the British destroyers had them dropped in their laps.

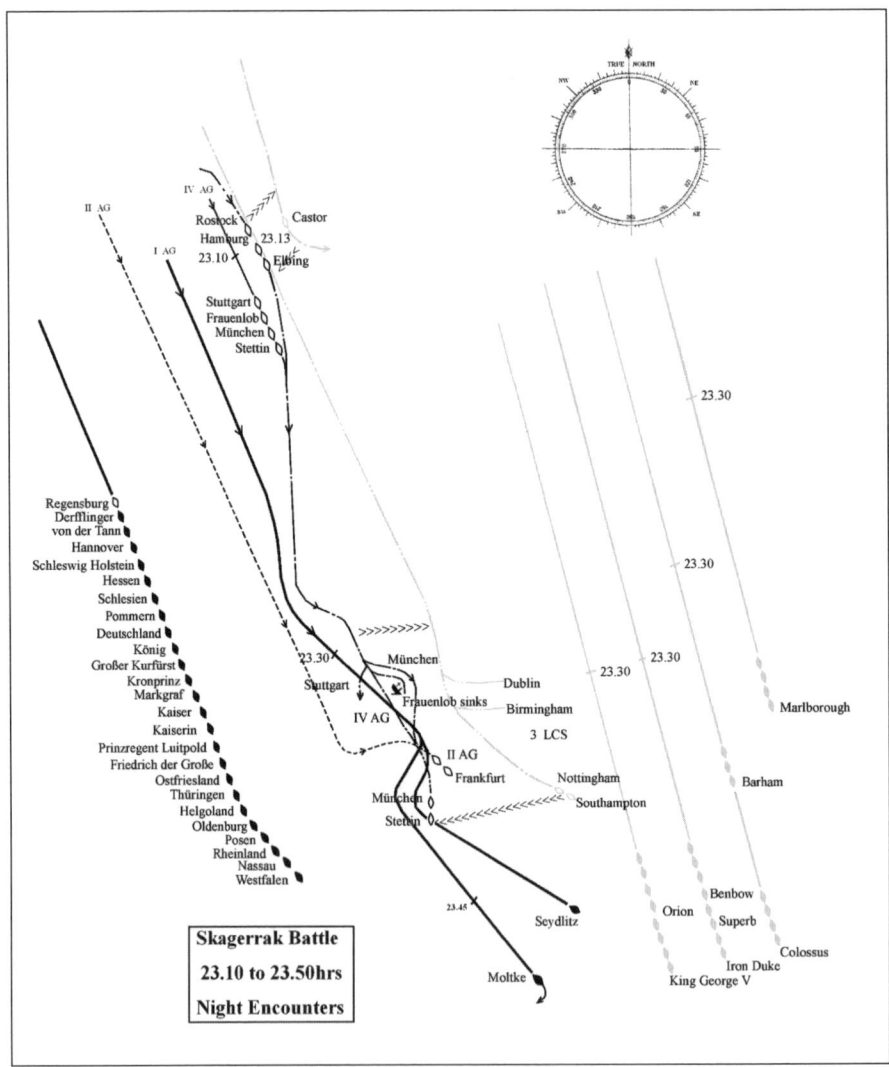

Towards 00.30hrs the British 4th Flotilla could make out a long line of ships to starboard, travelling southeast, with light vessels apparently overtaking them. The destroyers swung out their torpedo tubes and maintained course so that the range decreased to 1,000m, and then the Flotilla Leader, *Tipperary*, gave the recognition signal. A withering fire was the reply. The German battleships illuminated their searchlights and opened rapid fire from their medium and light calibre guns which immediately took effect on the hapless destroyers. To port of the German line the small cruiser *Stuttgart* lit her searchlights, but did

not open fire, whilst *Rostock*, *Elbing* and *Hamburg* all joined in with the battleships. Of the twelve destroyers at least seven were hit by shellfire, whilst *Spitfire* was also involved in a collision with *Nassau*. Return fire caused many casualties among the bridge and searchlight personnel aboard some German battleships. The German small cruisers however, were in a difficult situation as they were placed between their battleships and the opposing destroyers. When they recognized torpedoes being fired from the British destroyers, they found their escape blocked by the line of battleships. *Rostock* succeeded in passing between *Nassau* and *Rheinland* as the latter gave way, but *Elbing* was squeezed by *Stuttgart* and was forced to pass ahead of *Posen*. Because of the lively battle the commander of *Posen*, Kapitän zur See Lange, only belatedly realized that his ship and the small cruiser would unavoidably collide.

> There *Stuttgart* turned back to port very late, and *Elbing* was forced to break through (the line) ahead of *Posen*. From *Elbing* the situation did not appear dangerous. It was taken that *Posen* could well see the illuminated *Elbing* and correspondingly would give air to starboard. As the collision appeared inevitable, it was attempted, to avoid the stern with hard starboard rudder. As then it became known that *Posen* herself had laid hard starboard rudder, the rudder was taken off. The collision resulted to starboard aft and was relatively weak.[46]

At first the ship took on a list of 18°, but this could be righted by counter flooding. The starboard engine room filled with water, and after that also the port engine room. Because of this the steam condensed in the pipes to the rudder and generators, and the rudder and lighting failed. At first the port battery could still be used, however a report could only be conveyed by Morse signal as the wireless room had previously fallen out. The cruiser lay unmanoeuvrable to starboard aft of the German line and incapable of further action. About 02.00hrs the torpedoboat *S53* took off 477 men, leaving only a skeleton crew aboard to attempt to save the ship. This proved impossible and when towards 03.00hrs British destroyers and a cruiser were sighted Fregattenkapitän Madlung ordered explosive charges detonated to scuttle the ship, which sank by the bow. The Germans took to a cutter whilst the British cruiser fired a few shells into the sinking cruiser. The cutter drifted away and thereby soon found the exhausted doctor of *Tipperary* and hauled him aboard, and then found about 100 survivors from this destroyer drifting in the water. Fregattenkapitän Madlung did not hesitate to light a flare to try and attract the attention of the British ships. Five hours later the Germans were rescued by a Dutch trawler.

At around 00.40hrs the 4th Flotilla again approached the German battle line as they had resumed their southerly course, and again the Germans opened fire from their medium and light guns. During the following action *Broke* was hit in the bridge and went out of control, ramming next astern, *Sparrowhawk*, who was then also rammed by *Contest*. Nevertheless, *Contest* and *Ambuscade* had fired torpedoes and as *Rostock* attempted to break through the German line she was struck by one. The torpedo struck to port on the bulkhead between compartments X and XI, that is the IV and V boiler rooms. These two rooms immediately filled with water as did the wing passages, and because the torpedo was a shallow runner the upper bunker also filled so that there were 930 tonnes of water in the ship. The bows sank by 1.45m and there was a list of 5° to port, but nevertheless at first *Rostock* could follow the line at 17 knots. However, when *Rostock* was about 50 nautical miles west of Horns Reef it was observed that the boilers were salting and beginning to boil over. The cause of this was never found. The auxiliary machinery soon failed and the turbines had to be stopped, whereby torpedoboat *S54* took her in tow at a speed which at times reached 10 knots and it looked as if *Rostock* would reach harbour safely. Towards 03.00hrs the torpedoboats *V71* and *V73* arrived to assist. Nevertheless towards 04.45hrs what appeared to be two enemy cruisers were sighted, however actually it was *Dublin*, and as the airship *L11* reported further enemy forces in the immediate vicinity Kapitän zur See Feldmann decided to save his crew and abandon ship. The torpedoboats were called alongside and the crew was disembarked, then scuttling charges were detonated in the torpedo room and beneath the turbines. On the orders of the I FdT, Kommodore Michelsen, three torpedoes were fired at the ship to hasten the sinking, which occurred stern high at 05.25hrs. During the battle *Rostock* suffered eleven dead, and two others who died later in hospital, six wounded and one missing. She was struck by shellfire a total of seven times: once on the poop deck, once athwart ships above the turbine room, once through the fourth funnel, once on the belt amidships, once on deck behind the first funnel and twice on the forecastle. Five hits were from starboard and two were from port.

Even though the German cruisers played no further part in the action, there was still plenty to come. After the last attack of the 4th Flotilla, shortly after 01.00hrs, the German battleships sighted a ship with four funnels to port ahead. It was the British armoured cruiser *Black Prince*, and under the fire of at least four German battleships she was quickly set afire and after several smaller explosions was rocked by a single powerful explosion and blew up taking her entire crew with her. However, the German main body still had to break through the masses of destroyers of the 9th, 12th and 13th Flotillas. When the battle line came into contact with the 12th Flotilla there were terrible consequences. Towards 03.00hrs the battleships turned away to starboard to avoid torpedoes, but at 03.10hrs *Pommern* was struck by one, or perhaps two, torpedoes fired by the destroyer *Onslaught*. A series of powerful explosions followed one another at brief intervals and it was later thought that a 17cm magazine had detonated. From starboard, flames spread over the entire ship and reached past the mast heads. *Pommern* eventually broke in two and the next ship astern, *Hannover*, had to sheer out of line to starboard to avoid the floating stern half of the ship, on which the propellers and rudder towered high into the air. The entire crew of 839 officers and men perished. After that there was one more encounter with British destroyers before a certain quiet reigned over the German line.

Dawn on 1 June brought light rain, a southerly breeze strength 2 to 3 and quiet seas. It also brought an empty ocean. Nothing of the Germans was to be seen from either British flagship. Admiral Jellicoe expected the Germans to be to the northwest, while Vice Admiral Beatty expected them to be to the southwest. They were both wrong and at 03.30hrs the High Sea Fleet was 16 nautical miles west of Horns Reef, about 30 nautical miles northeast of Admiral Jellicoe. At 03.39hrs Admiral Jellicoe ordered his Battle Squadrons to turn north, and Vice Admiral Beatty's battlecruisers followed at 03.55hrs. At 04.24hrs Vizeadmiral Scheer ordered the I AG to return to harbour and at 05.08hrs he ordered the remaining forces to run in by their units. With that all hope of further contact vanished and the battle was over.

During the course of the morning the small cruiser *Pillau* was dispatched to *Seydlitz* to help pilot her home, and *Regensburg* was dispatched to relieve the four torpedoboats of *Lützow*'s crew.

A detailed analysis of the decisions undertaken or aftermath are not within the scope of this book, however a brief summary is necessary. The High Sea Fleet met and repeatedly attacked a Grand Fleet that outnumbered it two-to-one and inflicted losses on it in the reverse proportion, then the German Fleet executed a skilful withdrawal. On the evening of 1 June, without the post-battle spin of later years, the High Sea Fleet had carried the day. When the fleet returned to Wilhelmshaven Roads they were welcomed by cheering crowds lining the shoreline of the Roadstead. Across the North Sea the forces returning to Rosyth were greeted by jeering workers pelting them with coal from the Firth of Forth bridge. The attacking spirit of Nelson was gone. The Royal Navy no longer wanted to win, they just did not want to lose.

> There was a choice: to fight or not to fight. Ours, in the place of the Admiralty, would have been to fight. Theirs was not to fight. That decision fastened upon the British Navy an incubus of which it will not rid itself for many a year. Every British commander with an instinctive willingness to assume risks, which is the very foundation of naval and military greatness, will be confronted with a formidable library purporting to prove by every form of skilful plea and clever argument that Jellicoe won the World War without 'leaving anything to chance'.[47]

So let it be said that the Battle of Jutland was not a defeat, but also that the Skagerrak Battle was a victorious epoch of the High Sea Fleet.

Chapter 9

The Second Battle in the Helgoland Bight, 17 November 1917

After the Skagerrak Battle Vizeadmiral Scheer continued his policy of attempting to bring part of the Grand Fleet to action, in accordance with the guidelines given for the High Sea Fleet. At a meeting on 30 June 1916 with the Imperial Chancellor, Bethmann-Hollweg, Vizeadmiral Scheer learned that the Government was still unable to bring itself to sanction unlimited U-boat warfare against trade and the British economy, whereas Scheer advocated conducting the naval war with all the weapons available in the most effective way, regardless of political considerations. Although disappointed, Vizeadmiral Scheer knew this was a matter for the Cabinet and Naval Staff to decide and meanwhile he would continue to conduct offensive operations.

After the Skagerrak Battle all of the *Panzerkreuzer* (battlecruisers) and three of the battleships of the *König* class required repairs. Whilst these would mainly be complete by the end of July, the repairs to the cruisers *Seydlitz* and *Derfflinger* would take longer, being completed on 2 and 15 October respectively. Repairs to *Derfflinger* were extended because a new tripod mast was installed incorporating an artillery direction position, so that that smoke interference as occurred on 31 May would be reduced. Until the fleet resumed offensive operations several torpedoboat *Flottilles* were dispatched in turn to the Flanders base at Zeebrugge to continue active operations.

Meanwhile plans were developed for a further operation against the coastal town of Sunderland. As before U-boats would be deployed off the English coast to attack the Grand Fleet as it proceeded to counter the High Sea Fleet. For this advance the I Reconnaissance Group, *Moltke* and *von der Tann*, would be reinforced by the brand new battleship *Bayern*, and the other battleships *Großer Kurfürst* and *Markgraf*. A total of eighteen U-boats would take part and eight naval airships were available for reconnaissance. According to plan the High Sea Fleet put to sea at 18.00hrs on 18 August, with the I AG just 20 nautical miles ahead, instead of the 60 miles as on 31 May. At 06.00hrs the following morning the battleship *Westfalen* was torpedoed by the British submarine *E23* and was dispatched back to Wilhelmshaven by Vizeadmiral Scheer. Despite being concerned that the secrecy of the operation had been compromised early, Vizeadmiral Scheer continued his operation. Meanwhile British Naval Intelligence's Room 40 had decoded a message on the morning of

18 August saying that III Squadron would pass the outer Jade at 22.30hrs that evening and had already alerted Admiral Jellicoe, so that at 11.55hrs on 18 August he gave orders for the Grand Fleet to put to sea and assemble. All doubt had been removed when the wireless order: 'Gg 2750/0 takes place today', was transmitted on the morning of 18 August. Directional bearings were also taken on a number of U-boats and later on *Westfalen* after she was torpedoed. It looked as if there would be another battle in the proportions of the Skagerrak Battle as the High Sea Fleet approached the English coast and the Grand Fleet approached from the north. However, during the morning both Admirals Jellicoe and Beatty turned north for 2 hours because of U-boat contacts, but by 12.00hrs on 19 August the British and German Fleets had neared to within about 90 nautical miles of one another. Had not the British made the northerly turn there would probably have been contact between the fleets around 13.00hrs. Nevertheless, at 13.00hrs Vizeadmiral Scheer received a report from airship *L13* identifying heavy enemy forces to the south of the position of the High Sea Forces. Vizeadmiral Scheer now determined to abandon the bombardment of Sunderland and pursue the forces to the south, which *L13* identified as destroyers, cruisers and battleships at 13.22hrs. It appeared to be the isolated British fleet part that had evaded the Germans since 16 December 1914. In reality it was the Harwich Force of light cruisers and destroyers. From U-boat reports Vizeadmiral Scheer knew that the Grand Fleet lay to the north, and as he proceeded south it became clear that he was chasing a phantom force. Notwithstanding the chance of a night torpedo attack on the Grand Fleet, Scheer decided to call off the operation at 16.30hrs in the afternoon. Nevertheless, there had been some success for the Germans. At 06.56hrs the light cruiser *Nottingham* was struck by two torpedoes fired from the stern tubes of *U52*, under the command of Kapitänleutnant Walther. At 07.24hrs *U52* succeeded in hitting with a third torpedo and *Nottingham* sank. Likewise in the afternoon *U66*, under Kapitänleutnant Bothmer, hit the light cruiser *Falmouth* with two torpedoes and the cruiser remained stopped with a list. The destroyer escort successfully held *U66* at bay, but the following morning *U63*, commander Kapitänleutnant Schultze, had the opportunity to damage *Falmouth* with a further two torpedo hits and she sank just 5 miles off the English coast. In total the German U-boats fired a total of twenty torpedoes at British warships for a total of seven hits, that is 35%.

For the Germans the plan to draw the Grand Fleet out had again worked, but it was found that the reconnaissance by airships was unreliable and at times misleading. The trap set by U-boats had also worked, but had failed to catch capital ships. For the British the results of the 19 August operation were more far-reaching. Admiral Jellicoe, backed by Admiral Beatty, gave instructions that the Grand Fleet avoid going further south than latitude 55°30' North and further east than longitude 4° East unless it had sufficient destroyers as an antisubmarine screen. This represented a shift in strategic thinking which the Germans found difficult to comprehend. With the approval of the Admiralty the protection of the North Sea and the English coast south of Sunderland would be left to the local forces, that is the Humber and Harwich Forces and the 3rd Battle Squadron. It did not matter for the decision whether the Grand Fleet was based at Scapa Flow or Rosyth. From this moment on the North Sea south of the Tyne was under the domination and undisputed influence of the German High Sea Fleet. It would now take great pressure to bring the Grand Fleet to blows in this area.

A further German advance was planned for the beginning of September, however this was cancelled because poor weather made reconnaissance impossible. The next large-scale operation by the High Sea Fleet was postponed several times likewise because of bad weather but was eventually conducted from 18 to 20 October 1916. The advance continued into the middle of the North Sea and in addition to eight reconnaissance airships the small cruiser *Stralsund* embarked a seaplane reconnaissance aircraft. During the advance to the west, at 09.47hrs, the small cruiser *München* was torpedoed by the British submarine *E38*. *München* had been unable to avoid the torpedo as it was only seen late in the rough sea. The Leading Engineer of *München*, Ingenieur Zieb wrote:

> The alarm readiness still stood when about 9.45am the air track of a torpedo was recognized from the bridge of the small cruiser *München* to port. With hard rudder and the order 'Both engines three times Utmost Speed (AK) ahead' the Watch Offizier attempted to avoid the torpedo, however the range was too short. The torpedo struck amidships at the level of the second boiler room and rent a large hole in the hull. A giant water column, mixed with black coal dust and pieces of coal from the destroyed bunker, mixed with parts of sheet steel plates rose to the height of the mast tip and then heavily fell back on the ship. The fore- and aft ship strongly shook up and down, however the ship did not break apart.[1]

Eventually 500 tonnes of water entered the ship and after salting of the boilers she had to be taken in tow, at first by torpedoboat *V73*, and later by her sistership *Berlin*. Nevertheless, the following day Fregattenkapitän Tietgens was able to steer up the Jade under his own power and run into Wilhelmshaven Dockyard. On this occasion the Grand Fleet did not put to sea and apart from submarines there was no enemy contact. A further fleet operation into the area of the Hoofden planned for March 1917 came to nothing because bad weather precluded airship reconnaissance.

With the declaration of unlimited U-boat warfare on 1 February 1917 the axis of the naval war changed. The U-boat campaign was embarked upon to ruin Britain economically and its prosecution assumed paramount importance. Given that 'Jellicoe's offensive measures to draw out the Germans ceased after Jutland,'[2] and that the major part of the North Sea had been abandoned to the Germans, the Allies now embarked upon an extensive minelaying campaign in the German Bight to hinder the German U-boats putting to sea from their bases. The pivotal axis of the naval war between surface forces now changed to a battle between the British minelayers and the German minesweepers. Just as the minelaying stretched further and further to seawards and the German minesweepers had to operate further from their bases, the light forces of the Royal Navy attempted to disrupt the minesweeping and the escort *Flottilles* that took the U-boats safely through the mined areas. The Germans supported their minesweepers with forces which gradually increased in size as the battle over the minefields increased in intensity. After several small skirmishes this course of action resulted in the last major clash between British and German cruiser forces during the war.

Because of the work of British Naval Intelligence and Room 40 and the preference of the German command to transmit orders by wireless, the British forces generally had good knowledge of German minesweeping activity and could choose a time and place for an attack. The German minesweeping activity took two forms, one of maintaining the utilized channels mine-free and testing for new barriers in outlying areas, and the other of sweeping known mine barriers. The so-called 'test trips' in the outer parts of the blockaded area were the most vulnerable to attack. A test trip would usually consist of groups of trawlers fitted for minesweeping, specialist minesweepers of the M-type or old torpedoboats with light sweeping gear to locate mines, buoy boats to mark any mines found and *Sperrbrecher*–cargo ships made as unsinkable as possible with a cargo of barrels and wood–to trial the newly swept channels. This force was escorted by a group of torpedoboats, and by late 1917 was usually supported by a group of small cruisers. There was normally also a group, or file, of battleships or battlecruisers acting in distant support to the rear and a group of capital ships on Schillig Roads at 3 hours' notice.

On 16 August 1917 German minesweepers of the 5, 6 and 8 Minesweeper Half Flottilles were sweeping Route Yellow, one of the safe routes used by U-boats to put to sea. They were screened by three torpedoboats of the 12 Torpedoboote Half Flottille, supported by the small cruisers *Frankfurt*, Fregattenkapitän Rebensburg, and *Karlsruhe*, under Fregattenkapitän Tietgens. Route Yellow went northwest from Emden past the Dutch coast to the neutral free channel and the minesweepers lay in a broad search line abreast. To the south of the line lay the buoy boat *A36* and at 12.55hrs this boat sighted two groups of eight British destroyers and behind them three light cruisers *Centaur*, *Conquest* and *Canterbury*. *A36* fled to the northeast and a firefight began at a range of 5,300m, whilst *A36* also developed a smoke screen. *A36* soon encountered minesweeper *M28* but both boats remained undamaged and succeeded in withdrawing from the effective enemy fire. In conditions of poor visibility–it was just 4 nautical miles–the British destroyers next encountered the 5 MSHF which quickly slipped their sweeps and formed battle line on an easterly course for a passing battle which lasted from 13.10 to 13.25hrs. The British took the boats under a heavy fire. At 13.18hrs *M65* was hit and remained lying unmanoeuvrable because of a damaged main steam pipe. The destroyers approached to within 1,800m and hit the hapless boat twice more killing ten men and injuring thirteen, however she later escaped. The minesweepers *M4* and *M37* were each hit once. The logbook of H.M.S. *Centaur* recorded:

> 8.30hrs. Action stations. 9.45hrs, sighted enemy torpedoboat-destroyers right ahead. 9.47hrs. Opened fire with No.1 gun and increased to 25 knots. 9.50hrs. Five hostile ships in sight on port bow. Squadron alters course 4 points to port and *Centaur* immediately opened fire with whole broadside, closely followed by remainder of squadron. Enemy replied to our fire with small calibre guns, apparently 4.1 inch, and it became apparent we were engaging a squadron of minesweepers. A very heavy and effective fire maintained by *Centaur* for about ten minutes, enemy being repeatedly straddled and several direct hits were observed…The enemy made extensive use of smoke screens and succeeded in straddling us several times…[3]

Nevertheless the minesweepers successfully resisted the attack and there were no materiel losses. On the other hand, the supporting forces failed completely to fulfil their task of ensuring the security of the minesweepers. *Karlsruhe*'s commander wrote:

> The overview about the situation was difficult to obtain, and with the last report of the II Minesweeper Division, the actual strength and disposition of the Half Flottille were not accurately known. Apparently the 5 MSHF only consisted of 3 boats. Disturbingly this uncertainty was especially perceived with the failure of *Frankfurt* to lead, or give it to SMS *Karlsruhe*.[4]

For his lack of resolve the commander of *Frankfurt*, as senior commander, was relieved of his position in September. The Official British History does not mention this encounter.

On 15 November 1917 the German Fleet Chief issued a new order for a "test trip" on 16 November. The starting point would be Grid Square 058 beta, some 70 nautical miles northwest of Helgoland, at the end of the 'Route Mid'. The partaking forces were to be:

- 2 and 6 Auxiliary Minesweeper Half Flottille of the North Sea.
- 6 Minesweeper Half Flottille
- VII Torpedoboote Flottille with *S62* and *G87*

- 14 Torpedoboote Half Flottille with *G92*, *G93* and *V83*
- 12 Torpedoboote Half Flottille with *V43*, *V44* and *V45*
- II Reconnaissance Group under Kontreadmiral von Reuter:

  - *Königsberg*, Fregattenkapitän Feldmann
  - *Frankfurt*, Fregattenkapitän Seidensticker
  - *Pillau*, Fregattenkapitän von Gaudecker
  - *Nürnberg*, Kapitän zur See Hildebrand
  - *Kaiserin*, Kapitän zur See Graßoff
  - *Kaiser*, Kapitän zur See Loesch

Königsberg and *Nürnberg* were new cruisers, and should not be confused with the ships of the same name lost earlier in the war.

Kontreadmiral Ludwig von Reuter was born on 9 February 1869 in Guben, Brandenburg. He entered the Imperial Navy as a cadet in April 1885. He commanded the armoured cruiser *Yorck* before the war and at the beginning of the war he was appointed to the newly commissioned battlecruiser *Derfflinger*, which he commanded in the Dogger Bank Battle. In September 1915 he was appointed Leader of the IV Reconnaissance Group, which he led in the Skagerrak Battle, and in September 1916 was appointed Leader of the II Reconnaissance Group. He was promoted Kontreadmiral in November 1916. In January 1918 he became 2 Admiral of the I Reconnaissance Group, and then Commander of Reconnaissance Forces in August 1918, replacing Admiral Hipper who had taken overall command of the High Sea Fleet. His successor on *Derfflinger*, Kapitän zur See Heinrich, wrote:

> My predecessor, Kapitän zur See von Reuter, welcomed me. After a brief hand over I took over the ship and crew, whereby on such opportunities one usually spoke. For my predecessor, who had been appointed Leader of the IV AG, leaving the ship and his *Offizier Korps* was very difficult.[5]

On the evening of 15 November Kontreadmiral von Reuter decided to postpone the operation because of the bad weather. On the evening of 16 November he gave the new arrangements by wireless, giving the time of departure from Schillig Roads, and the time for the forces to be at the beginning point for the sweep. The Germans might as well have issued a written invitation to the British forces.

After learning of the intended German test trip sometime soon after it was arranged the British Admiralty decided to deliver a strong counterblow. A powerful force of cruisers was to intercept the German units at their commencement point and destroy as many as possible. The Royal Navy forces for this operation comprised:

- 1st Cruiser Squadron under Vice Admiral Napier:

  - *Courageous*
  - *Glorious*
  - Four screening destroyers

- 6th Light Cruiser Squadron, under Rear Admiral Alexander-Sinclair:

  - *Ceres*
  - *Calypso*
  - *Caradoc*
  - Four screening destroyers

- 1st Light Cruiser Squadron, under Commodore Cowan:

  - *Caledon*
  - *Galatea*
  - *Royalist*
  - *Inconstant*
  - Two screening destroyers

In immediate support was the 1st Battlecruiser Squadron under Vice Admiral Pakenham, who had overall command:

- 1st Battlecruiser Squadron:

  - *Lion*
  - *Princess Royal*
  - *Tiger*
  - *New Zealand* (attached)
  - *Repulse*

- Nine screening destroyers

Then finally further back were heavier supporting forces:

- 1st Battle Squadron

  - *Revenge*
  - *Royal Oak*
  - *Resolution*
  - *Emperor of India*

- *Benbow*
- *Canada*
- Eleven screening destroyers.

The battleships and modern light cruisers of the 6th LCS represented some of the most powerful ships the Royal Navy possessed, and yet the battlecruisers had been found wanting in the Jutland Battle and even the new additions were of doubtful value. A secret Admiralty document gave the following evaluation: 'The armour protection of "REPULSE" and "RENOWN" calls for serious consideration. With a belt of only 6 inches they are dangerously liable to destruction by a *single hit* and in view of their high-speed and powerful armament it is considered that, as soon as the new shell has been supplied to all battle cruisers, no time should be lost in fitting the additional protection which is now in course of preparation for them.'[6] *Glorious* and *Courageous* were even worse off with just 2 inches, or 52mm, armour over the outer skin. Although both classes of ships were armed with heavy 15-inch guns and were capable of high speed, their protection was totally inadequate.

Now once again the wretched staff work that had dogged the Royal Navy since the first Helgoland Battle revealed itself. Considering that the admirals involved were expecting to encounter the German quarry at the edge of the mined area they should have been given the latest appraisals of the mine situation to enable them to press the pursuit and bring about decisive results. However they were not so informed. The Commander-in-Chief had a copy of a chart showing Helgoland Bight mine fields prepared by the Hydrographer of the Navy, and which was issued monthly. Vice Admiral Pakenham had been shown this chart which showed clear water to the southeast of the starting point of his operation for a distance of 30 nautical miles. However, this chart had not been shown to his subordinate admirals. Vice Admiral Napier had concluded from information available to him that he could penetrate the blockaded area for just 12 miles. Rear Admiral Alexander-Sinclair and Commodore Cowan were less well informed and were ignorant about some of the minefields, their charts showing large areas of clear water that was in fact mined. The British official history summed up thus:

> There was also in existence a chart which showed not only the British and German mines in the German Bight, but also the approximate positions of the channels that the Germans had swept through them. The commander in chief possessed a copy of this chart, but he had not shown it to any of the Admirals in charge of the operating squadrons; nor had he included any of the special information contained on this chart in his operational orders. The paragraph in the orders devoted to 'enemy intelligence'…gave no indication of the probable routes and the general line of retirement of any German forces that might be met with on the outer edge of the barrier.[7]

As in the Jutland Battle the British forces were able to put to sea before their counterparts. The 1st Battle Squadron arrived in Rosyth during the afternoon of 16 November and the collected force departed at 17.30hrs. At 08.00hrs the following morning they were approaching the general rendezvous in the outer German Bight. At 00.30hrs on 17 November the II AG departed Schillig Roads and proceeded towards their 07.00hrs rendezvous with the minesweepers. It had been intended that *Königsberg, Nürnberg* and *Frankfurt* take aboard floatplanes on the afternoon of 16 November but the uncertain weather had meant that the aircraft could not fly to Schillig Roads. Likewise on the morning of 17 November four aircraft that took off for reconnaissance soon turned back because of mist.

The weather in the Helgoland Bight on the morning of 17 November was a light north to north-westerly wind, a slight swell and changing visibility in mist and haze. At around 06.00hrs the first auxiliary minesweepers arrived at the rendezvous and proceeded slowly to the northwest. As it was still dark they soon made a turn and at 07.00hrs they met the boats of the 5 and 6 MSHF at the rendezvous. The assembled minesweepers broke out their gear and were ready to begin work, but the trawlers of the 2 and 6 Auxiliary Minesweeper Half Flottilles were missing and were still 10nm to the southeast of the rendezvous. At 08.28hrs *Königsberg* turned back to the southeast to fetch the errant trawlers, leaving Kapitän zur See Hildebrand aboard *Nürnberg* in charge. Previously, at 07.40hrs *Pillau* had sighted seven smoke columns to the west. '270° true; 7 smoke clouds. They were not reported, as they were taken for downcast smoke from the minesweepers.'[8] Then at 08.28hrs *Pillau* sighted the enemy. '270°, at first 2 then 3 vessels in sight. 1 vessel approaches oneself at high speed, right a larger vessel, seemingly a battlecruiser or battleship, right of there further vessels.'[9] Shortly after at 08.35hrs the first shots impacted just 200m short of *Pillau*. Then the other ships could make out the vague outlines of several ships on the horizon to the northwest.

As the British forces approached the general rendezvous the look-outs aboard *Courageous* sighted the enemy at 08.30hrs. Visibility was better to the lighter east and three groups of German vessels could be made out, although erroneously they thought they could see submarines. At 08.37hrs[10] *Courageous* opened fire on *Pillau* with her 15-inch guns, followed by *Glorious* at 08.41hrs. *Cardiff* and her destroyers opened fire on the minesweepers and torpedoboats. The Germans were totally surprised as the impacts of numerous shells arrived amongst their vessels. Kapitän zur See Hildebrand knew his first priority was to protect the minesweepers and he immediately took *Nürnberg* at full speed ahead to place himself between the enemy and the sweepers, giving the signal 'Z, Zero', follow the leader. *Pillau* and *Frankfurt* followed on course 347°, but because smoke quickly obscured the range course was changed to west and at 08.40hrs the enemy could be made out at 110 to 120hm. An accurate fire surrounded the German ships, which was quickly answered.

When the minesweepers came under fire they slipped their gear and turned onto an easterly course. One of the marker boats, the trawler *Kehdingen*, was advanced ahead and was hit by shellfire. The boat was crippled and was soon sunk, the majority of the crew being saved and taken prisoner. Nevertheless it was fortunate that the 5 and 6 Auxiliary Minesweeper Half Flottilles had been late, as if the test trip had proceeded on time in a north-westerly direction they would surely have been cut off by the superior British forces. As it was they were able to quickly disappear into a thickening smoke screen.

Königsberg was pushing southeast when she heard the thunder of cannon and observed gun flashes to the northwest, then the impact of heavy projectiles 2 nautical miles astern. Nothing could be seen of the enemy as Kontreadmiral von Reuter turned his flagship to the northwest and at 08.53hrs made the signal 'Course SE, follow the leader'. At 09.00hrs *Königsberg* turned SE and reduced speed to 15 knots to allow the II AG to close on her.

The A-Boats of the Auxiliary Minesweeper Flottille fought an artillery battle at ranges of 92 to 98hm from 08.50hrs to 09.02hrs with the destroyer escort of the 6th LCS. The A-Boats believed they had seen hits on some of the destroyers after which they turned away. Between 09.05hrs and 09.30hrs the A-Boats took a Flotilla Leader under fire and after that returned to harbour without further trouble from the enemy. Likewise the M-Boats of the 6 MSHF were repeatedly in battle with British destroyers at ranges between 35hm and 70hm. At 09.45hrs the destroyers turned away from the M-Boats and the 6 MSHF returned to harbour without further enemy contact. The delayed boats of Auxiliary MSHF 2 and 6 made off to the southeast and later east and despite being in contact with British forces and being in great danger were able to escape into smoke.

As the running battle developed on a SE course Kontreadmiral von Reuter was unclear about whom his opponents were as visibility aft was obscured and distorted by smoke and haze. Now and again *Königsberg* could make out an individual battlecruiser, but the number and type remained unknown. The cruisers of the II AG ran in a loose line of bearing formation with a great distance between ships and developed a smokescreen, with *Nürnberg* and *Pillau* also throwing smoke buoys. About 09.05hrs the first shells impacted around *Königsberg*, however nothing could be seen of the enemy although at 09.08hrs she fired on a British destroyer with four salvos. From 09.14 to 09.31hrs *Königsberg* lay under straddling salvos of medium and heavy calibre which could only be avoided with course alterations. In poor visibility fire was returned at 130 to 100hm.

The other three cruisers of the II AG had lain in British fire since 08.35hrs and their advance towards the enemy had reduced the range to 110hm. As *Pillau* turned to port onto a SE course at 08.50hrs she opened fire on the forward battlecruiser at 60 to 70hm and the crew believed they had seen a hit on the forecastle. At 08.55hrs the I port 15cm gun, which was not engaged,

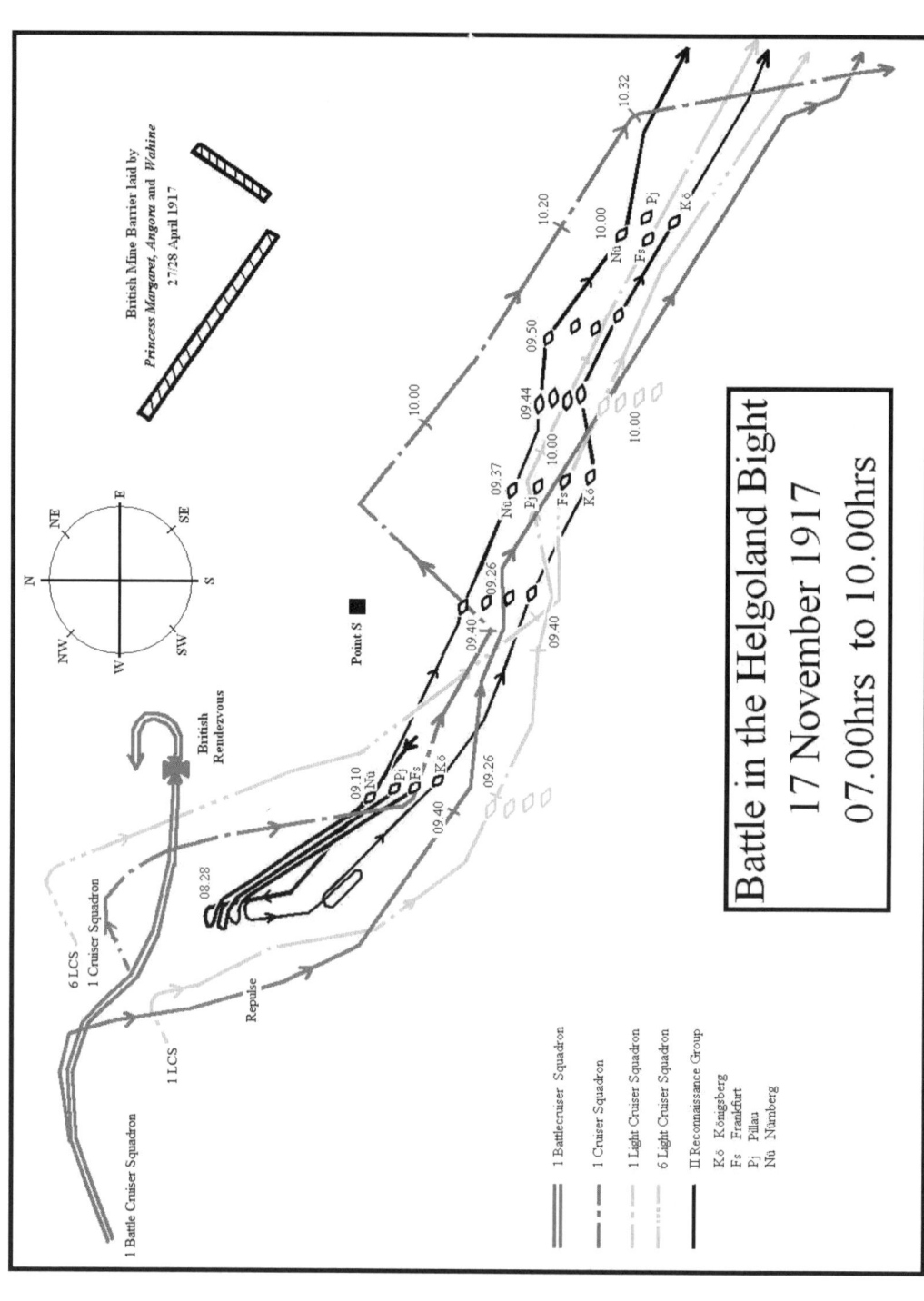

received a direct hit on the brow shield. Because of the destruction it must have been a 15-inch shell, however only the N°1 of the serving crew was killed and the N°3 and N°4 were thrown overboard by the blast, whilst the N°s 2, 5 and 7 were all slightly wounded. Although the cannon was out of action, after cauterization and chipping off impeding parts the gun was again rendered ready for service. At 08.55hrs *Nürnberg* opened fire at a range of 110hm but owing to smoke and fog the enemy soon disappeared from sight. Heavy, medium and light shells were also falling around *Frankfurt*, who returned fire as the opportunity presented itself.

Towards 09.00hrs *Courageous* was nearing the German smoke screen and therefore Rear Admiral Napier turned away sharply to the south. When he was clear of the smoke he could see three cruisers of the II AG on course SE and he resumed his pursuit. Vice Admiral Pakenham decided more support was necessary and at 09.07 he ordered *Repulse* to leave the 1st BCS and support the 1st LCS. At 09.10hrs *Courageous* and *Glorious* could reopen fire on the German small cruisers and at 09.12hrs *Cardiff* joined in. However, *Ceres* and *Calypso* could not get into range until 09.22hrs when *Inconstant* and the rest of the 1st LCS also opened fire. Therefore by 09.20hrs the II AG again lay under heavy fire. Now the destroyers *Vanquisher* and *Valentine* of the 6th LCS screen advanced to deliver a torpedo attack but at 09.23hrs *Pillau* obtained a hit on the left destroyer causing high flames, after which the destroyers turned away and *Pillau* changed target.

From 09.30hrs the Germans again cast smoke buoys and made heavy smoke from their funnels. As Rear Admiral Napier was approaching this smoke towards 09.35hrs he was also approaching the line which represented the limit of his advance into the mine fields. Therefore he turned the 1st Cruiser Squadron 8 points, or 90°, to port and crossed the wake of the 6th LCS. Rear Admiral Alexander-Sinclair and Commodore Cowan also made considerable turns to port soon after 09.40hrs so that between 09.40 and 10.00hrs all the British squadrons lost ground on the Germans.

The 6th LCS made the smallest turn and therefore took over the lead, and therefore *Cardiff* came under fire and soon received three hits in quick succession. At 09.50hrs one shell struck *Cardiff*'s forecastle and started two worrying fires. Soon after she was struck in the superstructure above the aft control position and a third shell struck the torpedo flat, without, luckily, causing an explosion. Now the smoke cleared a little and as Rear Admiral Napier could see the II AG still on course SE he determined to continue the pursuit and at 09.52hrs ordered an alteration to starboard. Nevertheless at 09.58hrs Vice Admiral Pakenham ordered a general recall but, as all the British ships had resumed fire and *Repulse* had also come into action, Rear Admiral Napier was reluctant to act on the recall and continued the chase for the time being.

Towards 10.00hrs *Pillau*, that was running well, passed *Frankfurt* to port. Between 10.00hrs and 10.50hrs the fog cleared considerably, and as the British were again approaching they could once more take the Germans under an effective fire. *Nürnberg* was under heavy fire from 15-inch and 6-inch shells:

> About 10am it was somewhat clearer. The fire of the enemy (aft most battlecruiser) increased in intensity and remained of the utmost violence until 10.45am. Shells of large and medium calibre–usually in salvos of 2 to 3 shells–struck in brief succession in the vicinity and next to the ship so that a zigzag course had to be taken and maintained near the English mine barrier.[11]

During this time *Nürnberg* suffered through splinter damage. One man was killed and four others were badly wounded, one of whom died later. Five men were lightly wounded and a rangefinder was damaged. Towards 10.40hrs *Nürnberg* ceased fire as the enemy disappeared in smoke and the enemy fire gradually slowed and ceased.

After *Pillau* had passed *Frankfurt* she began to slack aft a little and at 10.00hrs lay in heavy fire. At 10.10hrs *Frankfurt* fired a torpedo towards a light cruiser, which was avoided however. At 10.20hrs *Frankfurt* received her first hit from a 6-inch shell which put the IV gun and aft rangefinder out of action. Four or five cartridges of the ready ammunition burned and together with splinters caused some damage and killed two men. Two more were thrown overboard and ten men were wounded. At the same time a 6-inch shell struck the upper deck nearby and wounded five men. A further hit struck a spar of the main mast. The range to the British light cruisers fell to as little as 90hm and towards 10.00hrs *Repulse* could also intervene with her 15-inch guns. *Frankfurt* was forced to zigzag to throw off the aim, but this only reduced her mean speed.

Between 09.00hrs and 09.30hrs *Pillau* repeatedly came under heavy fire and used smoke to throw off the British fire. 'To starboard aft shot at approaching destroyers at 84hm, and light cruisers at 60–100hm. Enemy ships were out of sight several times because of the hazy fog of the torpedoboats and cruisers, therefore frequent target changes required. 9.15am: Order to engines: "Strong smoke."'[12] Between 09.45 and 10.07hrs *Pillau* also threw smoke buoys.

The German fire was partly effective. At 10.41hrs *Calypso* received a hit which penetrated the conning tower roof and detonated. Everybody in the conning tower was killed and on the upper bridge the commander, Captain Edwards, was mortally wounded and Navigation Officer was rendered unconscious. All those on the lower bridge were also killed. Damage to electrical leads and fire control apparatus caused *Calypso* to cease fire for the time being. This hit was apparently attributable to the fire of *Pillau* or *Frankfurt*.

Kontreadmiral von Reuter's flagship, *Königsberg*, was the furthest ahead. After initially firing on destroyers *Königsberg* changed target to a light cruiser or battlecruiser that was momentarily made out. At 09.30hrs this ship turned away. Then *Königsberg* changed over to the leader of the 6th LCS, *Cardiff*, and with the range at 85hm struck her at 09.50hrs, as related. At 09.33hrs and 09.50hrs *Königsberg* fired two torpedoes from the starboard above-water tube at a range of 105hm. Soon after this the starboard above-water torpedo tube was put out of action by a shell splinter. At 10.00hrs a light calibre shell struck the protective shield of the starboard I 15cm cannon. The shield was not penetrated but two cartridges of the ready ammunition were ignited, killing four men and badly wounding seven more, four of whom subsequently died. The losses were replaced and the gun continued in action.

Meanwhile *Courageous* and *Glorious* continued to lose ground on the German cruisers so that at 10.07hrs and 10.15hrs they had to check their fire because their shells were falling short. The cruisers of the *Galatea* class of the 1st LCS had found that their 4-inch guns were of no use in the long-range battle and only the 6-inch guns were effective. When at 10.32hrs Rear Admiral Napier reached the second, ultimate limit of his advance he changed coursed sharply to starboard and ran along the line that marked the limit of the mine dangerous area on his map. From this time on *Courageous* and *Glorious* were out of the battle. However, the light cruiser squadrons, with no such limits marked on their maps, continued the pursuit, as did *Repulse*.

At 10.12hrs Kontreadmiral von Reuter ordered his torpedoboats to attack the light cruisers. The available torpedoboats advanced and loosed torpedoes that for the greater part reached the British line. The first torpedo track passed close ahead of *Royalist*'s bow, and shortly afterwards a torpedo track was observed 30 metres ahead of *Cardiff*. For the next 10 minutes torpedo tracks were reported repeatedly by all three squadrons. One report states: 'The German light cruisers and destroyers fired about eight or ten torpedoes at ranges of 13,000–16,000 yards, one of which probably hit the light cruiser *Galatea* but did not explode.'[13]

Around half an hour after Vice Admiral Pakenham sent his general recall, Rear Admiral Napier made his turn to starboard and discontinued his pursuit, however he allowed the 1st and 6th Light Cruiser Squadrons to continue at their own discretion if they thought they could bring about a successful conclusion. He also ordered his heavy cruisers and *Repulse* to go no further. Therefore the 1st and 6th LCS continued their chase, but without *Courageous* and *Glorious* the chances of a successful conclusion were reduced. Shortly after, at 10.50hrs, any further thoughts of success were dispelled when heavy calibre shells began to impact around the British light cruisers.

The battleship file *Kaiserin* and *Kaiser*, under the command of Senior Commander Kapitän zur See Graßoff aboard *Kaiserin*, were intended by the Chief of the IV Squadron, Vizeadmiral Souchon, to serve as support for the test trip group. The morning of 17 November found this group far to the rear, too far to provide effect support. Kapitän zur See Graßoff determined on this rearward position as he was uncertain whether the test trip would return back through the middle of the German Bight or go around to the northeast and return on Route Blue. Therefore he decided to reach the departure point of the test trip, Point S, at around 10.30hrs, when he thought the minesweepers would be ready to return. Despite some of the numerous reports from Kontreadmiral von Reuter being incorrectly read, which served to confuse the situation, Kapitän zur See Graßoff hurried to his support, knowing that he would face enemy battlecruisers or fast battleships. He also reckoned that the British would have heavy support in the rear and that he faced a superior enemy. As the German battleships advanced to the northwest firstly torpedoboats came in sight and then the embattled cruisers of the II AG, however the enemy were hidden in smoke. By maintaining an easterly course Kontreadmiral von Reuter had the intention 'to draw the enemy behind myself on an eastern course through the English and German minefields and so catch them between the small cruisers and battleships. To the north and northwest he could only escape over mine barriers, and if he tried this movement to retreat to the west he would probably suffer losses to mines. His path west by reversing course must be cut off by the battleships.' Kontreadmiral von Reuter had cleverly drawn the British into a pincer grip formed by his II AG and the battleship squadron, but to achieve his intentions the battleships would have to continue northwest. However, as the two German groups rapidly approached one another Kapitän zur See Graßoff made a battle turn to starboard onto the opposite course and at 10.27hrs reduced speed to allow the II AG to catch up. Shortly after four the light cruisers of the 6th LCS were recognized. When Kapitän zur See Graßoff made out the tripod masts of the cruisers he imprudently believed he was dealing with battlecruisers. Kontreadmiral von Reuter's intensions were further thwarted when he attempted to signal *Kaiserin* about his plan, as his signals were late and incomplete when they arrived aboard the battleship. 'The signal department on *Kaiserin* was technically, in organization and personnel, not equal to the task.'[14]

Likewise the small cruisers were disappointed in their expectation that the battleships would bring relief, as heavy shells continued to fall around them. As his plan had been frustrated the leader of the II AG turned his cruisers in a southerly direction to join the battleships. At 10.41hrs *Kaiserin* opened fire on a faintly discernable light cruiser at a range of 160hm. After the next salvo fire was interrupted as the enemy disappeared in smoke, then reappeared on a north-westerly course. *Kaiserin* fired eight salvos in total and hit the leader of the 1st LCS, *Caledon*, once. The shell struck the waterline, however it failed to detonate or cause serious damage. *Kaiser* could only briefly make out the British light cruisers at 10.55hrs and briefly took them under fire. Rear Admiral Alexander-Sinclair immediately turned his cruisers 16 points to port and the

British soon vanished from sight. There was a short delay getting the message to retire through to *Repulse*, but soon all ten British ships were retiring northwest covered by *Repulse*. However, Kontreadmiral von Reuter had not yet given up and turned *Königsberg* to course NW and hoisted the signal 'follow the leader', hoping to take the battleships in that direction. As *Königsberg* was turning one of the last 15-inch shells from *Repulse*, her one hit out of fifty-four shots fired, struck *Königsberg* through the aft funnel at 10.58hrs. The raking shot penetrated all three funnels and detonated in the coal bunker above the IV boiler room. The result was a bunker fire with dense black smoke veiling the ship, which also had her speed reduced to 17 knots. Nevertheless the aft guns fired until 11.04hrs when the opponents finally disappeared.

At around 11.25hrs Kontreadmiral von Reuter ordered his forces to go to course NW whilst he would transfer to *Pillau*. In the meantime the Germans had been rushing reinforcements to the area, and at 11.35hrs the small cruiser *Stralsund* came in sight in the SSE, along with torpedoboats of the II Torpedoboote Flottille. They were also ordered to the northwest, and were joined by the small cruiser *Graudenz* at 11.40hrs. At 11.50hrs the first reinforcements from Wilhelmshaven arrived: the battlecruisers *Hindenburg*, Kapitän zur See von Karpf, and *Moltke*, Kapitän zur See Gygas. They pushed ahead and joined the battleships at 12.10hrs, advancing to the northwest. At around 13.10hrs the battleships *Friedrich der Große* and *König Albert* joined the ships under the command of Kontreadmiral von Reuter, and with that command was taken over by Vizeadmiral Souchon aboard the former ship. It was to no avail, however, because the British assembled their forces and withdrew across the North Sea without further incident, so that around 15.00hrs the German forces made a turn and ran in.

As far as the British were concerned the Commander-in-Chief, Admiral Beatty, was dissatisfied with the result. A large force had been allocated for the operation and was given information about the time and place to intercept the enemy. However, they had been unsuccessful in cutting off and destroying any German forces. He was critical of Rear Admiral Napier for failing to pursue the enemy at more than 25 knots, and for his first turn away from the enemy which lost much ground. However, the Admiralty declined to make Rear Admiral Napier a scapegoat, probably because it was embarrassed about the lack of information given him that was freely available. An Admiralty inquiry decided that the dissemination of information about minefields was disorganized in that some of the admirals concerned received no information at all. 'These considerations led to a question as to the efficiency of staff work in the battlecruiser force, but the Admiralty considered it was unnecessary to pursue the matter further, arrangements having been made whereby information regarding the minefields should in future be supplied by the Admiralty direct.'[15] British loses amounted to twenty-two dead and many wounded. In

206 The Battle on the Seven Seas

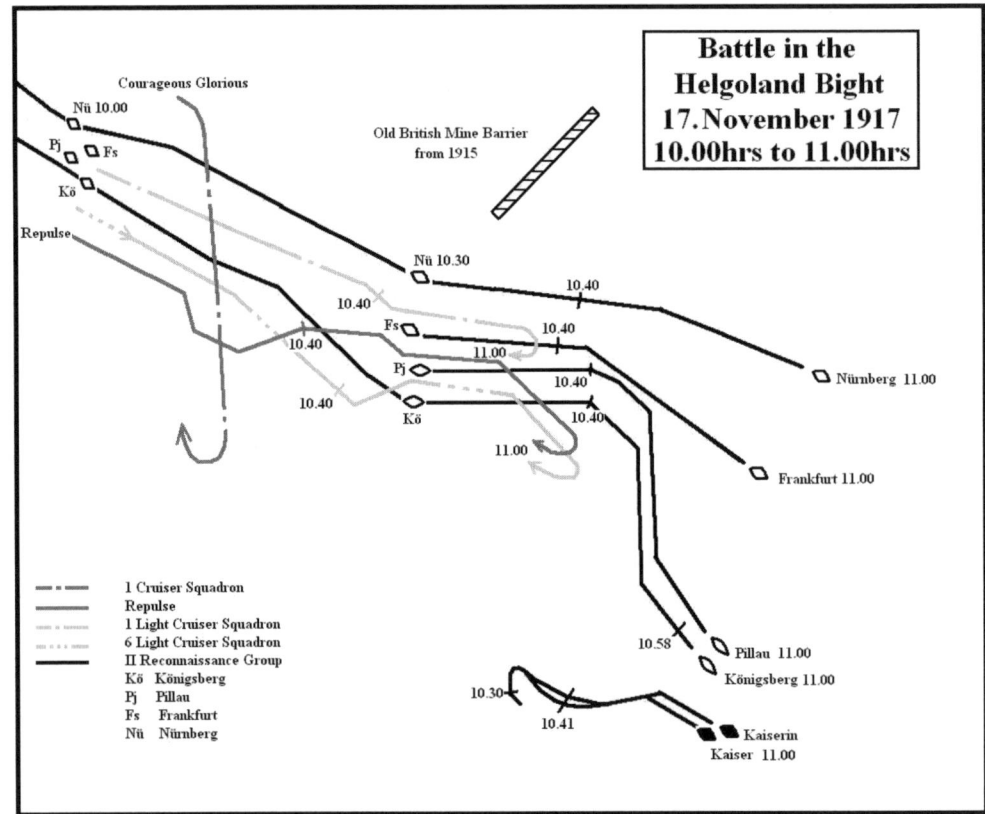

addition to the hits mentioned *Glorious* suffered splinter damage to the left gun of A turret.

German loses amounted to twenty-one dead and forty-three wounded, and in addition the survivors of the crew of *Kehdingen* were taken prisoner. Kontreadmiral von Reuter and his cruisers and torpedoboats had done an outstanding job in saving the slow minesweepers from total annihilation and had met the dangerous situation against a vastly superior enemy skilfully and with a good battle spirit.

In his report to the Kaiser, Admiral Scheer made the following conclusions:

The II AG and the torpedoboats have splendidly carried out their principal task: 'Covering the Minesweeper Unit.' The attitude of the forces involved earns full acknowledgement.

The battleship squad still arrived in time to stop the superior combat capability of the opponent. Unfortunately they did not succeed in utilizing the tactical situation aimed at by the Leader of the II AG. The commander of *Kaiserin* did not obtain an overview of the battle situation. The strength of the battleships was thereby not in the equation and the cover for the small cruisers was too late.

I remain undecided whether the intention of the leader of the II AG to draw the enemy to the east, and so bring them between two fires, had a chance and was fully understandable to the battleships, so much the more as the strength of the enemy was not reported. Despite all: the cruisers were heavily pressed. Course NW <u>must</u> therefore unconditionally be the thought of the battleship squad, until the enemy was brought to a halt. All considerations were against this turn.

The leader of the battleship squad could have brought us a success, that in great likelihood was to be expected. Because of this I have recommended the replacement of Kapitän zur See Graßhoff to the Chief of the Naval Cabinet.

Daytime test trips are only to be conducted in future with air reconnaissance (airship or flier)…The covering forces must be pushed considerably further forward. The covering forces must be stronger in future.[16]

In December 1917 Kapitän zur See Graßhoff was relieved of his command and appointed to the U-boat command in Austria. In February 1918 Kontreadmiral von Reuter was promoted to 2 Admiral of the I Reconnaissance Group.

Chapter 10

The Sea Battle Off Imbros, 20 January 1918

The Russian revolution in February 1917 had little or no effect on the Black Sea Fleet, which was spared the ravages foisted on the Baltic Fleet. Indeed it was not until 19 June that Vice Admiral Kolchak, the most successful Black Sea Fleet leader, was deposed by the assembly of delegates of the soldiers' and sailors' council. Nevertheless, the Russian Black Sea Fleet continued its successful campaign of sinking Turkish coal ships and merchant ships, and supporting their Army ashore. It was not until after the 'October Revolution' on 7-8 November 1917 (October on the old Gregorian calendar) that the Black Sea Fleet was placed solely at the disposal of the Central Committee of the Black Sea Fleet and all hostilities immediately stopped. After this armistice negotiations were begun at Brest-Litovsk and Germany and Russian concluded a separate peace.

With the exit of Russia from this theatre of the war, Turkish trade, and most importantly coal supplies from the mines at Zonguldak, again began to proceed unimpeded. However, virtually none of this coal could be spared for the Mediterranean Division, *Goeben* and *Breslau*, and even the monthly coal supply allocated and supplied from Germany failed to arrive on the ships, as it was given to the Anatolian Railway and transport ships to support and supply the Army Group in the field. The meagre amount supplied to the Mediterranean Division was consumed by day-to-day operation, and training and exercises.

In September 1917 the German Mediterranean Division received a new commander. The long serving hitherto commander, Vizeadmiral Wilhelm Souchon, was replaced by Vizeadmiral Hubert von Rebeur-Paschwitz. Vizeadmiral Rebeur-Paschwitz was born in 1863 in Frankfurt am Oder and joined the Imperial Navy in 1882. He commanded the cruiser *Arcona* and the battleship *Elsaß* before commanding cruiser formations and serving as Director of the Naval Academy. In 1913–1914 he commanded the 'Detached Division' of battleships that visited Africa and South America and during the early war commanded the III Reconnaissance Group and II Battle Squadron, before being appointed to Chief of the Mediterranean Division. On 2 December 1917 the Turkish Grand Headquarters reported to Vizeadmiral Rebeur-Paschwitz that two Allied divisions from Macedonia had embarked in Salonika and were bound for Palestine, and requested a U-boat attack on their transports. The Fleet Chief, however, had to report that no U-boats were operationally ready, but said it was possible for *Goeben* and *Breslau* to sortie in the direction of Salonika. The distance was just 120 nautical miles and he believed the ships could conduct the operation without meeting considerably stronger enemy forces. If the advance did not actually meet the transports then at least it would disconcert the Allies and cause them to reinforce their forces off the Dardanelles. This would give the U-boats more targets and perhaps ease the pressure on Palestine. A success at sea would also appease the loss of Jerusalem on 10 December 1917.

The Turkish War Minister, Enver Pasha, reminded Vizeadmiral Rebeur-Paschwitz of the great value of the cruisers to Turkey, both materially and symbolically, and of the existing danger from mines and submarines. Nevertheless the German Sea War Command and Turkish Army High Command approved an operation into the Mediterranean for the purpose of destroying Allied guard forces. With that the preparations for the operation began.

The composition of the German forces was to be: the battlecruiser *Goeben*, under the command of Kapitän zur See Stoelzel, the small cruiser *Breslau*, under the command of Kapitän zur See von Hippel, the four torpedoboats *Muavenet*, *Basra*, *Numune* and *Samsun*, and the U-boat *UC23*. To alleviate the coal procurement problem the ships themselves would travel to Zonguldak to replenish their bunkers. On 14 December the torpedoboats *Muavenet* and *Numune* went to Zonguldak, followed on 21 December by *Breslau*, which arrived back in Stenia on the Bosporus on 23 December with full bunkers. Procedures for *Goeben* were more time-consuming and complicated. Because the wharf at Zonguldak was too small to take *Goeben*, the battlecruiser would have to coal from barges on the roadstead. This would make events subject to the weather. Finally, after long negotiations with the War Coal Headquarters, *Goeben* was allocated 2,400 tonnes of coal for 14 January. On 15 January *Goeben* arrived on Koslu Roads at Zonguldak. For some days the weather had been poor with snow dominating. On the first day of coaling just 220 tonnes were taken aboard, whereas *Goeben* used 100 tonnes per day just lying with clear engines. Fortunately the weather changed for the better and after three more days *Goeben*'s bunkers were full so that on 19 January she again anchored off Stenia.

A major concern for the Germans was the presence of agents and Allied sympathisers in Constantinople who in the past had reported the movements of ships and other information. Therefore knowledge of the impending operation was limited to a small circle of *Offiziers*, and even Marshall Limon von Sanders, commander of the V Army, was not informed. On the evening of 18 January the order was given over the wireless for *Goeben*, *Breslau* and the flotilla to rendezvous at 2 o'clock in the afternoon on 19 January in the Sea of Marmora for exercises, a ruse intended to fool Entente agents. On the morning of 19 January the ships sailed down the Bosporus for the arranged rendezvous.

The German knowledge of the mine barriers off the entrance to the Dardanelles appeared to them to be extensive. So as not to arouse Allied suspicions it was determined not to employ extensive minesweeping before the operation. The immediate area off Cape Helles for 4 nautical miles due west had been swept by the minesweepers under Leutnant zur See der Reserve Semmler on three separate occasions in November 1917, but no mines had been found. Careful, continuous observation of the courses taken by Allied ships by the Coast Watch Service gave good indications of where the Allied mine barriers were. Known barriers were kept under observation by German fliers. A summary of all this information seemed to provide a good indication of which waters were free of mines. Then the day before the operation the Germans had a great stroke of luck. An English guard trawler ran aground off Enos Island and the maps aboard her passed into the hands of the V Army and were dispatched out to *Goeben* by Marshall Limon von Sanders. The map contained certain lines which corresponded to the probable positions of the English mine barriers. They were marked on the map in green. This map did not agree with German observations and repeatedly swept routes. When the German operational maps are compared to later Allied maps it is evident that the positions of the trawler maps' supposed mine barriers were incorrect, but nevertheless when the cruisers put to sea the captured map was referenced. This was to have fatal consequences as the Germans remained ignorant of the Allied mine barriers A, B, C and D (see map page 218).

Aerial reconnaissance also provided the up-to-date and accurate dispositions of the Allied forces. According to the latest aircraft reconnaissance reports[1] there were in Mudros Bay: two battleships of the *King George* and *King Edward* class, one armoured cruiser of the *Suffolk* class, one *Natal* class, one protected cruiser of the *Juno* class, a French battleship of the *Gloire* class, and additionally two destroyers, one monitor, one hospital ship, eleven steamers and thirty smaller vessels. British destroyers were seen to be patrolling off Imbros, where two monitors lay.

The German operational orders[2] called for the destruction of the guard forces off the Dardanelles and for the U-boat *UC23* to lie off Mudros Bay to ambush any forces putting to sea from there. The German forces were to put to sea during the night and were to be off Imbros at dawn, however, the torpedoboats were to wait at the entrance to the Dardanelles because of their low speed and poor offensive qualities. The German aircraft were to support the operation against enemy air attack. After destroying the forces off Imbros the cruisers were to move south against Mudros Bay on the island of Lemnos and attack ships there. The return was to be by sundown at the latest. Strict wireless silence was to be maintained until fire was opened.

The operation was quite aggressive in character, with *Goeben* and *Breslau* not only voluntarily braving mine-infested waters, but also looking for battle with two or three pre-dreadnought battleships, which were quite capable of inflicting fatal damage to the German battlecruiser. Nevertheless, the Germans were confident about their cruisers' ability to withstand punishment as on a previous occasion *Goeben* had suffered two mine hits in quick succession, and in July 1915 *Breslau* had safely returned to port under her own power after striking a mine in the Black Sea.

At 4 o'clock in the afternoon of 19 January 1918 the unit began the advance to the Dardanelles. The weather was especially favourable for the operation as the morning was clear, whereas the previous two mornings there had been fog that had continued until noon, which would have been cause enough to abort the operation. At about 03.30hrs the ships stood off the net barrier at Nagara. The latest observations of the previous day were brought aboard by the pilot *Offizier*, Leutnant zur See der Reserve Semmler, who was to guide the ships through the Turkish mine barriers. At the entrance to the Dardanelles the torpedoboats were left behind, as planned in the operational orders. At 05.41hrs Sedul Bahr was passed. At 05.55hrs *Goeben* altered course from 270° to 239° and threw a buoy overboard, to mark the return course for later. At 06.10hrs, whilst steering in the alleged mine-free channel, *Goeben* struck a mine in compartment X and XI to port. Vizeadmiral Rebeur-Paschwitz wrote:[3]

> It was a splendid Sunday morning, the stars still glistening, and shortly after dawn the sunlight magnificently bathed us from behind; everything pointed towards a good day. After their previous experiences the crew had much faith in their ship. 'She could take six mines', remarked one, whilst another was even more optimistic. I was standing on the command bridge when there came a shock, without a water column, and already a report from the *Zentral*, 'Mine explosion to port' It was an angry beginning. I dare not think about proceeding immediately…Should I turn back? A difficult decision. However, just as in peacetime, practiced a thousand times, the reports about the circumstances of the leak, the invading water quantities and the countermeasures taken, all came to us above…The Priest, who was not a party to this later told us: 'I was standing near a maschinist on watch, having a cigar, when the ship was shaken by a dull bang, followed by a huge vibration which shook through the big ships hull. "What is happening? What was that?" "Only a mine," replied the war experienced maschinist, "it does no harm, it just shakes us a little"'…My good friend, the ship's doctor, Dr. Moosauer, remarked we were more concerned with our cigarettes than with our lives.

Goeben had struck a mine adjacent to the bulkhead between compartments X and XI to port. The protective bunker filled with water and the bunker door to the 4 boiler room was bent slightly and leaked. This leak was soon closed with wooden wedges. Apart from that the wing passage also filled with water, and the common magazine on the lower platform deck filled, but otherwise there was little flooding as the torpedo bulkhead had limited the damage.

For the first time since that hot August of 1914 the German cruisers were loose in the Aegean Sea. At 06.32hrs course was again taken on Imbros and *Breslau* received orders to run on ahead to reconnoitre Kusu Bay to determine what vessels lay there, and to prevent their escape to the west. Kapitänleutnant Willi Nordeck, I Artillerie Offizier of *Breslau* wrote: "'Blinker signal *Goeben*", I heard the Signal Maat of the Watch on the bridge proclaim, and then his report, "*Breslau* run ahead according to plan". "Both engines utmost power ahead!" and we went past *Goeben* to the north, under Imbros.'[4] Whilst *Breslau* pushed ahead at high speed, at 07.42hrs *Goeben* opened fire with the medium artillery on the signal and wireless station on Kephalo peninsula. After four salvos the target was reported destroyed, whereon the heavy artillery opened fire on a ship with one funnel that was in Kephalo Bay. This steamer was of approximately 2,000 tonnes gross and received three salvos.

Meanwhile *Breslau* moved far ahead and around 07.40hrs two destroyers, *Tigress* and *Lizard*, rounded the northern tip of Imbros and took course ESE, but when their recognition signal went unanswered they turned onto course north. Kapitänleutnant von Nordeck continues:[5]

> Then there suddenly appeared–far ahead over 100hm distant–2 silhouettes off the island coast. And about the same time the report sounded from several different positions, 'Enemy torpedoboats 350°!' Quickly the Nr.1 of the Rangefinder, the Bootsmaat Grüning, gave me the range, then some short commands to the guns, and the first salvo of our 15cm guns thundered over the sea. The boats had luck, that owing to the forward firing direction only the forward two cannon could hold the target. With zigzag course and highest speed the enemy attempted to withdraw from our fire, and save themselves behind the promontory of the island. And again the boats had new luck, a new, more valuable target offered itself before our guns. At a range of 70–80hm, almost abeam, lay 2 enemy monitors, close under land peacefully at anchor, and especially difficult to see against the coast. They were only a few hundred meters from one another. 'Change target to the monitors 290°!' came the order from the Commander in the conning tower through the speaking tube to me in the artillery tower. '*Breslau* goes to half speed!'
>
> I cannot see the target in the first moments, the two flat monitors beside one another with their paint schemes are difficult to see against the rising coast close behind them. However, the efficient Obermaat Abraham near me, who directs the battery laterally, has already seen the enemy in his periscope and begins to target the larger of the two opponents. A view through the periscope and I also have the target.

It was the Royal Navy monitors *Raglan* (of 6,150 tonnes and mounting two American 14-inch guns originally constructed for the German-built Greek battleship *Salamis*) and *M28* (of 540 tonnes and mounting one 9.2-inch gun), which were hidden against the background of Kusu Bay. After *Breslau* opened fire *Goeben* also joined in at a range of 93hm. Both monitors replied to the German fire, but as the commander of *Raglan*, Commander Viscount Broome, later revealed it was only after *Breslau* opened fire on the two destroyers that she was recognised as a German ship. Kapitänleutnant von Nordeck wrote:

> The shooting was easy. *Breslau* had reduced speed, the range was not great–approximately 60-70hm–and the enemy lay still. Nevertheless, haste is required because the enemy had heavy artillery. One hit is enough to render *Breslau* unmanoeuvrable.[6]

The English fire fell short, causing huge fountains of water, but soon the accurate German fire had caused fires aboard *Raglan*. The larger monitor was soon engulfed in flames and began to sink. Later, when divers investigated the wrecks, an unexploded 28cm projectile from *Goeben* was found aboard the wreck of *Raglan*. Fire was now concentrated on the smaller *M28* and she too caught fire. A short time later, after the Germans had ceased fire on her, there was a dull explosion and in the place where minutes before the smaller monitor had stood there was now a high, black smoke cloud. The ammunition on the burning ship had exploded. Of the crews of the two monitors 132 men saved themselves by swimming ashore.

A little later a wireless message was heard being broadcast in plain English. It ran: 'Enemy ships at sea in the eastern Mediterranean. All merchant ships east of Malta go to nearest defended harbour.' The appearance of the two German cruisers had already achieved one of the raids aims: to disrupt Allied merchant shipping.

At 08.15hrs *Goeben* fired four more salvos on the vessel in Kephalo Bay, which took on a heavy list. Meanwhile *Breslau* took the air station at Kusu Bay under fire and soon the fuel tanks exploded with a powerful detonation. The two cruisers now reversed course and *Breslau* took station astern of the 'big brother' as the pair took course south back along the course they had approached on, to steer towards Mudros Bay in search of new targets. It was difficult to steer along the exact course as the mine detonation aboard *Goeben* had caused the gyro compass the read incorrectly, and therefore the ship had to be navigated using bearings taken on shore objects.

At 08.16hrs *Breslau* reported to the flagship 'Enemy submarine to port aft.' This report was in error, as there were no Allied submarines in the area. Then at 08.20hrs the two British destroyers again came in sight aft, and at 08.26hrs two enemy fliers were sighted. At this time *Breslau* was approximately 1,000 metres astern of *Goeben* and the flagship now gave orders for the small cruiser to take station ahead as *Breslau* had no Flak guns, only machineguns, and *Goeben* could bring her Flak to target the enemy aircraft without endangering her consort. The question now arises as to why *Breslau* elected to pass the flagship to port. Firstly convention says a ship overtaking should pass to port of the vessel being overtaken, and secondly *Goeben* had just previously been firing to starboard and her turrets were still trained in that direction, therefore Kapitän zur See von Hippel swung out to the port side to pass the flagship. Whilst *Breslau* pulled out to port the first bomb fell at 08.28hrs, 300 metres in the wake of *Goeben*. At 08.31hrs, whilst conducting the passing manoeuvre and when several hundred metres abeam of *Goeben*, *Breslau* was shaken by a heavy vibration. The speed immediately fell off and the bow turned to starboard. The helmsman was unable to check the swing and the order 'steer from aft' was not followed. An attempt to steer with the engines likewise failed and so the commander ordered: 'Both engines stop'. It was not clear whether the ship had struck a mine or torpedo, but then the Auxiliary Observer in the fore top, Leutnant zur See Eberhard Souchon, called: ' "Mines ahead!–Mines to starboard!–Mines to port!" The observer above could clearly make out the large, dark mine shapes in the transparent water.'[7]

Breslau had struck a mine to starboard aft, between frames 8 and 10, and the rudder, hand rudder and starboard low pressure turbine had all fallen out. Compartments I and II filled with water and apart from the dead, had to be abandoned. In compartment III, the aft ammunition chamber, the electric lights went out, the ammunition was thrown about and the crew were slightly injured. The shaft of the starboard low-pressure turbine was jammed in the aft ship and could not be moved. Some double-bottom compartments filled with water, and the *Oberdeck* and *Zwischendeck* were torn up.

At 08.33hrs *Goeben* turned to starboard and described a complete circle to come alongside *Breslau* to take her in tow. At this time another two bombs crashed into the sea 200 metres to starboard abeam. Vizeadmiral Rebeur-Paschwitz wrote:[8] 'The commander, Kapitän zur See Stoelzel, accomplished a perfect manoeuvre, so that a line could be thrown between the ships. The *Breslau*'s commander, my friend Kapitän zur See von Hippel, who was much loved and admired by his crew because of his fatherly and graceful manner, called across a warning to us, that between the two ships lay many mines.' However, all his seamanship skill came to nothing as at 08.55hrs, as the towline was being passed, *Goeben* was rocked by a heavy detonation to port. A water column black in colour towered mast high, before water and coal came crashing over the ship. 'In the crystal clear water I could see one just 2–3 metres away as the long ship glided past. However, the Commander, the Navigation Offizier and the battle Helmsman all knew their duty; not to allow the ship to deviate one degree from its course, and slowly we worked ourselves out of the minefield into free water,'[9] Vizeadmiral Rebeur-Paschwitz later wrote.

Goeben had struck a second mine to port between frames 65 and 78, adjacent to boiler room I in compartment VI. Once against the torpedo bulkhead stood firm, but the wing passage and protective bunker both filled with water, since these rooms were connected since the mine explosion in December 1914. Some leaks into boiler rooms I and II were sealed with wooden wedges.

After the first mine hit on *Breslau* the two British destroyers attempted to close the range, however they were fended off by the aft guns. Below inside the ship the Leak Security Service (Damage Control Service) under the direction of the I Offizier, Kapitänleutnant Homeyer, bravely fought to save the ship. All the men stationed below decks in the boiler rooms, engine rooms and magazines were in extreme danger from the pernicious enemy in their exposed positions. Meanwhile above, Kapitänleutnant von Nordeck was faced with a frightening sight:

> Helpless the ship drifted on the wind and current.
> I stood on the starboard wing of the command bridge, and coincidentally looked down at the water. Directly below me a mine moved a few metres distant from the hull side. I called my observation to the Commander, and whilst I reported this, a call from the foremast: 'Mines a few metres ahead of the bow.'
> The situation was bad. The only possibility remained to back the ship out. Long seconds pass, until the engine springs to life and the ship goes astern.
> Will we come free?
> We have luck! We escape these mines—and run onto others.[10]

At 09.00hrs the hapless cruiser detonated a further two mines consecutively, one below the 1 and 2 boiler rooms, in compartment VII/VIII to port, and the other below the port engine rooms. The electric lights throughout the entire ship went out and there was smoke and steam danger in the boiler rooms so that six boilers had to be shut off. From the ten men in boiler room 1 three came out, and of the crew of boiler room 2 and the starboard engine room in compartment V none were found amongst those saved. The crew of the port high-pressure turbine room also had to evacuate their positions. The 3 boiler room remained clear and held tight. Some of the gun crew of the port IV gun were injured, one with a broken leg, whilst two others were thrown overboard. The second and third mine hits had rendered *Breslau* completely motionless and she sank deeper by the stern and listed somewhat to port.

The Fleet Chief, Vizeadmiral Rebeur-Paschwitz, had meanwhile faced a most difficult decision. The area was deadly with mines, and there was the expectation that enemy submarines and heavy surface units would soon arrive. Under these circumstances the flagship could remain in the area no longer, as she was not only materially important but also politically important, and was the most powerful factor in the southeast theatre of war. The standing orders from the Admiralstab allowed him to stay no longer and so *Goeben* now departed the scene to return to the Dardanelles. At 09.04hrs the Admiral summoned the torpedoboats to the scene of the mining.

At this time the destroyers and fliers again approached the motionless cruiser. *Breslau* engaged them with cannon and machine-gun, so that the destroyers held back and the fliers' bomb aiming was put off and they missed their mark.

The ship drifted further, and at 09.05hrs a fourth mine detonated to port under the 4 boiler room. The 3 boiler room remained as the single water-tight room below the armoured deck, but it has also been abandoned. The *Oberdeck* above the detonation was torn up beside the port II gun, a coal hatch was thrown in the air and coal showered on deck. One man of the gun crew was killed instantly and several others were badly wounded. The ship listed over to port even further. Then a fifth mine detonated under the bridge and forecastle. An especially strong vibration was felt with this mine and it was thought that possibly another mine had also detonated.

The sinking was now only a matter of time, but *Breslau*'s commander would not give up his ship and wished to await the arrival of the Turkish-German torpedoboats. He would meanwhile have to hold the British destroyers at bay. Kapitänleutnant von Nordeck continued:

The cruiser lay strongly over to port.
There was no more doubt it now went to its end.
The last order was called over the deck: 'All men from the ship!' [Abandon Ship].
The *Breslau* was abandoned by the crew.
With 2 comrades I slid down the diagonal hull side into the water. We sought to quickly get away fast, in order to escape the notorious vortex.
Then a memorable view was offered to us.
The cruiser placed itself almost perpendicular, the bow stood steeply up, the anchor cables rushed out, and seconds long the ship stood as good as still. 'Three cheers for our ship, people and Fatherland,' called our Commander across the water at this moment. And under the cheering 'Hurrahs!' the ship slowly and majestically went in the depths at this moment.
It was impressively unforgettable for those who saw it.[11]

When *Breslau* struck the first mine the Torpedoboat Flotilla Chief assembled his boats, and on receiving the message from the Fleet Chief he advanced with his boats towards the accident site at high speed. The shortest route was across the supposed minefields. At 09.25hrs the two English destroyers came in sight to the north. The destroyers were superior in speed and armament and soon opened fire on the Turkish boats. *Basra* neared to within 500 metres of the sinking position of *Breslau* before she made a turn under heavy enemy fire. The boat received two 4-inch shell hits in the stern under water. Compartment I filled with water and compartment II, whose bulkhead was holed, was pumped out later. *Basra* returned fire and attempted to escape under an artificial smoke screen. The English destroyers attempted to cut off the Turkish boat until at 09.38hrs the shore batteries opened fire. At 09.45hrs *Muavenet* opened fire on a destroyer at a range of 80hm in an attempt to relieve *Basra*. According to the observations of *Muavenet* a shell from the forts struck one of the destroyers, and at 09.55hrs the enemy ceased fire on *Basra*. At 09.52hrs *Muavenet* ceased fire and after that the torpedoboats went to *Goeben* to secure her against submarines.

The battle of the destroyers and torpedoboats was observed by the surviving crewmembers of *Breslau* drifting in the water. From time to time errant shells impacted in the water in the vicinity of the survivors. Finally, after the conclusion of the battle between the light craft, the English destroyers *Tigress* and *Lizard* approached the drifting survivors, who by now had been adrift for 1½ to 1¾ hours. Because the water was so cold, just 8° Celsius, many of those who survived the sinking perished in the freezing waters from exposure. They passed without complaint, their heads just falling forward as they became stiff. Those who died in the water included the Commander, Kapitän zur See Georg von Hippel, the I Offizier, Kapitänleutnant Homeyer, and the Navigation Offizier, Kapitänleutnant Freiherr von Sell, and of the entire crew just 162 men were saved, whilst it was estimated that only 50 to 55 men were lost due to the mine explosions.

Meanwhile *Goeben* had abandoned the advance against Mudros Bay and began to retire. The flagship attempted to retrace the course followed during the morning, however, the buoys laid out could not be found. At 09.48hrs, in the vicinity of the first mine hit, a third mine was struck to starboard. The mine hit the side of compartments III/IV around frame 54. Water entered the wing passage and protective bunkers and the torpedo bulkhead was bent slightly but held. Once again the torpedo bulkhead had saved the ship from serious damage, and even after striking three mines the total water inside the ship was just 1,217 tonnes, and the list was 2¼° to port. The steadfastness of the battlecruisers design had been truly proved.

Whilst retiring *Goeben* came under further attack from enemy aircraft. Eight to ten aeroplanes continued the attack and at times up to twenty bombs landed around the ship, throwing up cascades of water. Finally at 10.05hrs German aircraft from Chanak arrived and a vehement air battle ensued, during the course of which a British aircraft fell in flames and a second was forced down and fired on from ashore. The torpedoboats had formed an anti-submarine screen for *Goeben* and they fired on the aircraft with rifles.

Goeben continued homewards and towards 10.30hrs passed the entrance to the Dardanelles, again under aircraft attack. Whilst negotiating their own mine barriers *Goeben* was unable to manoeuvre away from the falling bombs, but nevertheless was not hit. At 11.00hrs the last mine barrier was passed and the

218 *The Battle on the Seven Seas*

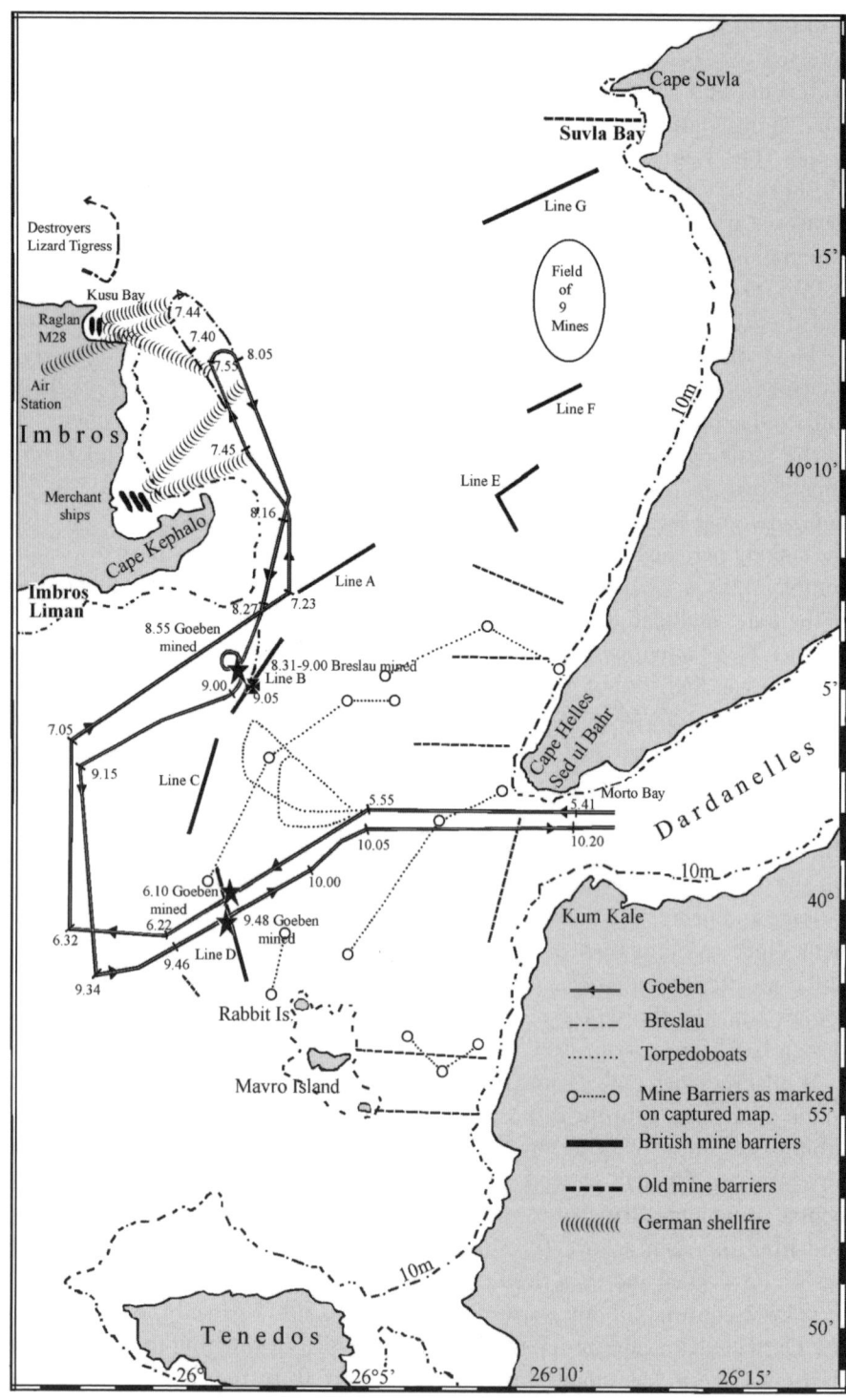

pilot, Leutnant zur See der Reserve Semmler, was dismissed. The High Command of the Narrows had provided handwritten charts of the net barriers and buoys for the ships, but these did not include Nagara Point and its marker buoy, which indicated the sandbank. Whilst putting to sea during darkness *Goeben* had not observed this buoy and Leutnant zur See der Reserve Semmler did not make the others aware of it. On the return, after passing the mine barriers and with the clear weather, the Fleet Chief believed there were no further navigational difficulties, and therefore dismissed the pilot before the ship had passed through the net barriers. Kapitän zur See Stoelzel and the Navigation Offizier, Kapitänleutnant der Reserve Brasch, did not foresee any difficulties and therefore did not oppose the dismissal of the pilot. On questioning from the Navigation Offizier the helmsman had confirmed to have the eastern buoy of the net barrier to port. As the Nagara buoy was not included on the sketch maps it was taken to be the eastern barrier buoy and was taken to port. Subsequently at 11.32hrs *Goeben* ran aground at 15 knots.

Vizeadmiral Rebeur-Paschwitz wrote:

After the fire grew silent and we seemed to have reached the quiet channel, I went with Korvettenkapitän Schlubach to my cabin to draft reports about the events, when suddenly the entire ship shook in all its joints, and the engines worked with utmost power astern, and then the *Goeben* stood motionlessly quiet. We went on deck and saw that the ship had seemingly pushed onto a sandbank, so went to the chart house to determine how this could happen. The mighty ship lay motionless, high and dry with three mine hits–and two others that were but poorly repaired–outside the anti-submarine barrier and therefore vulnerable to the English submarine, open to the enemy fliers and as good as powerless against the fire of the English dreadnoughts if they wished to bombard us from near Saros Gulf. It is to thank god that eventually only the fliers came. It looked truly that all the powers had sworn against us. Very soon the anchors were laid out to haul the ship free but this failed.[12]

Some weeks previously a steamer had been aground in the Black Sea port of Zonguldak and was got free by securing another steamer alongside and washing the sand away from under the stranded ship using her screw. It was determined to use this method to try and free *Goeben*, and the Turkish battleship *Torgut Reis* was quickly summoned to the scene. First the cruiser was lightened by removing ammunition, anchor chains, anchors and other equipment. However, there were frequent interruptions when submarine alarms were given, whereupon counter fire was undertaken, and when air raids occurred. More than 300 bombs were dropped on *Goeben* but only two hit the ship. One bomb struck the aft funnel mantel, and other struck a net box.

After 7 days of hard work, on 26 January, preparations for a towing attempt were complete. *Torgut* was secured alongside, and tugs were secured aft. *Goeben* got up steam and then all went astern at full power. Despite this the cruiser would not budge. Kapitän zur See Stoelzel then attempted to move his ship by working the engines unevenly. Slowly the ship began to turn about, degree by degree, a sure indication that it was sitting loosely. A second towing attempt was undertaken, from a different direction. All the hawsers went tight, and then the ship began to move, slowly at first, and then gathering speed. The lines to *Torgut* snapped like string and the tugs that could not rapidly cast loose were towed through the water at odd angles. Finally *Goeben* was free, and none too soon.

On Sunday 27 January the British submarine *E14*, Lieutenant-Commander White, departed Mudros and took course on the Dardanelles. At 03.00hrs on the following morning she passed the first net barrier and by daybreak was in the vicinity of Nagara Bank and began searching for *Goeben*. Unfortunately for the British submariners the cruiser had been gotten off the previous day, and after a fruitless search the *E14* began the return trip. Soon they discovered a transport ship and fired a torpedo at it, however after just eleven seconds the torpedo detonated, probably on the bottom, which caused all the lights in the submarine to extinguish and also sprang the fore hatch. As the boat was leaking badly the ballast tanks were blown and the submarine sprang to the surface whereupon she was taken under fire by the Turkish forts. *E14* dived again and continued towards the Dardanelles entrance.

Soon however, the boat got out of trim and soon went out of control. The resulting dive was checked and having only three air bottles remaining was forced to surface. Upon opening the lower hatch to the conning tower it was found to be full of water, whilst at the same time a heavy fire started from both sides. On emerging from the boat the crew found that the steering gear had been shot away and *E14* had to be steered from below. As she endeavoured to escape *E14* was hit repeatedly during the next half hour, and her commander gave orders to beach her. Before this order could be carried out Lieutenant-Commander White was mortally wounded and the submarine sank, taking twenty-three of her crew with her. *Goeben* had escaped further attack by a narrow margin.

In Turkey the first impressions of the loss of *Breslau*, known to the Turkish as *Midilli*, were of overwhelming sadness. The absence of the two cruisers caused a great restlessness in Constantinople, which was further fed by rumours of a German retreat from Sofia in neighbouring Bulgaria. Another view slowly awakened and won ground, however, which was that despite the grief at the losses there was a pride in a successful offensive. The appearance of *Goeben*, the Turkish *Yavuz*, on the morning of 27 January off Dolma Bay quickly changed the mood. Although the loss of *Midilli* caused grief, there was great rejoicing at the return of *Yavuz* and great pride that a victory had been won under the Turkish flag. The spell *Goeben* had cast in 1914 would last well into the 20th Century.

Notes

Chapter 1
1. *Der Krieg in der Nordsee*, Volume 1.
2. 1 hectometre (hm) equals 100 metres.
3. ADM 137/2067.
4. *Fearless* and 1st Flotilla *Acheron, Attack, Hind, Archer, Ariel, Lucifer, Llewellyn, Ferret, Forester, Druid, Defender, Goshawk, Lizard, Lapwing, Phoenix*, and attached to K force: *Badger, Beaver, Jackal* and *Sandfly*. *Arethusa* and 3rd Flotilla *Lookout, Leonidas, Legion, Lennox, Lark, Lance, Linnet, Landrail, Laforey, Lawford, Louis, Lydiard, Laurel, Liberty, Lysander, Laertes*.
5. Befehlshaber der Aufklärungsschiffe.
6. I Führer der Torpedobootes, or I Leader of Torpedoboats.
7. Later commander of the raider SMH *Wolf*.
8. RM92/3516.
9. Noted in the margin as *Fearless*.
10. *Der Krieg in der Nordsee*, Volume 1.
11. RM92/2400.
12. Quoted in *Tyrwhitt of the Harwich Force*, A. Patterson.
13. *Der Krieg in der Nordsee*, Volume 1.
14. RM92/3516.
15. RM92/3516.
16. *Naval Operations*, Volume 1, J. Corbett.
17. *Der Krieg in der Nordsee*, Volume 1.
18. Signal rating.
19. In *Auf See unbesiegt*, Volume 2, von Mantey.
20. RM92/2996.
21. RM3/4250.
22. In *Der Krieg in der Nordsee*, Volume 1.
23. In *Auf See unbesiegt*, Volume 2, von Mantey.
24. In *Auf See unbesiegt*, Volume 1, von Mantey.
25. RM47/607.
26. In *Auf See unbesiegt*, Volume 1, von Mantey.
27. *Der Krieg in der Nordsee*, Volume 1.
28. *Der Krieg in der Nordsee*, Volume 1.
29. RM92/2171.
30. RM92/2171.
31. RM92/3528.
32. RM92/3525.
33. *Der Krieg in der Nordsee*, Volume 1.

Chapter 2
1. *The Pursuit of Admiral von Spee*, Richard Hough.
2. *Before Jutland–Admiral von Spee's Last Voyage*, Korvettenkapitän Hans Pochhammer.
3. *On Lost Posts*, Korvettenkapitän Joachim Lietzmann.

4. *Before Jutland–Admiral von Spee's Last Voyage*, Korvettenkapitän Hans Pochhammer.
5. *Before Jutland–Admiral von Spee's Last Voyage*, Korvettenkapitän Hans Pochhammer.
6. *On Lost Posts*, Korvettenkapitän Joachim Lietzmann.
7. *On Lost Posts*, Korvettenkapitän Joachim Lietzmann.
8. *Der Krieg zur See 1914–1918, Der Kreuzerkrieg*, Vizeadmiral Raeder.
9. *On Lost Posts*, Korvettenkapitän Joachim Lietzmann.
10. *Der Krieg zur See 1914–1918, Der Kreuzerkrieg*, Vizeadmiral Raeder.
11. *Before Jutland–Admiral von Spee's Last Voyage*, Korvettenkapitän Hans Pochhammer.
12. *Life and Letters of David Earl Beatty*, W. Chalmers.

Chapter 3
1. RM40/276 *The Battle Off the Dardanelles*, von Rebeur-Paschwitz.
2. *German Battlecruisers*, V.B. Mukhenikov.
3. Utmost Power (AK) or Full Speed.
4. RM92/2544, War Diary SMS *Goeben*.
5. *North of Gallipoli*, George Nekrasov.
6. RM3/4717, *Report about Casemate Hit*.
7. *Ioann Zlatoust*, L. A. Kuznetsov.
8. RM92/2544, War Diary SMS *Goeben*.
9. N156, Souchon Nachlaß.
10. *Der Krieg in türkischen Gewässern*, Hermann Lorey.
11. *Der Krieg in türkischen Gewässern*, Hermann Lorey.
12. *Gangut* magazine Number 10, page 34.
13. *Der Krieg in türkischen Gewässern*, Hermann Lorey.

Chapter 4
1. *On Lost Posts*, Korvettenkapitän Joachim Lietzmann.
2. *The Last Battle of S.M.S. Leipzig*, Kapitänleutnant Schiwig, in *Auf See unbesiegt*.
3. *On Lost Posts*, Korvettenkapitän Joachim Lietzmann.
4. *Gallant Gentlemen*, E Chatterton.
5. *Before Jutland*, Korvettenkapitän Pochhammer.
6. *The Pursuit of Admiral von Spee*, R Hough.
7. *Before Jutland*, Korvettenkapitän Pochhammer.
8. *Der Krieg zur See 1914–1918, Kreuzerkrieg Volume 1*.
9. *On Lost Posts*, Korvettenkapitän Joachim Lietzmann.
10. *Before Jutland*, Korvettenkapitän Pochhammer.
11. *On Lost Posts*, Korvettenkapitän Joachim Lietzmann.
12. *On Lost Posts*, Korvettenkapitän Joachim Lietzmann.
13. *Der Krieg zur See 1914–1918, Kreuzerkrieg Volume 1*.
14. *Der Krieg zur See 1914–1918, Kreuzerkrieg Volume 1*.
15. Lieutenant Dannreuther quoted in: *The Pursuit of Admiral von Spee*, R Hough.
16. *Der Krieg zur See 1914–1918, Kreuzerkrieg Volume 1*.
17. *The Last Battle of S.M.S. Leipzig*, Kapitänleutnant Schiwig, in *Auf See unbesiegt*.
18. *The Last Battle of S.M.S. Leipzig*, Kapitänleutnant Schiwig, in *Auf See unbesiegt*.
19. *Der Krieg zur See 1914–1918, Kreuzerkrieg Volume 1*.
20. *The Last Battle of S.M.S. Leipzig*, Kapitänleutnant Schiwig, in *Auf See unbesiegt*.
21. *The Last Battle of S.M.S. Leipzig*, Kapitänleutnant Schiwig, in *Auf See unbesiegt*.
22. *Der Krieg zur See 1914–1918, Kreuzerkrieg Volume 1*.
23. *Gallant Gentlemen*, E Chatterton.
24. *Der Krieg zur See 1914–1918, Kreuzerkrieg Volume 1*.

Notes   223

Chapter 5
1. *My Memoirs*, Admiral von Tirpitz.
2. N162, Nachlaß Hipper.
3. *Der Krieg zur See 1914–1918, Northsea Volume 3*.
4. N162, Nachlaß Hipper.
5. *Der Krieg zur See 1914–1918, Northsea Volume 3*.
6. *Der Krieg zur See 1914–1918, Northsea Volume 3*.
7. See Chapter 6.
8. *Der Krieg zur See 1914–1918, Baltic Volume 1*.
9. Korvettenkäpitan Richard Foerster, I Artillerie Offizier, *Seydlitz*, in *Auf See unbesiegt*.
10. RM92/2931, *Kolberg* combat report.
11. *Doggerbank*, Korvettankapitän Kurt Gebeschus.
12. RM92/4250, Hipper combat report.
13. Follow the leader.
14. RM92/2307, *Derfflinger* KTB.
15. *Doggerbank*, Korvettankapitän Kurt Gebeschus.
16. *Doggerbank*, Korvettankapitän Kurt Gebeschus.
17. *S.M.S. Blücher in the Doggerbank Battle*, Fähnrich zur See Paulssen, in *Auf See unbesiegt*.
18. Signal group 'N D A'.
19. *Doggerbank*, Korvettankapitän Kurt Gebeschus.
20. Torpedoboats to the attack.
21. RM3/4250, Admiral Hipper's report.
22. RM3/4250, Admiral Hipper's report.
23. *Doggerbank*, Korvettankapitän Kurt Gebeschus.
24. *Doggerbank*, Korvettankapitän Kurt Gebeschus.

Chapter 6
1. Memoirs of A. A. Sakovich, published in the magazine *Sea Collection, 1931*.
2. Memoirs of A. A. Sakovich, published in the magazine *Sea Collection, 1931*.
3. Memoirs of A. A. Sakovich, published in the magazine *Sea Collection, 1931*.
4. *Recollections of a Naval Officer*, Captain 1st Rank Timirev.
5. *Report*, M. K. Bakhirev, reprinted Citadel press, St. Petersburg, 1998.
6. Abbreviated F.d.A.d.O.
7. *Der Krieg in der Ostsee 1914–1918*, Heinrich Rollmann, Berlin, 1929.
8. Flag–Flag-officer Wireless-telegraphy Office.
9. FT-Gast Wendt, RM5/4945.
10. One point equals 11° 15'.
11. FT-Gast Wendt, RM5/4945.
12. Report by Fregattenkapitän West, RM5/4943.
13. FT-Gast Wendt, RM5/4945.
14. *The Sea Battle Off Gotland*, V. Gribovski, St. Petersburg, 1998.
15. RM92/3388, Battle Report of SMS *Roon*.
16. From *Auf See unbesiegt*, Eberhard von Mantey, München, 1922.
17. From Goodhart papers.
18. On German vessels part of the damage control organization consisted of a Leak Countermeasures Gruppe, which was usually made up of stokers from the off duty watch.
19. Equivalent to Kapitänleutnant.

Chapter 7
1. Quoted in *S.M.S. Emden 1909–1914*, P.G. Huff.
2. Fregattenkapitän von Müller, quoted in *S.M.S. Emden 1909–1914*, P.G. Huff.
3. Quoted in *S.M.S. Emden 1909–1914*, P.G. Huff.
4. *Emden*, Franz Joseph Prinz von Hohenzollern.

5. *Cruisers Zhemchug and Izumrud*, M.A. Bogdanov.
6. Quoted in *S.M.S. Emden 1909–1914*, P.G. Huff.
7. *Emden*, Franz Joseph Prinz von Hohenzollern.
8. *Der Krieg zur See 1914–1918, Der Kreuzer Krieg*.
9. *The Official History of Australia in the War of 1914–1918*, Volume 9, A. Jose.
10. *Der Krieg zur See 1914–1918, Der Kreuzer Krieg*.
11. *Der Krieg zur See 1914–1918, Der Kreuzer Krieg*.
12. *Der Krieg zur See 1914–1918, Der Kreuzer Krieg*.
13. *The Official History of Australia in the War of 1914–1918*, Volume 9, A. Jose.
14. *Australian Dictionary of Biography*, Volume 9, p. 29.
15. *Der Krieg zur See 1914–1918, Der Kreuzer Krieg*.
16. *Der Krieg zur See 1914–1918, Der Kreuzer Krieg*.
17. *Der Krieg zur See 1914–1918, Der Kreuzer Krieg*.
18. *Der Krieg zur See 1914–1918, Der Kreuzer Krieg*.
19. *Der Krieg zur See 1914–1918, Der Kreuzer Krieg*.

Chapter 8
1. *Germany's High Sea Fleet in the World War*, Admiral Scheer.
2. BA-MA 162, Nachlaß Hipper.
3. *Elbing* combat report, RM92/2358.
4. Hermann Jung, *Skagerrak*.
5. *Der Krieg in der Nordsee Band 5*.
6. Leutnant zur See H. Kienast: *Mit Admiral Hipper auf der „Lützow"*.
7. *SMS Lützow in the Skagerrak Battle*, in Marinerundschau 1926, KK Paschen.
8. *Der Krieg in der Nordsee* Volume 5.
9. Vice Admiral J.E.T. Harper: *The Riddle of Jutland* (1934).
10. RM49/188, I AG War Diary.
11. Commander H.H. Frost: *The Battle of Jutland* (1936).
12. *The Sea Battle Off the Skagerrak*, Korvettenkapitän Foerster, In *Auf See unbesiegt*.
13. *Episode from the Skagerrak Battle*, Kontreadmiral Mahrholz.
14. Battle report SMS *von der Tann*.
15. Jutland Official Dispatches.
16. *Kiel and Jutland*, Korvettenkapitän Hase.
17. Kapitänleutnant Schumacher, II Artillerie Offizier *Lützow*.
18. *On Board SMS Lützow*, Seaman Fritz Loose.
19. *SMS Lützow in the Skagerrak Battle*, in Marinerundschau 1926, KK Paschen.
20. *Der Krieg in der Nordsee*, Volume 5.
21. *SMS Lützow in the Skagerrak Battle*, in Marinerundschau 1926, KK Paschen.
22. *SMS Lützow in the Skagerrak Battle*, in Marinerundschau 1926, KK Paschen.
23. *SMS Lützow in the Skagerrak Battle*, in Marinerundschau 1926, KK Paschen.
24. *Germany's High Sea Fleet in the World War*, Admiral Scheer.
25. Commander H.H. Frost: *The Battle of Jutland* (1936).
26. Leutnant zur See H. Kienast: *Mit Admiral Hipper auf der „Lützow"*.
27. *Kiel and Jutland*, Korvettenkapitän Hase.
28. RM92/2983, *Lützow* War diary.
29. Stabsarzt Florus Gelhaar died on 12.6.1916 aboard the hospital ship *Sierra Ventana*.
30. Hans Behrens, in *Das Volksbuch vom Skagerrak*, F.O. Busch.
31. *The Grand Fleet 1914–1916*, Admiral Jellicoe.
32. *Seydlitz* War Diary.
33. *Onboard S.M.S. Lützow*, Seaman Loose.
34. *SMS Lützow in the Skagerrak Battle*, in Marinerundschau 1926, KK Paschen.
35. In *Skagerrak*, by Hermann Jung, commander of A turret.
36. *The Engine Room Personnel of SMS Seydlitz in the Skagerrak Battle*, Oberstabsingenieur Looks.

37. RM92/3256, *Pillau* KTB.
38. RM92/3256, *Pillau* KTB.
39. RM51/335, Leader of II Reconnaissance Group KTB.
40. *Der Krieg in der Nordsee Band 5*.
41. RM3/4717. Report of Oberheizer Zenne.
42. RM92/3256, *Pillau* KTB.
43. The crew of *Frauenlob* had previously crewed *Danzig* until she was mined. The Imperial Navy suffered from a constant shortage of trained crew.
44. RM47/4753.
45. *The Last Eight*, Oberleutnant zur See a.D. Stolzmann.
46. RM92/2358, *Elbing* combat report.
47. Commander H.H. Frost: *The Battle of Jutland* (1936).

Chapter 9
1. In *Kleine Kreuzer 1903–1918, Bremen bis Cöln Klasse*, Koop and Schmolke.
2. Commander H.H. Frost: *The Battle of Jutland* (1936).
3. *Centaur* logbook ADM 53/37420.
4. *Karlsruhe* War Diary, RM92/2897.
5. MSg 1/2303, Nachlaß Heinrich.
6. CAB/24/62, The National Archives, Kew.
7. *Naval Operations*, Volume V, Corbett.
8. RM92/3257 *Pillau* KTB.
9. RM92/3257 *Pillau* KTB.
10. Here there is a two-minute discrepancy between German recorded time and British.
11. RM92/3186, *Nürnberg* KTB.
12. RM92/3257 *Pillau* KTB.
13. *From Dreadnought to Scapa Flow, Volume 4*, Marder.
14. *Der Krieg in der Nordsee*, Volume 7, von Mantey.
15. *Naval Operations*, Volume V, Corbett.
16. War Diary Commander of High Sea Fleet.

Chapter 10
1. *The Battle Off the Dardanelles* RM40/276.
2. RM40/276.
3. *Auf See unbesiegt, S.M. Ships Goeben and Breslau in the Last War Year*, Admiral Rebeur-Paschwitz.
4. *Experiences of Admiral a.D. von Nordeck on S.M.S. ,,Breslau" during the First World War*, RM92/3944.
5. *Experiences of Admiral a.D. von Nordeck on S.M.S. ,,Breslau" during the First World War*, RM92/3944.
6. *Experiences of Admiral a.D. von Nordeck on S.M.S. ,,Breslau" during the First World War*, RM92/3944.
7. *Experiences of Admiral a.D. von Nordeck on S.M.S. ,,Breslau" during the First World War*, RM92/3944.
8. *Auf See unbesiegt, S.M. Ships Goeben and Breslau in the Last War Year*, Admiral Rebeur-Paschwitz.
9. *Auf See unbesiegt, S.M. Ships Goeben and Breslau in the Last War Year*, Admiral Rebeur-Paschwitz.
10. *Experiences of Admiral a.D. von Nordeck on S.M.S. ,,Breslau" during the First World War*, RM92/3944.
11. *Experiences of Admiral a.D. von Nordeck on S.M.S. ,,Breslau" during the First World War*, RM92/3944.
12. *Auf See unbesiegt, S.M. Ships Goeben and Breslau in the Last War Year*, Admiral Rebeur-Paschwitz.

Bibliography

ADM 137/2067.
ADM 53/37420 *Centaur* logbook.
Auf der Spuren der Goeben, Matti Mäkelä. Bernard & Graefe (1979).
Auf See unbesiegt, Band 1 and 2, Eberhard von Mantey. J.F. Lehmans (1922).
Australian Dictionary of Biography.
Battlecruisers, N.J.M. Campbell. Conway (1978).
Before Jutland–Admiral von Spee's Last Voyage, Korvettenkapitän Hans Pochhammer.
Blücher in the Doggerbank Battle, Fähnrich zur See Paulssen, in *Auf See unbesiegt*.
CAB/24/62, The National Archives, Kew.
Cruisers Zhemchug and Izumrud, M.A. Bogdanov.
Das Volksbuch vom Skagerrak Hans Behrens, by F.O. Busch.
Der Krieg zur See 1914–1918, Der Krieg in der Nordsee, Band 1 to 7, Eberhard von Mantey.
  E.S. Mittler and Sohn 1920–64.
Der Krieg in der Ostsee 1914–1918, Band 1 to 3, Heinrich Rollmann, Berlin (1929).
Der Krieg in türkischen Gewässern, Hermann Lorey.
Der Krieg zur See 1914–1918, Der Kreuzerkrieg, Band 1 and 2, Vizeadmiral Raeder.
Die deutschen Kriegsschiffe 1815–1945, Erich Gröner. Bernard & Graefe 1982.
Die Deutschen Kriegsschiffe. Band 1–7, Hans Hildebrand. Koehlers (1979).
Die Großen Kreuzer von der Tann bis Hindenburg, Gerhard Koop, Klaus-Peter Schmolke.
Doggerbank, Korvettankapitän Kurt Gebeschus.
Emden 1909–1914, P.G. Huff.
Emden, Franz Joseph Prinz von Hohenzollern.
Episode from the Skagerrak Battle, Kontreadmiral Mahrholz.
From Dreadnought to Scapa Flow, Volume 4, Marder.
Gallant Gentlemen, E Chatterton.
Gangut magazine Number 10, page 34.
German Battlecruisers, V.B. Mukhenikov. St. Petersburg (1998).
Germany's High Sea Fleet in the World War, Admiral Scheer.
Goeben and Breslau in the Last War Year, Admiral Rebeur-Paschwitz, in *Auf See unbesiegt*.
Goodhart papers.
Große Kreuzer der Kaiserlichen Marine 1906–1918, Alex Greißmer. Bernard & Graefe 1996.
Ioann Zlatoust, L. A. Kuznetsov.
Jutland Official Dispatches.
Jutland, John Campbell. Conway 1986.
Kiel and Jutland, Korvettenkapitän Hase.
Kleine Kreuzer 1903–1918, Bremen bis Cöln Klasse, Koop and Schmolke.
Life and Letters of David Earl Beatty, W. Chalmers.
Lützow in the Skagerrak Battle, in *Marinerundschau 1926*, by Korvettenkapitän Paschen.
Marine Rundschau 1975/9 *von der Tann*. E. Strohbusch. J.F. Lehmans.
Marine Rundschau 1976/7 *Derfflinger*. E. Strohbusch. J.F. Lehmans.
Memoirs of A. A. Sakovich, published in the magazine *Sea Collection, 1931*.
Mit Admiral Hipper auf der „Lützow", Leutnant zur See H. Kienast.
MSg 1/2303, Nachlaß Heinrich.
My Memoirs, Admiral von Tirpitz.

N156, Nachlaß Souchon.
N162, Nachlaß Hipper.
Naval Operations Volume 1 to 5, J. Corbett and A. Newbolt.
North of Gallipoli, George Nekrasov.
Official History of Australia in the War of 1914–1918, Volume 9, A. Jose.
On Board SMS Lützow, Seaman Fritz Loose.
On Lost Posts, Korvettenkapitän Joachim Lietzmann.
Recollections of a Naval Officer, Captain 1st Rank Timirev.
Report, M. K. Bakhirev, reprinted Citadel press, St. Petersburg (1998).
RM3/3449, Lützow trials report.
RM3/4250, Hermann Fischer report.
RM3/4717, Report about Casemate Hit.
RM3/4717, Report of Oberheizer Zenne.
RM40/276, *The Battle Off the Dardanelles*, von Rebeur-Paschwitz.
RM47/4753.
RM47/607, Stoker Neumann report.
RM49/188, I AG War Diary.
RM5/4943, Report by Fregattenkapitän West.
RM5/4945, FT-Gast Wendt.
RM51/335, Leader of II Reconnaissance Group War Diary.
RM92/2171, *Ariadne* report.
RM92/2307, *Derfflinger* War Diary.
RM92/2358, *Elbing* combat report.
RM92/2400, *Frauenlob* War Diary.
RM92/2544, *Goeben* War Diary
RM92/2897, *Karlsruhe* War Diary.
RM92/2931, *Kolberg* battle report.
RM92/2983, *Lützow* War diary.
RM92/2996, Kapitänleutnant Tholens Report.
RM92/3186, *Nürnberg* War Diary.
RM92/3256, *Pillau* War Diary.
RM92/3257, *Pillau* War Diary.
RM92/3388, Battle Report of SMS *Roon*.
RM92/3457, *Seydlitz* War Diary.
RM92/3516, Battle Report *Stettin*.
RM92/3525, *Stralsund* War Diary.
RM92/3528, *Straßburg* War Diary.
RM92/3796, Battle report *von der Tann*.
RM92/3944, Experiences of Admiral a.D. von Nordeck on SMS „Breslau" during the First World War.
RM92/4250, Hipper combat report.
Skagerrak, Hermann Jung,
The Battle of Jutland, Commander H.H. Frost (1936).
The Engine Room Personnel of SMS Seydlitz in the Skagerrak Battle, Oberstabsingenieur Looks.
The Grand Fleet 1914–1916, Admiral Jellicoe.
The Last Battle of SMS Leipzig, Kapitänleutnant Schiwig, in *Auf See unbesiegt*.
The Last Eight, Oberleutnant zur See a.D. Stolzmann.
The Pursuit of Admiral von Spee, Richard Hough.
The Riddle of Jutland, Vice Admiral J.E.T. Harper (1934).
The Sea Battle Off Gotland, by V. Gribovski, St. Petersburg (1998).
The Sea Battle Off the Skagerrak, by Korvettenkapitän Foerster, In *Auf See unbesiegt*.
Tyrwhitt of the Harwich Force, A. Patterson.
Warship Profile 14, Seydlitz, Friedrich Ruge. Profile (1972).

Index

1 Cruiser Brigade 106, 109, 110, 117, 118, 120, 122, 126
1 Cruiser Squadron 19, 125, 179, 196, 201
4 Cruiser Squadron 30
7 Cruiser Squadron 4, 5
1 Destroyer Flotilla 3
3 Destroyer Flotilla 3
9 Destroyer Flotilla 153, 188
12 Destroyer Flotilla 188
13 Destroyer Flotilla 153, 160, 188
II Torpedoboote Flottille 180, 183
III Torpedoboote Flottille 150
V Torpedoboote Flottille 6, 7, 150
VII Torpedoboote Flottille 150
IX Torpedoboote Flottille 160, 178
1 Torpedoboote Half Flottille 150
12 Torpedoboote Half Flottille 193, 195
14 Torpedoboote Half Flottille 195
15 Torpedoboote Half Flottille 85
18 Torpedoboote Half Flottille 85
19 Torpedoboote Half Flottille 117
1 Battlecruiser Squadron 5, 82, 83, 87, 153, 182, 196
2 Battle Cruiser Squadron 87, 88, 153
3 Battle Cruiser Squadron 164, 165, 166, 178, 179, 180
1 Light Cruiser Squadron 4, 5, 27, 59, 87, 88, 90, 99, 196
2 Light Cruiser Squadron 90, 153, 184
2nd Admiral Reconnaissance Ships 29
2nd Admiral (Kommodore von Karpf) 107, 108, 109, 111, 113, 114, 117, 121, 122, 124
2 Battle Squadron 83, 174
3 Battle Squadron 87, 90, 99, 192
5 Battle Squadron 153, 158, 159, 161, 163, 164, 178
III Minesweeper Division 7
2 Auxiliary Mine Sweeper Half Flottille 194, 198, 199
5 Auxiliary Mine Sweeper Half Flottille 199
6 Auxiliary Mine Sweeper Half Flottille 194, 198, 199
5 Mine Sweeper Half Flottille 193
6 Mine Sweeper Half Flottille 193, 194
8 Mine Sweeper Half Flottille 193

A36 193
Abourkir 5
Acasta 165, 180
Acheron 221
Ackermann KzS 44, 47, 53, 54, 56
Admiral Makarov 106, 109, 110, 111, 114, 117, 118, 122
Alabama 43
Albatroß 80, 106, 107, 108, 109, 111, 113, 114, 115, 116, 117, 121, 122, 124, 125, 126
Aleksandr I 54
Aleksev Leitenant 120
Alexander-Sinclair Rear Admiral 196, 197, 201, 204
Allen Captain 64, 78
Alligator 109
Almaz 43, 44, 46
Amasis 61, 62
Ambuscade 188
Amethyst 5, 27
Amphion 3
Apel Oberleutnant zur See 140
Arabis 148
Arbuthnot Rear Admiral 165, 179
Archer 3, 221
Arcona 208
Arethusa 4, 8, 9, 11, 16, 17, 19, 20, 27, 88, 90, 99, 101, 221, 227
Ariadne 4, 21, 22, 24, 25, 26
Ariel 221
Astraea 139, 140
Attack 101, 221
Augsburg 104, 107, 108, 109, 111, 113, 114, 115, 116, 117, 118, 120, 122
Aurora 88, 89, 90
Australia 30, 60, 63
Ayesha 138

Baden (auxiliary) 61, 64, 80
Badger 221
Bakhirev Rear Admiral 106, 109, 110, 111, 113, 114, 118, 121, 126, 223, 227
Barham 153, 158, 161, 163
Basra 209, 216, 217
Bayan 106, 110, 113, 114, 116, 117, 122
Bayern 190

BdA 5, 6, 7, 10, 11, 14, 19, 25, 27, 85, 87, 89, 169
Beamish Captain 64
Beatty Vice Admiral 5, 16, 20, 40, 84, 87, 88, 90, 92, 94, 96, 97, 98, 101, 102, 149, 151, 152, 153, 154, 155, 158, 160, 161, 164, 165, 166, 173, 178, 179, 180, 182, 189, 191, 205, 222, 226
Beaver 221
Behring Kontreadmiral 85
Benbow 197
Benbrook 33
Beowulf 107
Berens Captain 2 Rank 118
Berger Kapitänleutnant 181
Bespokoinyi 53
Bethmann-Hollweg 191
Birmingham 5, 16, 88, 184
Black Prince 188
Blücher 13, 26, 85, 88, 89, 90, 92, 94, 96, 97, 98, 99, 100, 101, 223, 226
Bode Kapitänleutnant 167
Boedicker Kontreadmiral 148, 160, 177, 180, 182, 183
Boevoi 110
Bogatyr 43, 106, 110, 111, 113, 114, 118
Bothmer Kapitänleutnant 191
Brandt Captain 32
Brasch Kapitänleutnant der Reserve 219
Braunschweig 124
Breslau 41, 42, 43, 44, 46, 47, 51, 53, 208, 209, 210, 211, 212, 213, 214, 215, 216, 217, 220, 225, 226, 227
Bristol 60, 62, 64, 80
Broke 187
Broome Commander 213
Buresk 133, 137
Burnyi 110

Caledon 196, 204
Calliope 192
Calypso 196, 201, 202
Canada 197
Canopus 31, 33, 60, 61, 62, 63
Canterbury 180, 193
Caradoc 196

Index 229

Cardiff 198, 201, 203
Carnarvon 60, 62, 64, 66, 67, 69, 71
Castor 183
Ceres 192, 201
Chatham 141
Cherkasov Captain 2 Rank 128, 132
Cherkasski Captain 2 Rank 109
Chester 179
Chikuma 128
Christian Rear Admiral 4, 5
Christiansen Oberleutnant zur See der Reserve 143
Churchill W.S. 43
City of Winchester 139
Claus Stabarzt Dr. 69
Cleopatra 148
Cöln 4, 5, 6, 11, 13, 14, 15, 19, 20, 21, 22, 25, 26, 225, 226
Colossus 172
Conquest 148, 193
Contest 188
Conway Castle 80
Cornwall 60, 62, 63, 64, 65, 73, 74, 75
Courageous 196, 197, 198, 201, 203
Cowan Commodore 196, 197, 201
Cradock Rear Admiral 30, 31, 32, 34, 35, 40, 59, 60
Cressy 3, 5

D2. 5
D8. 5
D8 (Torpedoboote). 7, 11
Dannreuther Lieutenant 65, 72, 167, 222
Danzig 13, 22, 24, 25, 26, 184, 225
Dartmouth 141
Defence 39, 59, 60, 62, 165, 179, 180
Defender 10, 221
Derfflinger 31, 85, 88, 90, 92, 94, 97, 98, 101, 148, 150, 154, 158, 159, 160, 161, 163, 164, 165, 167, 170, 173, 174, 191, 195, 223, 226, 227
Derzki 44, 53
Deutschland 84, 124
Deutschland (Minelayer) 106
D'Iberville 131
Dreadnought 57, 225, 226
Dresden 30, 32, 33, 34, 35, 37, 38, 58, 59, 61, 62, 73, 80, 81
«Друид», «Дефендер», «Госхок», «Лизард», «Лэпвинг». *Druid* 221
Drummuir 61, 62
Dublin 184, 185, 188

E4. 5, 10
E5. 3, 5
E6. 5
E7. 3, 5
E8. 5
E9. 5, 109, 123, 124, 126

E14. 220
E22. 149
E38. 142
Eberhard Admiral 44, 46, 47, 51, 52, 54, 55, 57
Eckermann Vizeadmiral 84, 102, 150
Egidy Kapitän zur See 88, 102, 150
Elbing 150, 151, 177, 178, 179, 182, 183, 184, 185, 187, 224, 225, 227
Ellerton Captain 64, 81
Elsaß 208
Emden (I) 28, 29, 43, 127, 128, 129, 130, 131, 132, 133, 134, 136, 137, 138, 223, 224, 226
Emperor of India 196
Erdmann Fregattenkapitän 88, 100
Essen Admiral 106
Euryalus 5
Evan-Thomas Rear Admiral 153, 154, 158, 161
Evans Captain 64
Evstafi 43, 44, 47, 48, 49, 51, 54, 55, 57

Falmouth 5, 167, 152, 191
Falmouth 5, 167, 152, 191
Fanshawe Captain 64
FdAdO 123, 223
Fearless 3, 11, 17, 19, 221
Feilman Lieutenant Commander 3
Feldmann Fregattenkapitän 188, 195
Fenger Pfarrer 96, 157
Ferdinand Archduke 29, 42
Ferret 221
Fielitz Kapitän zur See 62
Firedrake 5
Fischer Stabarzt 96
Fisher Admiral 59
Force C 5
Force K 4
Forester 221
Francklin Captain 32
Frankfurt 150, 177, 178, 179, 180, 183, 193, 194, 195, 198, 201, 202
Frauenlob 4, 5, 8, 9, 11, 14, 15, 150, 183, 184, 185, 225, 227
Friedrich der Große 83, 84, 150, 151, 167, 174, 205
Fronde 131, 132

G9. 6, 10
G11. 10
G37. 176
G38. 176
G40. 176
G87. 194
G92. 195
G93. 195
G135. 113, 114
G194. 6, 9
G196. 6

Gaede Kapitänleutnant 129
Galanin Captain 1 Rank 44
Galatea 151, 177, 178, 196, 203
Gaudecker Fregattenkapitän von 195
Gebeschus Leutnant zur See 97, 223, 226
Geier 138
Gelhaar Stabarzt 224
Giseke Oberleutnant zur See 75
Glasgow 30, 31, 32, 34, 35, 36, 37, 38, 60, 62, 63, 64, 65, 73, 74, 75, 76, 80, 81
Glen Turret 131
Gloire 210
Glorious 196, 197, 198, 201, 103, 206
Glossop Captain 133, 134, 137, 138
Gneisenau 28, 29, 30, 31, 32, 33, 34, 35, 38, 39, 58, 59, 62, 63, 64, 65, 66, 67, 68, 69, 71, 72, 81, 87, 128
Goeben 41, 42, 43, 44, 46, 47, 48, 49, 51, 53, 54, 55, 57, 208, 209, 210, 211, 212, 213, 214, 215, 216, 217, 219, 220, 222, 225, 226, 227
Goltz Generalfeldmarschall Freiherr von der 53
Good Hope 31, 32, 34, 35, 36, 38, 58
Goodenough Commodore 5, 11, 16, 24, 48, 96
Goshawk 10, 221
Göttingen 30, 31
Graf von Spee Vizeadmiral 28, 29, 30, 31, 32, 33, 35, 36, 38, 40, 58, 59, 60, 61, 62, 63, 64, 65, 67, 68, 69, 80, 81, 127
Graßoff Kapitän zur See 207
Graudenz 85, 88, 177, 205
Großer Kurfürst 191
Gunther Marinestabsingeneur 125
Gygas Fregattenkapitän 108, 117, 118, 120, 205

Hagedorn Fregattenkapitän 95, 185
Hahn Oberingenieur 185
Hähner Oberleutnant zur See 116
Halm Fregattenkapitän 117, 118
Hamburg 150, 183, 184, 185, 187
Hannover 189
Harder Kapitän zur See 2, 3, 25, 27, 88, 150, 169, 176
Hartog Kapitän zur See 88, 150, 170
Hase Korvettenkapitän 160, 224, 226
Haun Fregattenkapitän 33, 36, 62, 63, 73, 76
Hawksley Commodore 183
Hebbinghaus Kontredmiral 88
Heidkamp Wilhelm
   Obermaschinistenmaat 95, 96
Heinrich Kapitän zur See and
   Kommodore 150, 160, 177, 178, 195, 226, 225

Hela 4, 11, 26, 28
Helmuth 140
Herm Oberleutnant zur See der Reserve 139
Heuberer Fregattenkapitän 177
Highflyer 80
Hildebrand Kapitän zur See 195, 198
Hind 221
Hindenburg 205, 226
Hippel Kapitän zur See 209, 214, 217
Hipper Kontreadmiral 5, 11, 13, 14, 26, 27, 83, 84, 85, 86, 87, 89, 90, 98, 99
Hipper Vizeadmiral 148, 149, 151, 152, 153, 154, 155, 158, 160, 161, 163, 164, 165, 168, 169, 174, 177, 178, 180, 195, 223, 224, 226, 227
Hoffmann Fregattenkapitän 185
Hogue 5, 27
Homeyer Kapitänleutnant 215, 217
Hood Rear Admiral 164, 167, 178
Hopman Kontreadmiral 106, 107, 121, 122, 125
Horton Commander 123, 124
Hyacinth 139, 143, 144

I AG 82, 83, 85, 87, 99, 148, 149, 150, 163, 164, 165, 167, 170, 173, 174, 177, 178, 180, 182, 189, 190, 224, 227
I Reconnaissance Group (I AG) 5, 82, 85, 148, 150, 190, 195, 207
II AG 85, 87, 88, 148, 150, 153, 154, 158, 164, 177, 178, 179, 180, 182, 183, 198, 199, 201, 204, 206, 207
II Reconnaissance Group (II AG) 5, 85, 147, 195, 225, 227
III Reconnaissance Group 208
IV AG 150, 182, 183, 185, 195
IV Reconnaissance Group 182, 195
I Battle Squadron 41, 147, 150, 182, 185
II Battle Squadron 89, 150, 173, 182, 208
III Battle Squadron 28, 84, 150, 16, 180, 182
I FdT 6, 11, 85, 88, 150, 177, 188
II FdT 150, 160, 177, 178
Ibuki 133
Idzumo 60
Inconstant 196, 201
Indefatigable 154, 157, 158, 159, 160
Indianola 125
Indomitable 88, 90, 94, 101, 173, 179
Inflexible 59, 60, 64, 65, 66, 68, 69, 71, 72, 81, 166, 173, 179
Ingenohl Admiral 2, 26, 82, 83, 84, 85, 147
Ingles Commander 139
Invincible 4, 5, 59, 60, 62, 64, 65, 66, 69, 71, 72, 81, 166, 167, 179

Ioann Zlatoust 43, 44, 46, 47, 49, 53, 54, 55, 57, 222, 227

Jackal 221
Jellicoe Admiral 4, 59, 87, 90, 102, 150, 161, 164, 173, 174, 178, 185, 189, 191, 193, 224, 227
Jerram Vice Admiral 128
Jung Kapitänleutnant 151, 224, 227
Juno 210

Kagul 43, 44, 46
Kaiman 109
Kaiser 195, 203, 204
Kaiser Wilhelm der Große 80
Kaiserin 195, 203, 204, 207
Kanin Vice Admiral 105, 106, 109
Karlsruhe (II) 193, 194, 225
Karpf Kapitän zur See and Kommodore 107, 108, 110, 111, 113, 114, 117, 120, 122, 150, 205
Kaskov Captain 1 Rank 44
Kaupisch Oberleutnant zur See 119
Kazanets 109
Keese Signalgast 15, 19
Kehdingen 199, 206
Kent 60, 63, 64, 65, 73, 74, 76, 77, 78, 80, 81
Kettner Fregattenkapitän 44
Keyes Commodore 3, 4, 5, 19
Kienast Leutnant zur See 152, 169, 224, 226
King Edward 210
King George 210
King-Hall Rear Admiral 139
Knispel Korvettenkapitän 48
Knoop Oberleutnant zur See 34, 36
Koch Oberleutnant zur See 146
Koehler Kapitänleutnant 73
Kolberg 2, 13, 14, 15, 26, 82, 85, 88, 89, 105, 223, 227
König 166, 190
Königsberg (I) 127, 138, 139, 140, 141, 143, 144, 146
Königsberg (II) 195, 198, 199, 202, 203, 205
Konstantin 44
Kretschet 104
Krokodil 109
Krosigk von Kapitän zur See 125
Krykhanovsky Leitenant 109
Kseniya 44, 54
Kulibin Leitenant 130, 132

L11. 188
L13. 191
Laertes 17, 221
«Лафорей», «Лоуфорд», «Луис», «Лидиард», «Лорел», «Либерти.», «Лайсендер», «Лаэртес» (каждый с тремя 102-мм орудиями в бортовом залпе, 30 узл. нефтяное отоплени. *Laforey* 221
Lance «Линнет», «Лэндр 221
Landrail 221
Lange Kapitän zur See 187
Langre 33
Lapwing «Феникс», «Бэджер», «Бивер», «Джекел», «Сэндфлай» (последние четыре были приданы отряду крейсеров типа «К») (каждый из 17 миноносцев по два 102-мм орудия, скорость 27—32 узла), «Люцифер», «Ллевеллин» (по три 102-мм орудия, 30 узл.). 221
Lark 221
Laurel 17, 27, 160, 221
Lawford 221
Legion 221
Leipzig 28, 29, 30, 31, 32, 33, 34, 35, 36, 37, 38, 58, 59, 61, 62, 63, 65, 73, 74, 75, 76, 78, 81, 87, 222, 227
Leipzig (1875) 87
Lemishevski P. V. 117
Lennox 121
Leonidas 221
Lettow-Vorbeck General 146
Levetzow Kapitän zur See 88
Liberty 17, 221
Lietzmann Leutnant zur See 35, 67, 221, 222, 227
Linnet 221
Lion 5, 88, 90, 92, 94, 96, 97, 98, 101, 153, 154, 158, 159, 161, 164, 165, 173, 196
Liverpool 5
Lizard 212, 217, 221
Llewellyn 221
Loesch Kapitän zur See 195
Looff Fregattenkapitän 139, 140, 141, 143, 144, 146
Lookout 221
Louis 221
Löwenberg Oberleutnant zur See 116, 117
Lowestoft 5, 10, 11, 24, 88
Lübeck 107, 108, 109, 111, 117, 118, 119, 120, 121
Luce Captain 32, 64, 76
Lucifer 221
Lüdecke Fregattenkapitän 33, 62, 73
Lukin Captain 1 Rank 44
Lützow 27, 148, 150, 151, 152, 154, 155, 158, 161, 163, 164, 165, 166, 167, 168, 169, 170, 172, 174, 176, 189, 224, 226, 227
Lydiard 17, 221
Lysander

Index 231

M28 (British monitor) 213
M4. 194
M28. 193
M37. 194
M65 194
Maass Kontreadmiral 5, 6, 11, 19
Macedonia 63, 64, 80
Madlung Fregattenkapitän 177, 187
Maerker Kapitän zur See 33, 62, 68
Magdeburg 85. 86, 104, 105, 143
Mahrholz Kapitänleutnant 157, 224, 226
Mainz 4, 5, 6, 13, 14, 15, 16, 17, 18, 19, 24, 26, 27
Makrel 109
Maksimov Leitenant 109
Malaya 159, 163, 174
Maltzahn Kapitänleutnant Freiherr von 18
Markgraf 190
Mauve Kontreadmiral 173
Meidinger Fregattenkapitän 19
Melbourne 133
Melchikovski Leitenant 55
Menche Kapitänleutnant 114, 123
Mersey 143, 144, 146
Meteor 99
Meyer Marineingenieur 67, 71
Michelsen Kapitän zur See and Kommodore 122, 123, 150, 188
Midilli 43, 220
Minotaur 132, 133
Mohawk 3
Moltke 13, 26, 42, 85, 88, 92, 94, 97, 98, 101, 147, 150, 154, 157, 158, 159, 163, 164, 168, 174, 182, 185, 190, 205
Mommsen Fregattenkapitän 8, 27, 177, 183
Monarch 172
Monmouth 31, 32, 33, 34, 35, 36, 38
Moore Rear Admiral 4, 5, 15, 88, 98, 102
Moosauer Dr. 211
Mousquet 128, 131
Möwe (Möve) 139
Muavenet 209, 217
Mücke Kapitänleutnant 133
Müller Feuerwerker 95
Müller Fregattenkapitän Karl 29, 127, 128, 130, 131, 132, 133, 134, 223
Müller Max Obermaschinist 184
München 13, 25, 26, 150, 182, 183, 184, 185, 192

Napier Rear Admiral 182, 196, 197, 201, 203, 205
Nassau 187
Natal 210
Nepenin Captain 1 Rank 104, 105, 110
Nerger Korvettenkapitän 7, 10, 21, 27

Nerpa 53
Neumann Oberheizer 20, 21, 227
Nevinski Leitenant 47, 48
New Zealand 4, 5, 88, 94, 154, 157, 158, 159, 160, 173, 196
Newbridge 141
Newburn 132
Newcastle 60, 134
Niese Kapitänleutnant 18
Nordeck Kapitänleutnant 212, 213, 215, 216, 225, 227
Nottingham 5, 10, 11, 24, 88, 184, 191
Novik 106, 109, 110, 111, 118
Novitsky Vice Admiral 44
Numune 54, 209
Nürnberg 28, 29, 30, 31, 32, 33, 38, 58, 59, 62, 63, 73, 74, 76, 77, 78, 81
Nürnberg (II) 195, 198, 199, 201, 202, 225, 227

Okun 107, 109
Oleg 106, 110, 113, 114, 116, 118
Onslaught 188
Onslow 165, 180
Orion 172
Otranto 31, 33, 34, 35

Pakenham Vice Admiral 196, 197, 201, 203
Pamiat Merkuria 43, 44, 46, 53, 54
Panteleimon 43, 44, 51, 53, 54, 55, 57
Partzech Sanitätsmaat 17
Pascha Enver 53
Paschen Korvettenkapitän Günther 152, 165, 166, 176, 224, 226
Paschen Wilhelm Kapitän zur See 15
Patton Captain 1Rank 109, 110
Pegasus 139, 140, 141, 143
Pelly Captain 94, 102
Penelope 148, 149
Petard 160, 161
Phaeton 151, 157
Phillimore Captain 64
Phoenix 221
Pilkin Rear Admiral 106
Pillau 27, 150, 177, 178, 179, 183, 189, 195, 198, 199, 201, 202, 205, 225, 227
Pioneer 143, 144
Pleiser Obergast 111
Pochhammer Korvettenkapitän 29, 30, 33, 67, 71, 221, 222, 226
Pohl Admiral 147
Pohle Oberleutnant zur See 18
Pokrov Rear Admiral 44
Pommern 124, 173, 188, 189
Porembsky Captain 1 Rank 44
Potemkin 43
Präsident 141
Princess Royal 5, 59, 88, 92, 94, 96, 101, 152, 153, 154, 155, 158, 163, 167, 173, 196

Print Adalbert 107, 121, 122, 123, 124, 125
Prinz Eitel Friedrich 30, 31
Prinz Heinrich 107, 121, 122, 125
Prinz Heinrich Große Admiral 86, 87
Prittwitz und Gaffron von Oberleutnant zur See 114
Putin Vladimir 132
Putyatin Admiral 44, 54
Pyramus 143, 144
Pyshnov Captain 1 Rank 118

Queen Mary 5, 153, 154, 155, 158, 159, 160

Raeder Fregattenkapitän 152, 222, 226
Raglan 213
Räsch Heizer (Stoker) 78
Rebensburg Fregattenkapitän 193
Rebeur-Paschwitz Vize Admiral 43, 208, 209, 211, 214, 215, 219, 222, 225, 226, 227
Regensburg 150, 160, 177, 178, 180, 189
Reiß Fregattenkapitän 26, 27, 177, 181
Rengarten Captain 2 Rank 104, 105, 109, 110
Renown 197
Repulse 196, 197, 201, 202, 203, 205
Resolution 196
Retzmann Fregattenkapitän 2, 14, 24
Reuter Kapitän zur See, Kommodore and Kontreadmiral von 88, 150, 182, 195, 199, 202, 203, 204, 205, 206, 207
Revenge 170, 172, 196
Rheinland 187
Riediger Leutnant zur See 75
Roon 107, 108, 109, 111, 117, 118, 120, 122, 223, 227
Roß Korvettenkapitän 100
Rostislav 43, 44, 49, 51, 54, 55
Rostock 13, 85, 88, 150, 165, 170, 178, 182, 183, 185, 187, 188
Royal Oak 172, 196
Royalist 196, 203
Rubens 143
Rurik 105, 106, 110, 111, 118, 119, 120, 122
Rybalotovski Leitenant 130

S13. 6, 7
S53. 187
S62. 194
S131. 107
S138. 122, 123, 125
S139. 122, 123, 124, 125
S141. 113, 114
S142. 113, 114
S149. 107
Sablin Captain 1 Rank 44
Sakovich Leitnant 105, 109, 223, 226

Samsun 209
Sanders Marshall von 209, 210
Sandfly 221
Santa Isabel 61, 64, 80
Scharnhorst 28, 29, 30, 31, 32, 33, 34, 35, 38, 39, 58, 59, 62, 65, 66, 68, 69, 71, 72, 81, 127
Scheer Vizeadmiral 13, 147, 148, 189, 150, 151, 164, 167, 168, 169, 170, 174, 180, 185, 189, 190, 191, 206, 224, 226
Schiwig Kapitänleutnant 63, 74, 222, 227
Schleswig-Holstein 173
Schlubach Korvettenkapitän 219
Schönberg Kapitän zur See 33, 38, 62, 76, 77, 78
Schottmann Obermaschinisten 23
Schröder Obermaschinisten 23
Schultz Kapitän zur See 33
Schultze Kapitänleutnant 191
Schwede Oberleutnant zur See 63
Seebohm Fregattenkapitän 22, 25
Seidensticker Fregattenkapitän 195
Sell Kapitänleutnant Freiherr von 217
Semmler Leutnant zur See der Reserve 210, 211, 219
Severn 143, 144, 146
Seydlitz 13, 21, 25, 26, 85, 88, 89, 92, 94, 96, 97, 101, 102, 148, 149, 152, 154, 155, 157, 159, 161, 163, 164, 167, 168, 170, 172, 173, 174, 176, 177, 182, 183, 185, 189, 190, 223, 224, 227
Seydlitz (Auxiliary) 61, 64, 80
Seymour Lieutenant 98
Shark 180
Sinop 46
Sipailov Michman 130
Skipwith Captain 64
Slava 106, 110, 118
Smirnov Leitenant 47
Somali 139, 141
Sommer Oberleutnant zur See 54
Souchon Kontreadmiral and Vizeadmiral 42, 44, 51, 52, 53, 203, 205, 208, 222, 227
Souchon Leutnant zur See 214
Southampton 5, 88, 94, 150, 161, 184, 185
Sparrowhawk 188
Spindler Kapitänleutnant 13
Steinbrinck Oberleutnant zur See 149
Stettin 4, 5, 6, 7, 9, 10, 11, 14, 15, 21, 22, 25, 26, 180, 182, 183, 184, 185, 227
Stoddart Vice Admiral 64
Stoelzel Kapitän zur See 209, 214, 219, 220
Stolzmann Fähnrich zur See 184, 225, 227

Storey Midshipman 160
Stralsund 2, 3, 13, 14, 24, 25, 26, 83, 85, 88, 89, 99, 148, 177, 192, 205, 227
Straßburg 2, 3, 11, 13, 14, 15, 16, 19, 24, 25, 26, 83, 227
Stratmann Kapitänleutnant 113
Street Commander 160
Sturdee Vice Admiral 59, 64, 65, 66, 67, 68, 81
Stuttgart 150, 183, 184, 185, 186, 187
Suffolk 210
Sultan Osman 42
Sutlej 5
Svyatoi Nikolai 54
Sydney 133, 134, 136, 137, 138

T29. 8
T31. 7
T33. 7, 9, 11
T35. 7
T36. 8
T37. 7
T40. 8
T73. 7
Tapken Kontre Admiral 26
Thetis 107
Tholens Kapitänleutnant 16, 17, 227
Tietgens Fregattenkapitän 192, 193
Tiger 88, 92, 94, 96, 98, 101, 153, 154, 157, 158, 161, 167, 196
Tigress 212, 217
Timirev Captain 1 Rank 106, 223, 227
Tipperary 186, 187
Tirpitz Große Admiral von 2, 83, 223, 226
Tirpitz Oberleutnant zur See 15, 16, 19
Torgut Reis 219
Tri Sviatitelia 43, 44, 49, 51, 53, 54, 57
Trotha Thilo von Fregattenkapitän and Kapitän zur See 88, 177
Trummler Kontreadmiral 41, 42
Tsarevitch 106, 110, 118
Tyrwhitt Commodore 3, 4, 5, 8, 9, 11, 16, 27, 88, 148, 149, 221, 227

U19. 2
U24. 2
U52. 191
U63. 191
U66. 191
UA. 122
UB18. 149
UC23. 209, 210
U-Fjord 177
Undaunted 88, 90
Undine 111, 113, 114

V1. 6, 7
V3. 9

V6. 6
V28. 160
V43. 195
V44. 195
V45. 176, 195
V71. 188
V73. 188, 192
V83. 195
V108. 122
V187. 9, 10
Valentine 201
Valentine (bark) 59
Valiant 158, 161, 163
Vanquisher 201
Vejs Captain 1 Rank 117
Verderevsky Captain 1 Rank 114
Vnimatel'nyi 110
von der *Tann* 13, 26, 84, 85, 150, 154, 157, 158, 159, 163, 164, 170, 172, 174, 190, 224, 226, 227

Wallis Korvettenkapitän 10
Walther Kapitänleutnant 191
Wami 143
Warrior 165, 179, 180
Warspite 158, 163
Wendt Signalgast 111, 114, 115, 116, 223, 227
West Fregattenkapitän 108, 109, 114, 115, 117
Westfalen 182, 190, 191
Weymouth 141, 143, 144
White Lieutenant –Commander 220
Widenmann Fregattenkapitän and Kapitän zur See 2, 26, 88
Wiesbaden 27, 150, 165, 169, 177, 179, 180, 181, 182
Wieting Korvettenkapitän 113, 114
Winter Captain 1 Rank 44
Wittelsbach 28
Witthoeft Oberleutnant zur See 127
Wolfram Kapitänleutnant 7
Wörth 87

Yarmouth 128
Yavuz 43, 220
Yorck (auxiliary) 30, 31
Yorck 195

Zarin Captain 1 Rank 44
Zélée 30
Zenker Kapitän zur See 150, 164
Zenne Oberheizer 181, 225, 227
Zerboni di Sposetti Korvettenkapitän von 125. *Zhemchug* 128, 129, 130, 131, 224, 226
Zieb Ingenieur 192